TREASURES OF WAR

—■—

CONCEALED BY THE EVIL ONES

—■—

DON STEWART NIMMONS

Copyright © 2002 by Don Stewart Nimmons

Treasures of War – Concealed by the Evil Ones
By Don Stewart Nimmons

Printed in the United States of America

Library of Congress Control Number: 2003103074
ISBN: 1-59160-460-5

All rights reserved. No part of this publication may be reproduced or transmitted in any form or by any means without written permission of the publisher.

Xulon Press, Inc.
10640 Main Street, Suite 204
Fairfax, VA 22030
1-866-909-BOOK (2665)
www.XulonPress.com

ACKNOWLEDGMENTS

To my beloved Barbara, for your love, courage ... and devotion to all of us.

For All World War II Veterans of the European and Japanese Holocaust and
Survivors of The Bataan Death March and POW Camps and
In Grateful Memory of All Who Died in the Service of Their Country,
Who inspired the book.

They Stand in the Unbroken Line of Patriots Who
Have Dared to Die that Freedom Might Live
and Grow and Increase Its Blessings.
Freedom Lives and Through It They Live.
In a Way That Humbles the Undertakings of Most Men,
Who are sources of continuing inspiration.

I want to begin by thanking my parents and friends who help me with my life – true friends who stuck by me during the failure periods – my father who taught me the values of initiative and honesty -- my mother who taught patience and basic values for a happy life – my teachers and professors who instilled the desire to reach my goals.

I would like to thank all the people who participated in the interviews with me, who provided me with information and photographs and who made it possible for me to take many pictures all over the world.

My predispositions are the product of a lifetime of questioning the source of wealth and its relationship to wars.

Finally, to the family members of the heroic soldiers killed in action – for their pain and suffering – changed lives forever.

This is a work of fiction. The events described here are imaginary; the settings and characters are fictitious and not intended to represent specific places or living persons.

CONTENTS

ACKNOWLEDGEMENTS	iii
INTRODUCTIONS	ix
PROLOGUE	xxi
Nazis SS Officers Hiding Loot in Argentina	20
Private Roy James Autrey, A. S. No. 38343655	63
First Meiji Constitution in 1868 – Asia War	89
Master Sergeant Arvil Steele	118
Filipino Guerrilla – Virgilio 'Bulldog' Hermano	141
Private William "Bill" F. Benson – "T" Patchers of the US 36th Infantry Division -- Battlefield Invasions – North Africa – Italy – France -- Germany – Austria	159
From the Jewish Ghettos Through the Partisan Battles – Erika Greenberg	167
"Private" Charles Robert 'Bob' Steele – **Brothers Fighting For Freedom**	218
Japanese KAMIKAZE – **SUICIDE Missions**	223
Colonel Frank 'Sport' Montgomery	268
Japanese Colonel Kiyoshi Stingy – Hiding Gold Bars For Himself and Japanese General Tomoyuki Yamashita - In the Philippines	273
Filipino Family Guarding Hidden Japanese Gold Bars For Years	283
Mafia During World War II in Argentina	290

CONTENTS / v

Sergeant Ronald **'Cherokee'** Osborne	300
Filipino Warrior Stories – Before – During – After – World War II	313
Japanese Surrender to the Allied Military Forces – September 1945	317
General Virgilio Hermano – Commander of Filipino – "Bulldog Guerrillas" -- **Retrieves** Gold Bars From Caves in the Philippines After World War II	341
Born of Privilege (BOP) Party and Initial Establishment of Supreme Commander Allied Powers in Tokyo, Japan – United States Senate – Office of the Born of Privilege Leader – (BOP) Leader – Washington D. C.	348
Global Banking Group – Created	351
Deputy Commander of Allied Powers – General Milton R. Salmon and BOP Party Chairman in Tokyo – Mr. 'Bert' Dover – Retrieve All Treasures from Emperor Zapp and His Family For **WHO**	394
Supreme Commander For the Allied Powers (SCAP) -- Issues the December 15, 1945 -- **SHINTO DIRECTIVE** – Abolition of State Sponsored Shintoism	402
The Compromise Agreements with Emperor Zapp and His Family	421
Shipments of Gold Bars and Other Treasures – From Japan and Philippines by **THE EVIL ONES**	431
CIA Attempts to Confiscate General Virgilio Hermano's Maps – and Gold Bars in the Philippines	436
Global Banking Corporation After World War II – Control – Control	447
Filipino Investments of Gold Bars in Argentina by Filipino -- Virgilio "Bulldog" Hermano Foundation	462

vi / CONTENTS

The US – Japan Agreement of 1951 – Article 14 and 15 of Chapter V –
    Claims and Property –**WHY! – WHY!**   490

Florida BOP Infighting and Herbert "Bert Junior" Dover, Jr. –
    Permission To Sell Illegally Held Gold --
    To Secretary of U. S. Treasury -- United States Senate –
    Office of Born of Privilege Leader (BOP-Leader) -- Washington, D. C.   500

The Mafia Continues to Roam in Argentina   506

Post World War II – Era – CIA In Fighting and Funds for Foreign Covert
    Projects From the Sale of World War II – Gold Bars   515

Late in Life Story of Master Sergeant Arvil Steele (Ret.)   526

EPILOGUE   529

1998-2002

I have written **Treasures of War – Concealed By The Evil Ones** in an effort to tell untold stories of the atrocities committed by military officers from several nations -- including a few American officers -- and how they siphoned off a great value of the war loot -- who sought personal wealth at the cost of their fighting forces. The political ideology of these individuals seized the Sovereign right to wage war -- to build a military for that purpose in an attempt to vindicate them.

Some of them taught their devout followers to fear and worship them as a Spiritual Leader or a God.

I know from experience how much life has changed over the past half century, and how that period of time so sharply contrasts with the present age.

Each story (chapter) in the book reveals how the heroic soldiers under command of their superior officers fought through anxieties and unimaginable horrors of war. I have attempted to bring this era in history alive as they lived -- and died.

The proof of this unholy alliance has incontrovertible evidence of collusion between America and other nations. America's role has been kept very, very secret. The deception and false front was played out with the public being led to believe "Warmongering would be dissolved – the Guilty would be brought to justice – Yet, Failure to hold everyone accountable – with a policy of exonerating the Evil God's – the final result.

Shortly after graduating from Baylor University in 1897, George W. Truett was called as minister of the First Baptist Church of Dallas. It was from this pulpit that he fulfilled God's plan for his life until his death in 1944, nearly five decades later.

Throughout his 50-year ministry, people clamored to hear him preach and did their best to follow his suggestions and emulate his example of Christian living. Though rewarded during his lifetime with many accolades and named to numerous responsible positions, including the presidency of the Southern Baptist Convention and the Baptist World Alliance, George W. Truett never sought to be anything other than God's messenger doing God's will, as God directed.

Dr. Truett had a simple explanation for his life, "I have sought and found the shepherd's heart."

George W. Truett was a man of faith – faith in God, faith in man, faith in the atoning death and triumphant resurrection of Jesus Christ, faith in the gospel as the power of God unto salvation to every one who believes, faith in the ultimate triumph of the good, faith to believe that the kingdoms of this world shall become the kingdoms of our Lord, and his Christ. This faith makes possible the victory that overcomes the world.

A MAN OF GOD[1]

George Liddell

Give me a man of God – one man
Whose faith is master of his mind,
And I will right ten thousand wrongs
And bless the name of all mankind.

Give me a man of God – one man
Whose tongue is touched with heaven's fire,
And I will flame the darkest hearts
With high resolve and clean desire.

Give me a man of God – one man
One mighty prophet of the Lord,
And I will give you peace on earth
Bought with a prayer and not a sword.

Give me a man of God – one man
True to the vision that he sees,
And I will build your broken shrines
And bring the nations to their knees.

[1] Reprinted by permission.

X / PROLOGUE

Instrument of Tyranny

Gestapo, its methods, and objectives are on the rise in Germany. The post World War I economic conditions and social climate are ripe for Neo-fascism and Neo-Nazism radicals to gain power in many countries besides Germany. The increase in the political power of the extreme right-wing parties under the rhetoric of fear and despair to destroy the fundamentals of Democracy led to its downfall.

Identity crises and social exclusion combined with the effects of globalization were the principle dispatch of the radical right-wing populist movements with openly fascist roots. Initially, the Neo-Fascist political candidates tailored their broadcasts to appeal to the essential voters in each region. At times it was very vociferate, venting the emotions of each segment of the voters; at other times the messages were softened.

Joining in the downfall of Democracy in Europe are the established parties being pressured into adopting Neo-Fascists fundamentals in order to maintain the support of their constituents and be re-elected. These conflicts between the parties resulted in public discourse on sensitive political subjects near and dear to the hearts of the Germans, such as race, unemployment, corruption, and the homeless, wages and international trading partners.

Often the established bureaucrats compromised their beliefs and positions on basic fundamental values because they feared the underground terrorist cells of the Neo-Fascists.

Europe was ripe for the ultra right-wing demagogues. The atrocities of the Geheime Staats Polizei, Nazi SS, Reichstag Fire, terrorist and Secret Police are determining the political makeup of the governments of Europe.

PROLOGUE / XI

Constitution of the Empire of Japan

On February 11, 1889, the proclamation of the Constitution of the Empire of Japan defined the Emperor as the constitutional monarch in a centralized unitary state. Never before in the history of Japan had the Emperor been worshiped as a living god – "the selfless wisdom of the universe." This was accomplished after the leaders of the Meiji Japan had engaged in 20 years of pragmatic political experimentation to redefine the imperial institution.

In this 1889 constitution, the Emperor was "sacred and inviolable," and sovereignty rested with him as the Head of the Empire of Japan. He was the sovereign and supreme commander of the Japanese armed forces, declared war, made peace, and concluded treaties; he had emergency powers to maintain public order and declare a state of siege. All laws required the Emperor's sanction and enforcement.

On December 25, 1926, His Imperial Highness Prince Regent Hirohito became the 124th Emperor of Japan and the new era was named Showa, "radiant peace".

The promotional publicity to the world from His Imperial Majesty Emperor Showa's (Hirohito) Imperial Palace during the first three decades of the 20th century was to portray him as a divine being with privilege. However, the samuriazation of the nation began to evolve during the third decade of the 20th century, from the concentration of power of the Emperor, to the local temples and villages onto the battlefields of Manchuria, China, Guam, and eventually Pearl Harbor.

Author's Photo

Emperor Hirohito appeared in uniform in public, reviewed troops, and issued imperial decrees and decorated soldiers and sailors. Prior to becoming The Emperor and after formal training in the military, he was promoted to high ranks in both the Japanese army and navy. Throughout the years between 1926 and 1945, he refused to take action to stop the war machinery build up and the expansion of the full-scale wars in Asia and the decision to wage war on the United States. Some of his own family members repeatedly attempted to stop the threat of fascism in Japan. He refused to remove The War and Prime Minister Tojo Hideki.

Shinto fundamentalism, and reaction against foreign origin religion-philosophical movements, Nationalism became a strong driving force of His Imperial Majesty Showa's (Hirohito) society. Nationalism was deeply burned-in as Japan was exposed to threats from abroad.

In *Shintoism,* the diverse religious cultures became the "Japanese Spirit", and became very evident as Japan expanded its powers in the Asian Wars in the late 1930's and early 1940's. The valiant Japanese soldiers became aware their spirit and loyalty caused them to look for the roots of their thinking habits, values and national identity. His Imperial Majesty Hirohito became the ruling force behind this "Japanese Spirit" throughout the battles to conquer and destroy its enemies. This "Japanese Spirit" enabled them to seek nothing at all for themselves, and be willing to discard body and mind and unite with The Emperor. The glorified thoughts of the "Japanese Spirit" so empowered the Japanese soldiers to die on the battlefield with assurance that the battle in which they were engaged is monumental majestic. They religiously believed the war was not a mere slaughter of their fellow-beings, but that they were combating evil.

"GOLDEN LILY"

God, The Evil One, Emperor Zapp, summoned His Imperial Highness Prince Major Snatch, his brother, to the Imperial Palace for the initial meeting with his inner circle of military advisors, underworld characters, businessmen and secret service. "Major Snatch, I designate you as my team Commander to lead the secret operations, code name "Golden Lily", into China for the primary purpose of controlling all looted treasures from our defeated victims. These will include all of the gold bullion, diamonds, gems and artifacts from the central bank vaults of each and every provincial government and the central bank of China, warlord's palaces, bank vaults, and shrines. I am the new God that the conquered people must worship. Buddha is no longer their God. I want each and every Gold Buddha removed from the temples and brought back to me. I will have them smelted down into gold bullion bars for my personal riches," **Emperor Zapp, the Evil God** gleefully announced and instructed.

"I am honored that you believe in me more than any other family member to head up this most important and secret team," Major Snatch replied.

"The looting has already begun. Some of my military officers and fighting warriors have not learned of their devotion to duty and to me and my long-term objective to conquer and have world dominance. You will be required to make examples of some of these men. Use the sword and have their heads cut off. This action should be done in front of the townships and our troops," **The Evil God** firmly pointed out to his brother.

"You must take whatever actions needed to remain in a low profile position with the Chinese," he continued.

"I will use a different alias for each major region that I collect the booty and conceal the method of transportation back to you here in Tokyo," Snatch divulged.

"You must supply me with coded authority to use with the commanding officers that I do not know personally," he added.

"I have given orders to Col. Oishi Tsuneo at my Army Staff War College to release the coded messages to all of my commanding generals in China, Hong Kong, Vietnam, Laos, Cambodia, Burma, Malaya, Singapore, Sumatra, Java, Borneo and the Philippines," **The Evil God** assured his brother.

"Your secret Imperial Palace code name is Bravest Warrior," he added.

"Excellent **Emperor Zapp**," Major Snatch stated as he bowed.

"Will you be sending any of my cousins or uncles to assist me in completing this mission?" he asked.

Hide it! – Hide it!

The enormous military might of the Japanese was used in its conquest of east and Southeast Asia. From these victories came immeasurable bounty. Gold and gems were confiscated from private citizens, fallen government central monetary vaults, churches, temples, monasteries, banks, corporations, and mining operations. The loot came from China, Indochina, Thailand, Malaysia, Borneo, Singapore, The Philippines, the Dutch East Indies, South Korea, Taiwan, Burma, Indonesia, Laos, Cambodia, Vietnam, Brunei and Hong Kong; a vast hoard of jewelry, gems, Gold Buddhas, Gold bullion, Gold bars, public and personal treasure. The military's booty was the accumulated overseas loot for more than a decade of conquest of the entire Japanese establishment. Speculation over the years on the total worth of this loot ranges up to over $ 100 billion valued on the 1998 markets.

What few people in the West grasped in the early 1950's was the amount of illicit funds, unreported assets, illegal earnings, criminal profits, black market proceeds, secret hoards of gems and precious metals, and other forms of black money that existed in Asia.

After, 1942, comparatively little of this loot actually reached Tokyo, perhaps less than a third. Most of it was thought to have gone no farther than the transshipment point of Manila; where its journey was interrupted by the war's changing fortunes, and had to be hidden.

The main reason very little booty reached Japan was the American submarine campaign, armed with effective new torpedoes, which cut the sea-lanes abruptly before the end of 1943.

The other reason the treasure failed to reach home was the Japanese criminal underworld, and the immensely clever and powerful people who were its patrons.

The great bulk of the booty appears eventually to have come under the control of senior Imperial Navy officers and was conveyed by them to Manila by sea. They kept it secret.

As the war reached a climax, hiding this huge treasure became a matter of urgency to senior Japanese navy officers in Manila who were responsible for its security and its shipment homeward.

Beginning in late 1943, some of the loot apparently was taken in truck convoys to the mountains, near the Benguet mines in Baguio, where it was hidden in tunnels or caves and sealed with concrete, and to other areas outside Manila, where it was buried in deep pits.

The secret treasure maps were kept in the headquarters of the Japanese high command in Manila until General Yamashita pulled out of the city in mid-December 1944 to new headquarters at Baguio.

PROLOGUE / XV

There were grisly stories about **Allied prisoners — mostly Americans, Australians, Filipinos and Britons,** --- being forced to dig these pits and tunnels during 1943 and 1944, only to be buried alive.

Japanese engineers rigged elaborate booby traps at each site, including fully armed 1,000 and 2,000-pound bombs, so that safe access to the treasure could be gained only if an excavator followed precise technical instructions described on secret maps.

A cruiser bound for Japan was disabled by a U. S. submarine. The cruiser escaped and had to dock for repair in the port city of "Top Secret" on one of the Philippine Islands. The incident is common knowledge to the locals and elders of this area of the island. After docking, the Japanese stayed for three months. They unloaded cargo and transported it to their main headquarters in the mountains on the island. The natives witnessed the soldiers place the "unknown cargo" in tunnels inside the caves. The Japanese Fourth Air Army Division defended this Island with 16,000 soldiers. The soldiers had pulled back to the mountain to make their final stand. The Battle of "Top Secret" happened soon thereafter and before the Japanese surrender, they sealed the unknown caves, which were in the vicinity of the mountain, by dynamiting the entrances to the caves closed. The Battle of "Top Secret" was one of the bloodiest and fiercest battles on the Philippine Islands and is suspected to have been such a great battle because the Japanese were protecting the "unknown cargo".

The two highest-ranking officers of the Japanese Imperial Navy in the Philippines were Rear Admiral Iwabuchi Sanji and Rear Admiral Kodama Yoshio. Rear Admiral Kodama Yoshio became known as Japan's criminal mastermind, who collected the loot over Asia and sent it back toward Japan by the way of Manila. Rear Admiral Iwabuchi Sanji became notorious as the "Butcher of Manila". He commanded the naval forces in the Manila area and was prepared to fight with the sixteen thousand marines and sailors under his command. He was determined to fulfill the standing orders given by naval headquarters in Tokyo not to let the Americans capture these treasured stocks and to keep facilities intact. Innocent civilians died in large numbers from heavy use of artillery by both sides. Japanese fighting men added to the carnage by murdering, raping, beating, or burning hapless civilians caught within their lines. About one hundred thousand Filipino civilians died in the battle in Manila. This was six times the number of soldiers killed on both sides.

Rear Admiral Kodama went back to Japan before the fall of Manila. Rear Admiral Iwabuchi was thought to have held his last stand in the Finance Building, the Legislative Building, and the Bureau of Agriculture and Commerce in Manila. He was presumed to have died in the rubble of the Finance Building when it was last silenced. Nobody ever positively identified Iwabuchi's remains in the finance Building. He may very well have slipped away through the tunnel system in the last stage of the battle, to survive the war in disguise. Many Japanese officers did vanishing acts. Perhaps the most famous was the brilliant Imperial Army Colonel Tsuji. After helping Admiral Kodama loot Southeast Asia, Colonel Tsuji eluded Allied capture by disguising himself as a Buddhist monk, and wandered through Southeast Asia and China for the next three years. After war crimes trial had ended and his friend Admiral Kodama had been freed from Sugamo Prison in Japan and could again pull strings, Colonel Tsuji returned to Japan and wrote a book about his adventure.

In 1984, after seventy-four years of unprecedented mischief, Admiral Kodama had a stroke and died taking his secrets with him. During his final years, he still manipulated events from behind the black curtain.

"MABUHAY"

Magellan, in the service of Spain, explored the Philippines in 1521. Later, the group of islands is named in honor of Prince Philip II of Spain. For 350 years, Spain retained possession of the islands.

The Filipino people through its political consciousness believed freedom from foreign rule was worth fighting for. Men warriors and many women sacrificed their lives and fought beside their husbands and sons to free their country from foreign dominance. One of the few woman freedom fighters that captured the imagination and respect of her countrymen was Melchora Aquino, popularly known as "Tandang Sora". A very attractive Filipino woman with many talents and strong character led her to be well received. Later, as a revolutionists in the late 1890's the Spanish captured and vigorously tortured her without any success in breaking her spirits or learning any warfare secrets. Many lives were saved as a result of her determination to win freedom. Later, the first U. S. civilian governor-general of the Colonial Philippines, William Howard Taft, offered her substantial rewards for her patriotic services during the war with Spain. She refused to accept them, because she was satisfied that her actions served her country. Her legacy for selfless devotion to freedom and country has been left behind for succeeding generations of Filipinos to equal.

With one exception, peace had come to the Islands in 1902. The Islamic Moros on the southern island of Mindanao remained in conflict with any foreign government or Filipino rule.

The culture of the various Tribesmen in the Philippines is something that most foreigners, including the Spanish, did not explore or care about. They spoke several languages such as, Malay, Spanish and English. Most of them had above average intelligence. The Spanish Roman Catholic Church and its missionaries had converted the Filipinos to Christianity.

Archipelago of over 7,000 islands lying about 500 miles (805 km) off the southeast coast of Asia, the Philippines became a very strategic colonial holding of the United States. Under Washington, D. C. plans and Governor Taft's leadership the number one objective was to establish an education system for the people of the Philippines. A large number of teachers from the United States were dispersed through out the Islands to teach English, American customs and history to the Filipinos rather than Filipino history and customs.

In 1916, the U. S. Congress passed the Jones Law that provided for the establishment of a Philippine Legislature composed of an elected Senate and House of Representatives.

Before the Filipino nationalists and the political forces in the United States could work out the differences between all special interest (Agricultural – sugar beets, tobacco, and dairy farmers) in the United States; who were worried about the hardships suffered by the Americans during the depression years and low-tariff products from the Philippines competing with U. S. industry - - concluding that it was in the best interest of the U. S. labor unions and others to "cut the cord" with the Philippines as a Colony of the U. S.

In January 1933, Manuel Roxas, a rising star in the Nacionalista Party and speaker of the House, successfully campaigned for passage of the Hare-Hawes-Cutting Independence Bill, which the Filipino Congress approved over President Herbert Hoover's veto. Manual Quezon y Molina opposed the legislation on the grounds that clauses relating to trade, the small number of Filipino immigrants each year, the guarantees of United States bases on Philippine soil and powers granted a United States high commissioner would compromise independence. After the bill was defeated in the Philippine legislature, Quezon himself went to Washington and negotiated the passage of a revised independence act, the Tydings-McDuffie Act, in March 1934 during the FDR administration.

The Tydings-McDuffie Act provided for a ten-year transition period to independence, during which the Commonwealth of the Philippines would be established. The commonwealth would have its own constitution and would be self-governing, **although foreign policy would be the responsibility of the United States.** Laws passed by the legislature affecting immigration, foreign trade, and the **currency system had to be approved by the United States president.**

Quezon had managed to obtain favorable terms on bases; the United States would retain only a naval reservation and fueling stations. The United States would, moreover, negotiate with foreign governments for the neutralization of the islands.

The country's first constitution was framed by a constitutional convention that assembled in July 1934. In May 1935, the voters for the entire Philippine Islands overwhelmingly approved it. This legal document established the political institutions for the intended ten-year commonwealth period. The first commonwealth election to the new Congress was held in September 1935. Under a constitution approved by the people of the Philippines in 1935, the Commonwealth of the Philippines came into being with Manuel Quezon y Molina as president.

Unfortunately, the islands were located in the sea-lanes dividing the South China Sea and the Pacific on the one hand --- the Malaysian, Indochina, Dutch and Thailand empires --- and China and Japan on the other --- and the lasting fact in recorded history that the weak are primary targets for overthrowing. The rise of Christianity hadn't changed matters very much. The classes of the people were the same. The Catholic Church did not attempt to educate the poor peasants. The Spanish did not want them educated. These conditions only made wars all the more bitter by the Guerrilla Rebels Revolution.

In 1938, the Philippine Legislature authorized Series No. 66 Victory Notes. These were in payment to the Philippines by the U. S. Government at the time the Philippines were under United States of America rule after the Spanish American War, for the Filipino Guerrillas heroic deeds to defeat the Spanish in the late 1890's and the rebuilding of parts of the country.

On June 14, 1938, President Franklin D. Roosevelt approved the issuance of Philippine Victory Notes in amount of more than Fifty Billion U. S. Dollars. **Under the U. S. Treasury Code, the President had sole authority to approve such dealings.** These approved Treasury Certificates certified that they were deposited into the Treasury of the Philippines, payable to the bearer on demand in silver or in legal tender currency of the United States of equivalent value.

Some months before Pearl Harbor, while the Philippine Islands were still under United States sovereignty, President Roosevelt issued an order making the Filipino army a part of the

American Army. Therefore, Filipino soldiers fought for their homeland as well as for the United States.

On Dec. 8, 1941, the islands were invaded by Japanese troops. Following the fall of Gen. Douglas MacArthur's forces at Bataan and Corregidor, Quezon established a government-in-exile that he headed until his death in 1944.

Vice President Sergio Osmeña succeeded him. U.S. forces under MacArthur reinvaded the Philippines in Oct. 1944 and, after the liberation of Manila in Feb. 1945, Osmeña reestablished the government.

The Philippines remained in this status until the eve of the Philippines' independence.

At the end of World War II, during July 1946, the constitution of the Commonwealth of the Philippines became the constitution of the Republic of the Philippines.

XX / PROLOGUE

Perónismo

In 1940, as an admirer of the Italian dictator Benito Mussolini, Perón traveled to Italy to study alpine military methods. He returns to Argentina in 1941. Later in 1943, he joined other officers in a secret military lodge and staged a coup d'état against President Ramón Castillo.

Publicly, the leading army officer in Argentina in 1945, Juan Domingo Perón, is admired by the Roman Catholic Church, the military, the industrialists, the vast landowners and the majority of the working people. In 1946, he ran for president and won by a huge majority.

Eva (Maria Eva Duarte) Perón, President Perón's second wife, met him in 1944 at a time when she is a very successful and popular radio soap opera actor. They married in 1945 and became his liaison with labor groups. She creates the Eva Perón Foundation (a social welfare institution) and establishes the women's branch of the Perónist party.

Religious leaders and the chief supporters of her husband literally worshipped her. Opponents despised her. Evita, as she was affectionately known, died in 1952.

Officers under President Perón's command supported the Neo-Fascists dictatorship. Together they instituted a program of revolutionary, nationalistic measures (known as Perónismo) instigated to lead the economy out of the doldrums and into both domestic and foreign trade recovery.

Now the Roman Catholic Church had excommunicated Perón, yet Perónismo remained the political reckoning force. In 1955, he was overthrown by a military coup. Terrorist acts of the loyal supporters of Perón created government disorder for many years.

After 18 years in exile, Perón returned to Argentina, and in 1973 he was elected president and his third wife, Maria Estela (Isabel) Martinez de Perón, was elected vice president. He died in office on July 1, 1974.

JAPANESE IMPERIAL ARMY – LEAD BY IMPERIAL FAMILY CONQUERS and LOOTS CHINA

Chiang Kai-Shek, also known as Chiang Chung-cheng, became commander-in-chief of the National Revolutionary Forces in 1925. The feuding warlords in central and northern China became the primary military focus of Chiang. He and his troops fought for three years before he succeeded in defeating the feuding warlords and reunifying China. Victorious, Chiang was elected chairman of the National Government of China.

The Evil God, the emperor, commanded his brothers and uncles to lead his armies to destroy Manchuria, China and all of East Asia. In 1937, Chiang took command of his Chinese military forces to fight the Japanese troops in Shanghai, Peking, Changsha, Chengtu, Siangtan, and Nanjing.

The eight-year War of Resistance by the Chinese was against the twisted religious philosophy that supported and fueled the Japanese military onslaught. **The Evil God** and his Imperial Family Members, in their capacity as military officers, **mislead the Japanese people and warriors to believe that they were the chosen people whose mission was to conquer the world.** As their God, the message was, "The Spirit of Japan is the Great Way of the Shinto Gods. It is the essence of the Truth."

Soon after the Allied Forces achieved the victory over Japan, the Chinese Communists launched an all-out rebellion and the civil war against General Chiang Kai-Shek was in full swing to overthrow Chiang's leadership in China.

The former Japanese colony, Taiwan, was transferred to China in October 1945. General Chiang Kai-Shek was the President of China at this time.

The Chinese communists took over the Chinese mainland and set up a communist regime in Peking in 1949, and after losing the civil war to the communists, General Chiang Kai-Shek fled to Taiwan.

TREASURES OF WAR – CONCEALED BY THE EVIL ONES

Chapter One

The Story of Nazis SS Officers Hiding Loot In Argentina

AUTHOR'S PHOTO

In 1943, due to the influx of the Italian and Spanish refugees escaping from the war in Europe to the coastal areas and Western mountain foothills near Mendoza, Argentina; it became a natural cover for the transpobation of people and goods from Germany to Argentina. These emigrants with expertise and money to develop the wine and olive industries poured into the country uniting with family members and friends who had immigrated to Argentina in the 1860s. They needed equipment from their homeland.

A pro-Axis neutral Argentina was one of the most attractive places in the world for the Germans to ship Treasures. Nazi intelligence negotiated lasting connections with many of the officials and military in Buenos Aires and the port cities of Mar del Plata, Comodoro Rivadavia and Bahia Blanca.

When President Ramón Castillo was overthrown in 1943, an army officer by the name of Juan Domingo Perón was on the rise to prominence. Army Colonel Juan Perón with a group of colonels seized power in 1944. With the support of the army, nationalists, and the Roman Catholic Church, Perón established a popular dictatorship. The popular and successful radio soap opera actor, Eva Duarte de Perón, his second wife, won the backing of the trade unions.

During the revolution fighting in Buenos Aires, Perón's men followed his order to destroy the symbol of wealth, the Jockey Club. The famous hand carved statues imported many years earlier by the Spaniards and located all over the Jockey Club were torn down by wrecking crews and tossed out into the streets to demonstrate Perón and Eva's misanthropic political position against the wealthy and to motivate the workers and army. Eva's (Evita, as she was affectionately known) popularity among the industrial working class was the major cornerstone of support for the Perón dictatorship.

Perón needed money to support his goals to maintain the office of president in the grand fashion he was accustomed too. He unabashedly admired Hitler. This information had reached Deputy Fuhrer, Heinrich Weise, back in Berlin.

TREASURES OF WAR – CONCEALED BY THE EVIL ONES / 3

The large blond and blue eyed Weise had learned that his wife's sister, who he had a romantic encounter with as a young teenager had moved to Argentina. After several months of writing letters to her, he received a reply.

"I was shocked to hear from you," she wrote. "I too have never gotten over you," she warmly expressed. "You have been so busy working on all of your projects for The Fuhrer that I did not know that you had time to even think about me," she pointed out.

Much has been written and made of the German submarine operations whose purpose was to ship death-camp booty to Argentina. After the Allied Forces pushed the German Army out of France in the fall of 1944, Deputy Fuhrer Heinrich Weise's self-preserving action was to escape from his headquarters by using one of the submarines at a pre-arranged site off of the Mediterranean Sea coast.

He summoned his driver to his office. "In the garage at the rear of this building is a captured U. S. Jeep. Go drive this Jeep around to the front and load these briefcases of mine in it together with these U. S. Duffle bags with our U. S. Army clothes," Weise ordered his driver.

"Where are the keys to Jeep?" Shultz asked.

"Here they are," as Weise tossed them to him.

These briefcases contained all of the documents of his Gold smelting operations in Germany and the establishment of Gold smelting operations in Argentina.

"Shultz, wait for me at the door of the Jeep out front," Weise commanded.

"Yes sir."

Weise made the rounds of his office one last time to be certain that he was not leaving any evidence of the looted treasures and his Gold shipment activities over the last few years. As he was leaving he noticed a lock on one of the file cabinets had not been un-locked. He looked through his keys and found the key that fit this file lock. He un-locked it and found several files of banking information, complete with account numbers, his bank signature copies, deposits and telegram bank transfers.

How in the world did I almost miss these crucial files? He thought.

He looked around one more time. Nothing else of importance was found.

He rushed out to his Jeep and opened one of the locked briefcases and placed the additional banking files in it and locked it.

"Shultz, you have the map of where we need to travel. Be very cautious. This Jeep should not present any problems for us to go through roadblocks in Germany because of my German officer's uniform," Weise reminded.

"When we get near the French border, you and I will need to change into U. S. military uniforms. I have several uniforms from U. S. POW's for you to try on and keep the ones that fit you best. I have already picked out several U. S. officer uniforms for me. Near the border you need to change into the uniform with the name Carpenter on it. I will change into the officer's uniform with the name Aubrey on it. I used the Red Cross to make up some papers last week for us in the names Carpenter and Aubrey. Your rank is Sergeant and mine is Colonel," Weise said enthusiastically.

"I have been told by intelligence that there are so many different divisions of Allied Forces coming across France in an attempt to push our troops back into Germany, that we should not have any problems traveling all the way to Marseille. I am depending on you to get us through the border crossings," Weise discussed with Shultz as he explained his escape plans.

"Heil Hitler," Shultz replied.

"No, no don't even think that, much less say it; Shultz, be careful about saying Heil Hitler during this trip."

"You and I should never acknowledge Hitler at any time during this trip. The border guards will attempt to confuse us by speaking "Hitler Trash" talk and trap us," Weise cautioned Shultz.

"Do you have enough ammunition for both of our guns in your case hidden up under the car?" Weise asked.

"Yes, I hope that we do not have to use it along the way," Shultz answered.

"During the trip, I will address you as Sergeant, and you will address me as Colonel Aubrey, and keep our final destination a secret between us," Weise explained.

"No problem, let's get the hell out of here," Shultz hastily said.

"Turn to the left at the main road, we should have enough gas to make it to our next rendezvous with my contact along the way to our port city destination," Weise instructed.

"Wake me up just before we get to the main border crossing," Weise ordered.

"OK, I will drive careful and not draw any attention to us," Shultz answered.

Weise leaned his head back in his seat and went to sleep. He was extremely tired and anxious from the days it took completing the plans to escape from Europe.

A few hours later in the day.

"Weise, Weise, wake up; we are approaching the border crossing roadblock into France," Shultz said shaking Weise by the shoulder.

"Wow, I must have been more fatigued than I imagined," Weise replied.

"Because of your snoring all of the cows along the road kept mooing and mooing as we passed them," Shultz said laughing.

"I do not snore," as they slowed for the crossing.

"May I see your identification papers and orders Colonel?" the American soldier asked as he saluted the Colonel's Jeep as they stopped at the border crossing.

"Yes, here is my identification and intelligence orders," Weise replied as he handed them to the young American soldier.

"Where are you going?"

O ur mission is classified top secret. Some Nazi SS troops were captured during some recent fighting south of here attempting to circle back behind our lines. I must find out just how much they learned and communicated to their headquarters. It is important that I get there as quick as possible to be able to interrogate them," Weise told the young American soldier.

"Are we on the best road to get to the Provence-Côte D'Azur region near the sea. Our orders are to find these captured Nazis SS officers at a special "classified" camp in this region?" Weise asked the American soldier.

"Yes, your driver has you on the best road for the fastest trip. Just keep on this road for another three or four hours, and you should find the region fairly easily. Watch out for the convoys of trucks with tanks and personnel carriers coming to the north," the American border crossings Sergeant told Weise (Colonel Aubrey), and Shultz (Sergeant Carpenter).

"Sergeant, we will need some fuel along the way," Shultz spoke up.

"About one hour down the road you will see the fuel depot. I have been told that they received a recent supply and should have plenty of fuel for you," the Sergeant replied.

"Good luck," the young American soldier said as he stamped their papers and motioned the guard to raise the gate and let them through.

"Thanks," Weise said waving as they drove off to the south.

As they drove down the road a mile or two Weise could not keep his thoughts inside.

"Why did I worry all week long about crossing into France?" Weise asked. "I never could have imagined that we would be lucky enough to have a young American soldier stopping us at the border. When he saw me as a Colonel in the U. S. Army and saw the Red Cross stamps already on my intelligence papers and orders, he could not think anything but good things about us."

Driving until they came upon the American fuel depot, Shultz drove off the main road to the area where the Jeeps and trucks were being refueled.

As they continued their journey and after more than five hours of driving over the rough roads, they entered the small town with the predominant church steeple pointing to the sky.

"Shultz, down the road a few blocks do you see the large oak tree on the right side?" Weise asked.

"Yes."

"When we get to the intersection just passed there, make a right turn,"

"See the second driveway, let me out here and circle the block," Weise continued as he pointed to it.

As Shultz drove near the house on his return from around the block; Weise opened the door of the house and waved for him to enter the driveway. Once they were both out of the jeep. Shultz went inside to meet with Weise and his contact.

"You, need to take these cans of gasoline, one by one, out to the jeep and fill our gas tank. Any full gas cans should be put into the side carriage of the jeep," Weise ordered.

"Yes, I will be careful as I fill the tank to be sure nobody is curious of what I am doing."

The two men completed the task at hand, had a brief meal and visit with their comrades. As they returned back to the main road leading south to the sea; both seemed very relieved that things were going so well without any major hang-ups.

As they drove in the night their speed slowed down by about forty percent of the daytime pace. After another five hours of driving with a few pit stops to relieve themselves and eat grapes from the nearby fields along the road; they entered the port city. Weise had made plans to go to one of his comrade's houses and attempt to contact by short wave radio the submarine out in the Gulf of Lion on a pre-arranged frequency.

When they arrived at his comrade's house on Place De La Joliette in Marseille, nobody answered the door. It was in the middle of the night. They decided to park the car at the back of the house.

"Shultz, take your flashlight and remove the guns from the hidden case up under the jeep. Put your stainless steel 9mm Lugar with the 4 inch barrel with the deep cut checkered walnut grips in your holster inside your suitcase. Bring me my stainless steel 9mm Lugar with my initials engraved on the hand carved ivory grips with the 6 inch barrel and Gold plated loaded chamber indicator," Weise instructed.

Shultz opened the trunk and took out his tools to un-bolt the hidden case under the jeep. He took his keys to un-lock the case. He removed his pistol and put it in his holster and placed it under the back seat.

"Heini, here is your pistol."

"Thanks, let's wait here in the jeep til morning, turn out the lights and maybe we can get some rest," Weise said as he jumped out of the front seat and got into the back seat.

The former Deputy Fuhrer, Heinrich Weise, escaped from Germany. Upon the arrival of his driver, 'Marty' Shultz, and himself at the port city of Bahia Blanca, Argentina, his first mission was to find Colonel Krause and locate the Gold Bars that he ordered shipped to Argentina years earlier. Then, he would investigate the status of the Gold Smelting operation near San Juan.

After meeting with the local front men of his company, Don Diego Limitado, in Bahia Blanca, Weise made arrangements to get he and 'Marty' some local identification cards and driver's licenses.

"'Marty', the company has several American cars out there in the yard for us. One is the 1939 Buick four-door sedan; the 1936 Plymouth is in good shape, or the 1938 Chevrolet. Which one do you think would be best for us to travel into Buenos Aires and across the country to the northwest?" Weise asked him as he tossed the keys.

"Where are they parked and can I test drive them?" Shultz replied.

"Give them a good testing and check-up; they are in the garage building number 3 out back."

"I will take a look."

Upon Shultz's return he had a big smile on his face, "Heini, that 1939 Buick with the gear shift in the middle of the front seat area has the most power of the three. I pushed the accelerator down to the floorboard, and it threw me back into my seat. In fact, the front wheels jumped off the pavement. It is attractive, big and has plenty of room for taking a trip."

"I will go into town and take the plane to Mendoza after you have first driven the car of your choice to Mendoza. You need to call me here and let me know when you have arrived," Weise commanded.

Once 'Marty' and Weise met at the Mendoza hotel recommended by 'Rudy' Krause, they were joined by Wolfgang Schmidt, Weise's personal confidant, and ate breakfast and decided to drive out to the Villavicencio Pass Hotel owned by Weise and his group.

"I do not want to go directly to the entrance to the hotel. You need to drive in front of the hotel and then turn up the road, which leads over a portion of the Andes Mountains overlooking it. We will stop at a lookout point about half way up," Weise calmly advised 'Marty'.

As they drove up the narrow winding rock road around some very tight cliff turns you could begin to see the picturesque view of the valley at the foot of the mountains directly below to the right and the road in the bottomland in the other direction toward the road to Mendoza. The clouds covered tops of some of the mountains. When 'Marty' stopped the car on the shoulder of the road about eighteen hundred meters up, they got out into a fresh cool breeze coming over the mountain ridge from the direction of Chile.

Author's Photo

"Look down at the huge hotel complex. You can see how deep the facilities go back into the mountain valley," Weise said as he pointed down to the site.

"Striking," Wolfgang Schmidt replied with a big grin across his face.

"As we drove on the road below in front of the hotel did you notice how high the support wall of the driveway entrance was and the two men standing next to the outer guard rail and looking out toward Buenos Aires?" Weise asked.

"Yes, from where we were traveling it looked very tall. In fact, looking up, the first part of the complex you notice is the wall and the top floors of the hotel. You don't realize how big and beautiful the hotel really is. From here you can see every part of the hotel complex," Schmidt answered.

"See how the hotel entrance driveway is constructed out over the ravine going in front of the hotel and the mountainside?" Weise asked.

"Yes, looking down from the hotel driveway that is about forty feet high at the edge of the outside concrete guardrail. The whole complex looks like some of the beautiful pictorial mountain hotels and palaces built back in Austria and the old country. From here it gives the appearance it grew or comes out of the mountainside," Schmidt answered with his personal observation with a bright smile coming from under his dark sun glasses.

TREASURES OF WAR – CONCEALED BY THE EVIL ONES / 11

"The primary reason I wanted to explain the surroundings here in Villavicencio Pass goes back to the map Colonel Krause sent to me via my sister during the war before I arrived here in Argentina. In the side of the wall below the hotel driveway now covered with greenery and vines is an entrance to a very large cave. Krause told me he stashed six thousand Gold Bars each weighing twelve and one half kilos in many different chambers of the cave going back under the hotel complex into the mountain. These Gold Bars were shipped from Amsterdam during the war. Before we began construction of the hotel I brought a team of demolition people here from Buenos Aires. I took them about five hundred feet into the cave and had them blast some rocks down from the ceiling and sides, closing the cave completely at that point of the cave. The first stack of Gold Bars are located more than twenty-five hundred feet back in the winding cave," Weise explained.

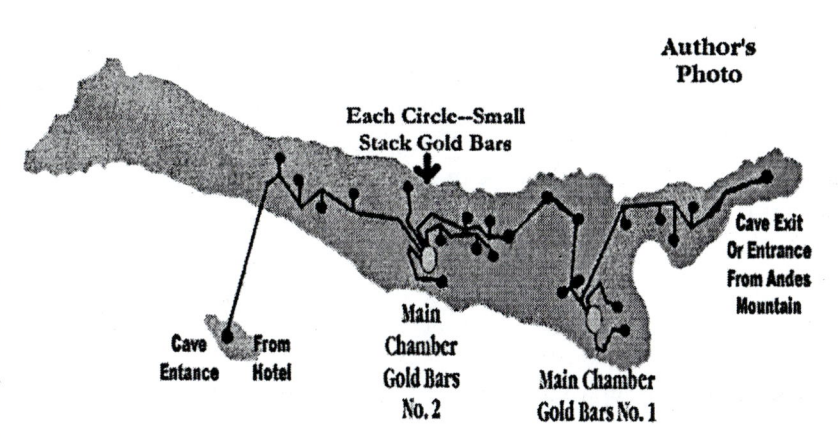

Author's Photo

Each Circle--Small Stack Gold Bars

Cave Entance From Hotel

Main Chamber Gold Bars No. 2

Main Chamber Gold Bars No. 1

Cave Exit Or Entrance From Andes Mountain

"What about the security of the Gold Bars in the cave?" Wolfgang asked.

"After the war, we just decided to bring in our architects from Buenos Aires and Germany and designed a basement under the driveway of the hotel. I wanted something built to permit me to enter the cave without having to divulge the whereabouts of this fortune to anyone alive," Weise frankly pointed out.

"Why in the world are you telling me all of this?" Wolfgang asked, completely dumbfounded.

"Schmidt, you have done me many favors and introduced me to some very attractive women that have met my needs since you and I met several years ago. We have had some exciting times together and back each other up every time we need to. I trust you. I have completed the formal membership of you into my central organization," Weise replied.

"Thanks! I don't know what else to say," as Wolfgang jumped up and gave Weise a kiss on both cheeks and an emotional hug.

"You and I have the world at our hands," Weise went on.

"We will party together."

"What is your plan for this project?" Wolfgang asked.

No negotiations regarding the identification and disposition of German external assets were undertaken in Argentina in the months immediately following the end of the war. Argentina created a historical commission to look into its relationship with Nazi Germany and the theft and disposition of valuables from Hitler's victims. The United States set about to establish more friendly relations following the criticisms contained in the State Department 'Blue Book' on Argentina in early 1946. American officials concluded that German assets were not identifiable by the Argentine Government and no looted Gold had reached Buenos Aires.

"Enough years have passed and all of the wartime claims against Germany have been investigated by the Allied investigators, and the disposition of German external assets were agreed upon by most countries and the Jews. A division of the proceeds from the liquidation of the German external assets has been completed by the Allies as reparations for wartime claims against Germany and given to the International Refugee Organization. This included the agreement on the restitution of looted Gold. I thought it would take forever before I could begin slowly moving some of this looted Gold back into the world's Gold market circulation," Weise further explained.

"You have kept this hidden for a long time. Who else knows about this? Wolfgang rapidly asked.

"I am not sure at this moment just how many insiders there are. I need to tie that down solid. I am proud of what I have done here and do not intend to let 'Rudy' take over," Weise replied as he put his finger of silence to his mouth and pointed to 'Marty'.

"Over the years Argentina has steadfastly balked at releasing any Argentine files about the disposition of millions of dollars in treasure looted from Europe and smuggled to Argentina. I made certain the primary conclusions for the government's position by paying off Perón and his people so they could enjoy some of the treasure for themselves," Deputy Fuhrer Heinrich Weise gleefully replied.

"Did you obtain one of those Red Cross passports before you shipped out from Germany with your original name, birth date and complete identification on it? I could not believe that the Red Cross was so gullible to issue them without doing any checking of my background," Wolfgang asked.

"Yes, I have one too! 'Marty' drive down the mountain road and return past the hotel entrance driveway and travel exactly three and two tenths kilometers to a narrow road to the left. This road will wind around until it comes to a dead end," Weise ordered.

Upon arriving at the designated spot, Weise ordered. "'Marty' you stay and guard the car. Wolfgang, grab two of those backpacks out of the trunk for you and let's go."

Weise and Wolfgang began walking on a path around two mountain ridges until they came to the secret cave entrance from the backside of the mountain. It would eventually lead all the way through the long cave to the hotel cave entrance at the other end, Weise said. "Here is a photo of the cave entrance that very few have ever seen up in these mountains."

Wolfgang asked. "Have you ever seen any mountain lions or vicious animals in this cave?"

"We will stay on the main cave trail until we get to the steel door blocking the entrance to the chambers leading to the Gold Bars shown on the map. I will show you the secret codes and locations needed to unlock the steel door. Mount two bright lights out of your pack, one on your head and one around your neck. Bring one of the hand flashlights, and we will turn all of them on once we get inside the cave, not before," Weise commanded.

"This cave has survived earth quakes and has apparently been here thousands of years. You must have been ecstatic when you discovered this enormous cave. How much further do we walk before we come to the steel door?" Wolfgang asked.

"Flash your light straight ahead. See the steel door at that narrow opening?" Weise asked in his excited voice.

"Watch me as I perform the secret maneuvers to unlock the steel door. After we go through the door, always re-lock it in this manner. Now, the tricky part of locating the various chambers of the cave comes into play. We will pass four offshoots to small chambers where Gold Bars are hidden at the end of them. The total distance to chamber number 1 is twice the distance we came to get to the steel door. We will walk through some shallow water. Don't be alarmed. You will not step off into any deep water. Most of the main cave has a height of more than four meters. We will arrive from the same direction into chamber number 1 that you would come from the hotel route. The very large stack of Gold Bars in chamber 1 is stacked on the hard rock bottom of the cave. You will notice a small opening around to the left side of the stack to another smaller chamber around the bend in the cave with Gold Bars," Weise said as they slowly walked through the cave to chamber number one.

"Indescribable, man, the glow from the Gold Bars is almost blinding. There must be a billion dollars worth of Gold Bars in this one cave chamber. I understand why you have kept this secret with you for these years. Anyone that worked on bringing the Gold Bars into the cave had to be dealt with harshly," Wolfgang said looking around chamber number 1.

"Yes, and you will not believe how many of the Gold Bars I personally brought here on a daily basis over the years from the hotel cave entrance area."

VILLA KRAUSE, ARGENTINA -- Former German Gestapo officers, who brought their wealth to this remote Northwestern Argentine town and employed many Argentina soldiers, police and peasants; were observed at various times to execute their own Gestapo soldiers without a trial.

TREASURES OF WAR – CONCEALED BY THE EVIL ONES / 15

Former Deputy Fuhrer, Heinrich Weise together with his driver 'Marty' Shultz began an attempt to locate all of the Gold Bars and Jewish Gold that Weise had shipped from Heidelberg, Germany to Argentina during the war. He ordered 'Marty' to Villa Krause, Argentina to bring Krause to Weise's special offices at the hotel in Mendoza.

'Marty' drove up the San Juan road at the foot of the Andes to Villa Krause. Upon his arrival he went to the Gold Smelting operation to find Krause. The man in the office told 'Marty' that 'Rudy' had taken one of the trucks and drove into San Juan for some supplies.

After waiting for about four hours 'Rudy' returned with a truckload of supplies. 'Marty' went back to the door of the warehouse, "Krause, 'Heini' wants you to come with me to his offices in the hotel in Mendoza for some important meetings."

As 'Rudy' continued to give instructions to the men unloading the supplies, "OK, let me finish getting these supplies unloaded."

"We need to get going as quick as possible," 'Marty' urged.

"Okay, let me drive my truck and follow you to Mendoza. Where will we meet in case I lose you?" 'Rudy' asked.

"Let's met in the lobby of the hotel. You know 'Heini's favorite hotel in town."

I bet 'Heini' wants me to tell him where all the Gold Bars are located now. 'Rudy' thought to himself.

After the one-hour drive to Mendoza, 'Rudy' set down at a table just outside the hotel and waited for 'Marty' and 'Heini' to meet him for a cup of Brazilian coffee.

Thirty minutes later, 'Heini' and 'Marty' came out looking for 'Rudy' and found him sitting at the table. "Welcome to Mendoza and the best Argentine wines and some of the best wines in the world," 'Rudy' said as he greeted them.

"I have purchased Les Vinos de Las Novias located less than three kilometers to the east of us. As you both now know, this is the wine capital of the Americas. I was looking for a unique place located nearby which would be handy to store some of the Gold Bars. Those huge wooden wine vats imported ten or fifteen years ago from Italy are extremely strong with steel bands around each of them. I have placed Gold Bars in two of them. Nineteen hundred thirty-six and thirty-four were good years. Do you get my drift? I have one of the Les Vinos de Las Novias grape hauling trailers out at the yard under tight security as we speak. Things were getting tough with the local fiscals up in Villa Krause, so I decided to establish operations here with only a few of my trusted security guards aware of the movement of the Gold Bars to Mendoza. When we finish our coffee here at the hotel, let's take a ride out to the winery. I believe that you will be pleased with my decision to operate here. There is a small airport with service to Buenos Aires twice a day," 'Rudy' elaborated.

"How many Gold Bars do you have here in Mendoza?" Weise asked.

"Finish up your coffee and we will go to the office and I will take the records out of my safe and give you an up-to-date inventory report. I have been well received by most of the good ole Italian and Argentine people here in Mendoza. Charity goes a long way with the peasants. You will see what I mean with the service here at the hotel," 'Rudy' bragged.

Upon arriving at Les Vinos de Las Novias, former Deputy Fuhrer, Heinrich Weise, stepped out of the car and looked all around the complex and said, "this is larger than I was expecting. Eight buildings with daily operations with the grape vineyard operators is a good long-term investment for me."

"I told you that you would be please," 'Rudy' replied.

"I noticed you have two armed men over there near the trucks and trailers. Which one of the trailers is the one with the Gold Bars in it?" Weise asked.

"Let's walk over to the one directly under the large tree, and I will introduce you to Escobar and Juan." 'Rudy' replied.

"Escobar and Juan, this is the big boss, Mr. Heinrich Weise, the man that I have been telling you about. You should do whatever he tells you to do when he is here and when I am not present."

Escobar and Juan immediately clicked their heels and stood at attention and Juan replied, "bueno, yo sí la criada, absolutamente."

'Rudy' walked around to the rear of the large trailer, untied the cover and lifted it a few feet and pointed inside. "See the Gold grapes ready for processing here at the winery."

Laughing, Weise replied, "bet you have to leave them a long time in the vats in order to ferment and become a year of some of the best drinkable wines. When are you transferring them into the Perseverancia?"

"Escobar, Juan and I are the only ones involved in this storage transfer. We will do it at 23:00 tonight."

"'Marty', looks like some of the missing Gold Bars have been accounted for. Let's take a look inside the Perseverancia and locate the two vats, years 1934 and 1936, the good wine years," Heini commanded 'Rudy'.

Entering through the small door into the Perseverancia and walking down the elevated wooden walkway between the three or four meters high wooden vats on each side of the chosen walkway and securely placed in the concrete saddles on the concrete floor, 'Rudy' led them to the vat marked year of 1936. He stepped off the main walkway and stepped up the wooden ladder to the large sealed opening in the center of the top of the vat. "Heini, the ladder is wide enough for three people. This opening at the top is where the wine is periodically tested. I will pull this opening off the vat and show you the Gold Bars in storage here as wine of the good year of 1936."

"'Marty', I believe that your inventory of missing Gold Bars has some corrections to be made to it. 'Rudy', how many Gold Bars are in this wine vat?" Weise asked.

"Here is a copy of the inventory sheet for the Perseverancia, including the ones in the trailer. A total of one thousand nine hundred and eighty Gold Bars weighing 12.5 kilos each are here."

"Are these some of the last ones that you re-smelted in Villa Krause and brought here or are they some of the Gold Bars removed out of the Villavicencio Pass hotel caves?" Weise asked.

"These are from the final shipment of Gold received from Europe which I re-smelted in Villa Krause over the past few years."

TREASURES OF WAR – CONCEALED BY THE EVIL ONES / 19

"We should leave and return to the hotel in Mendoza so that you, Escobar and Juan may continue your work here. I am very tired from the travel. The airplane stopped at every small airport between here and Buenos Aires. The dirt runway at San Luis was quite a surprise to me as we landed. Dust flew up everywhere. Just after takeoff from San Luis, we were at about two or three thousand meters up in the sky, and one gaucho just flipped his cigarette down the aisle with it still on fire. Obviously he had never been on an airplane before. I saw the carpet begin to burn, and I jumped up out of my seat and stomped the fire out. I must leave now," Weise commanded.

FOUR MONTHS LATER IN A MEETING IN MENDOZA.

Former Deputy Fuhrer, Heinrich Weise, summoned Wolfgang Schmidt to his private office at his hotel at Villavicencio Pass. Upon entering the office, Wolfgang rapidly asked. "What happened to Krause? Is he alive?"

"You remember the newspaper stories about unearthing the skeletal remains of the forty-two found dead at Villa Krause. Did I answer your question?" Weise asked.

Weise asked his secretary to bring two guest of the hotel to his office to meet Wolfgang. The two men entered the room and were introduced by Weise. "This is your new chief for our Western Argentina operations, Sr. Ernesto Kruger, and Sr. Dietrick Greenberg, our new chief financial officer, responsible for assisting you and I to make Gold Bullion deposits around the world."

"Greenberg, what Jewish Ghetto did you live in before the war?" Wolfgang immediately asked.

"Whoa! Wolfgang. I have done my due diligence on Mr. Greenberg and I know that he understands the confidential nature of his duties and responsibilities. What better way for you and I to prevent questions about where our source of Gold Bullion Bank Deposits originated? The new offshore corporate entity I established is British/American Investment Ltd. I am the Chairman and Chief Executive Officer; you are the Vice Chairman and President; and Mr. Greenberg is the Executive Vice President and Chief Financial Officer. Yes, I own sixty percent of the stock, and you own forty percent of the stock. The excellent salaries for Mr. Kruger and Mr. Greenberg with some special annual incentive bonuses will keep them in line. I do not have to remind them of the alternatives," Weise fully explained and warned.

TREASURES OF WAR – CONCEALED BY THE EVIL ONES

Chapter Two

The Story of Private Roy James Autrey, A. S. No. 38343655

Baby's Days

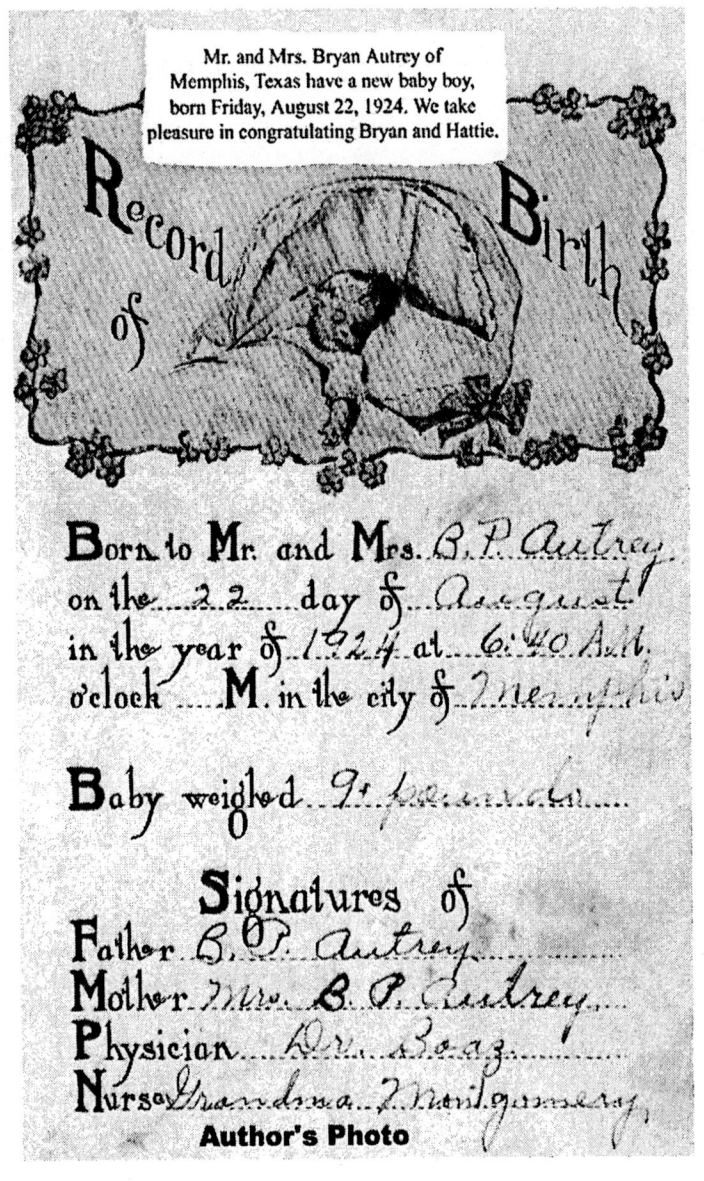

Mr. and Mrs. Bryan Autrey of Memphis, Texas have a new baby boy, born Friday, August 22, 1924. We take pleasure in congratulating Bryan and Hattie.

Record of Birth

Born to Mr. and Mrs. B. P. Autrey on the 22 day of August in the year of 1924 at 6:40 A.M. o'clock M. in the city of Memphis

Baby weighed 9¼ pounds

Signatures of
Father B. P. Autrey
Mother Mrs. B. P. Autrey
Physician Dr. Boaz
Nurse Grandma Montgomery

Author's Photo

Our son was born on Friday, August 22, 1924 in Memphis, Texas. On August 25th we named him Roy James Autrey. As parents, his father, Bryan P. Autrey and I, his mother, Hattie M. Autrey were so happy and felt God had truly blessed us.

He weighed a little over 9 pounds. My husband was a hard workingman. He was a master craftsman with many talents to later share with his newborn son. We had modest means, but a very strong Christian faith. Our goals in life were to devote our time to our faith, each other and the upbringing of our son. God had blessed us with so many talents, friends and family members that cared about each other during those hard economic times.

I kept a record of our son's Baby's Days in the book that I bought at the department store in town. One of the presents was from Zeb Jr. Some of the gifts were sweaters, comb and brush, powder puff, shoes, caps, bootees, hose, slips, clothes bag and rings.

TREASURES OF WAR – CONCEALED BY THE EVIL ONES / 23

Baby's first Kodak picture was taken when he was only eleven days old. We intended to take it when he was just a week old, but it rained and was too cloudy.

In the Mother's Record section of the Baby's Days begins with "Baby's first trip on the train was from Memphis, Texas to Pilot Point, Texas when he was almost four months old. We left Memphis on January 2nd. While at Pilot Point we visited in Dallas, Greenville, Whitewright. While on our visit to Pilot Point baby took the whooping cough. He was then six months old. We stayed there until he was almost over it and then came back to Memphis, Texas.

First Shoes – Baby wore his first shoes in 1924 presented by Aunt Rena.

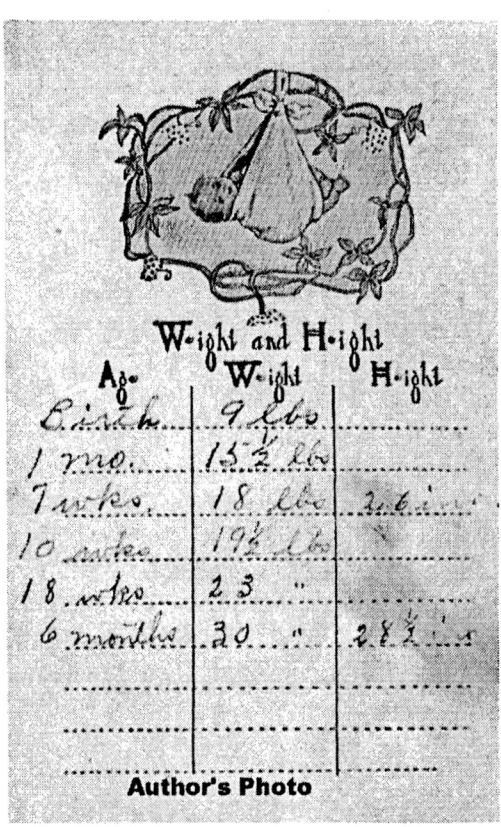

First Lock of Hair — Baby's first lock of hair was clipped by Mother on the 8th day of July in the year of 1925 when baby was nearly one year old.

Baby's Days – Remarks:

His baby ring was given to him by Aunt Sue Autrey on December 11th, 1924. Aunt Tinnis brought him another ring the first time she came to see him. He sat alone for the first time the day he was five months old. He crawled backward when he was six months old and did not learn to crawl forward until he was 9 months old. Began pulling up to things he could get hold of when he was nine months old. Would take a chair and push it all over the house and walk holding on to it.

First Word – Baby's first word was Da! Da! spoken at the age of eight months.

First Tooth – Baby's first tooth was discovered on 19th day of February in the year of 1925 when Baby was nearly 6 months old.

Mother's Record:

He is beginning to talk at 9 months of age. He says, Da! Da! Bye, go, and doll. He has eight teeth. Daddy is trying to sleep in the daytime, as he is working at night. Baby gets under the bed and goes up to his head and talks to him. So there is not much sleep for him. When he does get Daddy awake, he just laughs because he knows he will get to have a big romp. He loves to go take Daddy's dinner with Mother, just goes to jumping when we start.

On the 8th day of July 1925, Mother trimmed his hair for the first time. August 11th he made his first trip to the barbershop. He was 11 months old. Sat up in the chair real nice to have his hair cut.

First Step – Baby's first step was taken in the year of 1925 when our Baby was ten months old.

Photograph – 16 months old.

Remarks:

10 months old and is beginning to walk. Received a package today from Grandma that contained little sheets for his Kiddy Koop. Pillowcases, two new aprons and a big sack of "candy" from Big Dad. When he hears music, he tries to dance. 16 months old, when Mother steps out the door, he goes to the door and hollows for 'Too' (Aunt Sue) to let him in her part of the house. When he wants me to take him, he puckers up his mouth to kiss me and when I stoop for the kiss, he grabs around my neck and gets up. He says lots of words, shoe, car, go, doll, drink, Sue, Charles, candy, don't, choo choo (train), kitty.

Favorite Toys – His first toy was a green celluloid duck with a red head to put in his bathtub, given him by Aunt Sue Autrey. Dolls, ducks, rubber rings, rattles of all kinds.

First Christmas was December 25th, 1924. Baby was 4 months old when he celebrated his first Christmas. He received lots of rattlers, balloons and etc.

First Birthday:

Date: August 22, 1925 was spent at Pilot Point, Texas. Aunt Annie baked him a nice cake and placed a little pink candle on it. We took pictures of him with his cake.

Mother's Record:

Baby celebrated his second Christmas when he was 16 months old, tumbled out of bed in his little night gown and what a time he had when he discovered his "stocking" full of candy, fruit and lots of toys. Santa brought him a coaster wagon, a train that run on a track, a big auto delivery car with rubber tires, fiddle, pistol, engines, cars, picture book, wagon, new apron and baby plate.

Daddy has just bought a new car so baby asks for his hat and coat every morning, and has to go for a ride. He says "car" and "Daddy".

SEVERAL YEARS LATER

Daddy came home from across the road from working at the pipeline transmission company plant during one of those strong Texas Panhandle northern cold front that blew the door open and cooled everything in the house.

"Mom, I got a promotion to plant foreman. But it has a new assignment tagged along with it," Bryan told Hattie and Roy James.

"Praise the Lord," Hattie replied as she ran over to hug Bryan.

"Yes, we are going to move to the new plant being constructed in Shamrock," Bryan continued. "Just think, we will move out of the cotton capital county of Texas. Hall County has been good to us. Roy James, you were born here in Memphis, but it is time to meet the next challenge in our life. God has opened this door for us to go on down the road to new opportunities to serve him and have a good job during these hard times," He firmly spoke to his family.

"Let's take time to stop and give thanks to God for his blessings."

After giving thanks, Daddy went into the small living room of the company house and sits Roy James down and explained the details of the events of the day.

"Daddy, I have never lived anyplace but here

in Memphis. Mom and I have gone to visit Grandma Montgomery and Mam Maw Autrey back in Pilot Point. I won't know anybody in Shamrock. I don't want to move. Can't we stay here? I will miss my friends at Sunday school and church," Roy James sadly told his Daddy.

"Son, you and I must prepare for the challenges we will face in life as well as the ones during your education. If I decided to turn down this promotion in the company, future opportunities would pass me by. Shamrock is located on the main highway, Route 66. You are at the important age to learn as much of your basic fundamentals to grow up in a better world than I have achieved. Do you understand?" Daddy asked Roy James in his attempt to make the disturbing news easier to understand.

"What do you mean by a better world?" Roy James asked.

"When I went to Shamrock a few weeks ago to supervise the final fabrication and construction of the gas and oil gathering systems at the new plant, I nosed around to see what kind of schools, churches and growth was there. They have a Boy Scout Troop in Shamrock. Because of the businesses from all around the county are moving to Shamrock to be connected to the major railways, the progress from the oil and gas discovery boom, and the large number of workers building homes; new and very good schools are being built to make it better for young boys like you," Daddy explained to his son as Mom walked into the room to announce supper was ready.

"Sounds like Daddy knows a lot about where we are moving too," as Mom voiced her support to Roy James. "Let's wash up and get ready for supper."

"One other thing, you and I will go down to the North Fork of the Red River and try to catch some of those catfish," Daddy blurted out as he put his arm around Roy James on their way to the supper table.

"Red River, is that the same Red River that we go to fish near here?" Roy James asked.

"Yes, it is also near Shamrock."

TRIP TO HOUSTON, TEXAS IN 1933 TO VISIT WITH HIS UNCLE FRANK AUTREY AND GRANDMOTHER BENNIE AUTREY TRUETT AND OTHERS

"Mom, do we have everything in the car for that long ten hour trip down to see Mam Maw and all the family in Houston?" Bryan asked from the front door.

"It is so early my mind is not like your early to work brain. I packed everything that we put on the kitchen table last night plus the suitcases in Roy James' room and our bedroom. Yes, I think we have everything in the car," Hattie replied to Bryan.

Photo Includes Author's Mother and Grand Parents and Great Grand Mother

1933 Family Reunion Houston, Texas Roy with Grandma and Great Mam Maw

"I am going to pick up Roy from his bed together with the pillows and lay him in the back seat," Bryan said as he walked back into the home.

As Bryan laid Roy in the car he said. "He can sleep for another three or four hours before the sun comes up to see the country side."

The long trip was uneventful and everyone was glad to see them upon our arrival in Houston. Uncle Claud and Bryan's sister, Bennie, gave us their guest bedroom with a small fold away bed for Roy James to sleep. Bryan's brother, Frank Autrey, had driven over from Louisiana. But, most importantly to all of us was the chance to visit with Bryan's mother, Mam Maw. She was in good health and such a soft loving person. She would always teach all of us many good lessons about life. Roy James enjoyed sitting down at the piano and attempting to play from the beginners' songbooks. Family reunions were a special time in our lives. The kitchen at mealtime was a good time to catch up on the whereabouts of all the family members and write down some scrumptious recipes from all the excellent cooks in the family. I learned how to prepare fish and make in some unique delicious dishes.

The men and boys would talk about the church, business, sports, and who caught the biggest fish. Roy James was all ears and learned some valuable lessons.

A YEAR LATER – OUR VACATION TO GALVESTON, TEXAS.

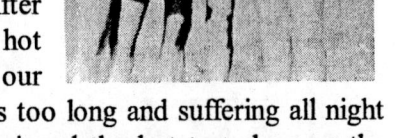

Some of my side of the family, the Montgomery and Mullinek families drove down from Pilot Point and Dallas to meet us at the beach in Galveston. We spent four days at a motel complex on the beachfront and enjoy the surf at every chance we could. After learning not to stay out in the hot sun in our bathing suits with our very white complexion bodies too long and suffering all night long from the sunburn, we enjoyed the last two days on the beach under the umbrellas the vendor had for us to rent. We would run out and jump into the gulf water and splash around and run back and get under these large umbrellas. Now, it was time to say our good byes and make the long drive north to Shamrock.

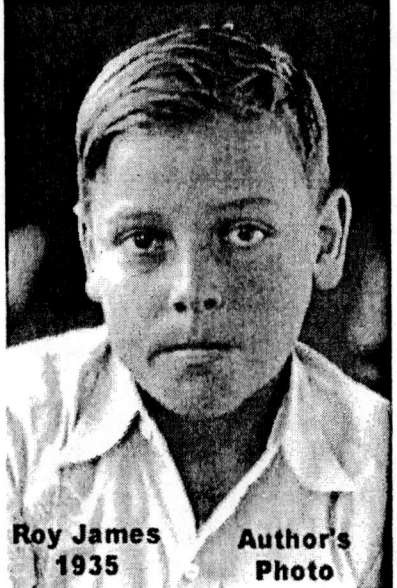

"Son, I went to the library and found a series of books entitled, *Scouting for Boys*. The books are some very good stories about young boys learning to hunt and spend time enjoying the Texas plains. I believe that next to studying your bible these books may illustrate the importance of scouting," Daddy explained as he handed over his notes from the library.

"Also, the name of the scoutmaster at the church, Mr. Ryan is on the paper," he added.

"Mr. Ryan, I know him. He is very nice. He taught my Sunday school class one time when

Mr. Clarkson was gone somewhere," Roy James said as he quickly dashed over to his dad to get the paper.

"Good son, I have offered to be a helper to Mr. Ryan and learn more about the scouting program. You and I will study the Boys Scout program together."

"I'm excited Daddy. I will stop by the library after school tomorrow and look at some of the books."

"Shamrock's Boy Scout Troop is Troop 1909. Mr. Ryan gave me a Scout leaders training guide to help me understand the important ideals of scouting, such as Its Motto, Oath, Law, Slogan and Outdoor Code. Here are the details of these ideals. I believe that a young man who lives by his Christian teachings and patterns himself after the Boy Scout Codes will learn how to deal with life." Daddy revealed to Roy James as he reached over and handed him the pamphlet.

Roy James turned to the section of the Boy Scout Handbook and began to read.

SCOUT LAW

A Boy Scout is:

- **TRUSTWORTHY.** A Scout tells the truth. He keeps his promises. Honesty is part of his code of conduct. People can depend on him.

- **LOYAL.** A Scout is true to his family, Scout leaders, friends, school, and nation.

- **HELPFUL.** A Scout is concerned about other people. He does things willingly for others without pay or reward.

- **FRIENDLY.** A Scout is a friend to all. He is a brother to other Scouts. He seeks to understand others. He respects those with ideas and customs other than his own.

- **COURTEOUS.** A Scout is polite to everyone regardless of age or position. He knows good manners make it easier for people to get along together.

- **KIND.** A Scout understands there is strength in being gentle. He treats others, as he wants to be treated. He does not hurt or kill harmless things without reason.

- **OBEDIENT.** A Scout follows the rules of his family, school, and troop. He obeys the laws of his community and country. If he thinks these rules and laws are unfair, he tries to have them changed in an orderly manner rather than disobey them.

- **CHEERFUL.** A Scout looks for the bright side of things. He cheerfully does tasks that come his way. He tries to make others happy.

- **THRIFTY.** A Scout works to pay his way and to help others. He saves for unforeseen needs. He protects and conserves natural resources. He carefully uses time and property.

- **BRAVE.** A Scout can face danger even if he is afraid. He has the courage to stand for what he thinks is right even if others laugh at or threaten him.

- **CLEAN.** A Scout keeps his body and mind fit and clean. He goes around with those who believe in living by these same ideals. He helps keep his home and community clean.

- **REVERENT.** A Scout is reverent toward God. He is faithful in his religious duties. He respects the beliefs of others.

SCOUT OATH

"On my honor I will do my best
To do my duty to God and my country
and to obey the Scout Law;
To help other people at all times;
To keep myself physically strong,
mentally awake, and morally straight."

SCOUT MOTTO

"Be Prepared."

SCOUT SLOGAN

"Do a Good Turn Daily."

OUTDOORS CODE

As an American, I will do my best to:

TREASURES OF WAR – CONCEALED BY THE EVIL ONES

Be clean in my outdoor manners;
Be careful with fire;
Be considerate in the outdoors;
And be conservation-minded

ONE YEAR LATER.

"This meeting of Boy Scout Troop 1909 is called to attention. Face the American Flag and Let's say the pledge of allegiance," Scoutmaster Ryan instructed the troop as he took charge of the meeting.

"I pledge alligiance to the flag of the United States of America and to the Republic for which it stands, one nation, indivisible, with liberty and justice for all."

"Be seated, we are going on a field trip to 'Big Red' Boys Scout Camp out at the river Friday afternoon. Some of you need to prepare for earning new merit badges while we are out there. I will go out to the camp shed ahead of time to make sure that the canoes are in good condition. Roy James, you need to bring your 22 rifle with the shells in a separate packge along with your camping gear. None in the rifle," Scoutmaster Ryan reminded him.

"Yes sir, Daddy and I have talked about what I need to do to earn my rifle shooting merit badge," Roy James seriously responded.

"Good, David, you need to bring your bow and arrows for earning your archery merit badge. That will give you a total of eight merit badges. That is very good," Ryan said with a proud voice.

"Thank you, I will be prepared."

"I have the merit badges each of you earned over two months ago. Come up here and pick up your certificates and badges. Then, when you leave here tonight, go home and do an extra favor for Mom and get her to sew them on your Boy Scout shirts," Scoutmaster Ryan said in his bragging Texas Panhandle manner.

"Mr. Ryan, my rabbit raising merit badge is not here," Curtis said as he looked through the remaining merit badges.

"Oh yea, I received a letter telling me that it would be backordered and mailed at a later date."

"I worked many hours building that rabbit hutch with the feeder and water holes. I took my Dad's wheel barrow down to Sullivan's Farm and Feed Store to buy the bales of hay for the fresh straw I needed to cover the floor of the hutch every week for more than six months. Raising those two different breeds, the California and Rex taught me many things like genetics of the best rabbit for show and best for selling the meat. Emptying that litter box every day was my responsibility. It was well worth it. I learned a lot and won the first place blue ribbon at the Wheeler County Fair."

"I saw your picture with you holding your champion rabbit in the newspaper. You did good," Scoutmaster Ryan replied with a big smile across his round face.

"Thank you."

"Boys, you have a good opportunity to perform and live up to your scout's slogan by doing a good deed everyday. Mrs. Skelton is recovering from surgery and needs someone to check on her at her home on Thomas Street. She may need help doing some chores around her home. She is not supposed to lift anything heavy," Mr. Ryan explained to the boys with all ears.

"Mr. Ryan, Roy James and I will check on her everyday," Curtis answered.

"Another need is for one or two of you to go down to the hospital and see old man Koenig. He is recovering from a broken hip. He fell off his tractor last week."

"David and I will visit him after school tomorrow," Ralph answered Mr. Ryan as he was pointing across the room to David, who was shaking his head in approval.

"Remember, you are a member of our Boy's Scout Troop and always listen and follow his instructions," Scoutmaster Ryan told the boys.

"Are there any other matters that we need to discuss?" He asked the Troop.

"OK, repeat after me."

"On my honor I will do my best
To do my duty to God and my country
and to obey the Scout Law;
To help other people at all times;
To keep myself physically strong,
mentally awake, and morally straight."

"You are dismissed."

FRIDAY AFTERNOON.

"Roy, it is time to load the pick up with our overnight camping, fishing and hunting gear for our trip to 'Big Red' Boys Scout Camp," Bryan instructed his son.

"Yes sir Daddy, are we going to sleep in the bunk house or in our tents?"

"You better prepare to sleep in either one."

"I will put the tents in the pick up."

As they drove down to church to pick up a few more of the boys for the camping trip, Bryan asked his son. "Have you studied your manual and learned all the possible questions that will be asked to earn your rifle shooting merit badge?"

"Daddy, I have memorized them all."

"Excellent son."

Each boy loaded his package bags into the various vehicles and off to 'Big Red' Boys Scout Camp they went. They were all very excited to be going for the overnight camping trip. It was a cold windy fall afternoon in this part of the Texas Panhandle. The boys were wearing their warmest clothes and boots. It took about thirty-five minutes to reach the campgrounds. After the boys grabbed their packs and camping gear Scoutmaster Ryan and Assistant Scoutmaster Autrey called all the boys around them and gave each of them instructions as to where they would be sleeping. They reminded the boys who had brought special equipment such as guns to place them on the table in the corner of Scoutmaster building.

"Martin, do you want to earn a portion of your fishing merit badge before dust?" Ryan asked.

Boy Scout Troop
Shamrock, Texas
1936

Author's Photo

Roy James Autrey

"Yes sir."

"Take your fishing tackle and box of hooks and lures over to that table over there near the large Mesquite tree," Mr. Autrey said as he gave directions to Martin.

"Yes sir." Martin said and picked up his rod and bait casting reel together with the box of hooks, weights, tools, knife and fresh liver his father had given him to catch some catfish in the river.

Martin patiently waited for Mr. Autrey to finish working out the details of the other Scouts. He noticed that others were given certain camp clean-up duties to perform. He felt very lucky to be able to begin earning his fishing merit badge.

"Alright Martin, pull out your spiral notebook and write down the answers to these questions. Do you have to have a license to fish in public places here in the State of Texas? Is there a size limit for each fish that you catch and may keep? Explain why we have regulations affecting fishing here where we live? The final question for today is, name and explain five safety practices you should always follow while fishing. When you finish your written answers, bring them to me in my cabin. Tomorrow, I will go over the remaining requirements. Do you have any questions about any of the questions so far?"

"No sir, I understood all of them," Martin replied.

"I leave it with you. Tell anyone that comes over to talk to you that you are doing your written portion of your fishing merit badge and can not talk to them until after you turn it in to me. Be sure your name, today's date and the merit badge name is on each page of your written answers."

"Thank you Mr. Autrey."

"You're welcome, keep up the good work. You have another merit badge test on Sunday, swimming. It will go toward reaching your goal to become an Eagle Scout."

Just as the sun was setting over the mountains in the west the Scouts gathered some dead wood and stacked it in the middle of the campfire area.

"Let me have a volunteer to light the fire without using a match or fuel lighter. Anybody!" Mr. Ryan shouted as he looked around the campfire. "OK, Carl you try your best to show us how it is done."

Carl ran into his cabin and brought some things from his camping pack. Then, he ran into the edge of the woods and picked up some dry leaves and straw. After a few minutes and his soft blowing on the red flame spots on the leaves he got the rich wood chips and leaves to begin to burn. All the Scouts clapped and congratulated Carl. It was time to tell stories of some of the interesting things that had happened to them or things unusual that they had seen. Rabbit hunting trips and how the rabbits ran from one burrow to the next to make you chase them until they finally stopped long enough to take a shot with your 22 rifle before they ran off into the woods to lose you, was one of the favorite stories that each Scout shared and attempted to top the other ones adventure. These stories included the learning process for field dressing the rabbit, skinning it to save the fur and cutting it up in preparation for cooking it in different ways, including with Mom's freshly make flour dumplings.

In the middle of some of the stories being told around the campfire, Mr. Autrey asked. "Roy James, David and Curtis, be very careful and not burn yourself, pull a few of the burning pieces out of the fire and put them under each of the pit grills, then, stack some of the dry firewood on top of it and fan it until you get a good fire going good. Mr. Ryan is getting the hamburger steaks ready for cooking. Any volunteers for becoming one of the chefs tonight?"

Every Scout in camp raised his hand except Dement. "Hey, Dement, go over to my pick up and grab one of those gunnysacks of potatoes. Bring it over here to this grill pit and I will show how easy it is to be a good cook."

"Yes sir, Mr. Autrey."

Mr. Ryan brought out a couple of trays of hamburger patties from his cabin. "There are three more trays of patties in the cabin. Some of you guys get them for me. Hey, Scouts, there are some bowls of my excellent spread sauce in there on the counter."

"Dement, take this foil and tear off pieces about twice the size of the largest potato. Wrap each potato in the foil and put it on the lower grill over the fire. No, No, don't reach in under that upper grill. Take your gloved hand and raise the top grill up against the brick smoke chimney end. Otherwise you might burn your arm from the hot top grill."

"Now I understand. Wow, this is a hot fire Mr. Ryan."

"Did any of you see my brushes next to the bowls of sauce? There is some more turning forks, flippers, spatulas, and the like in there. Bring them out here for each cooking crew to use at each pit grill."

The Scouts brought the cooking utensils out and put them on the old log tables next to the cooking grills. They worked as teams. One would put the hamburger patties on the grill, another would take the brush and baste the heavy sauce on them as it was grilling, and another one would take and turn over the patties and on and on until each one was done. They saw Mr. Ryan putting the cooked ones at the end of the grill with very little fire was burning.

"Do you Scouts want cold hamburger buns or do you like yours heated up?"

"Mr. Ryan, let's warm them before we put the patties on them.

"OK, go inside and get those boxes of buns that the Colonel's Bakery brought to me on his morning delivery this morning. The fire has died down and just put each side of the bun down on the grill and heat it. Mr. Autrey, would you please get the jars of mustard, pickles and the fresh tomatoes from the cabin?

"Yes sir"

ROY JAMES AUTREY'S HIGH SCHOOL YEARS.

Roy James was very active in his mechanics class. His father had taught him how to use all of his tools to repair things around the house, his bicycle, occasionally his friend's cars and our family car. The shop across the road from our house at the Gas and Oil Transmission Plant was equipped with just about everything in the world. Bryan, the master craftsman, taught his son how to weld both piping and structural steel and do pipe fitting.

Roy James had plenty of time to participate in both football and basketball for Shamrock High School. He was a four-year letterman in both sports. Due to the rapid growth in the county from the development of the oil and gas industry, many people from all around the Panhandle and other oil and gas areas like Southeast Texas and Southern

Louisiana moved into Shamrock. Roy James took it upon himself to make the new fellow high school students feel welcomed to the community. He would bring them by the house for a piece of my pecan pie and a glass of milk. He learned as much as he could about where they had come from and how many members were in their family. Being an only child was something that motivated him to seek out new friends at school. He invited most of his friends to go to church with him on Sunday. This usually happened during the week or if he forgot, he saw to it to invite them at the Saturday night drive end.

Before you could say 'what's-his-name', Roy James, my All-American son, and many of his classmates were graduating from Shamrock High School.

Shamrock, Texas - Class of 1942

Hattie Autrey and Son Roy James Autrey May, 1942 — Shamrock High School Graduation

Classmates - Class of 1942

My father and I talked about going to war. He had served in the United States Army in World War I. He rose to the rank of sergeant.

It was September 1942 and I had reached the age of 18 and decided to volunteer for the enlistment into the United States Army. As a young recruit, I passed the old 1, 2, 3 physical without any problems. I was assigned to the 79th Infantry Division and boarded a troop train to Camp Blanding in Starke, Florida for my basic training.

In early March 1943, our unit joined up with Second Army No. 1 Tennessee Maneuvers where we participated in the training. Due to the number of new recruits and space, I transferred to Camp Forrest, in

Tullahoma, Tennessee on July 19th, 1943.

The top brass had something special in mind for our unit and we were transferred one month later to Camp Laguna, Arizona for the Desert Training Center No. 3 California Maneuvers arriving on August 17th, 1943. This Camp's primary purpose was to prepare soldiers for combat fronts. No refrigeration or electricity, I lived in a tent with other guys. Having grown up in the Texas Panhandle I had experienced some harsh weather conditions. However, the Arizona desert is a place where you divide the men from the boys real quick. They wanted us to experience the most severe hardships and conditions that any soldier could face in combat. Most of my company were from parts of the US and had never experienced the heat of a desert. The daily routine had us up early in the summer sweltering heat and we almost froze to death during the cold winter nights. No mess hall, just canned rations was the norm. World War II was not going well on the battlefields in Europe and in the Pacific. Everyone knew that more fighting soldiers were desperately needed. Our division had done well in this inhuman training.

The Battle of Camp Laguna
(Author--Unknown Soldier)

We are the boys from Camp Laguna,
Earning our meager pay.
Guarding the people's millions
For one sixty-five a day.

Out in the windswept desert
Camp Laguna is the spot.
Fighting the terrible dust storms
On the land that God forgot.

All night the wind keeps howling.
It's more than we can stand.
Hell, folks, we're not convicts.
We're the defenders of the land.

For the duration we must take it.
Many the years of life we'll miss.
Don't let the draft board get you,
And for God's sake, don't enlist.

Out in the desert with rifles,
Eating and drinking the dust.
Doing the work of a chain gang
And too damn tired to cuss.

Out with the snakes and lizards,
Here's where the boys get blue.
Out in the windswept desert
Three thousand miles from you.

No one cares if we are living.
No one gives a damn.
Where we came from is soon forgotten,
For we're loaned to Uncle Sam.

We wash a lot of dishes
And peel a million spuds.
We have our hands all blistered
From washing dirty duds.

And when life is over
And we will work no more,
We will do our final dress parade
On the bright and golden shore.

Then Saint Peter will greet us,
And suddenly he will yell,
"Come in you boys from Camp Laguna.
You've served your time in Hell."

Mrs. W. E. (Jean) Stevens provided this written poem of a unknown soldier about the life in Camp Laguna that was found in the desert during World War II, by chance, and given to the historical society.

In late November 1943, we received our orders to travel army-style to Camp Phillips, near Salinas, Kansas. About five thousand of us arrived on December 4th, 1943. The weather reminded me of back home in Shamrock, Texas. Strong north winds so cold that you must wear long johns and an overcoat. We were assigned to the 44th Infantry Division.

Now we had completed the harsh desert training and the U. S. Army wanted us to focus on fine-tuning our artillery and gunnery skills during our advanced training at Camp Phillips. Private Autrey stood out as a skilled rifleman in Company 'C', 324th Infantry Regiment, 44th Infantry Division.

Christmas time provided a time to obtain a ten days furlough for all the men who were from the mid-west region. Roy James was eager to visit his parents.

Page Four

With Our Boys And Girls In The Service

Pfc. Roy James Autrey, who is now in Shamrock visiting his parents, Mr. and Mrs. Bryan Autrey, and his many friends and relatives, has completed his training at Camp Laguna, Arizona and is currently on his new assignment with the 44th Infantry Division at Camp Phillips, Kansas.

"Mom, Dad, here are some photos taken from Camp Phillips. As you can see some of the artillery cannons are very large. My best friend, Bud Gauerke is in the middle next to me on the right at retreat one day. Bud and I went down on Santa Fe Street in Salinas and had one of those quick I. D. photos in a booth made. Pretty good looking soldiers, right Mom?" Roy James asked as he pointed to the photos.

"Very handsome young men. Tell me more about your training?" Mom replied.

"We are awakened at 05:00 every morning and literally jump into our warm-up outfits and get in line for roll call, then, the master sergeant begins the daily routine of calisthenics, close order drill, organized athletics including ample physical exercise and stretching. Working up a good appetite, we march over to the mess hall for a good breakfast. They feed us plenty of eggs, bacon, sausage and sometimes steak with freshly baked bread.

At 07:00 we fall in formation in front of our barracks and march along the streets inside the Camp for anywhere from one hour to two. We are dismissed for thirty minutes to return to our barracks to change into our combat uniforms with backpacks and weapons."

"Mom, I only have two weeks home furlough during the Christmas holidays to make up for the year I have been in the Army. I know that you are very interested in learning what I have been through and all that, but I do not want to discuss most of it and I have been given orders to say very little about what we are doing and what our next assignment might be. I hope that you and Dad understand," Roy James interrupted the conversation.

"Roy, your Mom and I know that you will make us proud of you and since you are our only child we are eager to learn everything," Dad replied.

"We have always been a close family, and I have never kept anything from you up until now."

"Changing the subject, Roy you love football. Your cousin's team down in San Angelo beat two undefeated teams and won the state championship. Aunt Mary sent us the articles for both games. In the semifinals they pulled out a big upset of the Bobby Layne and Doak Walker team in Dallas. Highland Park's quarterback, Bobby Layne passed and Doak Walker ran and jumped out to a 20-7 third-quarter lead. You remember your cousin telling you about San Angelo Bobcats' teammates Milton Rathbone and George Graham as they were growing up?" Dad replied and asked.

"Yes Sir! When we were together throwing the football around the side yard at the last family reunion, he told me that Milt could throw the football more than 50 yards and hit the receiver."

"It must have been an exciting fourth quarter. Some headlines said it was the game of the decade. The Bobcats trailed the Scotties 20-14 and had driven down to the Highland Park 7-yard line with very little time remaining. The dramatic finish came when Rathbone threw a lateral to one of his halfbacks and the football bounced off referee Abb Curtis. With several players from both teams running and diving to get the fumble, Milt scooped up the ball and changed direction and ran around the left end for a touchdown. The extra point try would put them in the lead for the first time. George Graham, the fullback had made the first two extra points with Milt holding. His third extra-point of the game, won it for the Bobcats," Dad dramatically said as he played out the hand motions to the winning play and extra point kick.

"I sure would have like to have seen that game. Maybe it was more than the game of the decade," Roy replied.

"The next week San Angelo beat Lufkin 26-13 to win the state championship. Milt threw three touchdown passes and your cousin played on the championship team," Dad said completing the football stories.

Mom slipped out into the kitchen while Dad and Roy were talking football and began preparation of supper and some of Roy's favorite meals.

"Did Mom tell you that we are moving?" Dad asked.

"No Sir!"

"I have completed my assignment here and the plant is going well and company needs me to take over the Gas and Oil pipeline transmission station down at Goodrich, Texas."

"That's the plant where Uncle Frank has been constructing for several years?" Roy asked.

"Yes, the company wants me to complete the calibration of the controls for the movement of the fuels through the pipelines to the north and east. Afterwards, I have been told that I will become the plant superintendent. We will live in one of the company houses on the plant site."

"Great Dad, you will be doing your part to support these crazy wars with Germany and Japan. I bet the demand for crude oil for the refineries has made your job a twenty four hour a day task."

"Thanks son. Yes, the pipelines that supply our customers on the east coast are under heavy military security. I don't know whether you have been apprized of the secret information about the German U-Boats firing torpedoes and sinking some of the oil and fuel barges from the Texas and Louisiana refineries off the Florida and east coast on the way to ports on the east coast. The pipeline has become more and more important for the plants building military equipment and most critical, the transportation fuel for the ships, trucks, tanks and airplanes. Knowing that you are going to be fighting overseas, makes me aware that I have a personal interest in seeing that the fuel gets to where it is needed."

"Dad, you fought the Germans in the last war. What can you tell me about what I should expect over there?"

"Son, that was more than twenty-five years ago. I am sure that things have changed dramatically. The newsreels show a mighty German army possessed with the ideals of this Dictator Hitler. It is a very different war in many ways due to the intense SS leadership to control the world with its fascism. However, my best advice is to be prepared for the worst possible weather conditions and do the things that you believe is best to win the battles."

"I really appreciate your advice. We have a new commanding general who commanded the troops during the victory at Guadalcanal and Solomon Islands and had Infantry experience during World War I in France. Everyone seems to have a new enthusiasm to follow his leadership," Roy replied.

"What's his name?" Dad asked.

"General Alexander Patch," Roy replied.

"OK, I remember him as a Lt. Colonel in the war. He was a proven warrior," Dad said.

"Hey, you men ready for some hot supper," Mom said as she appeared from the kitchen.

"Mom, it smells good. Bet you fixed one of those smoked hams with sweet potatoes and a pecan pie."

"Almost correct, I have some of your favorite lima beans too. I will open a jar."

"Mom, I am excited for you and Dad getting to move out of the Panhandle to South Texas. You are

Private Roy James Autrey
Author's Photo

going to meet new friends and still have all the ones you have made here."

"That is going to be the hard part, leaving our long time friends here and the memories of you growing up to the young man you are today. But Dad knows that this is a good promotion as a reward for all of his hard work here. He deserves it and the new challenge is something God has provided for us."

"Mom here is one of my recent photos. Am I too serious in this one?"

"No, I like this one. You look like my young soldier."

"Mom here is my Texas drivers license. I can't use it in Kansas and really don't need it while I am in the military. Keep it for me until I return from the war.

On March 21st, 1944, Private Roy James Autrey and the men in 324th Infantry Regiment, 44th Infantry Division began packing equipment for their relocation and overseas staging on the east coast. They boarded a troop train at the railroad station for the long winding trip to Camp Myles Standish, Massachusetts. After stopping to pick up other soldiers from other camps along the way, they arrived on March 31, 1944.

Each man knew that he was through training and off to fight the Germans and Italians in Europe. It took two weeks at Camp Myles Standish to account for all of the men and their required battlefield equipment.

The Division embarked out of the Port of Boston on April 7th, 1944 for England. It took the ocean liner nine days to complete the voyage. The troop buildup in England was spectacular. The top brass was planning something big and Private Autrey and his company

TREASURES OF WAR – CONCEALED BY THE EVIL ONES / 45

confirmed that they had been assigned to the U. S. 7th Army under Lieutenant General Alexander Patch.

In July 1944, we were packing up again to travel directly by troop transport landing vessels from England to participate in the invasion of Southern France on the Mediterranean Sea coast near the Port of Cannes, France. On the voyage we learned that we were part of OPERATION ANVIL/DRAGOON, which was an invasion of Southern France in concert with OPERATION OVERLORD landings from across the English Channel earlier on June 6th, D-Day. We got lucky. The weather was good for an August 15th beach landing between Toulon and Cannes.

Once on shore, Free French forces joined us. Captain Berry told me that there were several other U. S. infantry divisions together with French commandos and U. S. airborne forces included in Operation Dragoon. On the second morning, he told our battalion that all we had to know was that we are going to keep the German forces occupied in Southern France and complement our other fighting forces in Italy and northern France.

The combination of the D-Day invasions at Normandy and a concentrated aerial bombardment on German Forces in Southern France caused them to pull back to the north and created a lot less opposition than everyone expected. Occasionally, the German Luftwaffe would make air raids during the cover of darkness. Lieutenant Carter pointed out an old church and we worked our way to the churchyard and set up camp. We had come approximately five miles inland and were awaiting our next orders. During the third night a good ole 'North Texas Thunderstorm' came roaring in and the downpour of rain caused us to seek shelter in the church. The next morning some of the French people came to the Church and greeted us with all the love and warmth in the world. They were obviously happy to see us and know the Germans had been removed from their town.

Lieutenant Carter told us that we were waiting for the American 8th Air Force Bombardment Group out of Lavenham, England to complete the bombing raids down the Rhome Valley to soften up the enemy. Day seven, we got our orders to move out. We were advised, "Don't forget your rear flanks."

As we pushed north the smell of death of dead horses and cows along the roads was something to wake us up. Now, we knew that we were in a war. The U. S. Army Air Force had bombed and strafed all vehicles and killed the retreating Germans. Frequently, someone ahead of us had buried a German soldier at a nearby gravesite, marked by a German helmet on something stuck into the ground.

As we marched up the roads near the river, Private Autrey kept gazing up to the high French Alps Mountains off to his right. The beautiful valleys had grape vineyards with row after row of grape vines alternating with rows of olive trees. The local French people provided us with places, such as warehouses, stores, and the palaces, to set up camp.

On September 7th, our orders were to take the town of Grenoble and Besanson. After locating the enemy, Lieutenant Carter asked for volunteers to take out the German garrison overlooking the town from a hillside. Private Autrey took his company with mortars and set up behind three boulders approximately 2,000 yards from the enemy. After zeroing in on the target, we blew up the German position. We liberated Grenoble and took a large number of prisoners.

As we approached Besanson, we came under some fanatical resistance. It was the first for Private Autrey. Through the sound powered phones, Lieutenant Carter directed me to draw the fire to locate the major battery firing upon our men. Carter told me to take a few of my buddies and run at a fast speed across an opening and then drop down. It worked. From Carter's position he located both the site of the German fire and noticed that hits in the ground were from large caliber shells. Then, the phone message came, "Begin a few fast steps and then slow down for thirty yards and stop when you hear the first shot."

The German artillery soldiers fell into the trap. They anticipated our fast running across the opening and the shells hit way out in front of us. Lieutenant Carter took control and ordered his other men to take out the artillery guns. We crushed the resistance and took control of the city.

Company 'C 'of the 324th Infantry Regiment, 44th Infantry Division, was a special trained and diversified unit with artillery, mortar, mine clearing and demolition squadrons.

After liberating these two cities, we enjoyed a few days of the local hospitality. American soldiers were something of a novelty and the French people were very excited to see us and gave us warmth that reminded me of the family gatherings back in Pilot Point, Texas. Families invited us to dinner. They dug out some of their finest wines that had been hidden from the Jerry's during occupation. We attempted to communicate with them with the best Texas sign language and a little Spanish that I had learned back in Shamrock.

A week later, Lieutenant Carter came by and told us to be prepared to move out at 07:00 the next morning. The last supper in Besanson was something very special for our Company. Apparently, some of the townspeople could see that our features had already changed to a more serious mindset and feel the change in our manners. The next morning in a drizzling rain, as we marched down the main street north to our next assignment, the streets were lined with the local families shouting, cheering and waving at us. It was a rewarding feeling for all of us.

It seemed to grow colder every mile further north. During a rest stop in the afternoon, Lieutenant informed us that our next major battle would be the liberation of large city of Lyon. Occasionally, a few 'lost' straggling enemy soldiers would attempt to slow us down with some rifle fire. Each time we opened up on them; they surrendered.

When we reached Lyon, we learned that the French Maquis had liberated this city of half a million people. It began to snow and the north iceberg like snowstorms came roaring over the mountains and through the hillsides and down into the valleys blanking everything white. We were not prepared for winter. Private Autrey needed insulation of his dark colored uniform. One evening he found some old newspapers in a building and stuffed them inside his clothes and army shoes. The winter of 1944 was the coldest, snowiest weather he had ever experienced.

Again, the hospitality of townspeople was unbelievably outstanding. We were treated to some fine places to stay for a few days, drank some fine wines and fed slaughtered beef and other livestock. The supplies lines from the Mediterranean Coast had began to catch up with us and more trucks and supplies were appearing each day. We jumped onto some of the new troop and supply trucks and rode out of Lyon on October 5th.

The German Luftwaffe made a few dives with guns a blazing as they past over us. Everyone knew that we were getting closer to the front battle line.

Surprisingly, when we reached Dijon the Germans had fled the city and done very little damage to the airfield. We drove out to the airfield and could not believe that the runways and taxi strips were in tack. We set up our tents just off the west end of the runway closest to the airport tower. Being near an airfield, the rumor was running rampant that we Americans would be home by Christmas.

Lieutenant Carter called us together and gave us his instructions. We were ordered not to talk to any of the local folks about our plans. Our orders were to be prepared to travel to Epinal, where we would link up with all of the 7th Army and all Allied Armies to conquer the Germans.

November 8th, east of Luneville, France, Company 'C' of the 324th Infantry Regiment, 44th Infantry Division took part in the Seventh Army drive to secure the Vosges passes in the Parroy Forest. The Vosges hillsides were covered with snow and ice in some of the worst weather conditions seen by the soldiers of the 44th. Kraut propaganda speakers sending out loud messages such as, "come on over to us, soldiers of the 44th, and have a hot meal". Some of the men gathered up some wood and built fires to warm their hands and feet and heat some fresh coffee. Ignoring the propaganda, the men ate their cold rations and drank the hot soothing coffee. Lieutenant Carter assembled all of his warriors and gave them some advice and warned them to be on alert for movement of the enemy in winter snowsuits. He told them that the United States Army Field Artillery Battalions would be pounding the Germans in the heavy fortified pillboxes, machinegun nest and dugouts and on the ridges and in the woods. He reiterated the important need for the communication soldiers to keep in constant contact with him of their position and the location of enemy firepower.

"We have four Battalions of Field Artillery backing us up. Let's use them. If you get a sniff of them, I want to blow them out of this world. Some of the large German 88's will be used against our tanks, I want to know when you spot one, then, especially the propaganda speakers," Lt. Carter assuredly told his men.

"You men understand the expression of making a charge like a herd of buffalos. The Field Artillery will begin tonight by firing more than 20,000 rounds. You will not get much sleep or rest, but neither will they. At 05:00 tomorrow morning, the 324th Regiment will be joined by the 71st Regiment to surprise the Jerry's by climbing up to the front lines along the edges of the woods. May God be with you and I know you will do what you have been trained to do and make me proud on everyone of you," Carter continued.

On the night of November 12th, the Field Artillery Battalions of the 156th, 157th, 217th, and 220th began to shower the Germans with constant pounding.

TREASURES OF WAR – CONCEALED BY THE EVIL ONES / 49

On November 13th, as one of Sergeant Cook's accurate hand grenade throwers, submachine gunners and tommygun marksmen, Private Autrey without regard to his own personal safety volunteered to risk his life to destroy the two German machinegun nests dug in about one hundred fifty yards apart. As only a trained fighting Infantryman must do in his lonely battle with the enemy shells bursting around him, he charged across the coverless terrain like a swivel hip college halfback at Notre Dame running for a long touchdown in the game against Michigan. A burst of machinegun fire was bouncing off the snow and ground all around him. About 30 yards from the first enemy nest he dropped to the ground and pulled the grenade pin and tossed it toward the nest making a direct hit killing four Germans. Immediately, he jumped to his feet at deadly close range and began firing his tommygun killing two more. The remaining 6 Germans through up their hands and surrendered. Using the six prisoners as a shield from the other German machinegun nest at the east end of the opening, Roy James marched the prisoners back to his Company 'C' who were dug in a ditch.

Private Roy James Autrey continued his relentless advance against the remaining German machinegun nest by circling from a different direction across the open field. Sixty yards from his target, he was struck by bullets from the machinegun and knocked to the ground. Wounded, he struggled to a crawling position and crawled to within twenty yards of the nest. On his back, Roy James pulled the pin on two grenades and tossed them back over his head. One grenade hit the bull's eye killing three Germans. He rolled over and sat up with his drawn tommygun in his uninjured arm. The other ten Germans surrender.

Private Roy James Autrey staggered to his feet and stepped forward ten steps or so until he stepped on an anti-tank mine. He fell mortally wounded.

Autrey's gallant fighting courage, heroic deeds and supreme sacrifice forced the enemy to leave the area and retreat, clearing the secret path for his company to march on to victory a few months later.

Some of those lifetimes during World War II were short.

Private First Class Roy James Autrey was awarded posthumously:

| Purple Heart With Bronze Oak Leaf Clusters | American Commendation | Army Commendation | European African Middle East Campaign | World War II Victory |

The Purple Heart was originally established in 1782 by Commander-in-Chief George Washington, revived again in 1932, and in 1942 President Franklin D. Roosevelt issued an Executive Order which provided that the Purple Heart would be made available to members of all US Armed Services who were wounded in action. Since then the Purple Heart has become one of the most highly respected decorations of the US Armed Forces. The decoration holds a very unique position in that the wound must have been received as a direct result of enemy actions. **The Badge of Merit.**

TREASURES OF WAR – CONCEALED BY THE EVIL ONES / 51

The telegram that every mother and father dreads to receive was received by Mr. Bryan Autrey on December 6th, 1944 from the War Department in Washington, D. C.

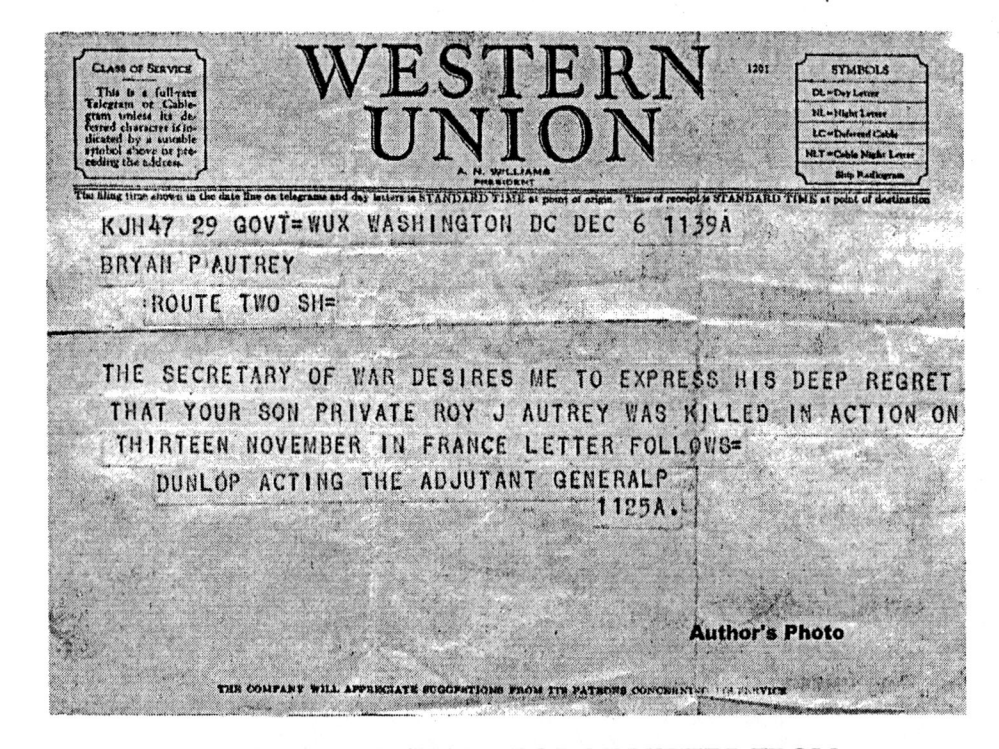

WESTERN UNION

KJH47 29 GOVT=WUX WASHINGTON DC DEC 6 1139A
BRYAN P AUTREY
ROUTE TWO SH=

THE SECRETARY OF WAR DESIRES ME TO EXPRESS HIS DEEP REGRET THAT YOUR SON PRIVATE ROY J AUTREY WAS KILLED IN ACTION ON THIRTEEN NOVEMBER IN FRANCE LETTER FOLLOWS=
DUNLOP ACTING THE ADJUTANT GENERALP
1125A.

Author's Photo

PRESIDENTIAL SEAL – TOP OF LETTER FROM PRESIDENT FRANKLIN DELANO ROOSEVELT

Author's Photo

IN GRATEFUL MEMORY OF

Private Roy J. Autrey, A.S.No. 38343655,

The Letter January 10th, 1945, from the Secretary of War informed Mr. and Mrs. Bryan P. Autrey of the posthumously awarding of the Purple Heart to their son, Private Roy James Autrey.

> January 10, 1945.
>
> My dear Mr. Autrey:
>
> At the request of the President, I write to inform you that the Purple Heart has been awarded posthumously to your son, Private Roy J. Autrey, Infantry, who sacrificed his life in defense of his country.
>
> Little that we can do or say will console you for the death of your loved one. We profoundly appreciate the greatness of your loss, for in a very real sense the loss suffered by any of us in this battle for our country, is a loss shared by all of us. When the medal, which you will shortly receive, reaches you, I want you to know that with it goes my sincerest sympathy, and the hope that time and the victory of our cause will finally lighten the burden of your grief.
>
> Sincerely yours,
>
> Henry L. Stimson
>
> Mr. Bryan P. Autrey,
> Route #2,
> Shamrock, Texas.

Author's Photo

TREASURES OF WAR – CONCEALED BY THE EVIL ONES / 53

The Memorial Service for Private Roy James Autrey, son and only child of Hattie Dohoney Montgomery Autrey and Bryan Perry Autrey, was held at Clay Funeral Home in Shamrock, Texas in January 1945.

"For God so loved the world, that He gave His only begotten Son, that whosoever believeth in Him should not perish, but have everlasting life." (John 3:16).

Author's Photo

CLAY FUNERAL HOME
SHAMROCK, TEXAS

54 / DON STEWART NIMMONS

WAR DEPARTMENT
OFFICE OF THE QUARTERMASTER GENERAL
WASHINGTON 25, D. C.

IN REPLY REFER TO: QMGMR 293
Autrey, Roy J.
A.S.N. 38 343 655

14 April 1947

Mr. Bryan P. Autrey
Route #2
Shamrock, Texas

Dear Mr. Autrey:

    Inclosed herewith is a picture of the United States Military Cemetery Epinal, France, in which your son, the late Private Roy J. Autrey, is buried.

    It is my sincere hope that you may gain some solace from this view of the surroundings in which your loved one rests. As you can see, this is a place of simple dignity, neat and well cared for. Here, assured of continuous care, now rest the remains of a few of those heroic dead who fell together in the service of our country.

    This cemetery will be maintained as a temporary resting place until, in accordance with the wishes of the next of kin, all remains are either placed in permanent American cemeteries overseas or returned to the Homeland for final burial.

Sincerely yours,

G. A. HORKAN
Brigadier General, QMC
Chief, Memorial Division

1 Incl
    Photograph

Author's Photo

U.S. MILITARY CEMETERY, EPINAL, FRANCE

IN GRATEFUL MEMORY OF

Private Roy J. Autrey, A.S.No. 38343655,

WHO DIED IN THE SERVICE OF HIS COUNTRY AT

in the European Area, November 13, 1944.

HE STANDS IN THE UNBROKEN LINE OF PATRIOTS WHO HAVE DARED TO DIE

THAT FREEDOM MIGHT LIVE, AND GROW, AND INCREASE ITS BLESSINGS.

FREEDOM LIVES, AND THROUGH IT, HE LIVES—

IN A WAY THAT HUMBLES THE UNDERTAKINGS OF MOST MEN

Author's Photo

Franklin D Roosevelt

PRESIDENT OF THE UNITED STATES OF AMERICA

On January 31st, 1945, The Secretary of War awarded the PURPLE HEART To Private ROY JAMES AUTREY For Military Merit and For Wounds Received In Action Resulting In His Death on November 13th, 1944.

THE UNITED STATES OF AMERICA

TO ALL WHO SHALL SEE THESE PRESENTS, GREETING:

THIS IS TO CERTIFY THAT
THE PRESIDENT OF THE UNITED STATES OF AMERICA
PURSUANT TO AUTHORITY VESTED IN HIM BY CONGRESS
HAS AWARDED THE

PURPLE HEART

ESTABLISHED BY GENERAL GEORGE WASHINGTON
AT NEWBURGH, NEW YORK, AUGUST 7, 1782
TO

Private Roy J. Autrey, A.S.No. 38343655,

FOR MILITARY MERIT AND FOR WOUNDS RECEIVED
IN ACTION
resulting in his death November 13, 1944.

GIVEN UNDER MY HAND IN THE CITY OF WASHINGTON
THIS 31st DAY OF January 1945

Author's Photo

BURIAL FLAG

Author's Photo

    Inclosed herewith is the same United States flag which was used during the burial services held at the time your loved one was permanently laid to rest in a United States Military Cemetery overseas. This flag, which is forwarded to you by the Government directly from the cemetery, is being presented as a token of sympathy and appreciation of a grateful nation with the thought that it may prove to be of sentimental value to you.

    In order that you may receive this flag in the shortest possible time it is being sent without detailed information relative to specific grave location within the cemetery.

    Within a short time you will receive from the Department of the Army a letter furnishing complete information concerning the cemetery, the grave location within the cemetery, and the headstone which will be erected at Government expense. This letter will be sent from the Department of the Army, Office of the Quartermaster General, Memorial Division, Washington 25, D.C.

TREASURES OF WAR – CONCEALED BY THE EVIL ONES / 57

327-A Silver lake Street
Oconomowoc, Wisconsin
August 2, 1945

Dear Mr. and Mrs. Autrey:

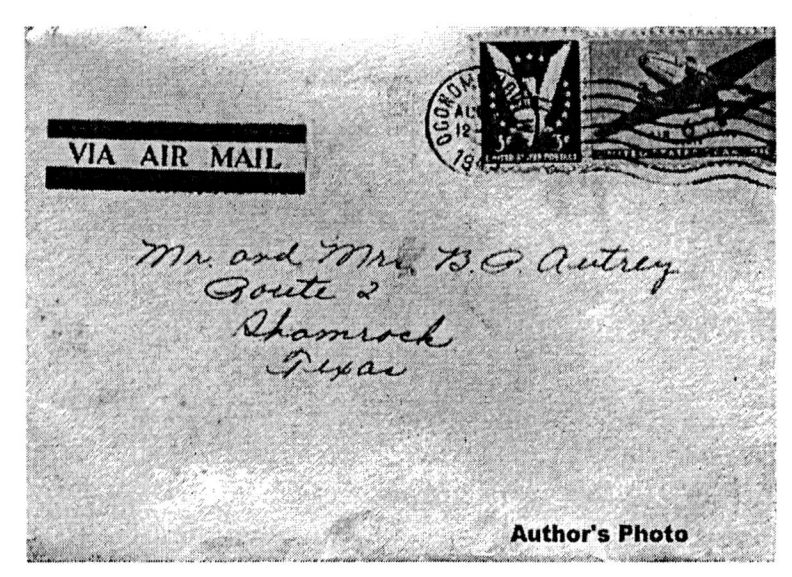

Your letter came last week, but so did Bud, which was reason I didn't write sooner. He arrived a week ago yesterday --- or the 25th.

When I hadn't heard from you for so long, I meant to drop you a line again; but I'd been working, which kept me rather busy. Of course, I'm not working now. But I am glad you are feeling better, and glad to know that wasn't what kept you from writing.

Regarding Rose Mary! I can't remember her last name, nor do I know her address. However, I do know she was from St. Louis, Mo.; and I believe she went with the Navy as a nurse. It seems the last I heard she was in California.

I meant to send you a picture of Bonnie Sue, but now I'll wait until I take some of her and Bud together. The ones I have now are all a few months old.

I'm going to let Bud finish this letter now, as he's sitting here anxiously waiting for me to finish. Next time I'll try to write more.

Sincerely,
Teresa

Hello Folks,

I'm very sorry I didn't write to you sooner, and I'm sure you have been very anxious to hear what I had to say. I did want to answer your letter as soon as I received it, but at the time I wasn't able to give you the information you so badly wanted.

Ever since I heard of Roy's death; I must speak frankly about it because there has been so much of it. I tried in every way that was possible for me to try and find out how it happened, and it wasn't until a week before we left France that I learned the facts, and at the time they were no longer accepting mail at the A. P. O. I did not talk to the man who saw it, but from another good friend of Roy's who had.

It is not a long story. Because in War I believe you know Mr. Autrey death can come very fast, and to Roy it did, but not without reflecting his courage and the stuff he was made of and it is something you, his mother and father can be proud of.

The day was one dreary sleety day as they all were in France just after one of the first light snowfalls, making it very tough for our boys. They were assigned the task of taking and clearing out the Parroy Forest, between Huneville and Sarrebourg. You probably never heard of it, but it was some of the toughest, most miserable fighting our division ever faced. It was the beginning of the battle that broke the German's back.

Roy's squad was assigned the task of taking a machine gun nest. Roy was carrying the B. A. R. One of our most feared weapons when carried by a man who knows how to use it, and Roy did. Well Roy's squad started across the open ground towards the woods and the machine gun. When a heavy mortar and machine gun barrage pinned them down. They stayed down for some time, and the Roy as you would know him to do, said, "We can't stay here all day" and started to make his way forward with the rest of the men following.

Roy was wounded in the leg by machine gun fire. This could have been the easy way out. The "Million" dollar wound Infantry Men talk about; but Roy, I hardly need to tell the rest you will know it as well as I. He refused to stay down and be evacuated. Hardly able to walk he hangs onto his B. A. R. He keeps going forward. He hadn't gone more than thirty steps and he stepped on an anti-tank mine. His death of course was instantaneous. That is where my relation of the facts ends. But being in the engineers where we handle German mines; I know just how terribly potent they are. It makes me very sad to have to recall this

TREASURES OF WAR – CONCEALED BY THE EVIL ONES / 59

heartache to you, and also to recall it to myself, because Roy was my best and closest friend, but I also know you would never cease trying to learn the truth of Roy's death. I'm sure you must agree with me that no man could meet death in a finer, more glorious way. Not that war and dying in it was looked forward to by him, but he loved life and his way of life so much that he fought to the death for it. I think that in passing the final test.

I want to say a few words for myself. I can't express how wonderful it feels to be back home with my wife and angel daughter. It seems as though I just arrived yesterday, and already more than a week has passed. And the thought of leaving again is staring me in the face, and to say so long the second time is well nigh onto impossible. And I'm hoping and praying every day that circumstances will arise which will make it un-necessary for me to make that Pacific trip.

As Teresa has already said, we plan to get some pictures taken and we want to send one of the family to you folks, and I'm hoping that someday after the War, soon, we will be able to make the trip down to see you. Roy always wanted us to do that. And I know we will enjoy it immensely.

This is all for tonight.
May God bless and keep you always.
          Love,
               Bud (Cpl. R. Gauerke)

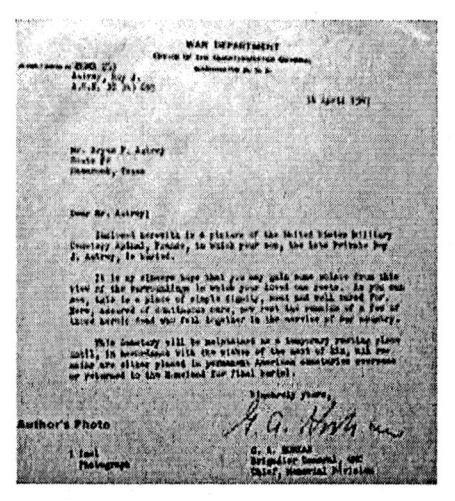

The World War II Epinal American Cemetery and Memorial is located approximately four miles southeast of Epinal (Vosges), France on Road D-157 in the village of Dinoze-Quequement. It can be reached by automobile via toll Autoroute A-4 eastward to the Nancy Exit. Take Highway N-57 and exit at Arches-Dinoze. Rail service is available from Gare de l'Est, Paris via Nancy, where it may be necessary to change trains. The journey by train takes about five hours. Air travel is available from Paris to the Epinal-Mirecourt Airport. Travel by air takes forty-five minutes. Adequate hotel accommodations and taxi service can be found in Epinal and vicinity.

PRIVATE FIRST CLASS ROY JAMES AUTREY

Is Buried -- Plot B Row 4 Grave 12

South Side Section of Court of Honor and Tablets of the Missing

The cemetery, forty-eight acres in extent, is located on a plateau one hundred feet above the Moselle River in the foothills of the Vosges Mountains. It contains the graves of 5,255 American military Dead. The 46th Quartermaster Graves Registration Company of the U.S. Seventh Army established it in October 1944 as it drove northward from southern France through the Rhone Valley into Germany.

The cemetery became the repository for the fatalities in the bitter fighting through the Heasbourg Gap during the winter of 1944-45.

The memorial, a rectangular structure with two large bas-relief panels, consists of a chapel, portico and museum room with its mosaic operations map. On the walls of the Court of Honor, which surround the memorial, are inscribed the names of 424 Americans who gave their lives in the service of their country and who rest in unknown graves.

Stretching northward is a wide tree-lined mall, which separates two large burial plots. At the northern end of the mall the circular flagpole plaza forms an overlook affording a view of a wide sweep of the Moselle valley.

On May 12, 1958, thirteen caskets draped with American flags were placed side by side at the memorial at Epinal American Cemetery. Each casket contained the remains of one World War II "Unknown" American serviceman; one from each of the thirteen permanent American military cemeteries in the European Theater of Operations. In a solemn ceremony, General Edward J. O'Neill, Commanding General of the U.S. Army Communication Zone, Europe, selected the "Unknown" to represent the European Theater. It was flown to Naples, Italy and placed with "Unknowns" from the Atlantic and Pacific Theaters of Operation aboard the USS Blandy for transportation to Washington, DC for final selection of the "Unknown" from World War II. On Memorial Day, 1958, this "Unknown" was buried along side the "Unknown" from World War I at the Tomb of the Unknown Soldier at Arlington National Cemetery.

Resurrection - South Facade of Memorial

World War II Epinal, France, American Cemetery and Memorial

It contains the graves of 5,255 American military Dead. The cemetery became the repository for the fatalities in the bitter fighting through the Heasbourg Gap during the winter of 1944-45.

Interior of Chapel, East End of the Memorial

Museum Wall Map (Left Section)

In the summer the cemetery is open to visitors daily from 9:00 am to 6:00 pm and in the winter from 9:00 am to 5:00 pm.

In honor of Private Roy James Autrey, cousin to the mother of the author, and the daily reminder of the ultimate price paid for freedom, the author has the collage as shown below hanging in his office.

Parent's broken hearts for the loss of their only son's life in a foreign land never to be able to see or talk to him again leaves them grieving each and every day for the remainder of their saddened and shortened lives.

Bryan and Hattie Autrey
Visiting Author's Parent's Home
Houston, Texas
1952

TREASURES OF WAR – CONCEALED BY THE EVIL ONES

Chapter Three

The Story of First Meiji Constitution in 1868 – Asia War

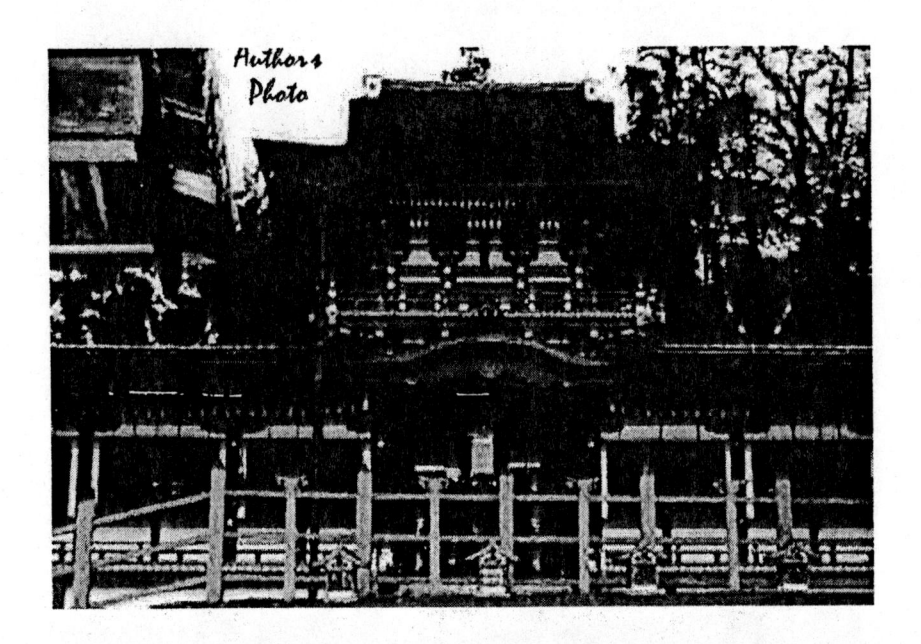

65 / DON STEWART NIMMONS

1868 THE FIRST MEIJI CONSTITUTION-SHINTOISM

Japan was the first country in Asia to have a constitution in the late nineteenth century. The Meiji Constitution established a constitutional monarchy and proclaimed the sovereignty of the emperor as a divine living god.

The religious cult and belief emerged as State Shinto and practiced in peoples' everyday lives. The word Shinto originated due to the competition of the traditional religion of Buddhism. Two Chinese characters are used to write Shinto. First, 'shin', is used to write the native Japanese word 'kami', meaning divinity, and second, 'to' is used to write the native word 'michi', meaning way.

On February 11, 1889, the proclamation of the Constitution of the Empire of Japan defined the Emperor as the constitutional monarch in a centralized unitary state. Never before in the history of Japan had the Emperor been worshiped as a living god – "the selfless wisdom of the universe." This was accomplished after the leaders of the Meiji Japan had engaged in 20 years of pragmatic political experimentation to redefine the imperial institution.

In this 1889 constitution, the Emperor was "sacred and inviolable," and sovereignty rested with him as the Head of the Empire of Japan. He was the sovereign and supreme commander of the Japanese armed forces, declared war, made peace, and concluded treaties; he had emergency powers to maintain public order and declare a state of siege. All laws required the Emperor's sanction and enforcement.

On December 25, 1926, His Imperial Highness Prince Regent Hirohito became the 124th Emperor of Japan and the new era was named Showa, "radiant peace".

The promotional publicity to the world from His Imperial Majesty Emperor Showa's (Hirohito) Imperial Palace during the first three decades of the 20th century was to portray him as a divine being with privilege. However, the samuriazation of the nation began to evolve during the third decade of the 20th century, from the concentration of the power of Emperor, to the local temples and villages onto the battlefields of Manchuria, China, Guam, and eventually Pearl Harbor.

Emperor Hirohito appeared in uniform in public, reviewed troops, and issued imperial decrees and decorated soldiers and sailors. Prior to becoming The Emperor and after formal training in the military, he was promoted to high ranks in both the Japanese army and navy. Throughout the years between 1926 and 1945, he refused to take action to stop the war machinery build up and the expansion of the full-scale wars in Asia and the decision to wage war on the United States.

Shinto fundamentalism, and reaction against foreign origin religious-philosophical movements, Nationalism became a strong driving force of His Imperial Majesty Showa's (Hirohito) society. One primary excuse preached and implemented by His Imperial Majesty depicted Japan being exposed to religious threats from abroad.

In <u>*Shintoism,*</u> the diverse religious cultures became the "Japanese Spirit", and became very evident as Japan expanded its powers in the Asian Wars in the late 1930's and early 1940's. The valiant Japanese soldiers became aware their spirit and loyalty caused them to look for the roots of their thinking habits, values and national identity. His Imperial Majesty Hirohito became the ruling force behind this "Japanese Spirit" throughout the battles to conquer and destroy its enemies. This "Japanese Spirit" enabled them to seek nothing at all for themselves, and be willing to discard body and mind and unite with The Emperor. The glorified thoughts of the "Japanese Spirit" so empowered the Japanese soldiers to die on the battlefield with assurance that the battle in which they were engaged is monumental majestic. They religiously believed the war was not a mere slaughter of their fellow-beings, but that they were combating evil.

The 1868 Meiji Restoration was one of the most significant historical changes in Japanese history. The country was united under the rule of the emperor. This change was a mental and spiritual one as well as institutional and political. They strayed away from Buddhism and turned to the older religion of Shinto.

State Shinto adopts those teachings, beliefs, philosophies and theories, which uphold the rule over other nations and peoples by Japan by the reason of:

(a)   The doctrine of the Emperor of Japan is superior to the heads of other states because of ancestry, descent or special origin.
(b)   The doctrine that the people of Japan are superior to the people of other lands because of ancestry, descent or special origin.

(c)   The doctrine that the islands of Japan are superior to other lands because of divine or special origin.

(d)   Any other doctrine which tends to delude the Japanese people into embarking upon wars of aggression or glorify the use of force as an instrument for the settlement of disputes with other peoples.

It became compulsory from the State for all Japanese people to believe or profess to believe in State Shintoism. It was mandatory for all Japanese national public officials and local governments and employees to inculcate the beliefs of militaristic and ultra-nationalistic ideology premeditated to bamboozle the Japanese people and to create an eternal being for all loyal subjects who were aggressive and fought the wars for the emperor.

The Shrine Board of the Ministry of Home Affairs included forced financial support, construction of Shinto shrines, ceremonies, rites, and observances would direct the doctrines of State Shintoism. The training of a Shinto priesthood, teacher's textbooks and manuals, commentaries, official writings, interpretations or instructions on Shinto was to be controlled by the State.

The God-shelves (kamidana) physical symbols of State Shinto was exhibited in all offices, schools, universities, institutions, organizations and central meeting places.

State Shinto is the only recognized religion for Japan followers. All Japanese, who worship other faiths, creeds or religions will not be protected, but persecuted by the State.

Within this Restoration the realm, the new Constitution, exalted the glorification, as deities of soldiers who died fighting for the monarchy became a military tradition with religious and cultural revelations.

In summary, the emperor ruled all branches of the Japanese government under the Meiji Constitution.

The emperor was aggrandized as the descendant of the Amaterasu Ohkami, the Sun Goddess, or the Great Glorious Goddess; and **Shinto became the state religion giving the government the superficial appearance of a return of the Age of Gods.** State Shinto became the patriotic ritual incumbent of all-Japanese. The Japanese government for its

The Koshitsu Shinto (Shinto of the Imperial House)

The Koshitsu Shinto is a general term for conclave rites performed by the emperor, (who is now the 'symbol of the state and of the unity of the people' under the Japanese constitution) in order to pray myriad deities centering Amaterasu Ohmikami (a Goddess who is the ancestral deity of the emperor according to the Japanese myth) and the Imperial ancestral deities for a long continuation of the state, for happiness of the people and for world peace, and it has an independent system. Daijosai, or Great Festival of Thanksgiving, is the first Niinamesai (a rite of Thanksgiving) performed by the newly crowned Emperor of Japan in a palace called Daijokyu, which is temporarily built inside the Imperial Palace. Besides this rite, rites performed at the Grand Shrine of Ise are to be included in this category, since Amaterasu Ohmikami is enshrined there.

Niinamesai is the most important Shinto rite, which is performed in order to make an offering of the first fruits of a year's grain harvest thanking the deities for their blessing and also sharing the food produced by these first grains with the deities. According to the Japanese myth, it was Amaterasu Ohmikami who performed this rite for the first time.

The clergymen and women called Shoten (men) and Nai-Shoten (women) are serving in order to assist the Emperor to perform the rites. The number of rites performed by the Emperor reaches ten to thirty a year including Genshisai, the first rite of a year. There are scholars who call the Emperor the king of the ritual. It is considered that the true nature of the Emperor is to be always with Kami (the deities).

69 / DON STEWART NIMMONS

CARRYING OUT THE BELIEFS OF THE EMPEROR – UNDECLARED WARS IN ASIA

Chinese Warlords battled the Japanese armies in the city of Shanghai in their attempt to save their wealth and power in the region. The Warlords did not understand the spirit of **The Evil God's** commandment to his warriors. Each warrior was prepared to sacrifice his life for **The Evil God**, Emperor Zapp, because this spirit was an eternal spirit. Japanese warriors believed absolute loyalty will result in no death.

It only took the Japanese invaders six weeks to control most of the city. When they captured an officer of one of the Chinese Warlords, he was taken to the nearest Japanese headquarters to be tortured. The torture was the "special" event of the day for some of the Japanese officers. The wild cruelty was never seen before in wars of the past.

"Col. Akirai, I have captured this Warlord Officer in the basement of the bank," Lt. Okochia announced as he came into the Colonel's temporary headquarters in the captured house.

"Well now, what is his name and the name of his Warlord?" the Colonel angrily asked.

"He will not tell us his true name. He expects the Chinese armies to come back and conquer us and win his freedom," Lt. Okochia laughingly responded. "He will not answer any of our questions."

"How unfortunate for him and his Warlord's treasures," Col. Akirai replied. "You men know exactly what to do to force out the answers that I want to know."

"Yes sir! Private Tao grab him by the hair and let's go into the yard for further torture," the Lieutenant gleefully said as they left to go out.

"Hang him by his arms to the post in the center of the yard. Where is my sword?"

"Let me run into your office and get it," Private Tao said as he bowed and ran to the office.

"Thank you! Private, begin the whipping with the steel chains." Lt. Okochia ordered.

TREASURES OF WAR – CONCEALED BY THE EVIL ONES / 70

"What is your name?" The Lieutenant asked the prisoner. "Make it easy for you and tell us everything we want to know about you and your family." he continued. "OK, Private Sakai, take off all of his clothes. Swing the chains across his upper butt and be sure they reach his front side," Lt. Okochia ordered.

"No! No! No!" screamed the prisoner.

Each time the chains whipped around the prisoner's body the blood flowed more profusely. The screams were weaker as time wore on from the beatings. Eventually, the prisoner fell unconscious because his brain could not cope with the pain from the beatings.

What should I do now? Private Sakai wondered to himself. Let me wait until he regains conscious. Maybe he is dead!

After learning that the prisoner was not responding, Col. Akirai went out into the yard. "Are you sure he's dead?" the Colonel asked.

"He is not dead but just unconscious," the Lieutenant answered.

"When he comes around, I want to know whether he has any daughters. Where they are? Tell him he can save himself; his treasures and his daughters; just tell us where everything is. I am betting on the fact that he is more interested in his life and his gold and gems than his family's safety," the Colonel continued.

"We will give him some liquor, bath him down and make him give us the answers that you need," Lt. Okochia stated as he bowed to the Colonel and tossed a bottle of whiskey to Private Sakai.

The Colonel returned to his room in the house of his temporary headquarters.

"Force some of that Whiskey down the prisoner, make him drink at least half of the bottle," the Lieutenant commanded.

"Yes Sir."

In the meantime, Major Hisaichi had captured another Warlord in a different section of the city and brought him to Colonel Akirai. The Major was wounded in the fighting to capture this Warlord.

"You are a true warrior of **The Evil God,** Emperor Zapp, he will be proud of all that you have done for him," Col. Akirai told the valiant warrior. "You know that you are combating these evil people and defeating the evil enemy," he genuinely spoke.

"Yes Sir," he said speaking for the first time. "May I go to the military clinic to have my wounds look at?" he asked.

"By all means," the Colonel replied. "What is your Lieutenant's name?" he asked.

"Lieutenant Sato, front and center," the Major ordered. "Colonel Akirai needs your assistance with this prisoner while I am gone to the clinic for medical treatment," the Major commanded.

"Yes Sir, what are your orders," Lieutenant Sato responded as he bowed to the Colonel.

"Bring this prisoner into my offices and put him in the back corner room with the window overlooking the side yard where the dead prisoners are laying on the ground," the Colonel said as he pointed to the door.

He grabbed the prisoner by the arm and led him to the back room. He seated him in a comfortable chair directed at the window.

"I know that you do not want to become one of those prisoners you see out the window," the Lieutenant said as he turned and looked out the window at the dead prisoners lying on the ground that had been killed by the sword of his men. "All you have to do is tell us your name and where your wealth is hidden," he demanded without giving him a chance to take a breath.

"If I tell you what you want to know, how can I save myself and family?" the frightened prisoner emotionally cried out. "I just want to live here and you can have my wealth. Just let me and my wife, sons and daughters live," he pleaded.

"Let me ask Col. Akirai about your pleadings," Lieutenant Sato assured him.

TREASURES OF WAR – CONCEALED BY THE EVIL ONES / 72

Lieutenant Sato left the prisoner under guard of one of his men as he went to see Colonel Akirai. "Colonel, may I come in?" he asked as he knocked at the door of the Colonel.

"Just a minute Lieutenant, I am writing my daily report to Emperor Zapp's brother," he replied.

After waiting in the hallway for about 30 minutes the Colonel summoned the Lieutenant into his office.

"The prisoner has made an offer to tell us about the location of his treasure and vehicles," Lt. Sato addressed the Colonel. "All he wants to do is live here in Shanghai with his wife, sons and daughters," he continued.

"Will he take me to see the treasure and vehicles that he has hidden?" Col. Akirai asked with a stern look on his face.

"Yes Sir, I believe he will. He just wants to live. The dead prisoners in the yard made a firm believer out of him. With your authorization I will proceed to have him take you and I to the hidden treasure and his vehicles. You could use a couple of good vehicles," the Lieutenant elaborated.

Daughters, Vehicles and Gold, what more could I asked for, he envisioned. *When Emperor Zapp's brother comes, I will be held in high esteem with him and his family.* Colonel thought.

"You have my orders to complete these negotiations with the prisoner," he guaranteed.

"Thank you Sir, I will let you know within the hour about where you and I need to go with this prisoner to claim his treasure and vehicles," the Lieutenant promised.

"Don't forget the daughters location also," the Colonel reminded him.

"Yes Sir, I will find out about everything," he assured the Colonel.

As the Lieutenant was going back to the corner office where the prisoner was being held, *the Colonel sure is very interested in knowing where the young daughters are located,* he questioned in his mind. *How do I convince this prisoner to give up everything in order to save the lives of his family and safely live here in Shanghai?*

"I got some good news for you, but you must act immediately," Lieutenant Sato forcefully told the prisoner as he burst through the doors to the room. "The Colonel has agreed to spare your life, but you have to pay for your freedom with your treasures and vehicles. He and I will follow your directions to the whereabouts of your treasures and vehicles. The Colonel will bring his forces to protect himself and carry the treasures back to his fortified bunkers," the Lieutenant said as he laid out the terms of the 'deal'. "What type and how many vehicles do you have hidden? Do you understand what you need to agree too?" He asked.

"May I keep a small amount of my treasures to buy food and necessities to live?" the prisoner humbly asked.

"No, do you think I am stupid. That was not part of the 'deal'. I need your correct name now! And, I need your agreement to the Colonel's offer to allow you to live, now" the Lieutenant forcibly expressed himself in the face of the prisoner.

With his head bowed, the prisoner spoke softly, "I am Ninh Zhao and I will take you and the Colonel to where you desire to go."

"Again, how many vehicles are there?" Lt. Sato growled. "My patience with you is gone. Where is your family? Answer all of my questions or you may end up having your head cut off with my sword like the others in the yard," He said heading out the side door to the yard.

"Wait, wait, I am ready to tell you everything; I just want to live here in Shanghai where I have lived all of my life," Zhao shouted. "There are two Daihatsui trucks and one four door sedan. They are two years old. My family is hidden out at my country estate some 30 kilometers from Shanghai," he told the young Lieutenant.

The Lieutenant did an about face and came running through the door and he promised Zhao. "If you are playing games with me and the Colonel and place us in danger from hostile elements from any of the few remaining Chinese Guerilla Forces along the way, and when the first shot is fired at us; the next gunshot that you will hear will be the last."

"I will draw you a map of the shortest way to get to both the treasures and vehicles in downtown and my family outside of town," Mr. Zhao assured Lt. Sato and he asked for some paper.

"Private Iwane, keep the prisoner under guard with your bayonet," Lt. Sato directed. "I am going to report to Colonel Akirai," he added.

TREASURES OF WAR – CONCEALED BY THE EVIL ONES / 74

The Colonel will love the new Japanese vehicles. The Lieutenant eagerly chuckled inside. He knocked on the Colonel's door. There was no answer. The Lieutenant fast stepped it outside to the recreation yard for the Colonel's troops. Across the yard under the overhang he saw the Colonel drinking some tea and eating his afternoon snack of fresh fish.

The Colonel looked up and saw Lt. Sato and motioned for him to come on over. "Is it time to cut the prisoner's head off?" He bellowed out for all to hear.

"Colonel, I have worked out your deal with the prisoner?" He replied.

"Colonel, the man's name is Ninh Zhao and he has agreed to leading you and I with our troops to locate the treasures and his two new Daihatsui trucks and sedan," Lt. Sato eagerly advised.

"Great news Lieutenant, but what have you worked out about his daughters?" Col. Akirai calmly asked.

Why is he pushing me to learn about the prisoner's daughters? Sato asked himself.

"He has three teenage daughters with the rest of his family hidden out at his country estate about 30 kilometers from Shanghai," Lt. Sato told the smiling Colonel.

Lieutenant, round up your battalion and get the remaining men of Major Hisaichi's battalion together out front at 16:00. Be sure you have enough trucks, at least two vehicles with mounted machine guns on them. Every soldier should be equipped with bayonets and grenades."

"Yes Sir, see you at 16:00."

LATER IN THE AFTERNOON.

"Colonel, Lieutenant Miyamoto Quickdraw from Major Hisaichi's unit has joined me with his battalion. I have all of the weapons and men that you ordered," Lt. Sato said as he bowed to the Colonel.

"Do you have the prisoner's maps?"

"Here they are Sir."

"Go get the prisoner and put him in my truck's middle seat beside me."

"Yes Sir," Lt. Sato said as he ran to the office where Japanese guards were holding prisoner Ninh Zhao.

Lt. Sato had Private Iwane bring the handcuffed prisoner and sit him in Col. Akirai's truck. The convoy of Japanese troops began to move out in an easterly direction toward downtown Shanghai. Colonel Akirai gave directions to his driver as they turned down several streets until they reached a warehouse building.

"Stop here!"

"Is this your building?" the Colonel asked the prisoner.

"Yes Colonel, you must let me enter the building by myself before you come in," prisoner Zhao replied.

"I did not get to be an officer of my ranking in Emperor Zapp's Army by being and doing foolish things."

"Lieutenant Quickdraw, take the prisoner and escort him to unlock the door to the warehouse. Lieutenant Sato, call all the men to attention around the outside of the warehouse and shoot anyone leaving the building," Col. Akirai sternly ordered his Lieutenants.

A chorus of "Yes Sirs" was heard. The men moved out and surrounded the warehouse. The prisoner went over to his secret place where his keys were hidden under a large stone and pulled out his keys and unlocked the main steel double doors. The Colonel and some of his men drove into the warehouse.

"Your map show that your treasure is hidden in some trucks down under that pile of steel beams over in that corner. Is that correct?" Colonel Akirai asked the prisoner Zhao asked pointing to the 20 feet high stack of steel beams.

"Yes Sir!" Zhao sheepishly replied.

"Sergeant Matsui, go get Private Tao and have him drive his heavy duty truck with the winch on it into this area," the Colonel ordered.

"Yes Sir."

Five minutes later, Private Tao slowly drove the heavy truck into position in front of the stack of steel beams.

"Sergeant Matsui, have the men attach the cables around each steel beam and pulled them over forty feet away from the current stack," Colonel Akirai ordered.

"Yes Sir."

Sergeant Matsui grabbed the heavy chain block with the large pulleys off the bed of his truck and showed his men how to rig it up on a beam of the warehouse directly over the stack of steel beams. He threw one rope to each man standing at each end of the beams and told them to tie the rope around each end of the steel beam as he raised the beam with the cable from his winch run through the rigged up pulley down to the center of the steel beam and guide the beam and keep it from moving sideways and hitting anything. After all of the steel beams were moved over the forty feet and placed in a new stack, Colonel Akirai could see the hidden short heavy duty steel trunks.

"Those trunks have chains locked together and around them," the Colonel observed. "Zhao, do you have your keys to unlock the chains?"

"Yes Colonel, I will get them out of my secret hiding place on the underneath of this chair in the corner and unlock the locks on the chains. Now, you may open the trunks."

The Colonel not trusting anyone and especially the Chinese stepped back some twenty-five feet and said, "Zhao, you open the lids of each trunk."

After Zhao successfully opened all of the trunks without an incidence, Colonel Akirai ordered Private Tao, "look inside and pick up one of the Gold Bars and bring it to me."

"Yes Sir."

Private Tao walked slowly up to the front of the first trunk and look inside not believing his eyes. He cautiously reached in and picked up the 6.5 kilos Gold Bars without setting off any expected booby trap. He turned around and walked over to Colonel Akirai and handed him the Gold Bar saying, "The trunk is almost full of these Gold Bars."

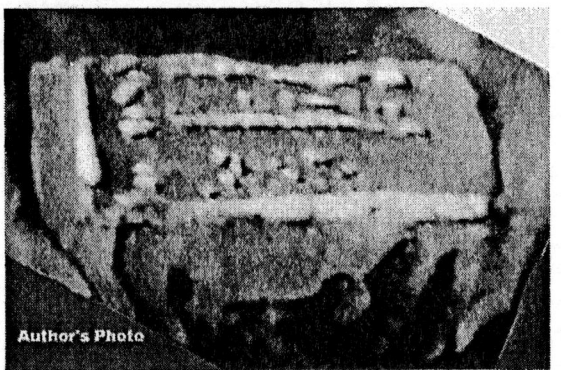

"Emperor Zapp and his brother who is coming to take over this military operation from my General next week will be very happy and pleased with what I have found for Emperor Zapp and his family," Colonel Akirai enthusiastically replied.

"Some of the trunks have swords, guns and uniforms," Private Tao said.

Why in the world is prisoner Zhao storing those things, Colonel thought.

Private Tao noticed Lieutenant Quickdraw had come into the warehouse from his security duties outside and motioned for him to come over to the open trunks. "Look at all those Gold Bars in that trunk and these things in those three trunks."

Lieutenant Quickdraw pulled out one of the uniforms and as it unfolded everyone noticed that it was a Japanese officer's uniform.

"Zhao, front and center," Colonel Akirai screamed at the top of his voice.

"You are a member and supporter of one of the Chinese Guerilla Units. You have hidden the uniforms and weapons of Japanese soldiers that you have previously killed."

"Colonel, NO, NO, NO, I do not know where those things came from. You must believe me. I am telling you the truth."

"You have already indicted yourself. This is the reason that you asked me to let you come in here by your lonesome self. You are as guilty as any criminal that I have ever known. Unfortunately for you, we have the evidence in your warehouse right next to some of your treasure."

"NO! Colonel, I am no guilty of ever killing a Japanese soldier. It must have been one of my workers."

"How many more Gold Bars do you have out at your country estate?" Colonel Akirai bitterly asked Zhao with a Japanese sword taken out of one of the trunks raised up in an attack position sticking into Zhao's chest.

"My family and I want to quietly live here in my hometown of Shanghai. I will give you everything to save my life. I beg you."

"Lieutenant Sato, get the troops in here to carry all of these Gold Bars to my truck over there at the doorway. Be sure you put some blankets down to protect the soft Gold Bars. After completing that order, have the men set up another defensive convoy to travel out to Zhao's country estate," the Colonel ordered as he walked around pulling Zhao by the ropes tied around his body.

TREASURES OF WAR – CONCEALED BY THE EVIL ONES / 78

"Zhao, you are a dead man if any of your guerilla friends show their faces on the way out to your country estate. My men know about the Japanese soldiers killed by wither you or your friends. The order from my General is very simple. If you discover Japanese pistols, radios, uniforms or any other souvenirs in the possession of the enemy, torture them, extract military information and shoot them before a firing squad or take my sword and chop their head off in front of all my men."

"Colonel Akirai, would you like to see some of the Gold Bars laid out on a cloth before we complete loading them onto your truck?" Lt. Sato asked and bowed.

The Colonel walked over to his truck and noticed the Gold Bars. "They are definitely smelted here in China. Look at those markings. Some of them must be many years old and the accumulation of successful business by Zhao's family over the last several hundred years."

"Lieutenant, have we gotten everything of value here at the warehouse?"

"Colonel, give me another fifteen minutes and both battalions will be prepared to receive your orders to move out."

Two battalions of men riding in trucks with the mounted machine guns were visible to everyone as they rolled down the streets and eventually on the road out to Zhao's country estate. As they approached the turn down the road to Zhao's place, some Chinese Guerrillas began to open fire on the rear truck. The Japanese gunner operating the rear machine gun immediately turned around and opened fire. Not one stalk of the cornfield was left standing and all of the Chinese Guerrillas were slaughtered. The convoy made the turn and sped up. As they came near the drive entrance to Zhao's place off to the right, everyone could see one of his Daihatsui trucks parked under a large tree with large branches shading the yard next to his house. The drivers had to slowly swing wide to make the turn to enter underneath the high archway and drive the 1,000 feet to the side of his house.

"Zhao, since we did not have a casualty back there at the turn, you live a little longer," Colonel Akirai said, as he turned to him face to face in the cab of his truck.

"Colonel, I did not have anything to do with those Chinese shooting at us. My family lives more than five miles down the road from there. Again, I beg you not to kill my family and me. I have agreed to give you all of my wealth."

"Us, what do you mean by us? They were shooting at us Japanese. You are not a part of us, and you never will become a part of us. Where are your daughters? Where is the other Daihatsui truck and sedan?"

"They should be in that barn over there with the double wooden doors. My family should be inside the house. I am sure that they have not shown their faces because they saw military trucks."

"Major Moto Torture, I am particularly concerned where the family and farmhands are presently hiding. Take prisoner Zhao with you and Lt. Sato and have him enter the barn in front of you. Should you see anyone with a weapon, shoot him on site. Unless a woman has a weapon, do not shoot any of the women. Move cautiously; remember the ambush down the road," Colonel Akirai ordered.

As Prisoner Zhao slowly walked up to the barn door he shouted out to anyone in the barn, "put down their weapons and raise your hands. They will kill you and me."

Zhao opened the doors and some of his farm workers walked out with their hands raised. Major Torture motioned for his men to take each Chinese farm worker and throw them to the ground and stand over them with their bayonets pressed against the back of their necks.

"Zhao, tell your farm workers that this land is declared 'off-limits' and is now 'state land' of my Emperor Zapp and the grandiose homeland of Japan. They must abandon this farm and go with my troops to wherever I command them to go. Anyone resisting Japan's occupation of China will be deliberately and methodically eliminated without civil, religious or any other gratification or privilege. You now owe your total allegiance to the sovereign State of Japan, Colonel Akirai announced to everyone in the yard.

Devastated, Prisoner Zhao raised his head with the tears streaming from his eyes. "I plead with you, Colonel, let me and my family live. See the other truck and the sedan in the barn. They are yours. Anything else here is now yours. Just let me go to Shanghai and live the remainder of my life under the authority and power of Emperor Zapp. I will worship him."

"What do you mean by anything else? What are you hiding out here on your country estate? You must have hidden some of your wealth out here too. Speak up now."

"May I go into the house and see my family and explain everything to them?" Zhao asked as he bowed to the Colonel.

"Major Torture, take a few men and go into the house and bring everyone out here in the yard," Colonel Akirai ordered as he held the rope around Prisoner Zhao.

Bowing to the Colonel, Major Torture and some of his men opened the front door and some of the men went to the back porch door and entered the farmhouse of this wealthy Chinese businessman. Shortly thereafter without incidence, the Japanese soldiers marched out with the two teenage girls and one teenage boy together with the Chinese woman and her domestic servants. The Chinese woman was looking straight at Zhao. Suddenly, Major Torture appeared at the front door and announced, "Colonel, these are the only people found in the house. But, look what I found on the fireplace mantle in the main living room. This Buddha is very heavy. I must set it down. It is made out of Gold."

Author's Photo

"Bring that Evil God of these Chinese here immediately. Emperor Zapp's orders are to ship all of these Buddhas back to him for melting down to pure Gold for his personal wealth and eliminate any God's in the world and I must instigate this right away," the loyal and lustful Colonel commanded.

Major Torture called some of his men over to the front door and ordered them to carry the Gold Buddha over to the Colonel's truck.

Sitting in a chair next to his truck with Prisoner Zhao near him he asked, "How many more of these Buddhas do you have on our new estate? And you had better tell me everything you know immediately or you may learn brutality of my men."

"I swear to Emperor Zapp that this is the only one out here on my estate, oh I mean your new estate."

"Major Torture, take Prisoner Zhao into the barn and order your men to run some water from the well and pour it into the tub with my special red pepper powder. You know the rest of the routine," Colonel Akirai ordered as he handed the can of red pepper to the Major.

Subsequently, the coughing screams from the barn could be heard in the yard where all of the people from the barn and house were standing under the watchful eyes of the Japanese Armed Forces. Eventually, Prisoner Zhao thought he was drowning and hollered out in desperation of the human spirit, "Okay, Okay, I will tell you where everything is located. Here in the barn, look up in each corner of the loft under the straw and you will find more Gold Bars and two Buddhas."

Major Torture brought the vomiting and coughing Prisoner Zhao out to Colonel Akirai. The attention was focused on what the men would bring out of the barn. Teams of two began carrying large Gold Bars in steel boxes and two Buddhas out to the yard in front of the Colonel.

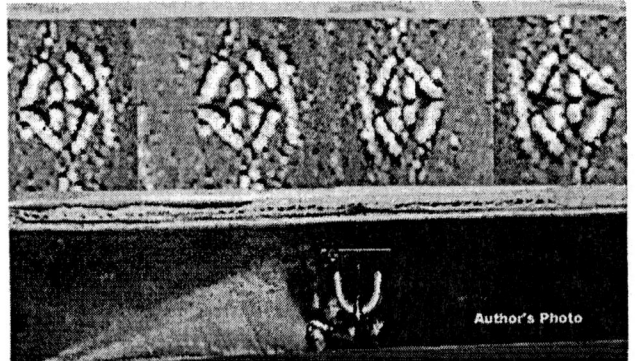

"You continue to amaze me Prisoner Zhao. Your repeated lies are adding up to your eventual resolve. How much do these open steel boxes of Gold Bars weigh? Is this your personal hallmark on all of them? How many Gold Bars have you hidden on your estate?"

"Colonel, these large Gold Bars each weighs 75 kilos, and those are the Chinese government's hallmarks. You should find 384 here. No, I mean 260 of the 75 kilo Gold Bars."

"Here you go again. If I do not find 384 Gold Bars here, you will wish you were dead," Colonel Akirai threatens.

Lieutenant Sato took a break from the barn duty to remove the Gold Bars and called the Colonel to the side. "Sir, if I am not mistaken the Buddhist here in China place gift offerings inside the Golden Buddhas for the local Buddhist Priest to remove and offer his blessings to the local family for their prosperity and large crops of rice. I am going to try to remove the head of the Gold Buddha that we took from Zhao's warehouse in town and look inside for treasures such as diamonds and money."

"Excellent idea Lieutenant. Let me know if you have any problems removing the head of the Buddha."

"Zhao, what are the ages of your two daughters? Ask them to come over here to me."

"Lo Lam is sixteen and Chik Benji is fourteen years. They are my sweethearts and daddy's little girls."

"Major Snatch, the Emperor's brother, will arrive here tomorrow. He will need female companionship while he serves **The Evil God, Emperor Zapp,** here in Shanghai. I will supply him your two daughters for his pleasures. You must instruct them to follow each and every desire he has."

Furious, Zhao could not control his emotions, "Be merciful, your lust for my young daughters is obnoxious to me. What kind of majestic person would lower himself to this level? Please let me, I beg you to let me replace my young daughters with the beautiful young women that work for me."

"Your arrogance will destroy you. My men and I will use the women that work for you for our ritual pleasure of our flesh," the Colonel replied.

"Zhao instruct all the women to go over there in front of the barn and remove all of their clothes," Colonel Akirai ordered.

"But Colonel, my wife is one of the women," Zhao emotionally stated.

"Major Torture, remember Japanese are a chosen people and it is our mission to control the world. After they disrobe, pick out one of the young girls for me and you and eighteen of your men take the others into the barn and have some fun. I will join you as soon as Lieutenant Quickdraw relieves me to hold onto my prisoner. Don't forget, Lieutenant Sato and his men need to have some recreation with the women after you men are satisfied," Colonel Akirai reminded his men.

Lieutenant Sato and three of his men successfully completed finding the combination to take the heads off of the first Gold Buddha and discovered several hands full of coins, diamonds and jewelry. Walking in double time steps, the Lieutenant arrived next to the chair in the yard where Colonel Akirai sat. "Look at the treasures I found inside of the Gold Buddha. These diamonds must be of great value for Emperor Zapp, **The Evil God.** This one must be at least 60 carats."

"Your knowledge of the Buddhist here in China has paid off. These things could have been lost in the smelting process back in Tokyo. By the way where are the two Buddhas from the barn?"

"Sir, I will take a look inside and find them."

"No Lieutenant, you guard my prisoner while I go and take some time to relax with my young female friend. We will look for the Gold Buddhas later. Get me some of the Chinese Opium out of my duffle bag marked with the letter O in the cab of my truck? I need to give this to my young thing? This will stimulate her sexual organs and make her perform well. I forgot to tell Major Torture about my supply for just this occasion. When it is your turn feel free to use some and give some to your men for their women."

Nearing the end of the day, all of the men were gathering together in the yard with bright smiles across their faces. Colonel Akirai strutted around the yard like a little Caesar. "My greatest glory will be to die for Emperor Zapp, **The Evil God.**"

"Lieutenant Sato, take three of your men back into the barn and find those two Gold Buddhas."

It took a little over thirty minutes before the Lieutenant emerged with his men and he carried the two Buddhas.

"Let me show you how to remove the heads of these. First, you lay them on their back, and second you grip the head by the ears and twist the head to the left. See, here are Emperor Zapp's additional diamonds," Lieutenant said as he pulled out his right hand full of diamonds.

"Outstanding, Lieutenant Quickdraw do you have the final count of the Gold Bars?" the Colonel asked.

TREASURES OF WAR – CONCEALED BY THE EVIL ONES / 84

Lieutenant did not want to be outdone by Lieutenant Sato so he went over to the truck where the Gold Bars in steel boxes had been loaded. After checking with his men he walked back to the Colonel and bowed. "We have counted 260 of them."

"Major Torture, take your special leather coat and lace it up as tight as possible around Prisoner Zhao. Pour the water on him and leave him tied up until morning. When that coat starts shrinking and the excruciating pains throughout his body indicate to him that he is going to die, he will barely be able to tell you where the other 124 large Gold Bars are located out here. You or one of your men needs to sit down next to him to hear his confession during the night. When that occurs, wake me up," Colonel Akirai ordered.

At 03:20 in the early morning Prisoner Zhao whispered to Major Torture, "I will tell you where the other Gold Bars are located. They are buried in the hill of dirt and rocks down behind the main barn."

Major torture went into the house where Colonel Akirai was sleeping with his new young Chinese lover. "Colonel, Colonel, the prisoner has described the location of where the other Gold Bars are located."

"Cut the lace leather straps on the leather coat and let him live so we have time to make sure to excavate the Gold Bars. Good night Major. See you in the morning."

"Good night Sir!"

The next morning the Japanese troops rounded up some pigs, chickens and one young yearling and butchered them. They built several good fires and began roasting each of them. The smell of the freshly cooked meal made the men enjoy the morning and forget for a short time that they were looting China. The smell of hot teas lingered all around the grounds in front of the barns. After eating just about everything that had been prepared, Major Torture called all the men to order and they fell in line. He described to the men the job ahead of them. He marched them around the barn and down the hill to the high bank of dirt and rocks. He ordered them to take their foxhole shovels and dig into the side of the embankment and locate the buried Gold Bars. The men began digging into the hard dirt and rocks. The digging was slow.

Surely Prisoner Zhao has some larger shovels, picks or other tools to dig with and make this task go faster, Major Torture thought.

He sent two of his men back to the barns to look for hand tools. Ten minutes later, they returned with four long handle shovels and two picks. Approximately, twenty minutes passed when all of a sudden his men let out a big 'YO'. When Major Torture climbed down to the bottom of the embankment and look up he saw more than twenty-five Gold Bars protruding from the bank.

"Emperor Zapp and Colonel Akirai are going to be very excited about this discovery."

"Keep digging men. There are more than 90 hidden out here somewhere. Private Tao go back to the barnyard and fill the large canteen with as much fresh tea that you can find and make some if none is made," Major Torture ordered his men and gave instructions to Tao.

"Yes Sir." Private Tao said as he bowed to the Major.

Before Private Tao returned with the tea for the hard workingmen and another man hollered 'YO' from over in a different direction from the first discovery. Major Torture double-timed it to the spot.

"Major, look at those Gold Bars next to the rim of the hillside near the big rock. When we finally dug the rocks away from the large rock next to it and put our ropes around the top of it to pull it down, look what we found when it fell. It appears that these large Gold Bars go back into the side of the embankment. Maybe there are some more."

"Excellent work men, keep it up. But, first let's take a break for some teas."

The excitement of finding Gold Bars for Emperor Zapp, **The Evil God,** created a frenzy of digging all around this area of the farm. Each team of Japanese soldiers looked at every crevice in the ground and hillside embankments. Without the use of heavy construction equipment, many of the Japanese soldiers that did not have shovels or picks dug with their bare hands. One team of soldiers was digging on a red dirt hillside when a loud 'YO' was heard around the farm. Six of the soldiers got down on their hands and knees and dug with their hands until they had uncovered a large number of 75 kilos Gold Bars.

These digging activities continued for five more hours. The 'YO's were heard each time Gold Bars were discovered. Eventually, all 124 Gold Bars were found, and the soldiers carried each one of them back to the yard and loaded them onto one of the Colonel's trucks.

The Colonel strutted over to the trucks with the Gold Bars and beamed from ear to ear. "Emperor Zapp and his brother Major Snatch, will rejoice to realize that all of you soldiers have kept your pledge of allegiance to **The Evil God.** Before we leave in the morning for our return trip to Shanghai to meet Major Snatch tomorrow upon his arrival in China, you have the rest of the day and the night to enjoy the Chinese girls and women. Some pouches of Opium powder are on the table in the house. You are dismissed."

During the evening and night loud screams could be heard from the barns and out in the fields. Some of the young Chinese girls were being gang raped by several soldiers.

At 11:00 Colonel Akirai called his troops to order and gave them the orders to take a group of the young Chinese girls out behind the barn and use his saber to cut their heads off. One by one you could hear the familiar 'YO' each time one of them was killed. Eventually, everyone had been killed except Prisoner Zhao, his young daughters Lo Lam and Chik Benji and his son Mao. He gave orders to bring them to the center of the yard.

"Prisoner Zhao, you have not obeyed my orders and attempted to keep some of your wealth from Emperor Zapp. You have committed blasphemy against our Supreme Being. I am committed to carrying out my orders from Emperor Zapp. Your two daughters will travel to Shanghai with me for the welcoming of Major Snatch, Emperor Zapp's brother. Your son will also travel with us to Shanghai for the purpose of telling the Chinese people to submit to the strongest people in the world, the Japanese. He will be a very good spokesman. He has seen first hand what happens when the Chinese do not worship the spiritual leader of the world, **The Evil God,** Emperor Zapp," Colonel deliberately and hatefully said.

"Colonel, Colonel!"

"Bow at my feet," Colonel Akirai said looking Zhao straight into his eyes. "It is easy for me to carry out the orders of Emperor Zapp because he will be pleased with my actions," the Colonel added as he raised his officer's sword and came down with him shouting a loud, "YO!"

IN THE MEANTIME A SPECIAL MEETING WAS CALLED IN TOKYO

"Major Snatch, my younger brother and devoted Godly servant, I need you to go to Shanghai and show the Chinese that they must cease fighting their guerilla wars against my Imperial Armies. My eminent desire through the use of every method imaginable including the theory of total war to conquer the world and all religions and receive all people total worship commitment to me as their only God will be carried out with your leadership in China," Emperor Zapp, **The Evil God,** demanded.

"Emperor Zapp, I will serve you undividedly. When do you want me to leave? Will the Kwantung Army be under my command for you?"

"Here are my written orders and detailed instructions. First, I need the Opium Monopoly Bureau's money to help finance my increasing war machinery. Make sure that all of your Generals receive the message to increase the addiction of the Chinese women and men to our harvested opium. The Chinese women will become addicted sex slaves to my Imperial Armed Forces until we conquer them and during the following years as sex servants for the pleasures required to keep my Imperial Forces content. I need to regularly supply them pleasures that will make them fight for anything that I demand and maintain their devotion to me. I understand that some of the looted Gold Bars and diamonds have been confiscated, and I need them here to further finance my war machine. Yes, the Kwantung Army will report directly to you. I have given the proper orders to the War Minister. He will notify all of his Generals. Remember your secret Imperial Palace code name is 'Bravest Warrior'. Remind the Generals everyday that I am the ruling force behind their men's "Japanese Spirit", and they will be constantly combating evil enemies and will unite with me in the hereafter immediately upon their death at the Holy Shrine," Emperor Zapp answered and deliberately explained his scheme to complete the conquest of China.

Bowing to Emperor Zapp, "I understand that some of the Chinese Guerrilla Units have not been executed. I will boil some of them alive as soon as I arrive. At this stage of the war in China, your Imperial Forces should not be having casualties. When I take my sword to the heads of some of the leaders, the message of your power will spread. The women will become our slaves to meet any of our needs. I will religiously enforce this. It is coming up on the next harvest season of the opium poppies growing on the farms up in the mountains. With my organization skills that I learned at the War College I will have your Imperial Forces direct the farmers to greatly expand the number of acres of their poppy crops. They will be ordered to keep records of the number of acres of each farmer and keep up with the harvest and downstream delivery of all buckets of opium white gooey stuff from the poppy seeds and the opium plant poppy seeds to our controlled processing plants for the mixing the white stuff with our chemicals to make the brick-size opium blocks and drying the seeds in the sun. I will give them orders to execute in the towns' center any opium poppy crop farmers with hidden crops from the Japanese Army Police. This will assist in stamping out smugglers and competitors. I will pay the legitimate opium poppy crop farmers a good price for their efforts and products.

"This is precisely what I need in China at this time. You need to leave for Shanghai as soon as you get your team together," an elated Emperor Zapp said.

Two days later, Major Snatch, the youngest brother of Emperor Zapp, boarded his plane with his chosen team of enforcers and flew off to Shanghai, China. Upon arriving at the Shanghai International Airport he was met by Colonel Akirai, Major Moto Torture, Major Hisaichi, Lieutenant Sato, Lieutenant Miyamoto Quickdraw, Lieutenant Okochia, Sergeant Matsui, Private Iwane, Private Tao, Private Sakai and seven battalions of Japanese soldiers.

The confiscated Daihatsui Sedan was used as the limo to take Major Snatch to his specially prepared hotel room overlooking the city. After resting from his coughing spells caused by the burning buildings, surrounding fields, forest and Chinese bodies, he met with his officers in the lobby of the hotel. Colonel Akirai bowed and spoke first. "Here are my daily reports since my arrival in China. My Emperor's Brother, we have carried out the Emperor's orders and taken possession of large numbers of Gold Bars, Golden Buddhas, diamonds, emeralds, turquoise, ruby, and many other treasures for the economic needs of Emperor Zapp. Let's go out this back door and see some of the treasures."

"Can we do something about this smoke everywhere? Cough! Cough! And where are my young Chinese women?" Major Snatch asked.

"We have two young women for you up in room 734 eagerly awaiting your arrival and desires. As soon as we see the treasure, I will take you up and introduce you to them," Colonel Akirai replied as he led Major Snatch out into the back parking lot.

"Major Torture, lift the loot cover and show Major Snatch the enormous riches of his brother, Emperor Zapp," the Colonel ordered as they approached the large truckload of Gold Bars and the Golden Buddhas.

"Unbelievable, astonishing, magnificent!" Major Snatch said as he proudly thrust himself up on the truck.

"I must immediately send word to my brother, Emperor Zapp, and request some special naval forces to carry this loot back to Tokyo. You men should await my personal orders for transporting this to whichever Chinese port is assigned by the Japanese Naval Forces for this very important task," Major Snatch added.

"Now for some deserved rest and sexual pleasures, let me take you to room 734 to meet your young Chinese virgins," Colonel Akirai suggested.

With the Japanese guards on duty at the end of each hallway of the hotel and upon reaching room 734, Colonel Akirai unlocked the door and bowed to Major Snatch as he opened the door for him. "Major Snatch this is Lo Lam Zhao, age 16 and this is Chik Benji Zhao age 14. Please enjoy the evening and night."

"Have room service send up some of the finest Chinese food, wines and liquors."

EMPEROR ZAPP CALLED ANOTHER BROTHER TO HIS PALACE

"Brother Mikey, I need you to head up the Secret Intelligence Team and learn of everything that is happening in the Chinese Expeditionary Forces in China. Since you have the training at the Military Academy and Military Staff College and are so young and completed your physical and intelligence courses at the top of your class, you will be given my personal authorization to see that your coded reports of the movement of the wealth of the conquered Chinese is religiously done and shipped back to me here in Japan. I need to have control over all of these assets. Do not hesitate to let me know of any person, family or military officer that you suspect of diverting the treasure to places for themselves," the **Evil God,** Emperor Zapp spoke with compassion to his young brother.

"Yes sir, and may I choose my staff from the various military forces?" Brother Mikey replied and asked.

"Yes, just give me their names and I will give my orders to the War Minister," **Evil God,** Emperor Zapp replied.

"Thank you, my Brother and **Divine God**, I will pack for the long haul."

TREASURES OF WAR – CONCEALED BY THE EVIL ONES

Chapter Four

The Story of Master Sergeant Arvil Steele

91 / DON STEWART NIMMONS

I was born in Linden, Texas, USA on April 22, 1920 out of the wedlock of my very hard working parents. My parents named me Arvil Leon Steele.

Every since my Daddy died in 1931 when I was only 11 years old and left my Mother with very little material things, my younger brother, Bob, and I worked many hours in the sharecropper's cotton fields plowing the land and turning up the burrows to make the rows to plant the cotton. Then, during the long hot summer days in Texas we picked cotton every day and got paid by the pound. My hands were so cut up and bleeding at the end of the day that I had to put them down in the cool creek at the end of the cotton field to reduce the pain and stop the bleeding before going to the bunk house to eat some of the fresh garden food and off to bed.

One of the happiest times in my life was at the age of 12, a year after my daddy's death, and my mother decided to have me and my 3 sisters and younger brother, Bob, move off the sharecroppers farm in Texas to her mother's big house up in Mena, Arkansas. Grandma Chambers had a large house in town.

My older brother Fred was 12 years older than me. He had gotten him a pretty good job in Texarkana, Texas and came to Mena to move Mom, my sisters, Bob and I to Texarkana just before school started in 1933. Later that year I finished grammar with very good grades. During my high school years I desired adventure and wanted to see the world. I decided to quit school before I completed my high school, and I joined the United States Army Air Force at the age of 16 in Fort Riley, Kansas.

In 1936, I decided to seek some adventure in my life and go join the military service. A friend of mine and I came up with the scheme to quit high school and go to the Union Station in downtown Texarkana, Texas and hitchhike a ride on the northbound freight train to Kansas City. From there we caught another boxcar over to Topeka, Junction City and on to Fort Riley, Kansas. On September 11th, 1936, I signed the Oath and Certificate of Enlistment in front of Major J. W. Carroll of the Second Calvary for a three-year enlistment. I lied about my birthday. I told them I was born on April 22, 1918 instead of 1920. I was 16 years old when I joined the United States Army. When the major asked me who my nearest relative and person to be notified in case of emergency, I told him my mother, Mrs. June Steele, and gave him her address back in Texarkana, Texas. I named her as my designation of beneficiary.

Since I was so weak and undernourished, my Sarge wanted to fatten me up. He let me and a few others stay in the barracks and drink malts almost everyday until we had built ourselves up for the forthcoming basic training that all 2nd Calvary enlisted men went through. I went through some very harsh training at Fort Riley, Kansas. The difficult and harsh military training that I went through would later be one of the most important things that had happened to me in my life. After basic training I earned the rank of Private First Class as an artillery gunner in Company B in the 84th Field Artillery.

Twice a week I made a commitment to write my mother a letter to let her know how I was doing and tell her how much I loved her for what she had taught me.

Sergeant Bob Turley called me into his office and gave me the good news. He gave me a 30 days pass and told me to go home and visit my mother and family. Springtime in Arkansas was the best time to get off the cold windswept plains of Kansas. Almost a year had gone by since I first arrived at Fort Riley. I was eager to go home for a while.

The bus ride home was not quick enough for me. I wanted to see Mom, sisters and brother Bob. My brother and I talked about everything that had happened to him in high school and the artillery training of mine at Fort Riley. I had gained about thirty pounds and was strong as an ox. Some of my former classmates and Bob's friends would meet almost everyday down at the Ozark Café and have a delicious chocolate malt and hamburger. After the fun in my overalls and non-uniform clothes it was time to get back to my duties at Fort Riley.

In the fall of 1938, I was given my second 30-days home furlough and went down to the bus station and bought my ticket to Texarkana, Texas. Excited? You bet I was. However, the old bus stopped at nearly every town along the way. It did not have much room for anything. By the time I made all the bus transfers, the trip lasted until midday the following day. Yet, the final few hours were on the highway through the beautiful Ouachita National Forest. The colorful leaves brought back some fond memories of when my brother Bob and I would go to the parks and lakes to picnic and have fun with our high school friends.

My brother Bob was working after school at the local grocery store. Bob knew that I had started to smoke. He told me that when the 'big folks' came into the store, they all smoked Lucky Strikes. So, I told him to get me a few packs of Lucky Strikes. He fondly called me Dub. Just like my previous furlough, Bob and our friends would meet down at Trader's Hamburger Shop and eat the big hamburger and drink chocolate malt. The newsreels down at the Loew's Palace Saturday movie matinee showed the Germans building up its military might. Everyone asked me what I knew about the possibility of our military and me going to war. I kept telling them that Texarkana was a long way away from the German war, and I was not worried.

Bob and I went fishing out at the lake a couple of times. He told me which girls that I should treat nicely. We caught a few catfish and took them home for Mom to fry for supper. Yes, time had gone by real fast. It was time to get my bus ticket back to Fort Riley and earn my pay as a soldier. Mom and Bob came down to the Greyhound Bus Station to see me off on the bus.

I trained to become an excellent gunner's mate in the 84th Field Artillery. Since I loved to read, something my mother infused in me, I read the instructions for operating and maintaining the artillery cannons, quickly. After completing my three years service in the United States Army, I was honorably discharged on September 10, 1939.

I told some of my smoking and drinking buddies goodbye and wished them well. Down to the old Greyhound Bus Station I marched in double time. I was eager to see my brother Bob before he made his final decision to enlist into the service. You bet, Mom's home style cooking was on my mind also. Girls, well yes, I had some unfinished business with my girl. After the long bus ride I was glad to hear the bus driver holler out.

"Union Central, Texarkana, Texas!"

As I stepped off the bus a fresh northern breeze hit me in the face. The bus driver opened up the luggage door and pulled out all the bags and suitcases for Texarkana. My duffle bag was not tossed out on the curb. Immediately, I stepped around the bags and stuck my head up under the open door and saw my bag way back in the right side of the compartment. I pointed to my bag. The driver crawled into the luggage compartment and tossed it to me. I wanted to surprise Mom so I grabbed my bag and walked all the way home. The front door was unlocked and I just walked in. Mom saw me and ran down the hallway and gave me one of her bear hugs.

"Arvil, why didn't you call me from downtown? I would have come and picked you up."

"I wanted my homecoming to be a pleasant and happy surprise."

"Arvil, you need to go down to Piggly Wiggly and meet with Bob. He wants to enlist in the service. You have learned many things during the last three years and can help him make his choice," Mom said in a very concerned motherly voice.

"Alright Mom, I want to take a good hot bath and change clothes first. I love you Mom. You are very special to me."

I grabbed my duffle bag and ran off to Bob's and my bedroom. Later, I walked into the kitchen where Mom was already baking some of my favorite fresh bread.

"Smells delicious Mom."

Mom turned around and smiled and said, "Don't you look good with that hair slicked down with your hair oil. Got something special in mind?"

Chuckling and with a suspicious grim across my face I replied, "A date with Kathy would make my homecoming begin on the right note. When I go to the store to visit with Bob, I just might look her up and see if she has any opening dates for me. All the eligible guys must be trying to keep her from missing me."

"Go talk to Bob. He is very serious about joining the service."

"I noticed that Fred's room has been taken over by Sister. What is he doing now?" I asked Mom.

"Yes, Fred worked so hard that he got the promotion at the Magnolia Petroleum Company service station and rented an apartment over on South Kinsey Street."

"Mom, does he continue to support you and the girls?"

"Oh yes, he just needed to have a life of his own and told me not to worry about anything."

"I wonder if he would loan me his old car to take Bob and our dates out tonight?" I asked Mom.

"Drop by the service station and ask him on your way to the store to see Bob."

"Great idea Mom. See you later. Keep those fresh rolls and lofts of bread warm in the oven," I said as I gave her another hug and walked out the front door.

I walked to the Magnolia service station and learned that my older brother Fred was out on a highway service call in the wrecker truck. His car was parked at the station. Nobody could tell me just how long it would be before he came back. I decided to walk on to Piggly Wiggly and let Bob know that I was home from the service. I walked into the store and the checkers told me that Bob was in the back unloading one of the supply trucks. When I walked through the warehouse at the back of the store, I could see Bob taking some boxes from the truck and putting them down on the dolly. Just as he completed loading the dolly, he grabbed it and turned around to take it into the warehouse.

"Dub, when did you get home? Man, it is good to see you," Bob said as he pulled up with the dolly stacked high with boxes of groceries.

Arvil ran the twenty feet or so and gave Bob a manly embrace and said, "Arrived in Texarkana three or four hours ago. Mom is already baking some of our favorite fresh baked loaves of bread and rolls."

"Why don't you wait around here with me for the next hour and fifteen minutes until I punch out? I have several important questions to ask you about joining the service," Bob requested.

"I don't have anything better to do at this time. We can plan our activities for this evening with the girls after supper at Mom's. You understand that I completed my three years service and received an honorable discharge?" I asked.

"You and I talked about that last year. You did not know exactly whether you were going to re-enlist or get out. There aren't any planes around here for you to repair. Business is real bad and most of our friends and school mates are taking the low paying and long hours jobs at the railroad or going away to find a better life," Bob reminded his brother.

"Maybe I need to reconsider and re-enlist in the service," I replied.

"Dub, I want to travel and learn a better skill as a master craftsman. Here in Texarkana there are no good jobs available. Let's go to the best place and join the army," Bob enthusiastically announced as he continued to unload the truck of boxes of groceries.

"The United States Army was good to me and I learned many things including how to be a mechanic and repair things with my hands. I heard that one of the best places to enlist is in Dallas. Bob, you and I could grab a passenger train and check it out. I have saved some of my military pay and will pay for the trip to Dallas," as I interrupted Bob.

"Fine, let me punch out on the time clock and tell Darwin that I am leaving. Then, we can go home and eat Mom's good cooking and go out and have some fun tonight with the girls.

"No objection from me," I replied to back up Bob's suggestions.

Subsequent to the daily routine in Texarkana for one week, the two Steele brothers were raring to 'get out of Dodge' and boarded the train at Union Station to Dallas. They checked into a hotel and looked around for work in Dallas. Due to the large amount of military contractors in the Dallas and Fort Worth area, they believed that jobs would be plentiful and easy to find. Everywhere they went, the cautious message concerning their draft age was repeated.

Finally, when the brothers decided to check out the opportunities at the U. S. Army enlistment office in Dallas, Bob was convinced that he wanted to join the Army. Bob registered and signed up. After passing his physical he was inducted into the United States Army's Fifth Cavalry and sent off to Fort Clark, Texas.

97 / DON STEWART NIMMONS

Missing the comradery of his military buddies and another chance to learn more of the world outside his travels, Arvil met with Major Lester M. Kilgarif of the Field Artillery and agreed to re-enlist and serve for three years in Fort Sill, Oklahoma beginning as a Private First Class. The physical exam indicated a small cyst on the small of his back had been removed at Fort Riley in July 1939. On September 21st, 1939, Dr. Wendel A. Stiles, Captain in the Medical Corps signed off on Arvil's physical examination.

And off to Fort Sill, Oklahoma to join Company B, 38th Infantry did I go. After checking into my barracks my new sergeant told me that I was going to go through artillery gunner training.

My top sergeant had been given all of the evil spirits that anyone could have imagined. He had us up early and doing double time marching for miles at a time to the rolling hills where the artillery cannons and mortars were. He had us training to shoot at targets in the distance. Accuracy was the only game in town. After weathering all the storms that Mother Nature could produce in the Oklahoma storm alley, the brutal training sessions every day, eating war time field rations, the sergeant marched us back to mess hall for supper and then right off to the barracks for the night.

On October 26, 1940, 1st Lt. William H. Littleton of the Army Medical Corps gave me my re-enlistment physical examination. He signed off that I was mentally and physically fit for service in the Army of the United States.

On November 1st 1940, Major William W. Ford of the 18th Field Artillery Brigade issued my new orders as I re-enlisted in Company B and received my orders to go overseas to Nichols Field near Manila, Philippines. The 30 days "Delay In Route" orders and passenger train tickets to go to Union Station in Texarkana, Texas and later to San Francisco, California was given to me by the Major. His orders called for me to report at the naval base in San Francisco Bay and take the voyage on the ocean liner Etolin to the Philippines.

The bus ride from Fort Sill, Oklahoma to Texarkana, Texas was much shorter that the previous ones from Fort Riley, Kansas.

Mom was excited to see me.

"Arvil, you just missed Bob," she sadly told me.

"We have kept up with each other in our letters through the mail. He has Colonel Patton training him down at Fort Clark. I met Patton back at Fort Riley when he was going through cavalry training and learning to ride a horse. He is a tough military officer," I went on.

"Bob was here on leave from Fort Clark. He looked good and had earned his sergeant stripes," she proudly told Arvil.

Not knowing exactly how long it was going to take him to make the passenger train ride to San Francisco, California, I chose to board the train and cut my home furlough short by ten days. The trip through the Rocky Mountains was eye catching and breathtaking. I had brought a new camera for such times. Upon arrival at the San Francisco Rail Station a few days before I had to report to the port and ship out to Manila, I decided to see the sites around the bay.

As it turned out, the Etolin was no ocean liner. The 100-foot steel hulled former Alaskan fishing vessel had been converted to a crews ship. All the cleaning chemicals available in the world could not have successfully gotten rid of that fish smell. As the eighty or ninety troops sailed past the federal prison on Alcatraz Island and under the Golden State Bridge out to the Pacific Ocean, I wondered why I had been so lucky to see so many things in my young life.

We stopped at Pearl Harbor in Hawaii to drop off some of the men joining their various battalions already stationed there.

The ocean voyage from Hawaii was done during the best time of the year. The captain told us that the cyclone season had passed some two or three months before. We were all glad to see land as the Etolin moved slowly across the Bay toward the Port of Manila. Upon disembarking I could not keep from noticing the number of Americans from the American business community that had come to meet the various ships at the docks. January 1941 weather was not what we were told to be expecting. The tropical heat did not exist. It was very pleasant and not raining. The troop truck from Nichols Field was awaiting us. I jumped on board the second one in line. For the next two months I learned my way around Nichols Field and Manila on the weekends. A squadron of P-40-E's at the airfield at Iba, Luzon, Philippines needed some modifications and maintenance. The Colonel put up a posted notice for all men to report to their Lieutenant if they had such training for further orders.

I reminded my Lieutenant to review my military records to see if I met the requirement for this opportunity. I had been trained as a Field Artillery Gunner in the United States Army. He was very firm and let all of us know Nichols Field was now an 'OJT' operation. Yes, on-job-training for P-40-E's maintenance. I asked him where Iba was and would this mean a promotion review for me. A week later the Lieutenant called me into his office and promoted me to First Sergeant and gave me my orders to go across Manila Bay and up the Island about sixty to seventy miles to Iba Air Base.

Hampered by the lack of military equipment to fight a war, during the final months of 1941, my Army Air Force mechanics squadron was assigned to make the modifications to update and properly outfit the P-40-E's with 50 caliber guns on the wings and in the nose. One of my primary duties was to install 3 of the 50 caliber guns on each wing and one in the nose of these single engine fighters. We had to calibrate the guns with the mechanical device controlling them to be sure the guns operated perfectly. The real tricky part of this was bore sighting the 50 caliber gun in the nose of the airplane to permit the gun to fire and miss the fast rotating propeller blade each time it passed in front of the barrel of the gun. In order to prepare and steady the aircraft for this calibration and timing of the gun and propeller, the P-40-E had to be hoisted up off of the ground and placed on racks.

Since I enjoyed the night life in Manila and needed to pick up more supplies and additional troops coming into the Port, I would sign out one of the Iba Air Base trucks and get a few of my buddies and go Nichols Field and make the very active social scene. We camped out at the hotel bars in the famous Manila Hotel with its' MacArthur Suite, Presidential Suite, Penthouse Suite and Honeymoon Suites and the clubs nearby.

TREASURES OF WAR – CONCEALED BY THE EVIL ONES / 100

Occasionally, we got to leave the air base on the South China Sea coast and get out of the heat and go up into the mountains to a recreation facility in Baguio City. Camp John Hay was the American Officer's favorite place to congregate for fun and games of golf. I learned that President Teddy Roosevelt was one of the forces behind building this cool place. The winding mountain road to Baguio was a severe test of your driving skills. For this Texas dude, I was scared to go very fast like some of the guys. When they got a chance on a short straight away, they would come zooming around me. Some of the cliffs on the edge of the rocky road were some two thousand feet or more. It usually took us most of the day to reach Baguio from Iba. Worth it? You bet it was. I met several Americans that had worked and lived in Baguio for many years. One particular man had operated one of the gold mines in Baguio and made a fortune. He was very nice to us during our visits. He told me many times that he had no desires whatsoever to return to the USA.

The duty in the Philippines was good. Due to the heat and rainy seasons we usually got up early and completed our workday around noon or 13:00. We had plenty of time for young men to play and meet the local girls.

Every so often when we were in Manila, the famous writer of short stories, Ernest Hemingway came by Nichols Field Air Base to visit us. He was in the Philippines writing some of his books. "Hey Steele, you still here?" He would ask me.

"Yes Sir, I am enjoying my life here," I replied. "Why are you coming to see us this time?"

"Have any of you seen my Filipino girl? I need her to do some work for me," Ernie asked?

I laughing said, "Girl, you mean girls don't you? You ought to have a drink with us and Mercy will probably come back through here. She was looking for you about an hour and a half ago."

"Smiling, Ernie said, "My reputation is not what you have read in the gossip columns. I am working hard and don't have any time to fool around."

"Give us a break Ernie. You now have a case of amnesia. Did you fall off your horse at the American Riding Club yesterday?" Arvil said slapping Ernie on the back as he ordered a drink for Ernie.

"What do you think about all this Jap crap? Do you guys think the Japs are going to take over the Philippines just like all the other countries around here?" He asked as he turned around and made a motion like he was going to shoot Arvil.

"Wait a minute Ernie!" I answered with a chuckle. Jumping up on the stool, "You know that we have a lot of Japanese people here in the Philippines. Do you think the Japs are going to come in here and kill some of their own?"

"I am leaving to go to Spain to complete some of my writings. I have really enjoyed you guy's friendship, fun times and the laughs we shared together during these last few months. I will miss you," Ernie revealed.

After the attack by the Japanese on Pearl Harbor, the Japanese Air Force would make air raids from the north from Formosa, and the **"first place and first ones hit by the Japanese was the American Air Base at Iba, Philippines"**. On the morning of December 8, 1941, the Jap Zero Squadrons came in low from the north on their way to Nichols Field in Manila. When they saw the American P-40-E's sitting up on the racks on the taxiways around the air base, they circled and made dives with their guns blasting most of the "sitting ducks" on the ground.

Americans dug in and set up machine gun installations and a few of the P-40-E's would scramble to fight the Jap Zeros. The American Pilots did not have a chance against the Jap Zeros. They were far superior fighters because the American military leadership was not prepared for the Japanese offenses in the South China Sea area at that early time of the war. Air superiority belonged to the Imperial Air Force. The American losses were mounting and we had to retreat from the Iba, Zambales,

Philippines to the south to Nichols Field near Manila. We had to defend the attack by the Japanese on Subic Bay and then Manila.

The Pre-World War II plan within the RAINBOW matrix for any future unilateral military conflicts between Japan and the United States was given in 1938 under the Military Code name of ORANGE 1, and ORANGE 2, and later in 1941, ORANGE 3.

I could not believe the **"WAR PLAN ORANGE"**, the code name for the defense of Manila. I learned first hand that the "ORANGE PLAN" had been drawn up by the U. S. Military leadership, who had not been in the Philippines since 1898, way back during the Spanish/American War and World War I. The medicines, rations, ammunitions, and artillery were stored all over Manila in many different places. Unfortunately, when the Japanese began their assault of the Manila area, we learned that all of these necessities of war, that we were relying upon, were so old that most all of them were no good to us at all. For example, that most of the artillery shells would not even fire.

We had to retreat to Bataan. Bataan was nothing but a tropical jungle. We fought the Japs from our constantly moving campsites in the jungle. Many of the men were killed each time they went out on patrol. Coming down from the northern invasion at Aparri, the Japanese Army of more than five thousand soldiers strong with a devotion to their Emperor Zapp, unlike anything ever imagined before in history and fully equipped, was something none of us wanted to face on a twenty-four hour sleepless and without food condition. However, all of us were willing to fight until our last bullet was spent and use our bayonets in direct combat. Many of us had to kill our game and catch a small fish to eat in order to survive.

Eventually, after knowing that we were not going to receive any of the promised supplies and manpower support from Washington, our General in charge negotiated a peaceful surrender to the

Japanese. On April 9, 1942 the fall of Bataan occurred. The Japanese took us Americans and the Filipinos as prisoners of war. The Bataan Death March began from Mariveles, Bataan, Philippines up through Cabcaben, Hermosa and on to San Fernando. We had to march approximately 110 kilometers under the most uncivilized conditions that any person would have to endure. The Japanese army that drove us was on horseback, bicycles, in trucks, and would shoot any American soldier that would show any sign of fainting or weakness.

During the Bataan Death March, I met the three Bostedt brothers from Iowa, twins Joe and Jake and the older brother Randy. I kept telling them not to show any signs of weakness in order to survive. In fact, one of the brothers and I walked on each side of Joe to hold him up and prevent the Japanese from shooting him and leaving him along the road.

Some of the Americans would see the rice fields and attempt to make a break for the rice fields to get a drink of water. If they were caught, the Japanese army guards shot them. Some of the men would make the dash to the rice fields and successfully get a drink of water only to become very sick from the diseases in the water.

Since I had the harsh training back in the states and had been in the Philippines for almost a year, the young American soldiers that had recently arrived in the Philippines looked up to me for guidance during the Bataan Death March.

Being one of the survivors of the Bataan Death March from Mariveles to San Fernando, I was packed into an old crowded rail car. I could not sit down and it was about 120 degrees in these old rail cars. Many of the American POW's died on the trains during the continuation of the Bataan Death March to Cabanatuan City. I was in the first company to arrive at Camp O'Donnell near Cabanatuan City, Ecija, Philippines. Cabanatuan "ONE" prison camp at Camp O'Donnell was where I had to perform burial duty. The large burial pits were used every day. When we first arrived, 20 to 30 American prisoners were dying every day. The prison camp had approximately 20,000 prisoners. The camp had only ONE water spigot for all 20,000 men to get a drink. We would wait all day long to get water.

We had a Japanese/American who acted as our interpreter. He obtained favors from the Japanese officers by ratting on the prisoners. We called him "Owl Face". The Japanese bad guy, we named "Little Glass Eye", gave the most severe punishment or execution orders. Many of the American prisoners got sick and I attempted to help them from dying by continuously telling them that they had to have the will to do what the Japanese asked them to do and take care of their eating and drinking habits.

One of my dear friends today, Mr. Monroe Ryan from Arkansas, had gotten diarrhea so bad that I told him to eat the burnt rice from the bottom of the cooking pans. I had learned first hand several times during training that eating old coals from fires would stop diarrhea. So, I thought that the closest thing we had in Camp One at Camp O'Donald was the burnt rice on the bottoms of the cooking pans. It worked for Monroe. He lives today to give me credit for saving his life.

When I had burial detail, I witnessed the blood flowing from the burial pit used the day before into the burial pit being used that day. I learned that the immeasurable and deliberate evil forces of Emperor Zapp, his militaristic Japan and Imperial Army and its tactics to destroy their enemy, "The Invading Asia--Wicked Americans and British", caused an enormous psychological defeat of many young American soldiers. Some of these young men did not have the will power or fortitude to continue the unbearable suffering and gave up the fight to live in conditions never before imagined by anyone. Were the brave dead soldiers the lucky ones?

The transportation during those days was mainly by rail. The Japanese had use of the captured trucks from the Americans, plus the trucks that they brought in during their landing. Most of these trucks were charcoal fueled.

The Japs refused to give any medication as the men became more and more ill and the wounds from the brutal beatings and horse-whippings during the Death March and from the rides in the cattle railcars, together with human filth all around us, caused infected open sores and extreme high temperatures from the diarrhea and dysentery among the POW's.

Shortly after we got to Camp One at Camp O'Donnell I visited the Bostedt brothers in the make shift Hospital ward. I told them that they had to eat the things that would help them get as well as they could expect to get.

I had worked hard and risk being shot by one of the brutal Jap guards to keep Joe alive during the Bataan Death March. Later, I was very saddened when I had to bury these three brothers in the shallow grave during one of my burial details.

Continuously, the Imperial Japanese Army officers searched our barracks and bodies looking for anything of Japanese origin. Seeking out possible killers of Japanese soldiers, surprise inspections were conducted several times each day by one of the Japanese officers. He was indoctrinated to believe that a prisoner who had something from Japan had killed a Japanese soldier to obtain it. He believed this action was directed against Emperor Zapp, their God.

Keeping us awake at different hours during the night prevented us from having a full night's sleep. Every night the guards would come into our barracks and wake everyone up. When someone did not respond, they were either dead or unconscious from the lack of food or due to illness. It was hard to go back to sleep knowing that someone in your barrack was dead and whom you would be burying the next day.

The guards got a great deal of enjoyment out of kicking a guy in the open sore or wound and laughed about it. Some of the very seriously ill men had huge holes in their legs, no flesh right down to the bones. Without any medicines we learned to improvise by putting maggots in the wound and wrapping it with rags. The maggots would eat away the entire pus and everything diseased. Again, this was done because the Japs would not give any medicines to the POW's. Some of the brave men were lying there dying and the flesh actually rotting off their bodies.

Most of us POW's were so undernourished that we became skin and bones. Some were down from one hundred eighty to seventy-five pounds. I could not believe what was happening to American Soldiers.

TREASURES OF WAR – CONCEALED BY THE EVIL ONES / 106

> **SLEEP MY SONS, YOUR DUTY DONE...**
>
> **FOR FREEDOM'S LIGHT HAS COME.**
>
> **SLEEP IN THE SILENT DEPTHS OF THE SEA**
>
> **OR IN YOUR BED OF HALLOWED SOD.**
>
> **UNTIL YOU HEAR AT DAWN**
>
> **THE LOW CLEAR REVEILLE OF GOD**

The poet is unknown. It is inscribed on the monument to the Pacific War Dead, in Corregidor, Philippines. Each May 6th, the sun is in such a position that it's rays fall into the center of the monument, exactly at noon.

On or about June 1942, due to the need for Emperor Zapp to win over the Filipino masses to support his hand picked Puppet Filipino Government to lead the Philippines and prevent the use of large amounts of Japanese resources and armies to fight lengthy battles, he ordered his armies to release many of the Filipino prisoners and separate them from the American POW's at Camp O'Donnell. The Filipinos POW's detained were moved to Cabanatuan Concentration Camp. The conditions for the Filipinos were greatly improved. They had adequate drinking and bathing water.

However, back at Camp One I convinced the guards that I was obeying them and attempted to help them get some of the POW's to be more submissive to the Guards, making their jobs easier. As a result, I received a work detail. In general, I was fearful of work details. Many of the men were worked to death in the hot sun on road construction duty. The Jap construction bosses used every kind of horrible torture to force the POW worker to work beyond anything considered humane.

A Japanese Lieutenant, educated in the United States who had been called home just before the attack on Pearl Harbor, noticed that I was doing my best working on his project when one of his men came over and began torturing me with his bayonet. For some Godly reason, the Lieutenant picked me out of the POW's and called me aside and told me some things that would save my life and others that would listen to me. He spoke very educated English.

"Remember, if you ever get knocked down by a Japanese soldier, jump up immediately."

Eventually, I was given the job of cleaning up his boss's office. This gave me the opportunity to talk to them about supplying the sick POW's some medicines that I saw in their supplies. I had been taught as a young sharecropper working hard in the cotton fields how to get the best rows to pick. Now, I had a Japanese officer that spoke fluent English, who knew the American way of life; and it became obvious to me that he did not agree with Emperor Zapp's brutal policies. The other officers watched me and some of them wanted me teach them English. One particular very devout Shinto officer was not liked by most of the other Jap officers because he was ruthless with the POW's. He would kill a prisoner for no apparent reason at all. The American educated Japanese Lieutenant and I were talking one day about something that had happened to him when he was attending the university in the U. S. He wanted to know how he could do the same to the ruthless Jap officer. I showed him how to 'short sheet' the bed. The next day most of the officers tried to tell me in a few words of English mixed with Japanese how they watched the ruthless Jap officer try to get to bed the night before. They laughed and slapped me on my back and ran over to his bed demonstrating the events of the night before. I understood that he got so upset that he ran out into the night and did not come back until after they had gone to sleep. This was another lesson learned that I could share with the other POW's in order to survive.

My work detail consisted of something like a trustee in a prison. I drove a truck into town and picked up food for the Imperial Japanese Army officers. Being accustomed to some of the Filipino foods was a very important asset for me. On occasion, I was asked to show the Japanese cooks how to prepare some of the local vegetables and pork items. This gave me a slight breather from the everyday routine at the Camp and daily burial duties.

TREASURES OF WAR – CONCEALED BY THE EVIL ONES / 108

In 1942, the Japanese began getting the POW's out of the Philippines before the return invasion by the American forces. In November 1942, I was on the first Japanese "HELL SHIP" named Nagata Maru (Ship In Japanese). During these shipments of prisoners from the Philippines to Japan, the U. S. Submarines, not knowing that Americans prisoners were on these vessels, sank several of these "HELL SHIPS".

The conditions on the "HELL SHIPS" were worse than the Bataan Death March. We were locked down in the bottom of these vessels and packed like sardines. The Japanese would lower a bucket down for us to get a drink of water. They would do the same with the food. They would not let us out to go on the deck of the ship. We would have to knock on the door to get them to remove our fellow comrades who had died during the past 24 hours. It was almost totally dark down in the hole of the ship. When they would let down the bucket for us to urinate in, most of the men could not see what they were doing and would piss all over the compartment. Same for taking a shit. We were treated as inhuman as anything you could imagine.

It is my firm opinion that the main reason that the Emperor Zapp had decided to remove the POW's from the Philippines and take us to Japan was due to the fact that Emperor Zapp was having to send all of his men, including his 14 and 15 year olds, to fight in war actions in the Pacific. This would allow the POW's to do the technical maintenance work at the mines, docks, Hydro Units and etc.

My HELL SHIP docked at the Port of Maji, Japan. I was taken to the Prisoner of War Camp in Mitsushima, (Also, known as Tokyo Camp No. 2) located at 11,000 feet altitude. The buildings were constructed out of thin wood. Our clothing was shorts from the hot tropics of the Philippines. It was winter and cold all the time. We had to sleep on straw beds. Many of the POW's caught the common cold, which led to pneumonia and 3 to 5 deaths each day. The reason that the Japanese wanted us here in Camp Mitsushima, Japan was to complete the construction of the nearby dam for the large Hydro Electric Plant. We had to assist the contractors to bore holes in the mountain for the water to flow through and pour the concrete for the dam that the water would flow over.

Thinking we could help win the war by sabotaging the work detail, all of us agreed to support our countries efforts as best we could. During the mixing of the concrete we would mix the contents of the concrete to sand so as to cause the poured concrete to breakup and wash away each time the water would flow over the dam. It worked and the Japanese never did understand why this was happening. The dam was never completed until after World War II was over.

The Photo to the right was taken many years after the end of World War II. The Japanese completed the project that we did not complete because of our efforts to sabotaged the construction process.

Photo Courtesy of M/Sgt. Arvil Steele US Army Air Force POW At Mitsushima, Japan

The prison officials respected good workers. I weighed about 90 pounds at the end of my POW days. But, I was very strong because of the fact that I had worked hard to stay alive and did what I was told to do. In fact, the prison officials would come to me to get me to straighten out some of the prisoners. I would make a big fuss at the American prisoner in front of the Japanese prison official and make motions to the prison officer that everything would work out OK. I was known as a "Hauncho", a foreman for the Japanese prison officials.

Warm jackets were very critical for the survival of all of us at Mitsushima-Tokyo POW Camp No. 2. After learning a few phases in Japanese and using objects and lots of hand language, I could communicate with a few of the Jap officers and guards. I finally got it across to them to get some warmer clothes for us or all of us would die and they would not be able to carry out the orders of Emperor Zapp and build the Hydro Electric Plant for him.

TREASURES OF WAR – CONCEALED BY THE EVIL ONES / 110

Emperor Zapp's pictures were hung in every Imperial Army officer's office. I would point to the picture and go through all kinds of motions, pulling on their warm clothes and jackets, pointing at myself and toward the other POW's, showing them that our shoes had holes in them, pointing again at Emperor Zapp's picture and then to the direction of the Hydro Electric Plant and on and on until they understood me.

Finally, one of the Jap truck drivers came roaring into camp one afternoon, honking his horn and jumped out and shouted something in Japanese. It must have been a planned action by the Camp's officers to get us to think they had done something special for us. Chuckie, our guard's name, hollered across the yard to us and motioned us to come to the truck. Upon arriving at the truck, I noticed some winter clothes. Because we had lost so much weight, the sizes were OK for most of us. Chuckie grabbed a few of the clothes and slung them out into the men and gestured with his head for us to take the clothes.

As I turned around with a few clothes that I thought would fit me in my arms, I noticed Col. Calvin, the name we gave the Camp's commander, was standing on the porch of his office watching all of these developments. I smiled and waved at him and told the men to turn around and bow to him to make him feel good about what he had done for us. Then, I pointed up into the heavens and waved my hands for a moment and began to clap. All of the men picked up on this and clapped with me. Col. Calvin was such a dedicated worshiper of Emperor Zapp as his God; I knew he got our message.

Most all of the Japanese guards at the camp were former warriors of Emperor Zapp and had fought in the conquest, raping of girls and women, and looting in China. They had been wounded in China and brutalities of any human being had become a way of life and were oblivious to the proper treatment of POW's. I learned that a few of the guards spoke good English from their education and training in the United States prior to the war. Again, I worked hard at keeping as many of my fellow (Photo Courtesy of Arvil Steele, POW at this POW Camp) prisoners alive. I preached the idea that we must do what the Jap guards asked us to do.

After several bad incidences between prisoners and Jap guards in which the prisoner was killed, I repeatedly told my comrades that "Even if the Jap guard spit in your face, don't retaliate. But, if you do and he hits you with something and knocks you to the ground, jump up as quick as you can. If you don't jump up quickly, the punishment will continue. You are sending a signal to the Jap guard that he is superior to you. And he most likely will continue until you are dead."

Jap Guard Watanabe, not pictured above, was given orders by Emperor Zapp to go to all POW Camps in Japan and torture the prisoners. He came by our camp several times. The Jap guards were motivated to dish out more torture during his visits. Since he could speak good English he would go up into the face of a prisoner and tell him, "You think Joe Lewis has a knock out punch – watch my knock out punch." He would slug you right in the jaw and knock you to the ground and laugh at you.

The most brutal Jap guard was Capt. Sukeo Kakajima, the one on the left side of the front row in the photo above. One of his brutal actions was when he took off his boot and slapped you across your face.

TREASURES OF WAR – CONCEALED BY THE EVIL ONES / 112

The Jap guard that was interested in learning more about America is the tallest in the center back row above. At lunchtime he would walk off away from the other Jap guards and motion for me to come over to him. He taught me some more Japanese and I returned the favor by teaching him some English. "Frog" was the name given to him. After a year or so he began to use me to resolve some of the problems with prisoners.

The burial duty was a lot different than back in the Philippines. Burial duty consisted of two of us POW's carrying the dead up to the Japanese burial grounds along the trail up the mountain. We had to find some wood and build a fire – put the body on the pit with the fire blazing – stay and watch until the body was cremated. Then, we walked back down the mountain trail to our POW camp. It was a cold duty more ways than one.

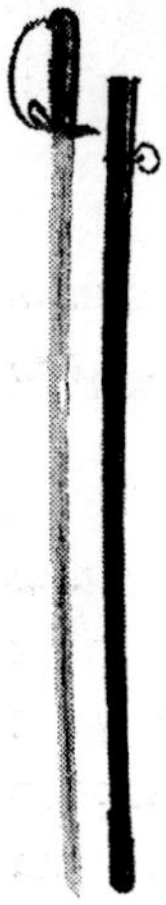

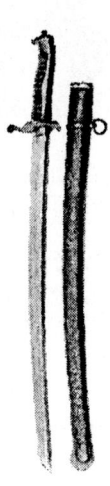

One of the things that the top Japanese prison officers would not tolerate was theft. When anyone of the prisoners got caught stealing something they would make a demonstration to the total prison population. One soldier took a pumpkin, and he was caught. The Japanese prison officer would remove his long **saber case** and use it to beat the prisoner all over his body. The soldier that had taken the pumpkin was put on display in front of all the prisoners of Camp Mitsushima. The saber cases were used to beat him across his head many, many times until his head was swollen 2 to 3 times its normal size and he turned purple. He died by noon the next day. I pleaded over and over again with the American prisoners to do what they had to do to survive. Most of them found a fighting heart to want to survive under the most horrid circumstances that anyone can imagine.

I keep telling myself that when I get home to Texas and Arkansas all I want to eat is a big Texas size hamburger with French fried potatoes and a thick chocolate malt.

All of these other guys dream of getting their favorite meal and a cool beer or whiskey on the rocks.

I can't let myself be overwhelmed by the horrible daily events. It's been almost three years and I could feel the confusion amongst the Jap guards. Something must be happening. All of a sudden, they are going down the mountain

TOKYO POW CAMP NO. 2
Photo Courtesy M/Sgt. Arville Steele

and bringing back much more food to eat. I got to think positive and continue to work hard to survive. Why did I receive my first Red Cross package a few weeks ago? All of these things made me wonder more and think about going home to see my Mom and brother Bob. I must keep the faith.

Here it was the first week of September 1945 and I almost passed out when the airplanes with that big STAR on the side of it flew over and dropped those barrels of food to us. The Japanese officers and guards came out and told us the Emperor Zapp had surrendered.

As we were marched down the mountain to the port city of Maji, I could feel the Jap officers that were very bitter and wanted to kill us. Then, I knew the Jap officers that were very glad that the war was over. 'Frog', together with his wife and children were at the bus station when I left. He gave me his tobacco pouch, pipes and leather jacket, and he and his family began to cry.

That guy thought the world of his tobacco he always smoked. And, he was proud of the tobacco blends in his unique pouch. He is attempting to say something to me at this critical time in his life, a defeated POW guard.

My first stop was Yokohama, Japan. The Army Air Force was going to fly us POW's on B-24's to Manila and transport us back to the U. S. on a special Army Transport Ship. We took off from Yokohama and got up into some very, very bad weather. It was so bad that the pilot had to change his flight and land on Okinawa. We were given some very special treatment at the airbase in Okinawa for a few days.

Finally, the Army Air Force personnel announced that we would be going on to Manila to catch our awaiting ship. We flew the same B-24 and landed at Nichols Field in Manila. I did not recognize any of the destroyed cities that I had known pretty well only three plus years before. I could not believe my eyes. Everywhere, most of the city was leveled.

How many people lost their lives here? I wondered.

TREASURES OF WAR – CONCEALED BY THE EVIL ONES / 114

Once we reached the docks at the port I saw this large Army Transport Ship. As I checked in with the boarding officer, I was told that I had a stateroom on the top of the ship.

"Hey Navy, don't kid around with me."

"Sir, I am not kidding you. You deserve a first class trip home because of what you have gone through. The nurses and doctors will take good care of you and get you back to better health," the young man said as he saluted Arvil.

"Thank you, I did not expect such a reception," Arvil said as he returned the salute and boarded the ship looking up at old glory flying above.

POW's from all over Japan were air lifted to Manila and put on this Army Transport Ship for POW's. I could not believe the way the Army Air Force was prepared to treat us and start the road to recovery from our many years of torture and slave labor work in Japan. Here I was in a high-ranking officer's suite receiving medical treatment deluxe. The doctors and nurses were working long hours to take care of our immediate needs. The comfort in the soft bed made it easier to rest during the day and night. Some of us could not believe it was the war was over. A few days out of Manila, the newsreels of the surrender by the Japanese officers was shown during mess hall. It was repeated a few more times during the long voyage home. Seeing General MacArthur signing the treaty on behalf of all of us gave most of us a good feeling. I still had some personal bitterness for him because of what had happened to me during December 8th, 1941 and thereafter in the Philippines.

The photos of some Emperor Zapp's officers that came to the surrender signing should have included the vicious officers that had run the POW Camps in the Philippines and Japan.

We stopped in Hawaii to pick up more supplies and reading materials and the like. Pearl Harbor was not the same as it was five years earlier. Looking at the tops of the sunken battleships made me realize that Emperor Zapp's plans to conquer the world beginning with the destruction of Asia and eventually leading to his ultimate desire and goal to defeat "The Invading Asia – Wicked and Evil Americans and British" by making the surprise attack on December 7th, 1941, took a consecrated effort on the part of all of us to defeat the true Evil God, Emperor Zapp and his Imperial Military Forces.

They passed out many of the newspapers from all around the world that had been published since our embarking from Manila. Many of the pictures in the newspapers and magazines reflected the emotions of the war ending and everyone coming home. The Troop Transport Ship pulled out of Pearl Harbor and headed east to San Francisco Bay. All of us were very impatient to return to the land of the free and home of the brave. I did a lot of praying, thanking God for protecting me from death during war and giving me a new start in life. Mom's teachings from the Bible to me as a young boy became very meaningful throughout the many trials and tribulations I encountered as a fighting soldier of the United States Army Air Force and as a Prisoner of War. I remembered the song that we sang in church many times, Onward Christian Soldiers.

Seeing the Golden Gate Bridge from the west looking east was something that I dreamed about. The tugs loud horns blew as they came out to greet us and attached themselves to our ship, and our captain let his return be heard all around the bay by blasting his louder whistles. This went on for several more times as we were being pushed up to the dock.

Eventually, we packed up our things and most of us walked down the gangplank to set our feet on the ground or pavement, as is the case in the U. S. for the first time in five years.

Army buses were lined up to take most of us to Letterman's General Hospital. After further medical examinations I was cleared to go down to the San Francisco Railroad Station for the trip home.

The United States Army had arranged for a special Red Cross Pullman Dinner Hospital Train for all of the POW's from Japan. The doctors and nurses issued us only pajamas hoping to keep us from jumping off the train at stops along the way to get whisky. That rule was violated at every stop from San Francisco to Texarkana. The former POW's jumped off the train in their pajamas and ran around town looking for a place to buy whisky. Then, they ran back to the train just before pulling out. Since the train cars were marked with very vivid Red Crosses, the word got out that some returning wounded army soldiers were on the train and most of the town folks wanted to show their respectful feelings to us. Most of the men in their pajamas running around town did not have to pay for anything that they desired.

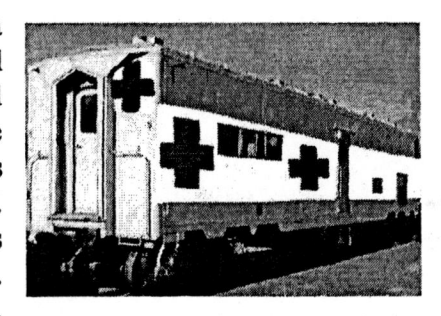

Mom had been sent a telegram from the War Department letting her know that I was on the train home. It was about 21:00 when the Red Cross Hospital Train arrived at Union Central Station in Texarkana, Texas.

As I stepped off the train in my new uniform issued to me while I was about one hundred miles from my final destination; Mom did not immediately recognize me. I weighed less than one hundred pounds. The last time she had seen me five years earlier, I weighed one hundred and fifty pounds. I had not received any mail sent to me, since the Japs on Bataan captured me on April 9, 1942.

"Mom, Fred, I am over here." I shouted.

"Arvil, Arvil, Arvil, you are safe and home at last. God has answered my many prayers. Praise God Almighty! Give me a big hug," Arvil's Mom screamed.

"Let's go have something to eat," she added as the tears streamed down her face.

"Fred, how is my big brother doing?" Arvil said as he embraced his older brother.

"Did you sisters dress up just for me?" Arvil added as he hugged both of them.

"Where is Bob? His war has been over almost six months now. Surely, he has been sent home by now. Where is Bob?" Arvil asked again.

"Arvil, like I said, let's go get something to eat," Mom nervously replied.

TREASURES OF WAR – CONCEALED BY THE EVIL ONES

Chapter Five

The Story of Filipino Guerrilla – Virgilio 'Bulldog' Hermano

Author's Photo

Back in the deep jungles of Northern Luzon Island our family was very poor during the time period around 1920. We did not have electricity, plumbing -- running water, private bath and flush toilet.

My father was one of the leaders of the local tribe, and my mother worked long hours every day. They named me Virgilio. We lived a few blocks off a country road in a one-room shanty. It was located in the heart of the township of Darat in the northern province of Ilocos Norte.

I had an unusual childhood, even by the standards of the culture. We spoke Malay, Spanish and English. My father obtained a one-school room education and had above average intelligence.

In 1936, my father, Manuel, was defeated in the county commissioners election. He had been elected in 1930, 1932 and 1934. In 1936 the opposition party had new leadership from the governor's office down to the local elections. The opposition party candidate, Romeo Tecson, beat my father. He only lived a few blocks from us.

On election night, Romeo did not even consider being a gracious winner. He road around town in a horse and buggy complete with a small marching band of his followers letting everyone know he was a better man than my father. Romeo had all of his group march in front of our home to rub it in.

I became so furious that I could not control my emotions. I grabbed my ole 22 rifle and left the house.

The leading news story a few weeks later was about Romeo Tecson dying of a gunshot wound.

The Central Luzon police authorities ordered the deployment of secret marshals into the region following the killing of Tecson. The secret marshals are plainclothes policeman.

The Spaniards converted the Philippines to Christianity. I thought.

Unfortunately, the islands were located in the sea-lanes dividing the South China Sea and the Pacific on the one hand --- the Malaysian, Indochina, Dutch and Thailand empires --- and China and Japan on the other --- and the lasting fact in recorded history that the weak are primary targets for overthrowing. The rise of Christianity hadn't changed matters very much.

The classes of the people were the same. The Catholic Church did not attempt to educate the poor peasants. The Spanish did not want them educated. These conditions only made wars all the more bitter by the Guerrilla Rebels Revolution.

The Tydings-McDuffie Act passed by the FDR administration in 1934 provided for a transitional period until 1946, at which time the Philippines would become independent. Under a constitution approved by the people of the Philippines in 1935, the Commonwealth of the Philippines came into being.

Some months before Pearl Harbor, while the Philippine Islands were still under United States sovereignty, President Roosevelt issued an order making the Filipino Army a part of the US Army. Of course, this made the Filipino soldiers who constituted that army a part of the Fighting Forces as much as were soldiers drafted in the States. After all, the Filipino soldiers fought for their homeland as well as the United States.

They remained in this status until the eve of the Philippines' independence.

Since the Philippines have become a separate nation, they may be reasonably expected to assume the continuing burden of caring for injured veterans among their own people.

VIRGILIO HERMANO – 'BULLDOGS' GUERRILLAS.

"Let me tell you one of the most vivid events in the early days as a leader of my underground guerrilla group, the 'Bulldogs'," Virgil explained. "The Japanese were forcing the Filipinos to disclose the secret hideouts of several 'HOOKS' guerrilla commanders," he went on.

The peasant guerrillas who fought the invading Japanese Imperial Forces are called "HOOKS".

"General Homma's campaign was to cut off local Filipino and tribesmen supporters," Virgil emotionally said. "No one would risk an arrest and torture by the Japanese Army or police. The Japanese Imperial Forces offered money and pardon, and the Filipino hostility toward Americans from the years of fighting them caused many partisans to surrender and to work for the Japanese."

"Three of my lieutenants from the highlands, Rogelio, Paul, and Rene were betrayed by their own people and killed by the Japanese leaders," he continued. "The Japanese made the most out of these victories and displayed severed heads of my lieutenants in the town center in order to intimidate the lowlands villagers into submission to their demands," Virgil emphasized.

"In the long-term these actions by the Japanese united the underground guerrilla movement, and the 'Bulldogs' won some important victories. The villagers began to risk their lives to come up into the hills and report the Japanese activities," Virgil proudly stated.

"I had to keep the 'Bulldogs' on the move from Badoc, Ilocos Norte to Mt. Sicapoo down to Claveria. We vacated our camps and fled to Mt. Lacob," Virgil continued.

The 'Bulldogs' had some 600 men at its peak in mid-1944."

"Col. Duque, the Cordillera Central mountain range is an ideal place for guerrilla warfare," Virgil suggested.

"Virgil, these mountains are covered with thick growths of jungle vines and trees," the Colonel explained, pointing to the mountains.

"But you need to take your army and locate a place along the river in order to have abundant fish for food," Virgil told the Colonel.

"Colonel, I know that there are a number of small highland villages on the slope of the mountains, very remote, inaccessible, isolated from the Japanese invasion troops," Major Virgil Hermano suggested.

"Colonel Duque, I am very familiar with the area between the villages of Lacob and Tineg. The highest mountain near there is more than 1,500 meters. The nearby Tineg River has two branches down in the lowlands with good fishing for food. We will set up camp on the southeast side at about 600 meters high on the mountain," Virgil elaborated.

"We will close down our camp here in the morning and move across the three mountains and reach our new camp site by dusk," Major Hermano confided to Colonel Duque.

"Sergeant Paygo go down to Agbulu and tell Major Mariano to come up and find us at our new camp," Virgil ordered.

Upon the arrival of Major Mariano two days later, the meeting began by issuing some concerns and warnings.

"I have learned that one of your men, Ricardo, left your camp site to return to his lowlands village, Piddig, and when he was captured by the Japanese he disclosed all he knew about your army," Major Virgil Hermano suspiciously stated.

This was shocking news to Major Mariano. "Ricardo was one of my best fighters," the Major Marino explained. "What happened?" he asked.

"The report I received from an old villager was that Ricardo's wife and young children were used to force him to spill the beans," Virgil said.

"Major, you must go back to your army in the highlands and lead them over the mountain and through the jungle and set up your new camp near the southern edge of Kabugao in the mountains overlooking the Abulug river. Let your men know that they are in danger of destroying themselves and their families when they return to their villages," Virgil instructed.

"Yes sir," the Major Marino replied. The major left that afternoon to return to his army camp.

"Sergeant, go over to Lt. Villacrusis' hut and see if he is free to meet with me in one hour," Major Virgil ordered.

"Major, Lt. Villacrusis told me to tell you he would be here in one hour," the Sergeant reported upon his return from the Lieutenant's hut.

"Sergeant how many times do I have to tell you to call me by my code name, "COWBOY?" Virgil scolded.

"I apologize sir."

When Lt. Villacrusis arrived for the meeting, Virgil was reviewing their current position.

"Lieutenant, I need to change my clothes and go down to Darat and commingle with the villagers and find some new recruits and financial support. You are in command while I am gone. I have some relatives in the Darat area that will hide me from the Japanese Army and police. I will take those gruesome photos depicting horrible things the Japanese have done to Filipinos --- getting heads chopped off --- skinned alive --- getting cut up into quarters --- and Filipino women's belly cut open," Virgil graphically described to the Lieutenant.

"I know the farmers and peasants language --- hopeless poverty, landlords, and loan sharks. I will wear my ragged peasant clothes. Therefore, I will smell like the peasants. I will take Leo, Jose, Chief, Cesar and Elmer with me. We will help the village peasants harvest the rice, cabbage, cauliflower, tomatoes, mangos, potatoes, and garlic; and then help them plant new crops," Virgil explained his plans.

"We will need several peasant packs with our pistols and grenades securely placed inside," Virgil emphasized.

Before Virgil and the five men left for the lowlands they gathered together for preparation and instructions.

"All of you must be conscious of Japanese snipers along the main trail. You all know the special sounds that are made between us to warn of sightings of the enemy. We will go in one straight line about 20 to 50 feet apart in total silence," Major Virgil instructed.

"That will work".

The team checked their packs and placed them on their backs and for some on their head. As they walked through the dense jungle, they came upon a fresh trail that appeared to have been traveled by the Japanese Army. Everyone was very scared and moved slowly along this trail. All of a sudden, "Chief" made the loud birdcalls to warn of a Japanese sniper. The team ducked into the jungle and took cover and slowly moved around the sniper. From his early days of hunting game, Major Virgil was a most accurate poison dart blower. He crawled through the brush to get behind the sniper. He took aim and launched the poison dart, and it struck the sniper in the back of the neck. The sniper tumbled out of the tree and landed near Virgil.

TREASURES OF WAR – CONCEALED BY THE EVIL ONES / 125

Virgil grabbed the guns and grenades from the dead sniper and ran about 200 feet through the jungle brush. He whistled for the team to re-group. They continued their travels to the village. They arrived at the village just before dusk. They located the home of Olivera, an old peasant friend of many years.

"Three of you are welcomed to sleep here tonight on the floor. The other three need to go down the road to the empty barn shed of the Ramon family just across the creek on the right. On the left side of the Ramon shed you will see a window, sleep there tonight. Last week, the elderly Ramon family were dragged out by their hair and shot by the Japanese army," Oli said.

The next day the guerrillas mixed and mingled with the village teenagers. They let them play with their pistols and showed them how the grenades worked. They told the teenagers combat stories.

"The pistol you are holding was used to kill six Japanese soldiers a few weeks ago," Cesar told the young men.

When they could touch the weapons and talk to the guerrillas, the new prospective recruits became more comfortable with the guerrillas. They learned that the guerrillas were not the bad guys that the Japanese would have them believe. The guerrillas did their best to look friendly and harmless to show the peasants not to be afraid of them.

The next day Oli told Virgil, "The rice crop of Pedro Mijares is ready to be harvested. Several of your men should go to the end of Crista road. You will see the thatch house. Pedro is expecting you. He will furnish each of you with a cycle to harvest the rice. He has two hectares to be harvested. He will donate twenty ten pound bags of rice to you," Oli genuinely spoke.

Virgil told Oli, "We need to have a mass meeting place for about ten to fifteen people so all attendees will have a chance to talk about new recruits. Since the church is used for meetings and has people coming and going, I suggest the church be used. You will be responsible for getting several young dependable kids to be positioned at a few locations to look out for people that will not be wearing the special cloth tag, which the young kids will know as the good guys attending the meeting. The kids should run to the meeting place to tell us when someone suspicious is coming down the street. If danger occurs, we will give signals along the way to tell the attendees to return home and not attend the meeting."

In the meeting six new recruits were ready to join the guerrilla group.

The next day Virgil called his team together and told them to meet at the Moreles farm up on the ridge above the river.

"We have two water buffaloes available to plow the potatoes out of the ground. Leo, you will work with one and Jose, you will use your skills to plow the ground with the rocks in the field. Elmer, Celso, Ben, and Ronell, you will get the sacks from farmer Moreles and pick the potatoes from the plants and put them into the sacks. You will carry the potatoes to the special storage place in the hills. Elmer, I told you about the place," Major Virgil ordered them.

"Keep your guard up for possible Japanese Army looking for food for their troops. Take the potatoes and bury them in the special sand at the site. This will preserve them for months to come. Farmer Moreles has offered us seven 10-pound bags for our guerrilla army. You should fill these seven bags and put in a remote place for us to pick up when we leave the village," Virgil interposed.

When the war began most of the remaining landlords and their managers retreated to Manila. The landlords now had three factions to fear -- the peasants, the Japanese and the guerrillas.

Virgil told Oli. "We will teach you how to organize to help each other, to stand together to fight for your common cause of freeing yourselves from the Japanese and the vicious landlords. We can teach your women many things that will enable them to be more active in their families and with their children. The women and children will be good for intelligence, collection and courier services for us."

Oli replied. "I will do my best to convince the villagers to back the movement to free ourselves of invaders and the 'Slave Owner' landlords."

"Oli, my team will be leaving tomorrow together with the new recruits. My guerrilla army will return to this village in about a month. We will be prepared to take over the village and prevent anyone from leaving or entering the village," Virgil told him.

The guerrilla team returned to their highlands camp. Approximately a month later Virgil's guerrilla army returned to Darat. The first thing they did was cut all outside phone lines. Guerrilla units were placed at key access points to ambush any Japanese army troops and landlords or their managers coming to the village.

All Japanese Army troops and pro-Japanese villagers and landlords were captured and tried in mass meetings at the church. Some of the Japanese offered maps to buried Gold Bars and other treasure that they had previously buried near Mt. Sicapoo and along the Laoag and Tineg Rivers in order to save themselves. The landlord's managers were first ridiculed, roughed up and tried before the villagers.

"You village leaders must distribute the landlords belonging equally among the peasants," Virgil instructed.

"Virgil, how am I going to get their maps of the buried Gold Bar treasures?" Oli asked.

"Before we execute the Japanese officers, let's torture them into telling us as much information regarding security and any rigged up booby traps to protect the buried Gold treasures and get the maps," Virgil schemed.

"There is a Lieutenant that speaks some English. I will call them all together and begin our torture routine," Ronell said as he left to fetch the Japanese prisoners.

The Japanese prisoners were brought to the church to begin their interrogation. Each of ten Japanese soldiers was placed in separate rooms.

Virgil went into the Lieutenant's room and began, "I understand that you speak some English. What is your name and where did you learn your English?"

"My name is Lieutenant Oskita and I studied at the University of California for one year before I was called home to enter Emperor Evil God's military."

"My men tell me that you have some maps to offer as ransom for your life. Do you have the maps with you? How do I know that this is not just some trick to save you and your men?"

Lieutenant Oskita bent over and pulled his boot off and slipped the folded map out and handed it to Virgil, "Believe me this is a genuine map. I was ordered to bury the Gold Bars that my superiors brought ashore about two months ago. My men and I chose the locations. I am under orders to keep this map and give it to my superiors after we defeat the Americans. My men know more of the details for each site."

"You can save yourself a lot of torture by describing each place where you buried the Gold Bars," Virgil shouted nose to nose with the Lieutenant.

"Chief, you and Ronell get some paper and write down everything these murderers say," Virgil added. "Are you men ready?"

"Yes sir!"

"Lieutenant, tell me what is meant by Island in River? Did you hide something there?"

"We found an opening in the trees in the center of the Island which had a some type of burial or gravesites on it. My men dug up the graves and buried Gold Bars in the bottom and put the graves back on top of them."

"Did you order the grave sites to be booby trapped or were any explosive devices such as land mines placed near burial area?"

"No Sir!"

"When I send one of my important men out there and I receive word that he was killed by your devious schemes to save these Gold Bars for Emperor Evil God, you will beg for us to kill you."

Author's Photo

"Sir, we only had room for the men and Gold Bars in the boat used to go to the Island in the middle of Laoag River."

"What about the site mark on the map up the Tineg Rive near Mt. Sicapoo? How did you get it up the river that far? Some of that river has shallow rock bottom."

"Let me call one of my men here?"

"Chief, take the Lieutenant to find his man and bring both of them back here as soon as you can. He can talk to this one man only. Do not let him talk to anyone else. Open each door and he will say yes or no and point out the correct man. He is not to say anything to that man before he returns here."

"Lieutenant, do you understand my orders?"

"Yes Sir!"

Upon their return, Virgil began again, "Lt. does your man speak good English?"

"He understands a little but does not speak much."

"Ask him the details of what was buried at the site near Mt. Sicapoo. I want to know every detail," Virgil asked as he pointed to the mark on the unfolded and smelly map.

Lieutenant Oskita quizzed his man and told him that their lives depended upon the accuracy and truth of his answers.

"Facing the three rock formations from the Tineg River, my men had some American POW's dig out a small cave until my men could walk back to a large room in the cave. This is directly to the right of the lower rock formation near the edge of the river. There are 1820 seventy-five kilos Gold Bars hidden in that one cave. The front of the cave was covered with large rocks and the demolition team rigged the rocks with explosives. Those demolition men have either been killed or moving north with the battalion. We do not know what to do with the explosives."

"What happened to the American POW's?"

"I was ordered to march them into the cave and shoot them. Their remains are in the cave."

"Emperor Evil God has caused you to become a vicious killer. Do you believe what you have done is moral?" Virgil suddenly asked.

TREASURES OF WAR – CONCEALED BY THE EVIL ONES / 131

"You do not understand our religious beliefs," Lt. solemnly replied.

"Who can tell me about the mark on the map on the peninsula on Laoag River toward the sea from Mt. Sicapoo?"

"I know all about this site. This is an old 1800 or older sugar mill plantation with some of the Spanish sugar mill ruins left as originally constructed. On the top of the mountain is the old sugar mill storage castle for sugar cane syrup and look out station for pirates coming up the river."

"What did you hide in the sugar cane castle? Surely the sugar cane was not stored in it any longer," Virgil replied.

"Believe it or not, we found eight feet of old spongy sugar cane syrup in the bottom of it. I ordered my men to gently remove some of the bricks of stones on the back side of the castle at ten feet from the bottom until we had a hole large enough to toss Gold Bars down into the old sugar cane syrup. A total of 3,241 Gold Bars weighing 6.5 kilos each were buried in the sugar cane castle. Then, I had my men cement up the rocks and bricks taken out of the side. No booby traps were installed."

"What else did you do at that location that you know so much about?" Ronell chimed in with his question.

"Yea, you better tell us everything," Virgil confirmed.

"Okay, down below the castle is some old Spanish sugar mill ruins built of stones and rocks. The large wide structure had a rock bottom. I ordered my men and some of the American

POW's to take the sledgehammers and bust up the flooring without damaging the sides of this old ancient landmark. They shoveled this waste up and dug a deep hole and buried 844 Gold Bars weighing 75 kilos each. We dumped the flooring back on top of them and threw some wet cement over everything. No explosives were used to defend this location. I knew the prospects of people walking on it would happen."

"What did you do with the American POW's?" Virgil asked.

"Since they had witnessed the burial of the Gold Bars, I had been ordered to kill any witnesses," Lt Oskita answered.

"No you don't understand. Where did you kill them and I bet you killed some Filipino POW's also," Virgil interrupted and added.

"I swear that I have never killed any Filipino, either soldier or farmer," the Lieutenant quickly replied.

"What God are you willing to swear to? Emperor Evil God is your God. Your English is better than I thought. Your willingness to swear on God does not ring true in my ear," Virgil cautiously warned the Lieutenant.

"Under military orders I marched the American POW's down to the Point at the edge of the Laoag River and ordered my men to shoot them. Some of them attempted to dive into the water and escape," Lt. Oskita proudly answered.

TREASURES OF WAR – CONCEALED BY THE EVIL ONES / 133

"I am a soldier. I must follow my military orders," the Lt. replied.

"What happened to the Filipinos? Did you shoot the Americans like shooting animals while they swam for their freedom?"

"The Filipinos, how many have you killed and how many of your men killed them?" Virgil repeatedly asked.

The Lieutenant did not reply.

"Ronell and Chief, to show our appreciation to the Lieutenant and his men for their cooperation in describing where the buried treasures are, take all of them down to Darcos's house and feed them the excellent barbequed pig dinners," Virgil ordered.

"Yes Sir!"

This was the secret signal for them to take the Japanese murderers and kill them.

The next morning Oli and Virgil met to discuss what had been learned from the Japanese.

"Oli, here are the marked maps indicating locations of the hidden Gold Bars and other treasure. Since it will take a large number of men to dig down and excavate these heavy treasures now, and we do not have the time to do this, you should turn over the maps and security information to my guerrilla forces and me. Also, other Japanese soldiers moving to the north could capture you risking it getting out that you have Lieutenant Oskita's maps. Later, when the war is over and we have time to search for the treasures, I will return the buried gold treasures to the village for you to distribute among the peasants and my guerrilla army," Virgil emphatically and assuredly stated.

"Virgil, I am entrusting these valuable maps to you for safekeeping until you return. When you and your guerrilla army are ready to search for the sites as indicated by the six gold marks on the maps and excavate the Gold Bars, I and some of the village leaders want to go with you and help you," Oli requested.

Virgil guaranteed, "You have my word Oli. I will do exactly what you have requested."

In a few weeks Oli, Virgil and the guerrilla army were confident the organization had completely won over the villagers and peasants. Because of their successful actions to free them from invaders and landlords, and to distribute the landlord's holdings and the understanding that after the war the Gold treasures would be shared by all of them, Virgil prepared to leave behind a few guerrillas and move on to their next target.

Virgil and the guerrilla army returned to their highlands camp near Tineg River. Shortly after arrival, Virgil led the army from the Tineg River camp over the Cordillera Mountains across Cagayan River through the Cagayan Valley up to the northern end of the Sierra Madre Mountains down to Palawig Mountain Range getting closer to the Babuyan Sea east of the original landing area of the Japanese Imperial Army at Aparri. They set up camp at about 300 meters elevation in the mountains near Mt. Cagua.

"Chief, you take your team and work down the Baua River by fishing out of rafts and gather as much intelligence on the Japanese army activity from the mountain to the sea," Virgil ordered.

"Yes Sir," Chief replied as he saluted Major Hermano.

"I will take my team and work our way down the Palawig River to the sea and since Port Casambalangan is between us, we should be able to determine what Japanese forces remain in the region," Virgil told Chief and the men in both guerrilla teams.

TREASURES OF WAR – CONCEALED BY THE EVIL ONES / 135

Virgil and Chief and their teams moved out early the next day. The weather was unusually cold for them.

After cutting down several small trees and making rafts for the team, Virgil encountered some very unusual activity coming up the Palawig River. He had his team direct the rafts around a bend in the river to a hidden cove. As the team watched, a flatbed Japanese's landing craft turned southwest up a stream coming into the river.

"Let's anchor our rafts and go up the hillside and see what is going on," Virgil told his crew.

It took them about two hours to secure their rafts and climb through the jungle to the top of the hill on the north side of the stream coming into Palawig River.

"Look", Virgil whispered to his men. "The river forks into a 'Y' and here comes two other landing crafts following the original Japanese craft. They are turning to the right in the wye. The first one is almost to the end of the cove. All three are obviously loaded with heavy armament or something," Virgil quietly continued.

"Looks like something important is fixing to go down," Celso softly spoke.

"We need to secure a better observation point and go around the hill on this side of the cove about fifty or sixty meters up the mountain side over there," Virgil pointed to his men.

Once 'Bulldogs' got in place they noticed that the Japanese Army Forces on the shoreline gathered some Filipino tribesmen and peasants together.

The first landing craft positioned itself toward the shoreline and docked. The front landing gate was lowered. 'Bulldogs' heard the Japanese army officer order the Filipinos onto the landing vessel to pick up heavy pieces to carry ashore.

"Wow!" Virgil whispered to his men. "Look at the size of those Gold Bars that they have uncovered. They each must weigh 50 kilos or more. That young boy can hardly lift the Gold Bar," Virgil continued.

"Why are they moving them up the mountainside toward us?" Jose asked.

"I do not know," Virgil replied.

After watching this chain of peasants pass each Gold Bar from one to the next all the way up to a ledge about forty meters from the edge of the stream, 'Bulldogs' noticed that the Japanese were ordering the peasants to sit down and rest.

Then, the Japanese officer ordered the peasants to stand up and began passing another bunch of Gold Bars up to the ridge.

'Bulldogs' watched this spectacular event for two days until all three landing crafts were unloaded. On the third day everyone in the 'Bulldogs' team was shocked to see the Japanese remove timbers and brush from the entrance to a cave near the site the Gold Bars were stored on the ledge.

They counted a total of 4,821 large Gold Bars.

"The Japanese officer is going to have the peasants carry the Gold Bars into the cave and hide them in stacks inside. I am very concerned about what is going to happen after they have completed stacking them in the cave," Virgil whispered to his men.

"What do you think they are going to do?" Ronell asked.

"The Japanese are going to kill the Filipino peasants in the cave," Virgil told his team.

"Why don't we capture and kill the Japanese murderers before this happens?" Jose asked Virgil.

Virgil thought for a moment.

"We know where the Gold Bars are located, and we only have a small force without very many automatic weapons like the Japanese men have. Also, the value of the Gold is extremely important back at port city headquarters of the Japanese officials. If these men do not return, their headquarters will send out a sizable force to investigate. The odds are against us; and we all would be killed," Virgil answered his men.

The next morning the Japanese herded the Filipino peasants into the cave and rapid-fire shots were heard all over the valley.

Jose pointed and whispered, "the cave entrance has a mountain stream coming out of it. See the water flow down the rocks to the edge of the cove. Look! The water is turning red from the Filipino peasants blood. It is flowing all the way down the rocks to the stream below now."

As 'Bulldogs' watched the edge of the stream below become colored blood red.

"We must return to our main camp on Palawig mountain range to keep our return meeting with Chief's team," Virgil reminded his men.

After securing their rafts, they paddled back up the river to their original launch site. As they began their climb through the jungle a local tribesman chief met them.

"Let me handle this. I will attempt to speak the tribe's language that I know and put them at ease. Do not make any comments or indications about the Gold Bars," Virgil ordered his men.

Virgil spoke to them in their tribe's language. "I told them that we were Filipino guerrillas fighting the landlords and Japanese Army and returning to our guerrilla camp in the highlands," Virgil explained.

The tribe chief told Virgil that he would support them with food and information.

LATER IN THE GUERRILLA WAR AGAINST THE JAPANESE.

"Behind us, we heard the burst of machine-gun fire ... We ducked and dove into the bunkers near our vehicles.... As soon as we identified the location of the Japanese, we took the offensive and finally drove them away with a continuous barrage of machine-gun fire of our own," Colonel Hermano explained to his Guerrilla Group after the skirmish.

In early 1945, Colonel Hermano requested assistance in delaying the retreating Japanese Army from Baguio to Tuguegarao Airfield and over the mountains to the Port of Aparri.

In evaluating the status of the retreating Japanese Army and the impending fall of the Japanese Navy in Manila, the U. S. military leaders sent word that an American team of demolition experts headed by Captain Donald Crow would be landed by submarine at the Port of Bauang, La Union.

Since Colonel Hermano was up the coast at Luna and his Guerrilla Team knew the roads and bridges in the region, they moved in to support Captain Crow and wait for his orders. Within two weeks he received his orders to lead Captain Crow's group up the coast highway to Batac and over the Cordillera Central Mountain Range road to Tuao. From Tuao they could divide into four groups and go south toward Baguio along the Chico river and blow up several bridges; back to Ramon and San Mateo along the Magat River and blow the main bridges leading to the Cagayan Valley region; further to the north down to the Cagayan River leading into the Port of Aparri to by blocking the highway with huge boulders and rocks from the dynamiting.

"Colonel Hermano, you are the leader of this operation, and we are the demolition experts with the many safe and successful battles under our belts to back you up. Let's get the job done and force the destruction of the remaining Japanese Army or make them surrender in due course." Crow concluded.

Due to the personal direction and leadership of Colonel Virgil Hermano to friendly locations in Tuao and the necessary planning for the sites that needed to be destroyed, complete with maps and friendly guerrilla camp sites in the region; Captain Crow and his demolition teams went on to carry out some raids on bridges, roads, and buildings which caused General Yamashita's Japanese Fourteenth Army and Imperial Navy Vice Admiral Okochi's Naval Forces casualties, equipment loss, and retreat into the Cordillera Central Mountain Range.

Upon the return from the mission, Captain Crow told General Allen, Commander of the U. S. Sixth Army battalions; "Colonel Hermano's leadership was the primary reason that our mission was discharged successfully."

TREASURES OF WAR – CONCEALED BY THE EVIL ONES / 139

"Your knowledge of these mountains and roads is invaluable. We have not won the war. But, you will continue to lead your Guerrilla Group and fight side by side with us until Emperor Zapp and his Imperial Armies and Navy is removed from the Philippines," General Allen thankfully replied. "Our intelligence has sent a message that the Japanese Army has some Forces down in the Nueva Vizcaya region. I want you and your men to take a look along the northern road and report back to me of your findings," Allen ordered.

On March 19, 1945, Colonel Virgil Hermano led an assault and demolition team to an unguarded section of road near Baguio, and mined it for half a mile. A dozen cars came down the road, one carrying the Japanese appointed Filipino President Laurel. Through binoculars, Colonel Hermano recognized Laurel and General Capinpin. He waited till their cars passed, and then fired his charges. All the Japanese in the convoy were killed.

Later, in April 1945, Colonel Hermano literally tumbled onto some of Yamashita Gold. Virgil was leading a patrol in Kayapa, a mountain district of Nueva Vizcaya Province. There he encountered a Japanese patrol of twenty men. Following them, he was led north toward the Ifugao rice terraces. One Japanese soldier was lagging behind because his pack was too heavy. Hermano raised his rifle and picked off the straggler. As he came out of the brush and walked forward to reach for the dead Jap Soldier's pack, a bullet from another Jap Soldier buried in the jungle up the roadway struck him in the back, and he pitched down the mountain into the jungle clinging to the pack.

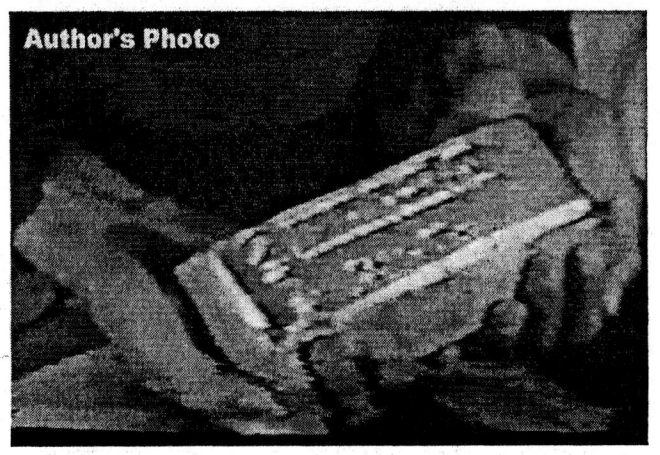

The wound was superficial, but the heavy pack contained three Gold Bars. Colonel Hermano opened it wider and the three shinny Gold Bars felt so smooth and beautiful to him. He reached in and picked one of the Gold Bars up and realized how heavy it was. He noticed that the markings indicated that it was from Sumatra. He knew that he was on the trail again of some of the Japanese Imperial Army's Loot stolen in the war for Emperor Zapp.

These Gold Bars are worth a lot of money but not as much as the large quantity of Gold Bars I saw being hidden in the cave near Palawig when the Japanese Army murdered all of those Filipino POW's after they carried them into the cave. Where did all these treasures come from? Emperor Zapp wants to rule the world with the accumulation of all of this wealth. Maybe, just maybe I will be able to withhold some of these Gold Bars for my future here in the Philippines. Colonel Hermano thought.

JUST REWARD.

After Colonel Hermano and his surviving Guerilla Fighters had fought the Imperial Japanese Forces all over the Philippine Islands and were gathering for a meeting with the invading American Forces; General Allen, Commander of the U. S. Sixth Army Battalions, called Colonel Hermano into his temporary quarters and ordered, "Colonel, I need you to work with two of my logistic aids and prepare a detailed report of the status of all Japanese Military Forces of Emperor Zapp on the Islands. This report is critical to our Islands Campaign strategy. Location, manpower, military equipment and movements should be the primary focus of the report. Lt. Cartwight will obtain any additional supplies or stenographers that you need. This report must be completed by 20:00 tomorrow."

Maj. Gen. Guillermo Francisco

Author's Photo

"Yes Sir! I appreciate your confidence."

At 20:00 the next day Colonel Hermano had completed the detailed report identifying most of the Japanese positions on the Islands. General Allen and his staff met to study the report almost around the clock for several days for Allied Forces Troop deployment to recapture all of the Philippines. At chow time three days later General Allen had made arrangements for Colonel Hermano to eat with him and his staff.

"Your detailed report is one of the most professional military battlefield reports that I have ever witnessed. I have issued orders to award you the Silver Star," General Allen said as he proposed a toast.

"Sir, I am humble to think of your fine gesture for my work. Many of my Filipino friends fought and died as members of my Filipino Guerrilla Forces. They and Major General Guillermo Francisco deserve much of this award. Some people have questioned my activities over the past few years, so this honor is especially gratifying to me personally."

"Men, we have a job to do. Let's get it done so we can go home to America," General Allen said as he stood up to leave the mess haul.

TREASURES OF WAR – CONCEALED BY THE EVIL ONES

Chapter Six

The Story of Private William "Bill" F. Benson

"T" Patchers of the US 36th Infantry Division

Battlefield Invasions - North Africa - Italy - France - Germany - Austria

**36th Infantry Division -- World War II Combat Casualties
19,466 Total casualties - 3,717 Killed in Action - 12,685 Wounded in Action 3,064 Missing in Action.**

As a member of the Texas National Guardsmen, my Unit was mobilized on November 25th, 1940 at Camp Bowie, Texas, as a member of the US 36th Infantry Division. My name is William 'Bill' F. Benson. Correctly known as Private 'Bill' Benson. Originally, known as the 'Texas' Division of the 36th Infantry due to the tens of thousands of Texans. Later, as the Selective Service draftees began coming into Camp Bowie from all over the Nation an All-American feeling existed. However, we Texans maintained the ownership of the 36th Division, better known as the 'T Patch' Division. Most daily training in the cold winter months in Central Texas included a series of Infantry and Field Artillery operations while learning precision armed fighting. Occasionally, I had to do my K-P duty.

I received my thirty days, 'Delay In Route' orders, from Battery "A", 133rd Field Artillery Battalion Commander at Camp Bowie to go home and report to Fort 'Swampland' Polk, Louisiana on June 14th, 1941. I went home and partied with my young friends and dated my true love, Rozella 'Rose' Vera Richter. Everyone back home was asking many questions about whether the US was going to enter the war and fight the Germans. I told them that all I knew was the 'Texas' 36th was training like we were already at war. 'Rose' and I decided not to get married with the uncertainty of the war. So much for the good time and a few Grand Prize beer sessions with my friends, my duties beckoned me.

Training under General Walter Krueger's Third Army in the muddy swamplands of southern Louisiana was something new for this Central Texas boy. The only mud we had was down at the banks of the rivers or the fishing pounds on the farms. Mosquitoes were as large as some of our U. S. Army Air Force B-47s. I learned to rub some of that stinking mud on my neck, face, shoulders and arms to keep them off. Several times I wondered which was worse. I began to think that somebody up there was trying to tell me something, but I did not know what it was. I thanked him for the fresh water showers when we got to return to Camp. Those Cajuns could entertain you almost as good as the good ole boys back in Central Texas. Since we outnumbered them, they did not challenge some of our bragging Texas tales about how much bigger and better everything was in Texas.

Right in the middle of one of those strong northern thunderstorms in February 1942, we received orders to jump on the caravan of Army trucks and travel all the way to Camp Blanding, Florida. I was stunned to learn that we were not shipping out to fight the Japanese. There was so many new recruits coming into Camp Blanding every day, space was not available for everybody. With all of our previous training I wondered why we were here.

I did not have to wonder very long, my orders called for me to travel overland again to the State of North Carolina. I spent the remaining warm summer months training.

In September 1942 I was given my orders to board a troop train with all my other 'T' 36th Infantry Division and travel up north to Camp Edwards, Cape Cod, Massachusetts. The Texans 36th Division fighting warriors were coming from all over the US to congregate way up north. So many men arrived that I was ordered to set up a tent for three and myself. I had never seen so many tents in the world.

Photo Courtesy of Pvt. 'Bill' Benson 'T' 36th Division 1942

I can see something big about to happen to my buddies, and me. I better take time to write 'Rose' and let her know what is going on, I thought.

Amphibious operations practices began early the third day after arriving at Camp Edwards. The Thirty-Sixth Division launched several mock invasions on Martha's Vineyard in twenty degrees below zero stormy winter weather on the Cape. I had been in some Central Texas blowing winter storms and tried to convince some of my Yankee Buddies that everything in Texas was bigger and better. I do not think that I convinced even one of them after going through the second mock invasion. *I guess I became obnoxious to them.*

My Company Commander, Lt. Ryo Rihn, came in and handed me a cup of coffee and gave me orders that I was not to write anything about my activities to anyone back home as we sipped the good hot coffee. He confided in me that all mail was being censored.

What more do I need to silently tell me that I should take time to write 'Rose" again and tell her some of the beauty of the new region of the US that I was getting to see and tell her not to worry, I thought.

It had been almost two years since I had been home when I received my orders on March 20th, 1943 to check out a complete combat pack with several types of guns. Later that day we were transported to the 36th Infantry Division's staging areas where all of us were gathering together. The military equipment was enough for a major campaign. After I watched the loading of our ship, I boarded the Thomas H. Berry Cruise Ship and we sailed out of the Port of New York. The ocean voyage was not completely uneventful. The Navy Destroyers had to take care of the German U-2 Boats on two different occasions. I could not believe that I did not get seasick like so many of the men did. I had never been out to sea or the Gulf of Mexico when growing up back in Texas. We arrived at the Port of Oran, Algeria eleven days after sailing.

Lt. Rihn led us down the landing stairs to the dock. Our 36th Division was given orders to be held in reserve and jumped on some of the troop transport trucks and go to some desert training camp about as far as Waco is from Dallas. Later on, I learned that the German General Rommel's Afrika Corps had been defeated by some of General Patton's Armies.

If we are in reserve, now we will have to relieve some of General Patton's troops, I thought

In the meantime, the US and British Military and Political leadership was meeting in an attempt to determine what the next best move would be made against the Axis Forces. Some of the Regiments and Division Headquarters traveled by truck back to the west and spent the summer around Casablanca. I have been in some dust storms in West Texas, but I finally found something that was bigger than Texas. A 4 to 5 hundred-mile trip by a convoy of trucks and the desert sand constantly blowing off the desert this time of the year was bigger and better than anything I had ever experienced in the Big State of Texas.

Later on, we 'T-Patchers' became the primary force of the newly organized Fifth Army's Invasion Training Center on the Mediterranean. Many months were spent training for several different invasions at Sicily and other Italian ports. I never will forget how we camped out on the beach for weeks awaiting the ships to come along the shoreline to pick us up for the campaign, which was to begin at Salerno, Italy. The Mediterranean Sea lanes and airspace toward the East from our Training Center at Arzew, Algeria was controlled by the Allied

Forces, and we could make the voyage without major encounters by the enemy. No naval or air bombardment had been taken against the Germans. Our Commander was Maj. Gen. Fred L. Walker.

Then, Battery 'A', 133rd Field Artillery Battalion of the Thirty-Sixth Infantry Division received its orders to sail east toward the southern coast of Italy. The Landing Craft Transports (LCT's) were loaded down with plenty of equipment, men and supplies for an extended and demanding campaign. The fleet was strung out for many miles across the Mediterranean. I did not have to guess what we soldiers were about to encounter. Just as my LCT began its early morning dash on September 9th, 1943 to the sandy beaches near the ancient port of Paestum, Italy without the support of the naval battleship guns or our P-40's strafing the enemy inland, I noticed that my breathing was very rapid and my heart was pounding almost out of my chest.

Maj. Gen. Fred L. Walker became the Commander of the first American division to invade the European mainland and test Hitler's and Mussolini's Axis Forces. Yes, I was a part of that historical event as a member of the Thirty-Sixth Infantry Division on my personal first as well as our Battalion's first combat mission.

Man, these Germans must have been warned that we were coming and are ready willing and able to kill everyone of us, I thought as the Kraut's artillery from all around the hillsides overlooking Salerno came exploding all around me.

As I moved off the shoreline Lt. Rihn had us double time it to our assigned forward observers post and set up operations. The constant flow of LCT's was unloading more troops, troop transport trucks, and tanks onto the beachhead. It was our responsibility to locate the machine gun nest, snipers and enemy artillery guns and to direct the 36th Infantry Division's courageous warriors during their initial fighting on foreign soil. Lt. Rihn pointed out some snipers firing from the balconies of some old buildings and the port's observation lighthouse. Pvt. Stevens and I worked our way to a position and timed their coming out in our attempt to take out a few of the snipers. But the snipers in the lighthouse could move from one side around to the other side away from us preventing us from getting a good shot at them. I told Pvt. Stevens and Pvt. Martinez to stay at this position and Pvt. Hunt and I were going to move into position on the other side of the lighthouse. I reminded them to fire their weapons upward at the lighthouse and we would be sure to do the same to prevent a friendly fire casualty.

As we dashed from one building and across open spaces we came upon a bunker with two machine gun nests facing toward the beachhead. I dropped to the ground and motioned for Pvt. Hunt to pull two grenades and toss them into the bunkers. The machine gun nests were wiped out. Some of my comrades would not be gunned down as they came ashore. I had to quickly move past the bunkers because I felt that the snipers had heard this commotion and would be looking down on Charlie and me. As we ran for cover on the other side of the lighthouse the snipers began to fire down on us. I had been trained that shooting down on a moving target was the hardest warfare that I would encounter. My drill sergeant had taught me that 9 out of 10 times I would fire over the moving target when I shot from above. Sure enough, he was right. The Jerry snipers were firing some four or five feet over my head. Hunt and I made it to an excellent location in an alleyway on the other side of the lighthouse observation ledge. The snipers apparently forgot where our comrades were and ran around to the other side where Syd and Raul almost immediately picked them off one by one. Some more of our 36th Infantrymen would now make it safely ashore from the continuous flow of landing crafts all day long.

Here it was the first day and I had killed someone for the very first time in my life. Yet, I knew that they were there to kill me. It began to sink in just what war was really all about. The officers had trained me well and I was prepared to do the killing rather than be killed.

TREASURES OF WAR – CONCEALED BY THE EVIL ONES / 148

1943 Sept. 9th.
Salerno, Italy Landing
Contributed by
US Navy Archive

The tank destroyers, two-tracks and tanks were continuing to be unloaded onto the beachfront. As Forward Observers, Lt. Rihn had ordered us to return to our assigned spot on the battlefield map. After our successful skirmish with the German snipers, Stevens, Martinez, Hunt and I prowled our way back to Lt. Rihn. Since he had received phone contact from Battery 'C', 133rd Field Artillery Battalion leader asking for some co ordinances of the Kraut's pillbox locations for their artillery and machine gun nest that were blasting the troops on shore, Lt. Rihn took Stevens and I with one of our tommyguns and grenades and went on our mission to hunt for the enemy pillboxes and radio back to Battery 'C' with their 105-mm and 155-mm howitzers down on the beachhead. We encountered some bloody hand-to-hand bayonet fighting along some of the streets into the city. The bitter fighting was all around us. Some of the freshly arrived 36th T-Patchers began to flood the combat zone. The Jerry's counterattacks were sometimes very frantic. After some of our grenades were thrown into some of the second story buildings some of the Germans would come wandering out into the open in a delirious state. When the ones that did not toss their weapons to the ground and put up their hands, we were not going to risk who was the fastest gun in the west. This was not a movie. It only took shooting one or two of them to get the firm message across.

Author's Photo

Some of the Italian underground met us head on and offered some gallant support. The German Forces in Salerno, Italy were smashed, sustaining heavy casualties, and our first campaign was won at the cost of a large amount of our blood on Italian soil and a tremendous number of US 36th Infantry Division casualties. Thank God for our furious training methods from the beginning until this invasion.

1943-After Battle at
Salerno, Italy
1st and Last Beer
Ration during the War
Photo Courtesy of
Pvt. Bill Benson with
His Comrades

Lt. Rihn issued us a ration of beer to enjoy. He told us that it was really our 1st and our last during the Italian Campaign. Every one of us would rather have had a good ole

149 / DON STEWART NIMMONS

Grand Prize or Lone Star from back in Texas, but none of us complained. Pvt. Stevens and Hunt did not understand our preference. With each sip of Lt. Rihn's issuance of beer, each 'Texans' 36th Infantryman expressed what Stevens and Hunt should taste. Being from the east coast, they did not know any better. We described the pure, cool and clear waters from the Hill Country in Texas that was used in our Texas beers.

I told Stevens that when he and I got through conquering the Germans and go home; I would invite him down to Texas and have him drink some real beer with some of our prized bar-b-que beef steaks.

A few months later all of us learned some soul-searching news.

Some of our comrades in other Battalions of the 36th Division in another southern Italy battle during the attempted and failed crossing of the Rapido River were slaughtered. Lt. Rihn told us that only a few squadrons out of approximately 700 or 800 36th Division Infantrymen returned alive.

Division Commander, Maj. Gen. Fred L. Walker was ordered by 5th Army Commander, Lt. Gen. Mark. W. Clark to regroup and leave Salerno and move up the Italian west coast onto the Anzio beachhead and join Gen. Lucas.

Gen. Walker's orders at Anzio was to eliminate the stalemated troops and begin offensive actions against German artillery positions and take charge of the American Troops and move forward all the way to Rome. Here it was the middle of February, 1944 and he knew that many battles had to be won in Southern Italy to make 'D' Day, June 6, 1944, a campaign that was critical to his success and the plans to defeat the Krauts.

Some of the 362nd Infantry Regiment of the 91st Infantry Division had captured a farmhouse above the east-west canal and west of Mussolini Canal between Conco and Cisterna about ten miles inland on the Anzio beachhead and needed forward observers with radio equipment.

At early, early light tomorrow morning, February 26th, Captain Galloway of the 362nd gave the orders. "You men work your way back to the farmhouse with Sergeant Steele of the 362nd. Lt. Rihn, the 36th Division and your seven men, Cpl. Anderson, Privates Benson, Stevens, Seamur, Martinez, Hunt and Caldwell have successful battlefield forward observers experiences in Salerno. They have the necessary communication equipment and plenty of guns and weapons. Tell Sarge that Lt. Rihn will take over the command of the post. You need to bed down in these fresh dry blankets tonight and get some rest between their mortar rounds. May God be with you on your mission in the morning, stick to the plan and contact me as soon as you reach your position at the farmhouse," Captain Galloway ordered.

TREASURES OF WAR – CONCEALED BY THE EVIL ONES / 150

The mission was successful without casualties. I could not believe the excellent observation location. First, I saw a few of the German Mark IV Tanks just over the levees. Sergeant Steele pointed this out to Lt. Rihn. These German Tanks had been used for the counter attacks on the beaches. Second, I noticed several 88-mm caliber artillery cannons in the distance. These were the most feared artillery guns of the Germans Artillery Divisions.

I obtained permission to contact Naval and Beachhead Operations and gave them the locations on the Anzio Invasion map as Aprilio. I told them to wipe them off the face of the earth. Within ten minutes, our batteries of Naval gunfire and fire from mortars and howitzers repeatedly destroyed the targets.

Later the next day, as some of us advanced to the destroyed sites, I came upon this destroyed German Tank with the initial 'T' 36th and USA written on it. I thought to myself, the only party that had told us that he was going to do this was Sergeant 'Shorty' Sowell of the artillery and tank maintenance Regiment of the 36th. Obviously, he had not left his initials on the destroyed tank. He might have been mistaken and shot when he wrote SS on the tank.

The Kraut Tanks that had not been destroyed immediately turned and ran toward Alban Hills. Lt. Kihn kept us moving at double time. He told us that he did not want the Jerries to sit back and pick us off. He instilled in us the primary goal was to keep the enemy on the run preventing counterattacks as had been the case for several months at Anzio.

At Velletri Gen. Walker had the 142nd Infantry infiltrate the German line by stealth. This action was so successful it was said '...it turned the key to the city of Rome and handed it to Gen. Clark'. By noon the main tank assault on the southern beaches had been brought virtually to a standstill. The Armored Divisions had helped to make the operations costly for the enemy, but to a large extent the battle had been fought by infantrymen and infantry weapons. Asked by one of his men, "What are we going to do if we run out of ammunition?" "Fight with the Rammerstaff!" was the Colonel's bellowing reply. German tanks lay shattered in fields nearby. Dumps were set up, exit roads were operating, anti-aircraft batteries were in position, and communications finally working. The 142nd Infantry moved forward in preparation for an attack on Altavilla and Hill 424.

As Battery 'A', 133rd Field Artillery Battalion slowly fought its way inland from Anzio in the long and bitter Italian Campaign, the need to use our 105-mm howitzers and fire from mortars helped make the enemy counterattacks costly to them. Our foot soldiers with automatic weapons made the big difference in defeating the Germans as we advanced. Repeatedly, our howitzers were used to fight off Kraut tanks at distances of 200 to 350 yards. In the majority of the encounters, when the German's Armor was destroyed, the enemy infantrymen turned and retreated north.

1944-36TH Infantry Division Destroys German Tanks
Along Road Inland From Anzio, Italy
Photo Courtesy of Pvt. Bill Benson

36TH Infantry Division Captured German Ambulance-Anzio, Italy
Courtesy of Pvt. Bill Benson

From our forward observation post we discovered the major peak of the Albans, Mount Artemisio, near the middle of the fortified German defense line, was practically empty of enemy troops.

We called in our engineers to prepare a safer traction to climb up to the top of the mountain. When we arrived early the next morning at the top, we surprised the four Germans and captured them without ever firing a single shot.

As commander of the forward Artillery observer team, Lt. Kihn immediately called for our artillery units to fire across the mountain onto the Kraut's supply trucks lined up on Italian highway 6.

The Texan 36th Division now controlled the region near Velletri, Italy. On May 25th, 1944, the Texan 36th Division broke through to the east of the Alban Hills, threatening to cut off the Germans.

However, the efficient Germans organized a rearguard operation and put up some fierce fighting to allow time for most of their units to escape to Rome and north of Rome.

On May 31st, the German Tenth Army retreated northeast and we drove down highway 6 to Rome.

Finally, on June 4th, 1944, two days before the D-Day Invasion at Normandy, Allied Forces, including the Texan 36th Infantry Division, captured Rome, the first Axis mainland Capital. This news rang bells in Rome and in the head of The Fuhrer.

I took some time to write Rose and let her know that I loved her and was eager to learn about her US Army Nurse Corps activities.

As we continued our fighting north of Rome, heavy fighting erupted as the German Tenth Army under Field Marshal Vietinghoff and eight to ten new divisions from out side of Italy that had been ordered directly by The Fuhrer to leave their respective battlefields and to reinforce Vietinghoff's efforts to retake Rome.

Photo Courtesy of Pvt. Bill Benson
Pvt. Bill Benson in Front of German
Texan 36TH Infantry 88-MM Artillery Cannon.
1944 Rings On Barrel Represents
Number of US Army Air Force Planes Shot Down

153 / DON STEWART NIMMONS

We found out that the Germans were well entrenched on the hillsides surrounding the battle lines with artillery and mortar fire. One of the most exciting times for me was when one of our heavy-duty trucks hauling a load of artillery shells was hit. Immediately, a fire flamed up on the opposite end of the trailer near me. Pvt. Stevens and I began moving kegs of powder and ammunition away from the fire as fast as we could move. We were able to save all of the ammunition and gunpowder to use at a later battle. Lt. Rihn had taken cover near one of our tanks and did not learn about the crazy thing that Stevens and I had done until later.

Lt. Rihn complemented us and issued orders to award us with the Bronze Star. His words of encouragement were always a great comfort during this horrendous war.

A rifle company slipped out of the thick brush and joined us. They had climbed their way out of the hillside vineyards where they had been dug in during the fighting. They were very glad to see us in our trucks pulling the artillery weapons. The heavy mortar shells that they were carrying for miles could now be loaded onto the trucks. Also, their rifle ammunition in the metal boxes in their backpacks was laid upon the truck beds beside each man. Many of us relished the moment to grab a long overdue snooze.

'T' Patchers of the 36th Infantry Division fought the delaying German Forces north through Lake Bracciano and then swung west toward the Port City of Civitaveechia where we encountered some brutal fighting with the Krauts near the Port City of Grosseto. After the capture of Grosseto, most of us climbed on board one of the troop carriers, tanks, trucks and jeeps and moved as fast as possible toward the port city with an occasional flare up of the Jerry rear guards.

On June 26th, Lt. Rihn called us all together and told us the good news that we had successfully accomplished our missions and were being assigned another extremely important task out of Salerno by the way of Rome. He told us that we would enjoy ourselves a few days in Rome and motorize on to Salerno to learn the details of our next mission.

Lt. Ryo Rihn   Pvt. Bill Benson   Pvt. Syd Stevens
1944--Anzio, Italy -- Forward Observers --
Photo Courtesy William "Bill" F. Benson--36th Division

Lt. Rihn was briefed on our Battalion's mission. He showed us the maps and aerial photos of our next amphibious landing in southern France and the invasion campaign to defeat the German Forces in France and crush them as far north into Germany and further, if needed.

It was one of the best-planned military operations that I had seen up to that time. The number of navy vessels, battleships, LCT's and destroyers was very impressive to all of us. On August 13th, 1944 the convoy of American ships sailed from Naples around 13:00. Two days later as the Army Air Force Bombers and the large cannons from the offshore US Navy Battleships pounded the French Riviera beaches between Marseilles and Toulon, our landing craft approaches our assigned beachhead. Our assignment was a demand to secure one section of the beach and push inland some 10 to 12 miles on the first day toward the Argens River Valley and meet up with the paratroopers that had been dropped behind the beachhead. The Germans were surprised and were not prepared for such an invasion force of this size. We lost a few good men, but the enemy lost many times more and once we captured the higher ground above them, the Krauts by the hundreds began to surrender. After fighting some special encounters to the rear of certain German Forces for three or four days to relieve some of our comrades cut off and pinned down closer to the their beachhead landings, we met up with the paratroopers and immediately advanced to the town of Draguignan where we captured the Commanding General of the German 62nd Corps together with his entire staff. This led us to follow our orders to high tail it to the French Alps town of Grenoble.

Lt. Rihn called our Battalion together and gave us our new orders. The 'T' Patchers 36th Infantry Division, including Battery 'A', 133rd Field Artillery Battalion, were to destroy the German Nineteenth Army's planned retreat from France and the remaining German Forces attempting to re-enter the fighting by coming across the mountain passes from Italy. He ordered us to accelerate our initiative and proceed to the hills north of Montelimar, the major town alone the Rhome Valley.

On August 23rd, we moved into position with our howitzers. The US Army Air Force bombers pounded the Germans and some key bridges down below us. One of our main targets was the large 380 mm railroad cannons and the German Panzer Divisions. These enemy weapons were lethal in everyway. On the 24th, we began to pound them with one round every few minutes day and night. This continued for more than a week up and down a stretch of the Rhome River for more than 10 miles. Destruction! We were destroying everything from buildings, convoys of German vehicles, trains, artillery pieces, tanks and the men operating all of them. In early September, we had captured Montelimar and demolished the German Nineteenth Army.

I lost my hearing for about a week. As soon as this battle was over we were ordered to fight our way north through Strasbourg, and the icy roads to Montbronn. We reached Montbronn in early January 1945. Cold, you bet it was. As we say back in Texas, it was cold as a Polar Bear's Bottom.

Hagenau is not far from the Rhine River and is eighteen miles north of Strasbourg. The airfield at Hagenau had changed hands several times in the bitter fighting. Its steel-concrete hangars and buildings had been thoroughly demolished. In the middle of January, we were ordered to attack a German offensive that had trapped the US 79th Division near Haguenau. We had a scrappy fight with some Krauts in one of the buildings on the outskirts of the city. Lt. Kihn ordered our machine gunner to blast away at the building. The 5 enemy soldiers waved a white flag out the doorway and surrendered. We found some German offensive plans and some very tasty German liquor.

The encounters in the city became kind of weird after the initial fight. As we moved through the city the Germans occasionally fired a heavy artillery shell in the almost deserted city. The 80 mile trip to Haguenau and the ensuing periodic battles and the more than 150 days of constant skirmishes and major campaigns since we came ashore in August was being felt in my weary aching muscles and down to my bones.

After moving toward Kurtzenhausen we found out why we had been ordered to the Haguenau, France area. A major German offensive was waiting for us. On January 21st, more than 15 German 10th SS Panzer Division tanks with supporting Infantrymen came out of the woods and fought until most were either killed or captured. The numerous skirmishes in the Haguenau Forest against a stubborn German 36th Division with its' Ordnance Company laying antipersonnel mines on the roads through the woods caused the US 36th Infantry Division many casualties all around me. I was fortunate to be riding with Artillery Company behind the lead troops. We conquered the German 36th Division.

The short winter days in France where the snow fell from time to time maintaining a depth of two feet or more, gave us an opportunity to use the captured German Liquor hidden under the stacks of coal in some of the basements of the liberated homes during our house to house encounters.

After the ground haze from the cold weather began to lift, the skilled US Army Air Force Mustang Fighter pilots gradually defeated the Luftwaffe aerial encounters until the enemy in March 1945 refused to enter any more aerial fights.

We fought on, and on March 20th, 1945, the US 36th Infantry Division won its last battle in France and entered Germany.

On April 2nd, Lt. Rihn called us together and told us that the German Siegfried Line of defense was our next encounter and that we were not to have any normal friendly relationships with any of the German citizens. But, for the time being we were ordered to our first rear guard duty in Palatinate.

Then, on April 24th, we received orders to re-enter the war and sped off toward the Danube River and on for another 350 miles with only occasional resistance. The Bavarian Alps was very scenic but very dangerous from some of the straggling and fleeing Nazi SS Troopers remaining convinced they could win the war. They dug in and fired sniper shots at us.

On May 4th, 1945 we fought our way into Austria and captured some ranking German Officers. At 18:30 on May 5th Lt. Kihn received the orders for us to halt in place and await further instructions. Germany had surrendered.

V-E Day was on May 8, 1945. The war was over, but we were still soldiers and we were still a long way from home.

It took several days after the end of the war in Europe to carry out the surrender directives. For my Battalion, May 8th, 1945 was the day that the Germans in this attractive tourists region of Austria drove their trucks into town and stacked their weapons in piles just in front of us. It felt good to finally begin to try to relax as much as I could. However, when I walked around I watched everywhere I stepped. I caught myself walking around suspicious places on the ground and pavement. When we entered buildings, hotels and vacant houses, we all continued to approach each new venture as though it was booby-trapped. I had survived the war without being wounded and knew the evilness of the enemy. I had seen some of my buddies, including Pvt. Stevens, get blown into several pieces. It ain't easy to forget more than a year of constant killings.

I was very enthusiastic about going home and see my Rose and find out whether she had survived her duties in the US Army Nurse Corps.

Lt. Rihn called me in and explained our latest orders. We were assigned the duty of assisting in the identification and resettlement of the mass numbers of displaced persons and the denazification of the region and get the enemy and our military weapons rounded up and placed in secure locations.

Three weeks after V-E Day the 'T Patchers' 36th Infantry Division assembled on Memorial Day in front of the City Hall in Kaufbeuren, Germany to honor the memory of all the fallen comrades. General Dahlquist gave a very emotional speech and reminded us the Naziizm had been destroyed together with the evildoers and evil it had brought to the world.

The next day, Lt. Rihn called me in and told me that since I had been a 'Point Man' during the war that I was going home today. He told me to pack my duffle bag and grab the next train west. My group traveled by train through Germany to the Port of Le Havre, France and boarded the Armitage Cruise Ship for New York.

I arrived in New York in June 1945 and was transported over to Camp Joyce Kilmer, which is about 30 miles south of New York City. The US Army Transportation Division was moving soldiers out by train and bus as fast as we could be processed. I remained at Camp Kilmer for a few days before boarding a train for Fort Sam Houston and checking into Brooke Army Medical Hospital in San Antonio, Texas. I had contracted malaria and they wanted to treat this for a few weeks before discharging me from the Army.

I was discharged from the Army in Dallas, Texas and went down highway 75 to my parent's home in Corsicana, Texas.

Some of the many medals awarded to Private William F. "Bill" Benson, of Battery "A", 133rd Field Artillery Battalion, 'T' Patchers, 36th Infantry Division of the US Army are as follows:

Bronze "V" Star With Oak Leaf Clusters And Two Arrowheads   **American Commendation**   **Army Commendation**   **Combat Service Commemoration**   **European African Middle East Campaign**

| European Victory Commemorative | Liberation Of France | Overseas Service Commemorative | World War II Victory Commemorative | World War II Victory |

The legacy of the 'Texans' 36th Infantry Division for its relentless fighting spirit and heroic deeds in some of the most brutal and difficult Campaigns of World War II in four countries, Italy, France, Germany and Austria will live forever.

My first job after the war was at Brown Ship Yard in Houston, Texas. Rose and I got married on April 13, 1946. The next job I got was with Humble Oil and Refining Company at its' Raccoon Bend Production near the Brazos River. We moved out to Bellville, Texas in 1947 and raised our family as I worked for Humble until I retired.

TREASURES OF WAR – CONCEALED BY THE EVIL ONES

Chapter Seven

From the Jewish Ghettos Through the Partisan Battles

The Story of Erika Greenberg

161 / DON STEWART NIMMONS

My father owned a bank. The Nazi SS Troops took our town and immediately began persecuting the Jews. Our house was marked as being owned by a Jew. They forced us to wear a large yellow Star of David on the front of all our clothes. Life long friends strayed from us to prevent their being ridiculed as a friend of a Jew. Jewish sympathizers were called down to the local Nazi SS office and warned of the danger of being classified as a traitor.

Since the Nazi SS Troops needed the ability to communicate with the international banking community because the Allied Countries were confiscating and blocking German government banks currency and gold transactions with the outside world, my father's Jewish Bank was ideal for them to use for payment of needed military supplies from outside Germany. Therefore, he earned a white armband with a blue Star of David, which entitled him to special privileges. He could travel freely around the country without the risk of being taken away to the work camps. The Gestapo created this identity for a group of Jews that were labeled as vital to the causes of the Third Reich.

One day I went by my father's bank and noticed this slick looking Gestapo dude standing outside the entrance to the door. I knew that they were just starting to take charge of his bank. This Kraut was so obvious to everyone in town. Later, I learned from my father that he would make random checks on the activities of the bank in his attempt to catch any Jew from removing his money or gold and silver from the bank. He had warned my father that he would be held totally responsible for such actions against the Nazi SS.

I decided to remove the Star of David from my clothes and become a normal attractive young lady the Geheime Staats Polizei would refrain from harassing.

I talked my mother and father into letting me move to my own apartment away from the Ghetto. They were known by all of our neighbors as Jews. I feared that it was only a matter of time before our neighborhood would be looted and my mother and father be beaten and forcibly taken down to the local train station and sent off to the camps in the 'East'.

Georgia, a childhood friend of mine, worked in the downtown city records department. She looked up people with Christian names with birthdays in the same year that I was born. She provided me with three different sets of I. D. documents with a recent passport photo on each of them.

In 1943, I obtained a job at a German Military products company. Since I was young and attractive lady with Christian documents, I could freely travel in town and to the countryside.

On one of my journeys a Partisan Group of Jews confronted me. They took me into the woods for interrogation. Eventually, I became certain that these Jews were fighting for the same cause as myself and dedicated to guerrilla warfare tactics against the Nazi Forces and stop the brutal killings and transportation of Jews to the 'East'. Once convinced, I reached down and took off my boots and pulled out my true Jew identity papers and presented them to the Group.

The Partisan Group asked me to spy for them to catch collaborators that were obtaining favors from the Gestapo in return for telling them where the Partisan Group was hiding. I only had to identify the collaborators. They would do the rest and take care of shooting them.

The primary focus and goal in everyone's life was to live even as a second or third class citizen. Every Jewish home and business was being looted of their jewelry, currency, coins, gold and silver, vehicles, store inventories, office furnishings and equipment, appliances, paintings prior to being torched and burned to the ground leaving nothing but ashes. The pictorial history of many Jewish families was destroyed forever. Photos, deeds and records all went up in smoke.

I often wondered where some of these Nazi SS troops were taking the looted things such as vehicles, tires, auto engines, brand new department store items and many other personal items such as appliances. They had to be taking many of these things for themselves and not for the Fuhrer's cause. Maybe it was for the Nazi SS Colonels and other officer's personal family usage. Many of them lived in the same town or in a nearby town. They could just order some squadron to go to a Jewish owned store and loot it – load up the truck and delivery it to the home or warehouse of one of the Nazi SS officers. The more items they looted -- the more favors and promotions could be expected.

I met one of my Jewish boyfriends from the past across town on my way to the countryside to meet with the Partisan Group. He told me about a large warehouse owned by one of the Nazi SS officers that was being used to distribute stolen Jewish vehicles to Nazi SS officers who resided in other nearby cities. He described how they would take an unloaded tank transport truck and drive two or three stolen vehicles on it and drive off for four or five hours before it returned empty.

The Gestapo soldiers were given orders to begin the extermination of my family's Ghetto. They came in teams of large Hercules type men. They were ruthless. When this occurred, protection was not part of anyone's vocabulary. Rumors were running rampant. The Jews in the Ghettos were out of all of life's necessities. Dressed in Jewish uniforms and no place to go except where the brutal Gestapo police commandeered them like cattle down to the train station. If you hesitated, you were shot. Most of them were completely demoralized. Besides seeing their earthly possessions taken away and homes burned to the ground, some had seen their spouse or children forcibly removed and taken away or killed right in front of them.

Author's Photo

The Nazi SS officers would offer a jar of sugar to blue Star of David Jews and Non-Jews just for the identification of a Jew or for any Jew turned into the Germans.

I was in good shape, but I was working for a bunch of cold-blooded murderers and preferred to live elsewhere. I was armed with a German Lugar. The head of the Partisan Group called us together and told us that we were going on a suicide mission. Some of you might want to back out, because some of you may not come back. It is strictly your choice. I will completely understand. Just step forward. No one stepped forward. All were eager to free our region from these Nazi SS killers and find our family and win the war.

TREASURES OF WAR – CONCEALED BY THE EVIL ONES / 164

The days moving through the cold wet forest were done under high tension as we heard and found German Panzer Troop movement toward the north. We had conducted so many Partisan Group maneuvers that everyone knew exactly what to do when the German Panzer Divisions and Infantry came through the woods of the forest. Subsequently, the German Infantry losses to the Partisan Guerrilla encounters changed the Krauts offensive routes. They stayed on the roads near the Tanks and Infantry Troops Carriers and refused to enter the woods.

David and Aaron were our expert messengers. Sometimes, they would walk or run all day long to get to a safe place and relay the activities of the Gestapo and Nazi SS Troops. Then, they would return with excellent intelligence information to help us.

We used the captured German guns, grenades, potato busters, rifles, and most importantly, ammunition to keep our Partisan Group with sufficient weapons.

Sheldon was our mine detector leader and knew how to disarm and re-arm some of the models. This proved to be a good combat weapon against the retreating German Panzer Divisions. They had recently moved forward on roads and made fresh off road tracks in the fields without being blown up. Only to come back along this same route and be blown up by the new installation of mines by our Partisan Guerrilla Groups. This crippled the movement and confused the battalion leaders. One time this Kraut tank ran over a mine near the edge of the forest and the impact was so strong that it picked it up and turned it up against this tree. The explosion of the shells stored inside the tank blew out the bottom of the tank and when each subsequent shell exploded the Germans must have thought the Allied Artillery had zeroed in on their location. We were positioned to pick off the scattering German Soldiers.

Each time we closed in on another Nazi SS Battalion the suspense grew tense. One of our best maneuvers was to slide by the enemy at night and attack them from their over confident rear. We rounded up German soldiers and took them as prisoners. The temptation to shoot them on site was overwhelming for many of us who had seen some of their fellow comrades shoot their parents or other family members. I decided that I would not stoop that low. Since the German had surrendered, I took him as a prisoner and held him for the Allied

Forces to take care of his disposition. I had been taught to respect life. The German prisoners could not understand the talking amongst our Partisan Group. When we knew it was to our advantage to speak in Yiddish, we did. We interrogated the Kraut prisoners in an effort to learn where our Jewish families and friends were being held and where the 'Death Camps' were located.

Here I was hundreds of miles from my home town fighting a Guerrilla War in my homeland when I noticed one of the German prisoners was a warrior, slightly injured, that I recognized from my hometown. Martin and I had played together as young children in the city's park during the summer months. When I approached him, he spoke softly, somewhat embarrassed. This young strong man had decided to worship the teachings of the Third Reich and follow the Nazi SS beliefs. Now, it was getting close to the Germans being defeated from all fronts. Martin told me the story of how the Nazi SS officers had looted my father's bank and removed all of the Gold Bullion for themselves. He had seen some of the loot with my father's bank's name on the crates on some trucks headed for the port city. One of the other German prisoners overheard our discussions about my father's looted bank, and he spoke up addressing me as Fräulein Erika. He introduced himself as Guenter. He described how some of the Nazi SS officers divided up the spoils of war by loading two trucks with Gold Bullion with the intentions to drive it to Switzerland. When the Partisan Group had captured these prisoners, they had not had sufficient water for several days. A chorus of wasser, wasser, wasser could be heard all around. At first I suspected Guenter was using his story to receive more water. But, as he went into details of some of the crates being divided between the trucks for the port city and Switzerland; I realized that he had first hand knowledge about my father's bank's looted Gold Bullion.

We were tired, but several of us were always alert to stand watch during a rest period – either day or night.

The decision to fight as Partisan Guerillas or turn ourselves over to the Nazi SS was an easy one. We had fought hard and repeatedly risked our lives and refused to be captured. I cannot tell you how many times I was scared to death.

Our efforts denied the Nazi SS the use of some roads.

One of the happiest moments of the Partisan Group's activities is when I met a new member from the East who was running from the Gestapo. Japheth was a handsome and very articulate young Jew two years older than I. After Jay joined our missions he began to show a comfortable liking to me. The love bug hit both of us, but we knew that we could not have a normal relationship and had to concentrate on our task, or risk being killed.

The atrocities of the Gestapo and Nazi SS Troops became so common and the censorship of the news media prevented the Jews from letting the majority of the world learn of their plight. The false worldwide newsreels and commentaries exploiting the virtues of the Third Reich in relationships to the Jews in my country delayed the combative response from outside Germany.

I have vivid memories of being persecuted and driven off my family's land and seeing our property destroyed and members of my family herded into train cars for shipment to labor or death camps.

The machination of the Nazi SS Troops became a spiritual justification for the brutal persecution and mass killing of the Jews. The new spiritual leader of Germany professed superiority against all unruly heathens, especially the Jews.

Even though some of my childhood Christian friends grew up to worship Nazism as soldiers, many of their wives and children were never told the truth about their campaigns of terror during the war that was unsurpassed in bestiality and savagery on mankind. They hailed their inhuman actions as heroism.

All of us were looking for signs of victory to renew our faith and give us a stronger purpose to return to our families. Suddenly, one early spring morning the American Battalions came rolling up the road and I could not stop crying for joy. Once we were certain it was the American Troops, we walked out of the woods with our hands held high to prevent them from mistaking us for the Nazi Ss Troops.

I never will forget this Major Williams from the Americans. He let us know that they had to double time it to catch up with the retreating Nazi SS Troops, but he ordered details assigned to stay with us, feed us some meals and take control of our captured German prisoners.

Restless, unwashed and the men unshaven with plenty of mental and physical fatigue to go around, we looked at each other not uttering a word. Then, the pandemonium began to encircle all of my Partisan Group. My hope for survival had come to reality. The persecution was over.

All of us wanted to learn the whereabouts of our loved ones. The assigned American Troops drove us to the nearest slave labor and concentration camp. I searched for a familiar face among the few surviving Jews. The ocean of hatred and tormenting pain surfaced immediately. Eventually, we were led into the area of the gas chambers and furnaces. I stood there petrified from what I saw.

The memories of my family will live through me forever.

TREASURES OF WAR – CONCEALED BY THE EVIL ONES

Chapter Eight

The Story of "Private" Charles Robert "Bob" Steele

BROTHERS FIGHTING FOR FREEDOM

M/Sgt. Arvil Steele
April 22, 1920 ---

Feb. 22 1922 — Sept. 13 1944
Staff Sergeant Charles Robert Steele

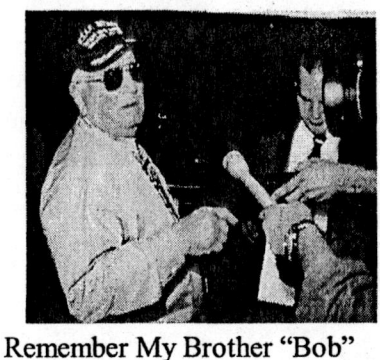

Remember My Brother "Bob"

"Bob" Steele

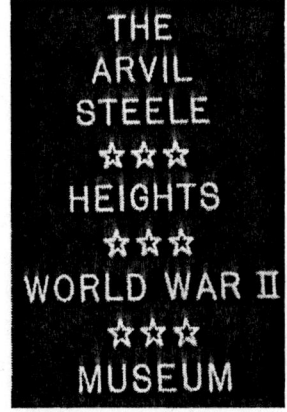

THE ARVIL STEELE ★★★ HEIGHTS ★★★ WORLD WAR II ★★★ MUSEUM

"Bob" Steele

169 / DON STEWART NIMMONS

I was born on February 22, 1922 in Linden, Texas. My name is Charles Robert Steele. My Daddy died when I was 10 years old. The depression years were very hard for my mother, three sisters and older brother, Arvil. Our Daddy did not leave us much in the way of material things. Mom got $200.00 insurance money when he died. We worked in the fields as sharecroppers. My brother, who was just one year older than I, and I picked cotton from sun up until sun down every day during the harvest season. The long summer months in Texas are very hot. My hands were so cut up and bleeding from picking cotton at the end of the day that I had to put them down in the cool creek to reduce the pain and stop the bleeding.

During the school year we all walked down the dirt road to the little schoolhouse. Our mother encouraged us all to learn to read as much as possible. After we got our chores done, I grabbed an old used book and learned to read about the world many things that I did not even imagine. I was fascinated to see how airplanes flew and took people to the big city. The only thing that my brother and I knew anything about was the freight trains. Reading had to be done in the late afternoon. We did not have electricity out on the sharecropper's farm. The kerosene lamps were used sparingly because of the cost of the fuel. Usually, we used the kerosene lamps on the little wooden table at suppertime.

Mom would ask us to wash and dry the supper dishes. She had us organize a routine on a daily basis where one of us would clean off the supper table. My brother or I would go out to the well and pump a couple of buckets of water and bring it into the kitchen. My three sisters would take turns washing and drying the dishes. If anybody broke dishes, they were in deep trouble with Mom.

Mom had a strong Christian faith. She taught all of us about the Bible. On Saturday evening, my brother and I would go out to the well and pump about ten buckets of water and bring them into the back room and pour them into the tub. During the summer time we enjoyed the coolness of the water. Cold winter days, he and I first poured the buckets of water into the large heavy steel pot outside. We gathered some wood from the woodshed and got a blazing fire going under and around the blackened pot. Arvil and I stood as close to the fire as we could to keep ourselves warm. Occasionally, on a windy evening a spark from the fire would blow onto our pants and burn a hole in them. After the water began to boil, we took turns dipping the buckets with steel handles into the hot water. We ran up the back porch into the back room and poured the steaming hot water into the tub. Back and forth we ran for about fifteen minutes. After almost filing the tub with hot water I would check to see if the water was still hot. If it were too hot, I would go out to the well and pump a bucket or two of the cold water from the well.

Saturday evening baths began. Afterwards, Mom would read us versus from the Bible. She reminded us that we had to get up early and do our chores and then get dressed for Sunday school and church.

After chores and fresh breakfast, Sunday morning was a delightful time. Several of our Sharecropper's field hand neighbors, Mom, Arvil, my three sisters and me would all get together and walk down the road about six miles to go to church.

The fellowship at the church was one of the high points of the week for me. I learned to read along with the Pastor and sing the hymns from the hymnals in the pews at the church. Mom had a good voice and she would lead us with her strong voice. I learned the importance of prayer during the church services. One of my Sunday school teachers gave me a little Bible to read.

Christmas time, the only thing that we received was a pair of overalls and some underwear. Every few years we would receive a new pair of shoes. Toys, not anything but maybe an empty sewing thread spool that my brother and I could use as a truck or car and play in the sand or dirt.

At the age of 11, a year after my daddy's death, Mom decided to move off the Sharecropper's farm in Texas to her mother's big house up in Mena, Arkansas. Grandma Chambers had a two-story house in town. This gave my brother Arvil and I a better opportunity to learn more adventures and seek some of our young goals to further advance ourselves.

I learned to use the school library and read about things that interest me. We worked around town doing odd jobs for some of the neighbors. One day while we were down town near the railroad tracks I saw some men jump up into one of the open doors of the freight train boxcars. I pointed to Arvil and told him to sit down and let's watch what happens. The train's engine was running and I knew it was about to start moving. Sure enough, after about one hour and fifteen minutes the train's conductor began to blow the loud whistle and the train slowly started northbound. The men in the boxcar were not discovered and had a free ride to somewhere.

Arvil and I planned a trip out of Mena during the Thanksgiving Holidays. I was 13 years old and he was 14 years old. We told Mom that we had a ride to go to another town with some friends. She agreed to let us make the adventurous trip. She warned us about our behavior and told us to be back no later than Sunday night. She knew it was good for us to grow up and that we wanted to see the world.

Sure enough, Friday afternoon we heard the train's conductor blow his whistle for the south side road crossing going northbound. Then, we heard the second whistle, which meant the train, was going to stop and take on freight and mail at the station. Arvil and I grabbed our small bag and told Mom goodbye. She reminded us about her previous instructions.

Arvil enjoyed the trip more than I did. He was planning his next adventurous trip down the line to the south. Mom pushed me to go downtown and find a job during the Christmas Holidays. During the depression years the federal government had to employ some men to keep a watch over the Ozark and Ouachita National Forest near our community. The Civilian Conservation Corps was responsible for constructing all-weather roads in Ouachita National Forest and building some buildings around the campgrounds, picnic areas and swimming lakes.

I went down to Dierks Lumber Yard. Sure enough, Mr. Dierks hired me to work out in the lumberyard loading lumber on the trucks that were going out to the CCC projects. It did not take long for me to learn that a good pair of gloves was something that I needed badly.

Mom went into town and bought me a pair of the muletrain leather gloves with the long sleeves to keep the lumber from cutting my forearms. Man, what a difference it made. I wanted to show Mr. Dierks that I was a good worker and could do many different things around the lumberyard. Summer vacation jobs were not plentiful. Mom taught me to be on time and not get into any arguments with other workers and say, 'Yes Sir' and 'No Sir' to the men in the office. I got stronger every day I worked. When it was time to return to my high school classes, Mr. Dierks called me into his office and told me I would be considered for a job during the summer months. I told him that I was and thanked him.

My older brother, Fred, was 13 years older than me. He went off to Texarkana, Texas and worked his way up to station manager for Magnolia Petroleum Company. The Mobil Station was doing well and Fred came to Mena to move Mom, my sisters, Arvil and I to Texarkana just before school started in 1933. I was very saddened to have to go down to Mr. Dierks lumber yard and tell him that we were moving to Texarkana and would not be working for him anymore.

The schools were better in Texarkana and we met new friends. Arvil and I worked around town doing odd jobs for some of the merchants and warehousemen. The rented house was a little nicer. Arvil and I shared one bedroom. Coming from a small town, the local boys with influential fathers had the advantage over us 'out-of-towners'. Mom encouraged us to set new goals and apply ourselves and not worry about the politics.

In the fall of 1936, Arvil and a friend of his decided to quit high school and join the army. He was only 16 years old. Mom did not think the army would take him because of his age. Later she found out that he had lied about his age and had gone to Fort Riley, Kansas and enlisted.

It was spring of 1937 and the trees were beginning to bud its green leaves all around the hills and mountains. My brother, Arvil, got a 30-day furlough from the United States Army in Fort Riley, Kansas and came home on the bus. He looked excellent. He had gained around thirty or forty pounds. He told me all about the training during the past year. One of the stories was about some of our top officers in our military had come to Fort Riley to do their training for the Calvary. He talked Field Artillery guns and ammunition powders and how they had to pull the cannons around by horses. The details of the trained horses were very interesting to me. Arvil had found something that was extremely interesting to him. He seemed content from his hasty decision to hitchhike off to the army the year before.

Since I was in high school and could not stay home with him, Arvil and I would meet some of his previous school friends and some of mine down at the Ozark Café to enjoy a chocolate malt and hamburger. We would all plan to go out to Shady Lake on Saturdays. Occasionally, we would go down to Iron Springs to swim and picnic. Yes, Sundays, Mom had us all in church.

Time flies when you are having fun. Yes, Mom, Fred, Sisters and I strolled down to the Union Station to see Arvil off to Fort Riley.

After I graduated from high school, I prayed about what God wanted me to do. Mom encouraged me to set my goals and she would back me no matter what I decided. Knowing the opportunities in Texarkana were very limited and my brother, Arvil had been honorably discharged on September 10th, 1939 from the U. S. Army at Fort Riley,

Kansas and was home, and he could not find any good job either, we decided to go down to Union Station and jump on the passenger train and go to Dallas, Texas. Everywhere I went I found out that I could work for one of the military contractors in Dallas or nearby Fort Worth. During most all of my interviews the boss would tell me that a man of my age and in my physical condition was subject to the military draft in the near future, and they did not want to train me and then I be called up for the draft.

After checking out the opportunities at the U. S. Army enlistment office in Dallas, I was convinced that I wanted to join the Army. Finally, after several days of meditation, I went down to register and sign up for the United States Army. A few days later I got my physical and afterwards I received my orders and a bus ticket to Brackettville, Texas.

'Dub', as I called my brother Arvil, reenlisted and was assigned to Fort Sill, Oklahoma.

From the bus station in Dallas, the bus ride took some twelve hours through San Antonio down the roller coaster U. S. 90 highway to Fort Clark. I saw many of the good cowboy western movies at the theater back in Texarkana, but I had no idea that I was going to learn how and why the U. S. Cavalry was trained.

Here it is November 1940, and I am in the United States Army's Fifth Cavalry living in the old stone fort buildings right in the middle of rattlesnake country. Big time! Ranch land was abundant. The cool flowing spring water was the best thing God had delivered to that part of the country. Dusty! I could not imagine dust in that many layers. It was thick as the smoke from the forest fires back in Ouachita National Forest, Arkansas, maybe a little bit thicker. The barracks were two stories and built out of some hardwood from somewhere in Texas and stonewalls.

My Sergeant Culpepper was as tough as they came. I was told that he had fought the Germans in World War I. The top man was someone from West Point. He had a liking for tanks and horses. When he came out on that balcony overlooking the quadrangle at the fort, he had the total respect of his officers and men. He let us know exactly what he expected of us and told us to be prepared for some very rough duty. During the second day of training while riding down one of the dusty trails this tank came out of the brush and scared me to death. Sarge screamed out to warn us that Colonel Patton was driving it and was going to fire the cannon near us. About that time the boom from the 75 mm tank cannon caused my horse to jump sideways and threw me off into a ditch with briar bushes with thorns as big as my mother's sewing needles.

Sarge Culpepper controlled his mount and took off after my horse. As this colonel clattered by in his tank sitting there with a big grin on his face looking down at me picking thorns from my butt and legs, he shouted. "In the rigors of actual war you would be dead. Be alert at all times, think ahead."

Here I was all full of holes from the thorns, dusty as ever, dirt everywhere, up rides the Sarge with my horse.

How am I going to jump up on that horse's saddle with my butt bleeding and full of pain?

The Sarge reminded me what the colonel had told us a few days earlier and cautioned me to control the horse that was in training also.

I did not believe that a commanding colonel would unexpectedly show up in maneuvers and especially the dusty brush country of South Texas. Every day he let us know it was very likely that we would have to go into some battle conditions worse than he was training us. I believed him and wanted to do my best to become one of his fighting men.

'Dub', as I fondly called my brother Arvil, missed visiting with me by a few days just after I left Texarkana to return to Fort Clark. A few days later he came home on his thirty days, 'Delay In Route', from Fort Sill on his way to San Francisco to ship out to the Philippines. He visited and enjoyed Mom and Sisters and our mutual friends in Texarkana before taking off on his first overseas trip.

Oh well, he and I will have many days to sit down and tell our stories to each other of our military training and the girls we meet during our journeys to the various cities when we both get out of our enlistment time period.

'Dub' and I wrote to each other several times each month. He shared his stories about his new promotion to Sergeant at Nichols Field, Philippines during his new on-job-training for an Aircraft Armament Technician for fighter planes. I told him about my rigid war games training in the dust. He let me know that he enjoyed my stories about going out on the rancher's ranch and doing some deer hunting.

Especially, the one when the rancher put me in a deer stand back in the brush overlooking a drinking water trough. I thought I had died and gone to heaven. Two big bucks came out of the brush from two different directions to get a drink. I raised up with my rifle to take a shot at the bigger one, when all of a sudden this huge buck with at least sixteen points came snorting up the trail to the water. He was taking claim to the water for himself and wanted all to know it. I took aim at his neck and boom he fell over like the cannon had shot him. I was amazed. The other two bucks were not spooked from the shot. They came out of the near brush to get a drink of water. I picked out the larger one and boom; he stumbled and limped off into the brush with blood flowing along the ground. The smaller one turned to look around and faced me; boom, I hit him right through the heart and he dropped immediately. Shortly after dust the rancher came driving up in his pick up. A few of his men helped me field dress the bucks and load them for the drive back to Fort Clark. Rancher Kinney's hands had killed a couple of bucks to go along with mine.

When we arrived at the Fort, he told his men to hang all of them up on a low oak tree limb. I thanked him for his hospitality and let him know that it was a good break away from our daily vigorous training. Sarge was very pleased to see my kill and told me to take care of skinning the deer, cutting them up, and that he wanted a back strap steak. "Get some of the K P guys to help you." Some of the mess hall cooks knew how to prepare some good venison back strap and rump roast with some cheap red wines.

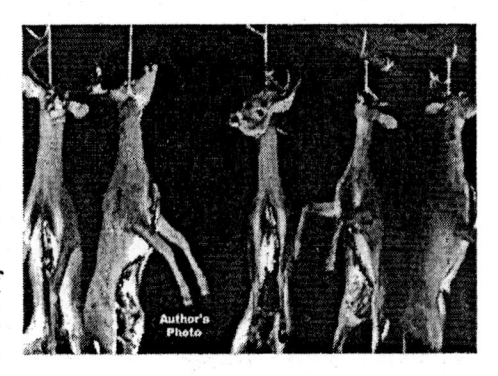

At reveille, one spring day in 1941, Colonel Patton came out on the balcony and announced that he was being transferred to Fort Myer near Washington, D. C. He also told us to get packed up because the 5th Cavalry was being transferred to Fort Bliss near El Paso, Texas.

TREASURES OF WAR – CONCEALED BY THE EVIL ONES / 176

Mom kept me informed of things back in Texarkana in her letters and included comments from Arvil from the Philippines. It sounded like he was in love with some young Filipino girl. His soft duty was something that I had not enjoyed. The West Texas dust and heat was not a tropical paradise.

Then, December 7, 1941 came and changed my life forever. Sergeant Culpepper stopped our daily maneuvers and told us that the Japanese had made a surprise attach on our bases in Hawaii. We all knew that our future training would be more intense. At parade rest in front of Sarge, we looked at each other and wondered out loud how this would affect our dusty training.

Wow, where is Dub in all of this? He is way past Hawaii. The Japanese had to fly past the Philippines to reach Pearl Harbor. I could not wait to get back to the barracks and write Mom and ask questions and also let her know of my support.

When the United States entered World War II, Fort Bliss was the home of the largest horse cavalry force in the nation. The First Cavalry continued to patrol the border during the early years of the war. The Army converted Fort Bliss into a mechanized infantry unit. Fort Bliss had begun its transformation into the nations largest antiaircraft artillery-training center.

Artillery units were coming into Fort Bliss from all over the nation. The War Department had purchased more than one million acres for expansion for these operations. From a few thousand acres Fort Bliss became roughly seventy-five miles long and fifty-four miles wide. It encompassed parts of Texas and most of its area lies in New Mexico. The fort became primarily an artillery post.

In 1942, I was stationed at Fort Bliss, Texas. The sandy and rolling hills and mountains around El Paso, Texas in the hot Texas and southern New Mexico summer were the conditions for our mock battlefield maneuvers.

Guess who came roaring into Fort Bliss to train the tankers for desert warfare? Remember that colonel who fired the tank cannon at me back at Fort Clark. Now, he was a general.

177 / DON STEWART NIMMONS

He drove us hard, sometimes out in the battlefields of New Mexico for three or four days at a stretch without us getting much shut eye.

We engaged in quick mountain and open desert maneuvers supporting the tankers. I learned to become the best fighting warrior in my platoon. I knew that because of our intense assault training that we were going to be sent to the battlefields where no normal soldier wanted to be. I rose to the rank of Staff Sergeant in the 2nd Armored Division in the 7th United States Army. This was General Patton's unit.

On September 12th, Lieutenant Galloway called me into his office and gave me my 30-days 'Delay In Route' furlough. I jumped at the opportunity to grab an eastbound troop train and go see Mom and my three sisters in Texarkana. My orders were to catch another troop train and report to Newport News, Virginia naval station on October 12th. He told me not to tell anyone anything about my orders and where I was going. He told me to be prepared for an early overseas assignment shortly after I arrived in Virginia.

When I arrived in Texarkana, Mom was so excited to see me, Grandma Chambers and Mom went down to the Piggly Wiggly Store and bought five large sacks of groceries. They cooked my favorite pork chops, sweet potatoes, collards and pecan pie made from pecans from this year's crop.

After supper, she set me down and pulled out a recent newspaper clipping and showed me the photo of the Prisoners of War during a Death March from Bataan. It told all about the battles that were fought between December 8, 1941 and April 9, 1942 keeping the Jap Armies busy and delaying them from moving on against the Allied Forces in the Pacific region. The American general in charge worked out the surrender to the Japs in order to save what was left of his men. Mom told that thousands of men had been shot and tortured to death. She could not get any information from the War Department as to what had happened to Arvil. She said. "Everybody's attention at the War Department was focused on winning the war against the Germans and Italians."

TREASURES OF WAR – CONCEALED BY THE EVIL ONES / 178

Mom and the family took me to church on Sunday. The pastor spent several moments talking about the war and the servicemen and women serving from his congregation. He asked me to stand and be recognized. He told me. "Everyone at the church is praying for you and your brother Arvil's safety."

Author's Photo

I nodded my head and saluted them before sitting back in the pew.

The next two Sundays, Mom, my sisters and I all attended Sunday school and Church. I could not have imagined how many of my friends were now going to church. The place was packed. Being in a U S Army uniform with my sergeant stripes caused almost everyone to come up to me and express their warmest thoughts and prayerful comments. They assured me that they would look out for Mom and Sisters while I was on duty.

Just before I was to leave for the east coast, Mom received a telegram from the War Department informing her that the Red Cross had learned that Dub was alive and survived the Bataan Death March and was at a POW Camp somewhere in Japan.

At the most, the troop trains were taking about one week to travel from Texarkana to Newport News, Virginia. So, it was time for me to determine when the next one would be coming through Texarkana to Dallas. The Union Station manager told me to be there on September 6th to catch the next east coast bound troop train.

At Union Station, Mom asked me. "Why are you going east?"

"Mom, I have orders from my commanders to say nothing of my next assignment."

She began to cry and gave me a big hug and told me. "Do not forget who you are, keep your strong faith in God and be yourself. You will be OK and I will be waiting for you here when you return from where ever you are going. I will write you every day and let you know what I learn about Arvil."

"I love you Mom. You have worked hard to show your love for me. I have been trained to do an important job. I will carry out my duties. When I get back, bake me your best cherry pie with whipped cream all over the top of it. Bye, Mom."

The train began to move out and I stood there holding onto Mom and Sisters as long as I could. I saw the caboose moving toward me and I pulled away from them just in time to grab the handrail and jump up onto the rear platform. The troop train was one of the nicer ones. It was a Pullman Sleeper train. I walked about four cars toward the front of the train until I found an empty sleeper.

The troop train ride from Texarkana to Newport News, Virginia, took five long days and nights. At the train station there were U S Army officers standing along the platform asking each of us what our outfit was. I told this Lieutenant.

"I am Staff Sergeant Robert Steele from the 2nd Armored Division of the 7th Army. I am transferring from Fort Bliss, Texas."

"Sergeant, jump onto one of these transport trucks, go directly to the port and find the *USS Augusta*. There is more than one ship at the docks. Find yours, and report to the receiving officer on deck. He will direct you to your quarters."

"Yes Sir."

I grabbed my duffle bag and backpack and jumped on the next truck in line.

Where in the world am I setting sail? No wonder Lieutenant Galloway ordered me not to talk to anybody about this mission. Here it is late dust and I have not seen any of the sites around Newport News. Maybe we will be allowed to go ashore for a day or two after all these men board the ships and before we ship out.

As I walked up the gang blank I looked at this monstrous size troop ship. I had never seen anything like it. Men were pouring onto the ship. As I got to the edge of the ship this sailor saluted me and asked.

"Name and regiment?"

"Sergeant Charles Robert Steele, 2nd Armored Division, 7th US Army."

He gave me instructions and directions to find my bunk down in the hole of the ship. Sure enough, when I found my bunk some of my men were already there.

"Hey Sarge, when are we going to get to go see the town tonight?" Private Snelling shouted across the noisy room.

"You should remain here until I receive further orders from Lieutenant Galloway. Secure your rifles, pistols and grenades. No live ammo in the firing chamber. The johns are out this door to the right and down the hall," I said turning and pointing toward the door to the left of where I was standing.

An echo of "Thanks Sarge" rang out from the room.

"Have any on you men been on a ship before? I asked.

"I will find out where sick bay is for any of you guys that might need to settle your stomachs," I reminded the men.

At 18:00 Lieutenant Galloway came into our bunks and one of the soldiers rose and called all of us to attention.

"At ease, has Sergeant Steele arrived?"

"Lieutenant, over here."

"Sergeant, grab all of your things. I need you up to my cabin for the voyage. Your bunk will be in my quarters."

When we arrived at his quarters, he showed me where I would work and sleep. There was a more secure and organized place for us to work.

"Sarge, this convoy of ships will leave within the next 12 hours for carrying out *Operation Torch*. This unknown mission will be a direct amphibious combat invasion of a foreign country from this troop ship. When Sergeant Culpepper arrives on board, you and he will find the Navy supply man and make sure that all of our equipment and supplies on this list are on board. Do you understand the importance of this order?

"Yes Sir."

"I need to let the troop ship's naval brass know immediately when all of our fighting equipment has been loaded on this ship. If it did not get loaded, then, you will be given orders to get our men off this ship before it sails," Lieutenant further ordered.

"Yes Sir, I will jump on this right now."

One hour later, Sergeant Culpepper and Steele met and went over the Lieutenant's order. We walked around the ship until we located the Sailor combat supply officer. Together, we compared the Lt's list with one of his men's list. All of us agreed that all but a few insignificant items were on board. We double timed it back to our quarters and told Lieutenant Galloway what we had determined.

"Fine! Culpepper get Steele to take you down to our men and give them orders to be prepared to get a good nights rest when orders are announced by the Naval Brass."

"Yes Sir, should we take roll call to see if all of our men made the trip here and got on board?

"Good idea Steele. There must be more than 10,000 men on this ship."

Later, just as we had completed roll call.

"ATTENTION EVERYONE, NOW HEAR THIS! ALL LIGHTS OUT AT MIDNIGHT"

Culpepper and Steele looked at their watches and had less than ten minutes to get back up to their quarters. We scurried about answering a few more questions and down the hallway and up the stairs almost getting lost in the flurry of movement of Army and Navy men. We reported that all of the men were accounted for and ready to roll.

During the night we heard all types of strange noises from the harbor. At 0600 the attention notices kept blaring out over the intercom system calling each division or battalion to mess hall near each one's bunk area.

It was about 08:30 the USS Augusta Troop Ship began to pull away from the dock. We decided to go out on deck to see all the activities of the launch of the ship. It was a very clear October day with the crisp cold wind blowing out to sea. Most of the men had never seen much less been on a Troop Ship. We slowly moved out into the Atlantic Ocean and watched some of the other Naval ships join us.

Five days out to sea several aircraft carriers, destroyers, and four or five battleships and additionally Troop Ships joined us.

We are going to war, big time. All those prayers that Mom taught me will come in handy. I am going to look back on this rough ocean voyage as a piece of cake. I wonder if the mail would get back Texarkana after we win our first battle on land. Tonight, I must take time to write Mom as I had promised her. I owe her eight days of letters now, Steele reminded himself.

"ATTENTION ALL PERSONNEL! NOW HEAR THIS! GERMAN SUBMARINES HAVE BEEN SPOTTED IN THESE WATERS! NAVY GUNNERS, TAKE YOUR STATIONS! ALL OTHER MEN BELOW DECK WITH LIFE JACKETS DEPLOYED!"

As I scrambled off the deck I noticed over near the edge of the horizon the Navy destroyers were zig zagging back and forth and firing some it's booming depth charges into the ocean. Holly Moses, they don't waste any time protecting the ships and us. My heart is running as fast as it was the day I was thrown by the horse at Fort Clark when Patton fired his tank cannon over my head. Bet many of the men will be so upset that sick bay will be full in a few hours and the bunks will be full of seasick men, Steele thought.

Eleven days later, Lieutenant Galloway received his orders and called us together in his quarters.

"Steele, you and Culpepper prepare the men for a full scale invasion force. All of their battle gear consisting of ammunition, gas mask, bayonet, steel helmet, rifle, grenades, field rations and first aid kit must be loaded into their field pack. Make the arrangements for all items that must be taken from the hole from the sailor combat supply man. Remind the men to secure their packs according to my previous training orders. Keep a record for me of each and every soldier. It will take you about three days to complete this."

"Yes Sir, it appears that our battle is not too far in the future," Steele replied.

"Correct! This is what you have trained so hard for. The Colonel gave me my orders and with a quote from our commander, General Patton. 'AS DESPERATE A VENTURE AS HAS EVER BEEN UNDERTAKEN BY ANY FORCES IN THE WORLD'S HISTORY', Lieutenant Galloway confidently replied.

"Excellent, we will work together with our men and be prepared to go to battle in short notice," Sergeant Steele replied as he grabbed Culpepper by the arm and left the quarters.

On November 8th, our Troop Ship was sailing in some rough seas off the French North African coast in the Atlantic Ocean.

"ATTENTION EVERYONE! NOW HEAR THIS! THIS INVASION FORCE IS GOING TO INVADE THE PORT OF CASABLANCA, IN THE PROVINCE OF MOROCCO IN FRENCH WEST NORTH AFRICA."

Most of the men began to wear their life jackets all the time. I noticed that our Troop Ship had come to a stop and was anchored off the coast. Apparently, some of the Troop Ships had moved on up north to the Straits of Gibraltar.

"ATTENTION ALL PERSONNEL! NOW HEAR THIS! PREPARE FOR BATTLE!"

All of us put our battle gear on with the heavy backpack and went to our assigned locations awaiting further orders.

"ATTENTION ALL TROOPS! NOW HEAR THIS! GO OVERBOARD BY WAY OF ROPE LADDERS!"

We climbed down cargo nets into the bobbing Higgins boat with the two-inch thick armor plate front drop ramp. The Sailor driving the boat gave the command to release the boat as he turned toward the shore. When we got closer to shore we could hear the machine gun fire bouncing off of the front ramp.

Lieutenant Galloway gave the command. "Keep your heads down. Sailor circle this boat to the south."

TREASURES OF WAR – CONCEALED BY THE EVIL ONES / 184

We all crammed on top of each other to prevent the shore installations from shooting us before we got to shore. After, the diversion to the south, I noticed that the attack from the French Troops and shore installations had ceased. The shelling from the big guns from the battleship had also ceased firing. We later learned that General Patton's personal effort, in which he took control of some of the invasion forces on the northern side of Casablanca completing the encirclement of the French Troops, resulted in the French leaders to order a cease-fire and surrender. Once ashore near Safi, we marched into Casablanca with only a few snipers firing at us occasionally. When we returned fire and killed a few of them, they quickly gave up.

Why in God's name are the French Troops trying to kill us Americans? Aren't we over here fighting the Axis Troops to free France, Italy, and all the other countries from Fascism rule? Maybe some day I will know why. Steele thought to himself.

"Culpepper, gather our battalion together. Roll call! Report!" Lieutenant Galloway ordered as he moved to the side of the dirt road out of the path of the trucks and heavy tanks.

"Yes Sir."

It took about one hour for all of the men in the battalion to report. No one was wounded or killed in the invasion. A few of them lost some of their gear during the landing.

"Lieutenant, all are present and accounted for, no casualties," Sergeant Culpepper reported to the Lieutenant.

"Good job well done. Now, let me flag down one of the Troop Trucks that has been unloaded at the port coming down the road. We need four or five of them to carry all you men and equipment. This battle has just begun."

Operation Husky, Seventh US Army under Lt. General George S. Patton, Jr., amphibious invasion to liberate the western half of the Island of Sicily. On July 10th, 1943, covered by gunfire from the Western Naval Task Force and Aircraft of the Twelfth Air Force, they landed on the shores of Sicily.

The U. S. Seventh Army rapidly moved forward over the west and north of the Island, with the British Eighth Army on its right.

Sergeant Steele looked down on the German infantry battalion from his foxhole on the hill above the road to Palermo. The enemy began firing a concentration of artillery at the hill. After an hour and half bombardment from the artillery shells, Bob worked his war into a better position to defend the 7th Army lines and move his remaining platoon around to flank the German mortar fire. Sergeant Steele slowly crept and crawled down to a shallow ravine and motioned for his platoon to come to his new position. Before they crawled down, Bob was struck by shrapnel from a blast from an artillery shell against a boulder overhead. He was wounded in his face and right leg. Bleeding and suffering severe pain, Bob went on the offensive and moved to a shallow draw to throw a grenade into the mortar fire bunker, silencing the weapon and blowing up all in it.

Immediately, the German infantrymen from two machineguns and one sniper across the hillside pinned him down by grazing fire. He motioned for his men to stay down and take cover. Crawling along the shallow draw, he made his way to within hand grenade range of one of the machinegun nest, he tossed two grenades into the nest destroying it and killing the Germans. Sergeant Steele crawled to the opening in front of the enemy's nest. Grabbing the rim with his right hand he pulled himself up and rolled over into the bunker. Looking around the destroyed machinegun nest he saw some German potato-masher grenades laying about twelve feet on down the foxhole entrance into the machinegun nest. He began to toss two at a time of their grenades down on the other German machinegun nest until all were killed.

The German sniper had been diverted while watching Bob perform his gallant and unselfish acts of bravery waiting to get a clear shot at Sergeant Steele. Bob's platoon moved into position to take out the sniper by a single rifle shot.

Sergeant Steele's platoon reached him and called for a medic to stop the bleeding from his face and the deep wound in his thigh. As Bob screamed, the corpsman pulled the six-inch piece of shrapnel out of his leg and wrapped it tightly to slow the flow of his blood. Then, the corpsmen lifted Bob to the ground and put him on a Jeep and transported him to the nearest field hospital tent.

The Army nurses calmly took charge and began treating his wounds and giving him some pain medicine. Bob learned to respect all of the Army nurses working long hours at the field hospitals. They had him up and walking around the perimeter in two days. Fortunately, Sergeant Steele did not require surgery.

As the battle for Sicily was moving rapidly to an end and victory by the Allied Forces and the Evacuation Hospital Nurses were desperately performing unbelievable stabilization procedures and evacuating the high number of serious and critically wounded casualties from the battlefields, many of the nurses got very little sleep and spent days at a time trying to save the wounded men.

Due to the lack of space on one of the hospital ships, Bob knew he could get back to the front line with his company.

Sergeant Steele hitched a ride on one of the division officer's jeep to the headquarters in Palermo. There he located his company who had advanced on to Messina.

On August 17th, the German general ordered a full-scale evacuation of the remaining four German Divisions and the few Italian soldiers from the island by ship across the Strait of Messina to Italy.

The expeditious Operation Husky campaign liberated the Island of Sicily in 39 days.

The victory by the Allied Forces at Sicily became the first piece of the Axis homeland capture during World War II. Allied Forces established the large military base to begin the invasion of Italy and train the enlisted men and officers for future amphibious landings throughout Europe.

Surprisingly, the defeat at Palermo caused the political opposition in Italy to oust Mussolini as dictator and begin the breakup of the Rome-Berlin Axis.

General Patton was very aware of the soldiers suffering from heat exhaustion brought on by the temperatures of over 100-degrees and the relentless push to Palermo and beyond under battle weary conditions. He replaced some of the infantry with fresh troops, allowing Sergeant Steele and his men to rest and recuperate before their next assignment.

HEADQUARTERS SEVENTH ARMY
APO #758
U. S. Army

GENERAL ORDER, 22 August 1943: NUMBER 18

Soldiers of the Seventh Army:

Born at sea, baptized in blood, and crowned with victory, in the course of 38 days of incessant battle and unceasing labor, you have added a glorious chapter in the history of war.

Pitted against the best the Germans and Italians could offer, you have been unfailingly successful. The rapidity at your dash, which culminated in the capture of Palermo, was equaled by the dogged tenacity with which you stormed Troina and captured Messina. Every man in the Army deserves equal credit. The enduring valor of the Infantry, and the impetuous ferocity of the tanks were matched by the tire-less clamor of our destroyer guns. The engineers performed prodigies in the construction and maintenance of impossible roads over impassable country. The services of Maintenance and Supply performed a miracle. The Signal Corps laid over 10,000 miles of wire, and the Medical Department evacuated and cared for our sick and wounded.

On all occasions the Navy has given generous and gallant support. Throughout this operation, our Air has kept the sky clear and tirelessly supported the operation of the Ground troops.

As a result of this combined effort, you have killed or captured 113,350 enemy troops. You have destroyed 265 of his tanks, 2,324 vehicles, and 1,162 large guns, and in addition, have collected, a mass of military booty running into hundreds of tons.

But your victory has significance above and beyond its physical aspect- you have destroyed the prestige of the enemy.

The President of the United States, the Secretary of War, the Chief of Staff, General Eisenhower, General Alexander, and General Montgomery have all congratulated you.

Your fame shall never die.

G. S. PATTON --- Lieut. General, U. S. Army, Commanding

While in Palermo, the 1st Battalion began to reorganize, restock all supplies and train each day for the amphibious landing for the invasion of Italy. Bob's 362nd Infantry Regiment of the 91st Infantry Division received assignment orders to the US 5th Army.

Over the next few months Sergeant Steele and his Regiment got to learn why the Sicilian people, although liberated, continued to live in poverty from the years of Mussolini Fascism. It was obvious that Sicilians did not trust their neighbors. Some had been silent Fascists party members and committed atrocities against their neighbors just to survive the cruel games of life that the Italian and German Armies played.

Everywhere Bob and his American buddies went brought new bountiful friendships with the Sicilians. Nearly every family on the Island had been affected by the war and especially during the fighting and bombardment when Allied troops and Sicilians lost their lives. Getting the food network organized by the Allied Forces and the new political leaders was one of the first and most important agendas facing Sicily. U. S. Army Corps of Engineers began the task to rebuild some of the bridges and temporary crossings around the island for the wagons and trucks to bring the wheat, grapes, olives and fruits from the orchards, fish, and the livestock to the marketplace.

Sergeant Steele found time to learn as much as possible about this multicultural society. He took time to visit some of the medieval cities with Romanesque Gothic cathedrals, fortresses, castles, and churches built many centuries before.

Sicily had been a Greek colony, a Roman province, an Arab emirate and a Norman kingdom. Eclectic cultures and races from Europe, Africa and Asia best describe the people of Sicily. Bob was not accustomed to such a variety of beautiful people and customs. His intrigue led him to want to take advantage of his free time and meet some of the local families and learn the language. He met a man named Alfredo Siracusa at a restaurant on the plateau overlooking the southern coast in Agrigento. Siracusa had studied in Europe and spoke very good English. He rose from his table and went over to Bob's table and said,

"Welcome to Agrigento. My name is Alfredo Siracusa and I have a summer place near here that you men are welcome to visit and enjoy."

A God answered prayer, Steel thought. "My name is Sergeant Bob Steele and here are some of my buddies in the 91st Infantry," Bob replied as he stood up and shook hands.

"Your offer sounds very intriguing to us, but we need some help on communicating with the locals," Bob replied, hiding his enthusiasm.

"Just learn vino, bistecca, gamberoni, panino, pesce, pollo, vitello and you will not go hungry while you are in Sicily," Siracusa said smiling.

"Vino, pesce and pollo I have already learned. What were the others?" Bob asked.

"Where are you guys from in the States?" Siracusa asked.

Wondering why he asked the question, Bob answered. "I am from Texas. Most of us are from the Mid-West."

"Then, you need to know the word for beef. It is pronounced vitello. You know wine, fish and chicken. The others are bistecca for steak, gamberoni for shrimp, and panino for sandwich. Everything here is cooked in olive oil, and the olives are made into a delicious paté, which we spread on our sandwiches or eat as an appetizer."

Knowing he would not remember, Bob asked. "Would you please write those words in English and in Italian?"

"Sure!" Siracusa said as he turned to the waiter and asked in Italian for a piece of paper. He wrote the words on the paper and handed it to Bob.

"You originally said that your place here in Agrigento was your summer place. Where is your home the rest of the year?" Bob asked.

"I reside in Palermo. I have a food export company. Or should I say had one. The Italian and German Forces occupation and the war have completely closed me down. I still do some business with some of the local merchants. The farmers have some products that were not destroyed by the bombing and fighting, but are not sure what tomorrow will bring. That is the reason why I came over to check on my southern beach place," Siracusa sadly replied.

"We know, we know, we would like to take a look at your place and maybe we could rent it from you so as to give you a little money during these hard times. We do not know how long we will be staying here in Sicily, but we know the future calls for us to be ready to fight the Jerry's on the mainland. So, we want to enjoy the times we have available to us. Let's go see your place," Bob said as they got up and left the restaurant.

As they walked outside, Siracusa said, "You men are generous. You have risked your lives to free us from them and now you want to help me. Remember, this restaurante will always served good food. My place is down that next street. We can walk the short distance."

"No, Alfredo, jump up on the truck with me and my driver will drive wherever you tell him too," Sergeant Steele said as he stepped up onto the back bed of the Army truck.

They rode around the corner and down the street to his street and turned left on the beach road rising some fifty feet above the rolling sea. The breeze was from the south off the water. The driver stopped when instructed.

Jumping off the truck and walking around the beach house to the cliff over looking the beach, Bob said, "Bet this place was very active a few weeks ago when our forces came ashore."

"Si, Senor! I imagine it was very loud here." Siracusa replied.

"Have they removed all of the land mines along the shoreline yet?" Bob asked?

"The other day I was startled and thrown against the wall when your ordnance regiment blew up a pile of the land mines on down the beach a ways that they had accumulated. I thought the war had began again until I went outside and found a man that had been warned that the land mines were going to be destroyed at a certain time. Those Krauts were here a long time and took advantage of that time to lay them everywhere. I hope that the experts find them all and destroy them. Yet, I imagine our people will accidentally step on them for years to come, just like the horror stories from Europe after The Great War where innocent children and grown-ups were either killed or mangled for life."

"Yes, Siracusa, some of our buddies have died from them. It is not a pretty site to witness."

All went inside and look around the nice furnished beach cottage. *We could bring some of the girls back in Palermo over here and enjoy ourselves.* Sergeant Steele thought.

"How much do you want for renting it for the next month?" Bob asked in his newly found Italian negotiating voice.

Just like his true spirit and from years of trading for food products, Siracusa replied. "Whatever you wish. I leave it up to you and your men."

"How about some US dollars? They are worth a lot now. We don't have very many liras," Bob responded.

Sheepishly, Siracusa replied. "Dollars would be good. I think I might be able to use them."

"OK, here is fifty dollars rent money for the next month. We want to be able to rent it for another month if we have not shipped out."

"Thank you, thank you. I will have one of my laundry girls come by each week and clean your laundry items. Her name is Rosita."

"You have a deal," Bob said smiling and thinking about the fun times ahead for him.

Upon completing the survey of the yard and walking down the rocks to the beach and checking things out, Sergeant Steele and his three buddies jumped into the truck and drove back across the island to their barracks near Palermo.

On the drive back, Bob told his buddies, Cpl. Dennis Shoulders, Privates Johnny Coskey and Bert Hawkins to keep their secret rendezvous among themselves. Dennis, Johnny and 'Hawk' agreed not to share their find with anyone.

Many of the Divisions in the US Fifth Army shipped out on September 9th, 1943 for the beach landing near Salerno.

Fortunately for Sergeant Steele and his company, they were left to train in Sicily and spent Christmas time with local friends and enjoy the special meal, including both vino bianco and vino rosso, prepared by the families.

TREASURES OF WAR – CONCEALED BY THE EVIL ONES / 192

Lieutenant Galloway was awarded several accommodation medals and received his captain bars. He was glad to see Sergeant Steele recover fully from his wounds.

Midnight on January 20th, 1944, Capt. Galloway entered the barracks and gave the orders.

"Men, prepare for the immediate embarkment of Sicily and fall in at 03:00 in front of station 44. You will be seated on the trucks for transportation to the troop ship at the port. The U. S. Fifth Army and the British Eighth Army that had left here four months ago are battling their way northward in Italy. One of our objectives is not to allow the Krauts to attack them from the rear. The enemy will have to defend their rear from our inland advance from Anzio."

It was a beautiful and warm day with very few clouds in the sky when the commands were given, "man your landing crafts."

When that front landing ramp was lowered into the calm beachfront sea, every Infantryman that ever rushed out into the potential machinegun fire wants to make it to shore and not be cut in half by the enemy guns. The German resistance was very light, not what had been expected, and Sergeant Steele and his company advanced some four miles inland at the end of the day.

Captain Galloway gathered his men together and set up camp.

"Sergeant Steele, how many men did we lose?"

"All have been accounted for and Private Hawkins has a flesh wound to his left arm. The medics have treated him and think he will be fine tomorrow. We were blessed today," Sergeant Steele replied.

"All of you men need to dig in before you bed down tonight. We have obviously surprised the Germans today, and they now know we are here. The 33rd Field Hospital and 96th Evacuation Hospitals landed today and are setting up operations near the beach. Many of our LST's have returned to Sicily to bring more men and supplies to us for our march to Rome. Although you may have some questions, unless they are critical, save them for later," Captain Galloway ordered.

In the successful landing of Allied Forces under the command of Major General John Lucas of the US Army VI Corps amounting to some 35,000 plus men, supplies and tanks, trucks and artillery weapons behind the German defense line across Italy forced the Krauts to regroup and return a large number of artillery, tanks and infantrymen supported by the Luftwaffe aircraft. Field Marshal Kesselring order his Commanders to block all roads that led from Anzio to Alban Hills, the next targeted invasion town on the Allied Forces plans. By mid morning on January 22nd battalions from five divisions were on their way to Anzio. Field Marshal Kesselring wanted to stop the advancing Allied Forces before they made an easy breakthrough at Alban Hills without much opposition all the way to Rome. To his surprise, his commanders sent messages in the early evening of the 22nd from 12 miles from the Anzio beachhead. Kesselring could not believe why the Allied Forces had not pushed forward when very little resistance existed. Battle hardened troops moved into excellent defensive positions.

Nobody understood why General Lucas made the decision not to speed onward from the successful surprise landing inland. He made one of the crucial mistakes in the Battle for Italy and World War II.

On the 24th, the day at Anzio began by hearing the German bombs falling all around them. Then, the long-range artillery, most likely the 88's, and mortar shells came raining down on the beachhead causing many casualties on shore and sinking a destroyer offshore.

During the night, while the Medical Staff and nurses were evacuating the casualties several Luftwaffe pilots came flying down pass the beachfront and dropped their bombs on two of the Red Cross marked and clearly lighted hospital ships making direct hits and sinking one of them.

Captain Galloway and Sergeant Steele witnessed this barbaric and cowardly act upon these defenseless wounded soldiers, doctors and nurses.

Sergeant Steele and his squad had entrenched themselves on a plateau near the Mussolini Canal overlooking the beach to the rear of them and directly beneath the enemy up above them. The next few days the Jerries counterattack was a constant shelling all day and into the night. The German officers chose to make a stand from the rugged hillsides surrounding the beachhead. Field Marshal Kesselring had plenty of supplies and ammunition with more coming in by the hour and was ready for a long battle. His main defensive line covered the total distance of the beachhead, complete with several German divisions, leaving no position open to flanking maneuvers. Relentless mortar attack onto the Americans forced them to take cover and move around in the mud and new artillery shell craters. Sergeant Steele's platoon was pinned down and receiving many casualties by the hour. He noticed a farmhouse off to his left that the Germans were using as a communication center directing the artillery and mortar fire to American positions. Having a few men in his platoon spread out and follow him, he led them to the farmhouse without any casualties. Upon receiving soft spoken orders from Sergeant Steele, each man followed him as he ran by the two windows on the east side of the farmhouse and tossing one grenade in each downstairs window and one through the upstairs windows. They immediately took cover along the base of the building and waited to see the expected counterattack. There was none and Sergeant Steele and his men cautiously took over the farmhouse. Once inside, they found all of the Germans dead and the radio equipment destroyed on the first floor. As they started upstairs, the two Kraut soldiers who had been deafened dazed and wounded by the repeated grenade blasts attempted to come down the stairs with bayonets drawn. Their wild shots did not hit Steele or any of his men. They returned fire and killed the remaining enemy soldiers.

Sergeant Steele set up a routine of constant patrolling from at least one window on each side of the farmhouse. He knew that it would not be too long before the news that the communication center in the farmhouse was silent or had been eliminated by the Americans. This would bring a tank or platoon of Krauts to investigate the situation. Unfortunately, Steele did not have a radioman with him to let the brass back on the beachhead and offshore know of the captured farmhouse.

Sergeant Steele turned to Cpl. Shoulders and ordered him, "Dennis find me a platoon radioman back toward the canal and tell the platoon leader that we are here and need his radioman and equipment. If you find one already dead and his equipment is working, check it out by communicating a message of our position to the brass or anyone. You bring the working radio back to me as soon as possible. From up here we can make a difference and let the guys know when and where some of the Kraut tanks are moving around and where they will come up over the train tracks, dunes and canal levee. Give it your best zig-zag run. If enemy fire starts up around you, drop down and dig in until you feel ready again. This is important. We need to keep this foothold."

"Ok Sarge, I am faster with my tommygun. I will leave my other weapons here. I need to be as light as possible."

"Excellent! I need you back here. You are too valuable to me. We have been through so much over here."

"Thanks Sarge!"

Calculating the most circumspect time, Cpl. Shoulders slowly crawled over to a trench and worked his way back to the American's position. Upon reaching his company commander, Captain Galloway, he pointed out on the battlefield map Sergeant Steele's position in the farmhouse above the east-west canal and west of Mussolini Canal between Conco and Cisterna.

"How in the world did you men make it up that far and capture that farmhouse?" Galloway asked in astonishment. "Let me radio Operations and tell them of his position immediately," the Captain added.

"Sarge led the five remaining in his platoon. Steele told us that we could just sit in the mud holes and get hit by the mortars and die or fight the Krauts and possibly take some of them with us. We all knew what he wanted to do and we followed him. The ten Germans must have been looking out the windows on the opposite side of the farmhouse that we attacked or someone fell asleep on watch. We killed all of them and knocked out the communication center they set up," Shoulders exhaustingly replied.

"What do you need Corporal?"

"Sergeant Steele ordered me to bring back a radioman to transmit messages back here and to Operations of the enemies movements of tanks, artillery and mortar locations."

"At early, early light tomorrow morning, you work your way back to the farmhouse with Lt. Rihn of the 36th Division and his four new men, Cpl. Anderson, Privates Benson, Stevens, Seamur. These men have some battlefield experiences in North Africa and another part of the Sicily campaign. All of these men have forward observers experience and the necessary equipment. Tell Sarge that Lt. Rihn will take over the command of the post. You need to bed down in these fresh dry blankets tonight and get some rest between their mortar rounds tonight. May God be with you and the men tonight and on your mission in the morning, stick to the plan and contact me as soon as you reach your position at the farmhouse," Captain Galloway ordered.

Lt. Ryo Rihn   Pvt. Bill Benson   Pvt. Syd Stevens
1944--Anzio, Italy -- Forward Observers --
Photo Courtesy William "Bill" F. Benson--36th Division

Early in the morning of the 30th, the weather was to the advantage of Lt. Rihn, Cpls. Anderson and Shoulders, Privates Benson, Stevens and Seamur. They made their way north up the Mussolini Canal past the east west canal entrance and turned northwest across the battlefield lined with mortar and artillery shell craters. The fog and low clouds early in the morning prevented their movement from the normal Luftwaffe Messerschmidt's strafing each morning as they came in over the hills from the north.

The large build up of the German troops from the region and from as far as north of Rome down to the high ground above Anzio allowed the Germans an excellent view of the entire beachhead. So the efforts of Sergeant Steele to establish a communication outpost with Lt. Rihn and his men of the 36th Infantry Division was a defensive victory of sorts for the static Operation 'SHINGLE' at Anzio under General Lucas.

Several weeks went by and the men of the VI Corps fought to save the five to seven miles inland of shoreline that it held and defend the Port of Anzio. Then, on February 16th, the Krauts launched their all out attack against the VI Corps in an attempt to drive them back into the sea. With only a few undamaged motorized infantry, armor and tank destroyers brought to the front, the men were forced to dig in, insert their bayonets for man to man combat and fight some of the most furious combat ever known to man. Lt. Rihn and the forward observers ordered a steady mortar attack on the advancing German machinegun nest, mortar and artillery positions. The standing orders were to repel all counterattacks and force the enemy to withdraw from any gains, but do not chase them beyond current positions held.

On February 22nd, on orders from Lt. Gen. Mark W. Clark and because General Alexander thought General Lucas was tired, worn out, exhausted and defeated, Lucas was relieved from command of the VI Corps one month after the landing at Anzio.

For the next four long months the VI Corps continued to courageously dig in and fight under the dominating high ground position of the Germans. Occasionally, some of the troops were ordered to attack certain positions and advance. Often, the Americans fought their way forward only to be ambushed from both flanks. Repeatedly, the field radiomen called for specific support of their battle location. More often than not, the support never came. Many American platoons were entirely wiped out or only a few survived. The Germans were so organized it frustrated the US Squad leaders who were losing their men in every skirmish.

The main German defenses near the city of Campaleone were built around the 29th Panzergrenadier and 26th Panzer Divisions with the rest drawn from Generalfeldmarschall Albrecht Kesselring Army Group C. Their positions were organized in considerable depth but lacked good lines of supply and reinforcement.

On the morning of April 12th, a combination of men from the 91st Infantry Division and the 36th Infantry Division fomented a surprise action against the most recent German counterattack in two directions at once using the newly arrived support equipment including the flamethrowers. Sergeant Bob Steele charged a key enemy position and destroyed a machine gun nest with hand grenades. He frantically motioned for his flamethrower gunner to come to his location. Steele pointed to a bunker of German soldiers firing mortar rounds toward the beach at the Americans. He gave the order to pull the trigger on the flamethrower. The hidden enemy foothold did not remain hidden, the long flame of death arced and hit two enemy bunkers immediately creating a blazing inferno and exploding ammunitions. Those Krauts not instantly killed came jumping out of the bunker entirely engulfed in flames. The screams from these men on fire could be heard several hundred yards around the battlefield. All of a sudden the enemy began appearing everywhere with hands raised and white flags on the end of their rifles.

The most immediate American objective was to conquer the enemy at Albono and open up the road to Rome and deal with the threat of the Germans retreating to fight at another more organized battlefield in Rome or beyond. The port city of Anzio was thirty-five miles due south of Rome. Major General Lucian K. Truscott, Jr. believed that the need to concentrate on a logistical base at Albans Hill for all American activities had first priority.

The German Luftwaffe began to counterattack with low flying strafing of the advancing American Troops. Our battalion learned that the best way to stop these attacks was to take our machine guns, elevate them, fire a stream of rapid fire, and hit the flying target with a few of the bullets. Also, some of our new men brought ack-ack guns ashore to the front lines. These were very good weapons against the low flying Messerschmidts. It was important to knock down all of them and prevent them from returning to their bases with our advancing troop's positions.

I slept in a mortar crater wrapped in my blanket. Early on the morning of May 3rd, mortar shells blasted my Company. Private Coskey was hit. He screamed. I jumped over to his trench. His right leg was torn off. I grabbed him and picked him up and ran across the open field several hundred yards dodging mortar shells landing nearby and around craters until I got clear of the position being attacked and finally made it to the medics. They lifted him from my arms and laid him on a cot and immediately gave him a shot of morphine to stop some of the excruciating pain. As I watched, they knew exactly what to do. They trimmed his right thigh, cutting off all the parts tangling down and bandaged up his stump leg. As I turned to leave knowing one of my men was alive, this nurse pulled down her surgery mask from her face and rushed over to my side and softly told me that they needed to take a look at the back of my left leg. Fresh blood was seeping though my pant's leg and from around the area where my left pant's leg was tucked into my boot. It was not from the Pvt. Coskey's splattered blood as I carried him.

The Army Nurse sat me on the side of a field hospital bed, and I loosened my belt, unzipped my pants, and pulled them down. Sure enough, the nurse was correct. I looked around and could see that I had received some kind of flesh wounds in my hip and thigh. I guess I was so scared and concerned for Coskey, I had not felt anything.

Army Doctors and Nurses laid me down and gave me some local pain injections and fished around to determine that all I needed was some medication to prevent infection and sewed up where the bullet went in and out for two different holes. I attempted to talk the Colonel over the field hospital to let me go back to the front with my Company. He learned from the nurses that I had admitted the freshly healed shrapnel wound that I received in Sicily. He insisted that I needed to go with the other wounded evacuees for transportation to a hospital in Naples. The hospital ship was very pleasant, mainly because the Army Nurses were so caring for every one of us. I told them that my most recent sweetie was an Army Nurse by the name of Lt. Sallie Cotton from Missouri that I met back on Sicily. One of the nurses, Lt. Mary Broussard, from New Orleans, Louisiana, knew Sallie from Lillie Jollie School of Nursing at Memorial Hospital back in Houston, Texas.

I felt like I was not supposed to be with the brave men that they had to carry off the ship and to the hospital in Naples. Those warriors had received wounds that would affect them for the rest of the their lives. Some had no legs and arms. Some had their bodies wrapped from head to toe from explosive burns. Some had been shot through the face and their eyes destroyed beyond replacement. Some had their private parts blown away. I just hoped that their families would accept them and truly understood what they had given up for their freedom.

Every day or so, the US Army Burial detail would perform their solemn duties and carry out those brave men and women that had died. I could not help myself wondering, *who were the blessed ones, the dead or the critically wounded that would live the rest of their lives severely handicapped.* I admired those guys on burial duty. They were some of my heroes. I saw a lot of field battles with some dramatic acts of heroism, but these guys had to do this duty every day for months at a time. When they came into my hospital ward, they would stop and talked to the most critically wounded and cheer them up. Then, go to the bed and quietly remove the dead comrade.

It was time for me to sit down and write my Mom. I had not received mail call for several months and needed to know what if anything she had heard from my POW brother, Dub. The nurses supplied me with an occasional magazine and newspaper. I learned that the Allies were winning some battles in the Pacific, but nothing was mentioned about the Japanese POW camps.

After writing Mom, I asked Nurse Lt. Brossard to mail the letter and find out the current whereabouts of Lt. Sallie Cotton and whether her military address had changed from Sicily. Later in the evening, Lt. Brossard looked me up in the lounge area where I was reading and told me that Sallie had been assigned to the 12th Evacuation Hospital Tent Hospital in England.

"If you want to write Lt. Cotton, give me the letter and I will put into the proper mail pouch and she should receive it in a week," Lt. Brossard kindly offered.

"Thank you Lieutenant. Sounds like she is getting ready for the northern campaign. You gals are so brave and put yourselves in danger every day," Sergeant Steele replied.

"Yes, I have heard a few air raid sirens since coming over here. You should keep the northern campaign and your units campaign information out of any of your letters, but you can send my best regards to her. Tell her that she and I need to get together after we win this war at the lunch counter at Woolworth's on Travis Street in Houston. We used to walk the few blocks to Woolworth's and enjoy a break from our nurse's training. She and I made our plans as to which boy we would accept a date or blind date from to go to the Majestic Theater near the nursing school on the weekends. The nursing school was strict. We could go out only on the weekends and had to answer roll call by 22:00. She and I had to jump out of our date's car and run to the desk and check in just before or at 22:00 more than one time. The guys wanted to sit out in their cars and fog up the windows during the winter months, and never could understand the 22:00 roll call time on the weekends," Lt. Brossard explained.

"Sounds like you gals learned military defensive tactics during nurse's training," Bob jokingly replied.

"You bet, with some of those guys we had to use more than military defensive tactics. We learned in our nurse anatomy courses about some of the more sensitive organs of the male body in case we needed to weaken the opponent's offensive tactics," Lt. Nurse Brossard said laughing as she turned to leave to make her rounds.

I need to go get some more paper and write Sallie. I must let her know that someone loves her very much and wants to spend the rest of his life with her when this mess is over, I thought as I walked back to my hospital ward.

The next day Pvt. Johnnie Coskey came by my ward in a wheel chair and told me that he had received orders to transfer to a rehab hospital back home. "Sarge, my hospital ship will be at the docks tomorrow and I will be on board. I know that you don't think you are a hero, but you will be my hero forever. I now know that I would have bleed to death if you had not done what you did back there on that battlefield. I guarantee you, my first born son will be named Robert," Private Coskey emotionally said.

"Johnnie, if it had been me I know that you would have done the same. One of these days when we win this ugly war and you and your future wife have that first son, you had better let me know it. Being a Godfather to your son will be a true honor for me. I will come and visit you and see the handsome young child," Sergeant Steele guaranteed Private Coskey as he bowed down and hugged him in his wheel chair.

After writing my letters to Mom and Sallie, I sought out the medical doctors to obtain my release from the hospital and orders to return to the front lines with my Platoon. Later that evening I saw Colonel Shofner, one of the chief surgeons at the Naples Hospital, coming from the wings of the hospital. I walked up to him and saluted him and asked him for a moment of his time. He was very gracious and listened to my emotional request to get back to the fighting. I explained that I had a brother in a POW Camp in Japan and wanted to defeat the Germans so that I could go to the Pacific and free him.

Most of my wounds were completely healed and I saw no reason to pass my time at the Hospital when I could be helping my men do their job of driving the Krauts out of Italy. Col. Shofner agreed to release me for returning on the next Hospital Ship to Anzio.

"When you arrive at beach headquarters at Anzio, let me know what Lt. Col. Adamson thinks about the need for you to rejoin your unit. If he gives his approval, you need to follow his orders. He has a better feel for current campaign movement and conditions," Col. Shofner deliberately ordered.

"Sounds good, Colonel. I really appreciate your understanding my urgent purpose to do something to finish this war here as soon as possible and volunteer for the front lines in the Pacific War," Sergeant Steele reiterated.

"No problem, I see your point. Maybe you need to slow down and not take as many chances when you are fighting the Krauts. What good will you be to your brother if you get wiped out here? I understand that we have them on the run and pushed them north of Rome," Shofner insisted.

"What do you mean? When the Allies win the northern invasion and together with our great offensive maneuvers from down here will squeeze those Krauts until they cannot find a way out. Most of the bloody battles are over. I will be back in the States by September 1st. If I had any money I would bet you on the merits of that statement," Bob eagerly replied.

"Okay. I pray that you are one thousand percent correct in your predictions. You know what goes on here and all the changed lives crawling around." Colonel Shofner replied as he shook his head and signed the battlefield assignment orders for Sergeant Steele.

Early the next morning, June 25th, I took a troop truck to the docks and boarded the returning Hospital ship for the voyage to Anzio. As I went ashore, it was very noticeable that the beach was not under attack as it was when I left for Naples Hospital six weeks earlier. I reported to 91st Infantry Division headquarters. I asked the desk sergeant, "I need to give my orders to Lt. Col. Adamson for his review before heading for the 362nd Infantry Regiment location and Captain Galloway's Battalion."

"Lt. Col. Adamson is in an officer's meeting until at least 14:00. Is this your first time here at Anzio?" the desk Sergeant asked.

"No Sir. I was here with the initial landing forces and led my Platoon to the forward observation post during four months of fighting until I was wounded and sent back to the Hospital at Naples."

"You must have nightmares about those frantic days of battle. I just arrived from the states as a logistic replacement. Why don't you go over to the canteen and relax for a few hours until Col. Adamson returns? I will be sure that he knows you have returned. In fact, I will come over to the canteen and get you for your meeting with him."

Sergeant Steele nodded as he asked where the canteen was located. Later in the afternoon the desk Sergeant came to check the whereabouts of Sergeant Steele.

"Sergeant Steele, I have some good news. Col. Adamson will see you at 15:30 in his office. He is looking forward to meeting you and reviewing your transfer orders."

"Thanks Sergeant."

Upon reporting to Col. Adamson's office, I was immediately welcomed into his office. After formalities, I handed him my orders from Col. Shofner.

"At ease Sergeant Steele. My desk Sergeant told me some things about you and your experiences here and where you want to relocate. Let me begin by some very sad news. Captain Galloway was killed during some very strong counterattacks some three weeks ago. Your new commanding officer for your Regiment is Lt. Col. Jordan."

"Man oh man, wow, terrifying, Captain Galloway and I went through some fierce encounters together. I cannot believe he is gone. I am in total shock. How did it happen?"

"I understand that he was hit by a 88-mm shell."

"Thank God he did not suffer."

"Sergeant, I will find the exact location of your unit and let you know day after tomorrow at 09:00. In the meantime, I have assigned you to tent number 780."

"Yes Sir."

Colonel Adamson realizes that I need some time to get my head clear from the tragic and sudden news of Captain Galloway's death.

Three days later, I received my orders to hitch a ride on one of the US Fifth Army's replacement troop transports up the west coast road of Italy north west of Rome to Grosseto. As the truck pulled up at the tent camp the new troops apparently wanted a veteran to show them the way. One of the men opened the cab door and told me to lead the way. I learned from the truck driver that most of these men had never had any combat experience. When we had traveled some seven or eight miles inland on the road through the battlefield, I noticed that the old farmhouse that I had used as a forward observer's position at the time Pvt. Coskey and I received our wounds had been leveled by enemy mortar or artillery fire. I had a very peculiar feeling to see this site, remembering that Captain Galloway had sent me some men and equipment to battle the Krauts. We passed over the famous Alban Hills area on our way to Rome. Everywhere I looked you could see the scars of some furious and savage battles. The farmhouses had been ravaged and most of the store buildings in the towns were in ruin. A few of the survivors did not known what to do or where to go, and remained on their farms with only a few scattered livestock and tools for starting over again. Most of the innocent civilians were traveling along the roads with just about everything personal possession that they owned wrapped in some type of bedspread or the like. However, they would turn to us as we passed and give us a big joyous smile and wave to let us know they were happy to know the Germans had been driven out of their land.

I asked the driver to stop a few times when I noticed that some young boys and girls without parents were walking along the dusty road. I told the men on our truck not to go to near them to prevent the possibility of disease transfer. It was an event that touched your heart to see some of them in wartime conditions. Most all of us left as much food and some chocolates as we could spare with them along the roadside and waved to them. They scrambled to get the food.

As we traveled north of Rome through the town of Bracciano a few German snipers began firing at the truck convoy. I told the driver to pull to the left side of the road and stop. I grabbed my tommygun and slowly opened my door and ran to the other side of the road and took cover in the ditch. I shouted for the men to take cover on the other side of the truck. I worked my way behind a fallen tree to get a better look at the snipers location. When the first sniper raised his head to fire at the truck, I waited for the second sniper to come out from the terrace. He used his rapid-fire weapon and opened up on the far ditch in an attempt to kill the men. Before he could duck down in the terrace, I opened up with my tommygun striking him in the chest. The force of the blast tossed him backward. Almost immediately, the other sniper through up his hands and surrendered. I shouted for one of the new Infantrymen to run forward down the road about 30 yards and draw his weapon and come in from the other flank to be sure there were only two snipers. Fortunately, these two enemy stragglers were the only Krauts left behind to attempt to slow our forward supply efforts coming up this road.

"Sergeant Steele, you taught us some important lessons today. Hey, you have some blood on your pants leg. You must have been hit. Medic, Medic, front and center," the Platoon's Lieutenant pointed toward his calf and called for the Medic in his gung ho voice.

Looking down at my right leg I noticed a slight flesh wound. I had felt something nick me as I made my way to the fallen tree.

"Lt. you need to bring the prisoner over here and interrogate him. We need to know when his battalion moved out and which direction they were going. Don't leave those weapons over there for someone else to come along and use. You need to assign a detail to bury the dead sniper on the edge of the field and mark his site with a stick with his helmet on it." Steele issued his experienced advice to the Lieutenant.

More confidently aware of the fact a war was going on all around them the replacement troops and I drove up the west coast road until we entered the town of Grosseto. Since my orders were specific to locate my Battalion and the new replacements had their separate orders to relieve certain other fighting men, I asked them to drop me off near the center of town. After asking a few of the American Troops where my 362nd Infantry Regiment was set up, I caught a ride in a jeep to our campsite. The first guy from my Platoon that I ran into was Cpl. Shoulders.

"Sergeant welcome back. Sir I have really missed you and your comradeship these past couple of months. I guess you heard about Captain Galloway. He fought a gallant fight saving his men and wiping out many of the enemy," Shoulders emotionally announced.

"Yes, I was told before I left Anzio. Sergeant Dennis Shoulders, congratulations, Sarge. They waited too long to promote you."

"Thanks Bob."

"Where is this Col. Jordan?"

"Bob, let me take you to his temporary office in an old Catholic School building."

"He ain't no Captain Galloway. You better get used to his way of fighting this war. He likes his men to go ahead of him," Sergeant Shoulders advised Bob.

"How are Sergeant Culpepper, Private Bert 'Hawk' Hawkins, and the other men in my old Platoon?" Bob asked.

"Sergeant Culpepper received a field commission and is now a 2nd Lieutenant with his own artillery Platoon. You will see 'Hawk' later tonight. The casualty rate for our men is forty percent. Killed in action, twenty-five percent and the rest wounded," Dennis regretfully elaborated.

"What happened to Pvt. Coskey?"

"The physical wound healed, but you and I know that he will live the remainder of his life without that leg and the emotionally scars from not having one. He recovered and was shipped back to the states on one of the many Hospital Ships. He was very gracious to me and told me that his first born son would be named after me," Sergeant Steele said turning to Dennis with a grin.

"I am happy for him to be able to get out of this inhumane war."

The men walked up the sidewalk to the Old Catholic school building partially bomb out by the Luftwaffe and into the hallway outside Lt. Col. Jordan's temporary office. Upon learning that the Colonel was in an officer's meeting both men sat in some wooden chairs and waited for him to come out. Some fifty-five minutes later, Sergeant Steele was introduced to Lt. Col. Jordan. The Colonel received his orders from Col. Adamson to report to his Platoon.

"What is that blood on your pants leg?" Jordan asked pointing.

"Oh, it was a little nick by a Kraut sniper along the road from Anzio. The medic gave me a tetanus booster and bandaged it. No problems, I am fine." Steele deliberately replied.

"I don't want any crippled men up here. Sergeant Shoulders show Steele where his space is in any of your tents."

"Yes Sir!"

Sergeant Shoulders and Steele did an about face and doubled timed it out of the building.

"I see exactly what you mean. He wants to keep a wall between him and his men. I got a job to do and won't let that stop me. This is the first sinister commander that I have had." Steele suggested.

Everybody was going over the Arno and Gothic Line Campaigns to the north with our next major skirmish the Port City of Livorno. Being a part of Truscott's US Fifth Army, our main objective was to gain control of the Port. It would be the first northern Italy port captured by the Allies. US Intelligence estimated Jerry's strength at less than 5,000. The plans called for the US Fourth Army to move north up the west coast road four days ahead of Truscott's troops.

On the afternoon of July 5th, 1944 US Fifth Army moved out northward toward the town of Gavarrauo just below some high ground up on the eastside of the road. The enemy defensive positions were strung out along a thin line between Roccastrada and Cannetto.

Apparently, the German high command out smarted our commanders and let US Fourth Army go north without engaging them. The unmolested 4th made it to Cecina before encountering fierce resistance. The Germans planned on out flanking them from the rear, but here enters the US Fifth Army from the south. For the next several days the 5th was battered from the eastern hill and mountain positions. Some of the caves made for excellent strongholds and the large rock boulders fortified their machine gun nest.

When the US Fourth Army in the north desired to move from Cecina eastward toward Florence they fared much better. They had called in Allied air support to destroy any Kraut counterattack forces. As the military plans called for, the Americans fought their way across the mountains down into the valleys south of Florence to await for other Allied troops to make the big push across the Arno River.

Gradually, the US Fifth Army fought through a few German positions to reach critical high ground. Ordered to move eastward away from the initial north route to Livorno and force a left flank attack penetration to force the Jerries to retreat over the mountains toward the US Fourth Army's and British Eighth Army positions. The US Army Air Force's P-51 and P-40 fighters strafed the enemy's critical machine gun positions.

The US Fifth Army was now free to proceed with the capture of Livorno. By the time they arrived, the opposition forces consisted of a few remnants of German defenders. On July 18th, General Truscott and his US Fifth Army liberated Livorno (Leghorn).

By the middle of July 1944, General Truscott's US Fifth Army had liberated the City of Livorno (Leghorn). During the time his troops were reorganizing and bringing fresh supplies through the captured Italian northwest coast port city, Lt. Colonel Jordan made a rare barrack's check in the port warehouse building and learned that Sergeant Robert Steele had received another grazing scalp wound. He summoned Sergeant Steele to his offices. Upon arriving the Colonel attempted to lay down the law.

"Sergeant Steele, you have been wounded four times in this war. I am going to issue orders for you to return to the Field Hospital down at Anzio or get on the first Hospital Ship that arrives here in Livorno."

"Colonel, I am not injured enough to prevent me from carrying out my duties."

"Your opinion is not what I base my decision. I base it on the book training that I obtained at military schools while growing up. Any wounded soldier should be prevented from front line duty. You will not return to the front lines. Do you understand?"

"Colonel, I have a brother that was captured in 1942 before I came over here. He survived the Death March of Bataan. He is somewhere in a POW Camp in Japan. Not you or anyone else is going to keep me from doing my part on the front lines to end this war over here as quick as possible and my getting assigned to the Pacific to whipped the Japs and free my brother. Do you understand?"

The startled Colonel replied, "Sergeant, my orders will be final."

"Colonel, do you have an older brother that you are very fond of and did everything together as you struggled through hard times growing up? Did he give you the shirt off his back? Did you and he go fishing at the river and camp out all weekend? I bet you are one of those kids that had everything and do not know what brotherly love is all about. Didn't you say a military school? Was this high school? You despise men like me. One of the rich kids, huh?

As the Colonel put his nose directly into my face and grabbed me by my shoulders, he said, "Steele, do not force me to have you thrown in the brink."

"You can have me court-martialled or whatever. This is not the front lines and no legitimate fighting officer would ever throw me out of the US Army because of your claims."

In frenzy, the Colonel grabbed my left bicep and spun me around and shoved me toward the door.

My reactions were natural. I whirled around and threw a combination right and left to his jaw, knocking him to the floor.

"Private Steele, you have just lost your stripes. You want to fight so much, try it as a private for the rest of your military career."

After the altercation with Colonel Jordan, I was assigned to Sergeant Shoulder's Platoon. It could have been worse, but I was determined to stay on the front lines and fight. The Engineering Regiments were performing miracles at the port. Within less than ten days, the US Navy ships came in from the Ligurian Sea, now patrolled and under the control of the US Navy, to the port. The US Navy Freighters and LCT's were unloading mass amounts of military equipment and some new replacement troops. You did not have to be a genius to understand that a strong push north to Germany was in store for us. My new Platoon leader was Major Lindsey. He seemed to be a fair and intelligent leader. Time would tell. In some of our Platoon meetings he told us that the US Fifth Army Command had changed its initial plans to cut off the Germans allowing the Krauts to escape north and organize with eight divisions from outside of Italy. But, we had accomplished some great feats in our push to Livorno. Our next objective was Arno River crossing. Major Lindsey told us that the French Moroccan Troops and the British Eighth Army had gallantly fought the German positions north along the Adriatic Sea Coast and Central Italian across the Italian Peninsula.

On August 23rd, Major Lindsey entered our barracks and told us the fun was over and we were moving out against the Germans across the Arno River and on to Bolgona. Our mission was to push them from our left flank toward the center of the Italian Peninsula and crush through the famous Gothic Line of German Defense. Intelligence had briefed him and he told us that four of those eight Kraut divisions had been withdrawn back to Germany because our guys were winning the many battles in France, Germany and elsewhere. He also reminded us that the Jerries were desperate and wanted to make these battles last until the forthcoming winter months stopped the fighting. This would give them time to regroup.

August 25th, 1944, my orders were to move out. I was not used to my new rank of Private. The scattered German defense attacked us near the crossing of the Arno River. With three divisions of troops and plenty of tanks, two tracks, artillery guns, and mortar units we destroyed the enemy quickly. After crossing the river at the town of Pisa, my unit came under machine gun fire from on top of an old building. The Krauts had used sand bags and some bricks to defend the excellent high position. All of us were pinned down. I noticed that the backside of their position was not fortified at all. They must have run out of sand bags or something. I hollered at Major Lindsey and motioned to him that I was going to work my way around to the backside. Major Lindsey gave me thumbs up and ordered his men to open fire on the machine gun nest. Using this valuable time, I worked my way to the rear of the building and tossed grenade over the roof and wiped out the three Krauts.

All of us bedded down for the night in those warm US Army blankets. Maj. Lindsey came over to my ditch and told me that I deserved special recognition for saving many men.

I told him that it was my duty to do what I had done. It was my butt also.

For the next few weeks the 362nd Infantry Regiment, 91st Infantry Division fought its way toward Pistoia, Italy under heavy German counterattacks. There were bombed out German tanks all up and down the roads for several miles. Major Lindsey told us we had accomplished our goal to outflank the Germans Gothic Line and our next objective was to capture Futa Pass north of Florence. The mountains became our worst nightmare. The Jerries were deployed in the critical high positions. On September 9th, I was forced to take cover in a trench near a German stronghold. They were firing repeated rounds from their machine guns. The ground above me was being constantly splattered for some fifteen minutes at least.

They sure must be defending something very important ahead of us. The best way to kill these guys is with the flamethrower, I thought.

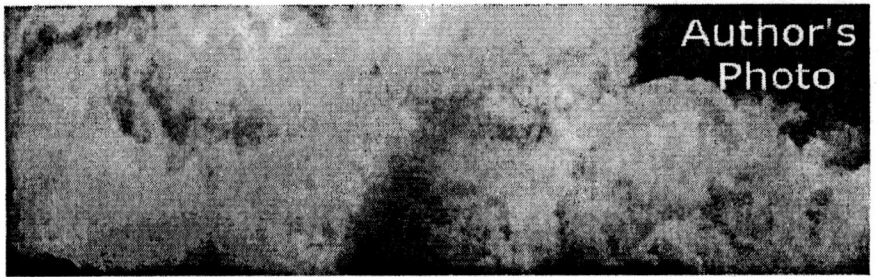

It was getting near dusk and my best choice would be to wait until it got dark. I motioned for the Platoon to stay put. Using a code word, flying horse, after dark I called for the flamethrower to join me. While waiting for Private Kidd to join me, the Krauts kept up a constant verbal barrage asking me to come on over and have something besides my cold rations to eat. One of them had very good English, but I had heard and seen that song and dance before. Private Kidd worked his way very quietly over to the trench. I asked him if he had every done this before. He said no. I pointed out exactly where I wanted him to fire the flamethrower. I told him after you follow my motion command, fire it and drop back down into the trench. Kidd was shaking so bad I wondered if he could pull the trigger and kill the enemy. Just first time jitters. When I gave the signal, he rose up and immediately pulled the trigger. The whole night sky lit up. The enemy's ammunition exploded like a 4th of July celebration back in Texarkana. All of the German soldiers in the machine gun nest had been killed and we won this little skirmish.

Next morning, no counterattacks for breakfast, the Jerries had retreated and I could see them in the far distance moving up into the mountains. Major Lindsey gathered all of his men together and told us to expect stiff resistance. As soon as the US Army Air Force completes its bombing raids and relays intelligence reports of the German Panzer Divisions locations, we must be ready to advance toward our targets. At 11:00 he gave the orders to cover the north side of the valley and move out. Sergeant Shoulders led his Platoon across the bottomland and we slowly advanced some eight miles receiving an occasional weak counterattack before nightfall. Major Lindsey and Sergeant Shoulders chose a cove up some two hundred feet above the valley floor on the northeastern side of the mountain for our campsite. It was a very good site and protected from direct shelling from the retreating enemy to the east.

At 06:00 on the morning of September 11th, Major Lindsey gave the intelligence report. We learned that the Germans had 88-mm long guns, the 16th SS Panzer Tank Division, mortars and machine gun nest located another four to five miles in front of us on both sides of the valley. Our orders were to clean out as many positions as possible and secure the number one stronghold guarding the narrow pass on the road to our targeted destination. He pointed out the crucial road junction at the town of Lorenzo. At 07:30 Sergeant Shoulders called our Platoon together. He checked to see that everyone had their complete supply of weapons and ammunition. Shortly thereafter, all was well and we moved out. With the aid of a few converted Italian guerillas that knew the mountains all their lives and that joined us during the night, we advanced a mile and half before the initial defensive fight of the Germans began.

Sure enough, the enemy's artillery shells constantly came exploding down on us. Additionally, the Italian perennial autumn rain poured down on us. The rough mountainous terrain together with the gumbo mud created some bad cases of 'here I am, shoot me' conditions. Some of our Division's Tank Battalions, Two Tracks motorized artillery units pulling 155-mm howitzers and 105-mm howitzers became sitting ducks for the well positioned Germans.

On September 12th, the US Army Air Force air strikes resumed due to much better weather. The fighting became more furious. Jerry mortar shells rained down on us. Casualties began to mount. The only thing we could do was returning a steady fire on the enemy positions. This forced the Krauts to slow the number of offensive attacks against us. Major Lindsey finally made contact with headquarters to learn of this morning's intelligence report. He called Sergeant Shoulders and I together and ordered us to concentrate on this one main enemy position on the other side of the valley.

"Major, I need to take four men including Private Kidd with his flamethrower with me. Sergeant you and everybody in the Division on this side of the valley must fire mortars, machine guns, rifles, and any artillery pieces not yet destroyed at that general area. Do not order any of our troops to open fire from the other side of the valley. I need the Krauts to be focused on this side of the valley," Steele announced.

"Steele, what are your plans?" Major Lindsey asked.

"I will lead our men down below our current position and over to the boxed canyon almost directly across from their position. We should be able to find cover there. Then, it is my intention to slowly crawl or walk in the high water in the canyon to the creek in the center of the valley," Steele further guaranteed the Major.

"Okay, you are now in the middle of the valley in a creek with rushing rainwater. What next?"

"If our men across the valley open up on them, the chances of us being seen will increase. From your constant shelling and firing from this position will keep them looking up here. I will lead the men up the other side to the rocks underneath that enemy position. From there I will play it by ear. I will destroy that critical location," Steele promised.

"Steele, the Jerries are up there on those peaks in some well-fortified concrete dug-outs and you are going to be exposed most of the time until you reach your destination. If you are successful in taking out that very critical position of the Krauts, you will surely save many lives and allow us to move forward to a less exposed position,"

Major Lindsey cautioned.

"They are picking us off like birds on a telephone line. Our casualties are mounting. I am ready to move out now. Moving out this evening will give us better cover with less bright sunlight," Steele replied.

"Good luck! Sergeant Shoulders, you and the other Platoons get into your positions and begin your constant firing to support these guys upon my command. Do not let up until I give the orders," Major Lindsey told his men.

I called my team together and told them to follow me only when I motioned them to move forward. Each man knew exactly what his duty was to capture the enemy's position. After the Battalion began firing just about every thing they had including mortars, I began working my way down the side of the mountain some 200 yards behind our troops location. Once all of us made it to the creek bottom in the valley, I slowly worked my way in front of our troops and on to beneath the Kraut's positions up on the opposite side of the mountain. Each of the men gradually made their way to my location. I took a very long look at the terrain up the side of the mountain to plan our safest route of attack. I had about another hour and half before nightfall to make my plans for movement during the night hours. There was a shallow ravine coming off the mountainside that could cause us problems should there be any Jerries hiding along the way up. I decided to wait until 01:00 to make the first phase up the mountain. I quietly told Pvt. Kidd with his flamethrower to take Bilnoski and Akins with him and move up the ravine watching for enemy soldiers until they reached the right side of the boulders some 30 yards below the target.

I told Kidd that Pvt. Saunders and I would work our way up to the left side of the boulders and wait until Major Lindsey located us and began the support firing in the morning. Pvt. Kidd, Bilnoski, Akins and Saunders and myself slowly crawled up the two routes and met about 03:30 on the exposed side of the boulders to the valley.

Here it is September 13th, 1944, and I am up here on this barren rocky hillside and outnumbered some 100 to 1. I got to figure out a way to fight our way up the ten to twenty yards closer to the Krauts fortified location and stop their assault on our Battalions across the valley. Will the enemy be able to shoot almost straight down the hillside at us if I toss a grenade from here and it lands outside their pillboxes? Surely they will immediately send someone to flush us out, I thought.

As the morning sun peaked over the mountains to slightly light up mountainsides all around us I got a better look at how I could lead our men to destroy this critical German location and move further through the mountains and on to Bologna. I told Kidd to follow me with his flamethrower around to the left front of the pillbox, which was away from our men across the valley. I am going to toss two grenades into the pillbox and as soon as they explode, I want you to stand up and pull the trigger and blast them with the flamethrower until he hears my command to stop. I told the other men to kill any Jerries that made a move away from the immediate area.

At 05:45 I attempted to locate Major Lindsey with my binoculars. Finally, I spotted his agreed upon location and signaled him by taking my mirror and directing the sunlight beam across the valley back and forth several times. It took them some four or five minutes to begin firing at the area above us. Now was the time for Pvt. Kidd and I to move out. I crawled off to the enemy's left flank over the rocky open hillside to approximately ten yards below the windows of the main German pillbox. Kidd, the rugged and extremely strong kid, was carrying the heavy flamethrower on his back and reached my location. After nodding to him and receiving his confirmation nod that he was ready, I stood up and tossed the one grenade into one window and the other grenade into another separate window of the pillbox and immediately dropped down. Both grenades exploded and Pvt. Kidd jumped up on the side of this hillside, braced himself, and pulled the trigger of his flamethrower until just about everything above us had exploded. The Germans must have had enough ammo to last three months.

My promise to Major Lindsey has been accomplished, I thought.

I signaled Major Lindsey to cease firing at the location and have his troops advance up the hillside on both sides of the valley. After the smoke had blown away from the mountain and as I gathered my men around me on the rim of the destroyed pillbox some of the German troops positioned all along their second defensive positions for the next mile or so along the high rim of the mountaintop began to open fire at us. Pvt. Bilnoski was stuck in the right leg. All of us were pinned down again. At the risk of life above and beyond the call of duty, I picked up my tommygun and quickly ran 20 yards up the barren but rocky hillside to a new and better position. After exchanging fire with the Germans and preventing repeated advancement attacks, I ordered my men to cover me with fire so I could move to a higher and better position to wipe out the enemy's nearest machine gun nest with 4 machine guns.

I fired a grenade from my rifle and hit one enemy's machine gun nest. The remaining German machine gunners opened up with burst after burst of concentrated fire on me. The bullets were zinging all around me with pieces of rocks almost covering my body. I remained calm during this barrage of constant firing.

I have three more grenades with me. I must choose a time to use them against the Krauts and protect my men from slaughter, I thought.

During a lull in the enemy firing, I rose to my knees and tossed one grenade into the nearest machinegun nest and as the explosions from the direct hit were occurring, I threw the second grenade at the German machine gun nest slightly to the left of the first one. Before I could drop down, the third machine gun nest opened with a burst of fire.

"Oh, My God!"

Later in the day, Major Lindsey and some of his men had worked their way up to the excellent high position that Pvt. Steele had almost single-handedly captured.

"Where is Steele?" He immediately asked.

Pvt. Kidd sadly responded, "Steele was mowed down by machine gun fire from the third machine gun nest after killing everyone in the first two Kraut machine gun nest."

Major Lindsey immediately summoned his radioman and got on the phone to his artillery officer across the valley. He ordered them to concentrate artillery and mortar shelling just 50 yards in front of his position. The second round was adjusted to hit closer to Major Lindsey. The German machine gun crew in the third nest took a direct hit. The Jerries not killed began to abandon their next. Major Lindsey shouted for them to halt and surrender. Then, he told Pvt. Kidd to fire his flamethrower straight up into the air. When the Germans on this mountainside heard the blast of the flamethrower, they all threw up their hands and surrendered. Major Lindsey ordered some of his support squad to take over the prisoners. Then, he went over to the spot where Pvt. Kidd told him that Steele fell mortally wounded. Steele lay face down. Major Lindsey rolled him over and saw that he had been almost cut in half.

"Pvt. Steele, you have been a hero many times over. I will see to it that your final ranking will be your highest achieved during your military career no matter what Colonel Jordan has to say," Major Lindsey utter to himself and the men around him.

215 / DON STEWART NIMMONS

Major Lindsey issued the orders to headquarters to promote Pvt. Bob Steele to Staff Sergeant. Over the next few weeks before the harsh winter months set in Northern Italy and stopped all military fighting by both sides, the gallant and brave sacrifices demonstrated by Pvt. Steele and his spirit to conquer the Germans and volunteer to go onto Japan if necessary to win freedom from the POW Camp for his brother, Sergeant Arvil Steele, inspired many other buddies to show their similar fearlessness while facing almost certain death.

Some of the many medals awarded posthumously to Private Charles Robert Steele, No. 180054000 of the 362nd Infantry Regiment, 91st Infantry Division of the US Army who was killed in action on September 13th, 1944 are as follows:

Silver Star   **Bronze "V" Star With Oak Leaf Clusters And Two Arrowheads**   **Purple Heart With Bronze Oak Leaf Clusters**   **American Commendation**

TREASURES OF WAR – CONCEALED BY THE EVIL ONES / 216

| Army Commendation | European African Middle East Campaign | World War II Victory | Combat Service Commemoration |

Our nation's third highest award is the Silver Star for gallantry in action.
The Bronze Star distinguishes Valor and Heroism with subsequent awards being denoted by Bronze Oak Leaf Clusters.

The 'Badge of Merit', The Purple Heart is awarded to those who are wounded in action.

Pvt. Steele received a Silver Oak Leaf Cluster in lieu of Five Bronze Oak Leaf Clusters.

Unfortunately, Major Lindsey's orders to promote Pvt. Steele back to his highest ranking position of Staff Sergeant during his brief military career was not approved. **Private Charles Robert Steele** in buried in Plot A Row 3 Grave 17 at the Florence, Italy American Cemetery.

217 / DON STEWART NIMMONS

Florence American Cemetery and Memorial

American Battle Monuments Commission

The World War II Florence American Cemetery and Memorial is located on the west side of Via Cassia near Florence, Italy. The site covers seventy acres on the west side of the Greve River. The wooded hills around the cemetery make a very picturesque frame of the rectangular shaped cemetery. More than 4,400 American military Dead are from the US Fifth Army burials originally made between Rome and the Alps after the capture of Rome by the Allied Forces in June of 1944. Pvt. Charles Robert Steele, 91st Infantry Division is buried in Plot A Row 3 Grave 17.

The memorial has two open courts joined be the Tablets of the Missing upon which is inscribed the names of 1,409 Americans who gave their lives in the service of their country and who rest in unknown graves.

Military Operations Map

Chapel Interior

TREASURES OF WAR – CONCEALED BY THE EVIL ONES / 218

Statue of 361st Regimental Soldier Overlooking Plot B

363rd Regimental Soldier Overlooking Plot A

Tablets of The Missing

TREASURES OF WAR – CONCEALED BY THE EVIL ONES

Chapter Nine

The Story of Japanese KAMIKAZE – SUICIDE Missions

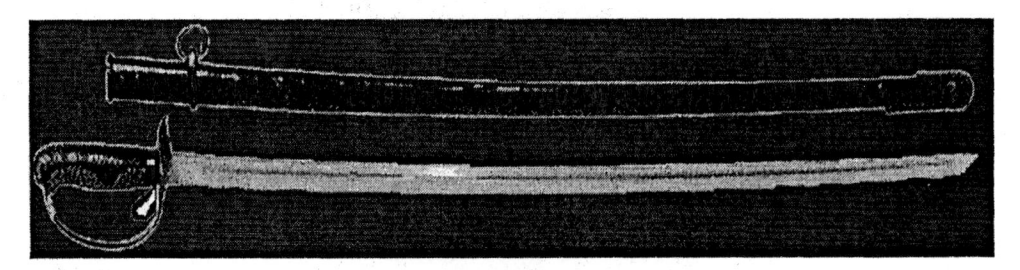

神風

KAMIKAZE – SUICIDE MISSION

Emperor Zapp was **The Evil God** who led the militaristic Japan by his Imperial Orders to his Imperial Army. He taught the instructors in the schools and later in the military academies the first priority in educating and training the young men was to brainwash them to be devoted to The Emperor, their God, and to the country. The education of the young men began in schools with a daily worship service where they were taught to die for The Emperor.

A special forces of the Imperial Army, known as the 'Kenpeitai', acted as the silencers of any radical outcry against The Emperor or the military. Similar to the activities of the Gestapo and SS officers in Germany, they censored much everyday activity of the Japanese soldiers and the public. The parents of many of the soldiers killed in action had to wait until after the end of the war to learn of their children's deaths. Battles lost by Japan were kept from the public.

Late 1944, The Diary of a Brave Japanese 18 Year Old Soldier.

"I volunteer for the sacred duty to carry out a suicide mission and become a happy soul mate of Emperor Zapp, My God, and be praised in the Yasukuni Shrine by the Emperor.

I am being rewarded for my deliberate work during my student years and the high grades in all my subjects. Many of my fellow classmates have not been accepted for this holy mission.

My pilot training has been less than six months. My flight instructor has flown more than 50 fighter missions for Emperor Zapp. I know that I will never be the ace fighter pilot that he is.

My honorable efforts to build a 'FREED ASIA' and conquer the wicked world against us at all cost will be my legacy.

I can't wait to fly my mission in the next major air battle against the American aircraft carrier.

If I do not return, I believe that my death will change the world, save you from the wicked Americans and lead Emperor Zapp to victory."

TREASURES OF WAR – CONCEALED BY THE EVIL ONES / 221

His Final Letter To His Family Before His Suicide Mission.

"Mom and Dad, I have been promoted to Corporal and given my orders from Colonel Coldblood, the commander of our Tokkotai squadron.

I thoroughly enjoyed my visit with you last year. Each of you looked good and was happy to see me. Mom, you cooked my favorite fish meal and I could not eat enough.

Any accomplishments of mine I owe to both of you because of how loving you have been and your direction to receive my religious strengths from the Emperor's Shrines.

How is Little JoJo coming along with his studies in elementary school? Has sister been accepted in the medical school? She is the top student in her class. Tell both of them that I love them.

Mom, your brother, Uncle Budd, will not be forgotten during my forthcoming mission. He and many other Japanese military leaders killed in the war will be very proud of my mission.

I must say good-bye the sergeant just stuck his head in the door and motioned for me to come.
Love you in the name of Emperor Zapp,

Your devoted son."

In 1944, the Japanese Imperial Army established a glider plane fortress, complete with large bomber aircraft, in Barangay Cacutud, Mabalacat, Pampanga (Central Luzon, Philippines). A rocket tube in its tail, equipped with high explosives, propelled these gliders. The large bomber airplanes were to be used to pull the gliders close to their targets and release them, and their pilots would guide them into the Allied warships. Lt. Sickbrain led the Shimpu Attack Units as they were known. Some of the highest leaders of Shintoism in Japan were sent to the base in Cacutud.

The Filipino native tribe known as the Aeta tribe had lived in the Zambales Mountains for several hundred years. One of the leaders of the Aeta tribe was Digimo "Moses" Reyes.

"According to 'Moses', he witnessed the operation of the Cacutud airfield from up in the mountain jungles nearby," Major Francisco explained.

Each morning Lt. Sickbrain would call his bomber pilots and Shimpu Attack Units together for a ceremony to dedicate their lives to His Majesty, Emperor Zapp and the land of the rising sun, Japan. These young Japanese airmen went through their religious teachings and worship, then, military training several times each day for more than three months.

Moses noticed some of the bombers were unloading bombs and small heavy crates. Also, he noticed small crates were being loaded onto trucks, which drove up a small mountain road across the valley from him and disappeared for hours at a time. Several of the large aircraft were cargo carriers. These planes came in from the south from Manila and other Philippine Islands. Each plane carried these small heavy crates. The small heavy crates were spread out on the beds of the Japanese trucks in order not to be too heavy for traveling across small bridges along the road. Each load was estimated to be between eighteen to twenty thousand pounds.

In Moses observation, he saw the bombs mounted onto the Shimpu Attack Gliders. The bombs never left the airfield.

Moses held a meeting of tribe leaders on each full moon. During a meeting in September 1944, near the top of High Park Mountain, the chief of the Burgos Aeta tribe told him about many trucks coming near them on the Agno River through the town of Santa Ignacia. He noticed each truck had several heavy small crates, which were unloaded near the riverbank. The Japanese Army had set up a fortress nearby and posted Japanese police at the guard stations around the fortress. The Burgos Aeta Tribe Chief saw American and Filipino POW's being used to build the fortress and to carry the small heavy crates inside the fortress.

Moses told the Burgos Aeta Tribe chief to watch for any movement of small heavy crates and to send a messenger to his base camp near the Cacutud airfield should any further movement be made of these crates.

The Allied forces in the Pacific were battling their way across the Pacific Ocean, Philippine Sea and South China Sea toward the Philippines in mid 1944.

Meanwhile back at Cacutud airfield the Japanese Imperial Army was preparing for its first Kamikaze unit attacks against the American forces invading the Philippines. On October 20, 1944, the Shimpu Attack Glider Units became world famous as the Kamikaze unit. This morning was no different than each morning for the past several months.

TREASURES OF WAR – CONCEALED BY THE EVIL ONES / 223

Unbeknown to the Japanese Kamikaze pilots, Emperor Zapp had his special medical teams to develop a new drug to be put into the customary pre-flight shake drinks. This drug would cause the pilots to get very excited and eliminate any fears for their safety in the hereafter. Lt. Sickbrain called his men to assembly and led them in their religious ceremonies, roaring yells, hail to Emperor Zapp and commanded them to their bombers and gliders.

The crews were lined up with one bomber towing one Shimpu Attack Glider with one Kamikaze pilot at the controls. For the next four or five hours the planes took off toward the Pacific Ocean and the Philippine Sea.

In the evening about half of the bombers returned and only Lt. Sickbrain's fighter plane returned. All of the young Kamikaze pilots had either committed suicide missions by diving their planes into Allied warships or been shot down by the Allied Forces before successfully completing their single mission.

All of these men believed their patriotic duty were one of a 'Spirit Of Dying Rather Than Being Defeated' all in the name of Emperor Zapp, **THE EVIL GOD.**

TREASURES OF WAR – CONCEALED BY THE EVIL ONES

Chapter Ten

The Story of Colonel Frank 'Sport' Montgomery

Courtesy US Army Air Force Archives

225 / DON STEWART NIMMONS

I was born in Cleveland, Tennessee on May 28th, 1920. My parents named me Frank "Sport" Montgomery. As soon as I completed high school in June 1938, I sat down with my parents one Sunday afternoon.

"Dad, I want Mom's and your permission to joined the United States Army Air Force?" Frank asked his parents.

"There is nothing here but working on the farm and occasionally getting on the horse and riding to Farmer Master and his wife's place three miles down the road around the bend. They are good old folks and have lived here more than seventy-five years.

The most excitement is when one of us runs into one of those long timber rattlesnakes crawling across the road and his head is in the ditch on the left and his tail is still in the ditch on the right. Do you remember that time that Sis and I were going over to The Masters' place to pick some beans in their garden? We thought a timber had fallen off the logging truck. We started running up to push it out of the way when all of a sudden we heard the rattling of this enormous snake. When we tried to kill it with those large rocks and it kept striking at us, I sent Sis running to the house to get you Dad. You brought the shotgun and blew its head off. And you know that the only child the Masters had was bitten by one of those big rattlesnakes and died many, many years ago. At least that is the story you told to Sis and I over and over again to warn us about the dangers of these big timber rattlers." Frank nervously explained his desires and reasons to go away from home as he walked back and forth.

"Son, yes I remember the excitement every time anyone of us kill a snake, bear or mountain lion. This is home for you. You have learned how to milk the cows, ride horses, plow the garden and fields, fish in the streams and ponds, hunt for rabbits, squirrels, and bobcats and take care of your horses, hogs, cows and everything. What else do you need to live a good life?" Dad asked.

"I have been reading about flying airplanes and learning how to be a mechanic to maintain them," Sport answered seriously with a smile on his face.

"Airplanes, what in the world would you do with airplanes around here in these mountains?" Mom quizzed, speaking for the first time.

"Mom, my heart set goals in life are not to waste my time out here on the farm. I know that you and Dad want me to be the one to take over the farm in about thirty or forty years from now," Frank went on.

"What's wrong with that?" Dad snapped.

"Nothings wrong with that. But, I want to make you proud of me by learning new things. Trust me Mom and Dad." Frank pointed out.

"Sport, you know that President Roosevelt is spending a lot of money on the development of the Tennessee Valley Authority. There are all kinds of jobs that will be near us here at home, good paying jobs. I bet they will need mechanics to repair the heavy equipment. You could go somewhere to learn how to become a mechanic with the TVA," Dad suggested.

"Where will you have to go to learn about airplanes and how to repair them?" Mom asked.

"Mom, I think that the best place for me to learn about planes is to join the United States Army Air Force. They will train me and pay me while I learn all about planes. They will supply me with my clothes, a place to stay at, and the pay," Frank responded.

"Army, you want to be a soldier?" Dad quizzed.

"Yes, I have to be a soldier for a few years while I learn all about flying and repairing airplanes and get paid for it. Not a bad deal!" Frank replied.

"Sounds like a pretty good thing. The country is not at war. You should be safe while the government teaches you something you are interested in. Mom what do you think?" Dad commented and asked.

"Son, if you are sure you want to go away on your own and learn about airplanes. You have my OK," Mom tearfully whispered.

"Great, I will catch the bus and go into Chattanooga tomorrow and enlist in the US Army Air Force," Frank spoke as he hugged his Mom.

"Dad, you and Mom will have to go with me to sign the enlistment papers," Frank informed them.

A month later.

"Son, the mailman came by today and left a letter for you from the US Army Air Force," Mom told Frank as he came in from the barn after milking the cows.

"Where is it?" Frank asked.

"Over there on the fireplace mantle."

"Wow, they want me to report to Southeast Air Corps Training Center at Maxwell Field in Montgomery, Alabama in two weeks for initial flying training as a cadet," Frank told his Mom after reading the letter.

"Maxwell Field, where in the world is that?" Mom asked with a sadden face.

"As I remember from my geography and history lessons, that is not too far from Tennessee," Sport assured his Mom.

"How will you get there?" Mom asked as Dad came in from the corncrib.

"How far is what? Dad asked.

"Sport got his letter from the US Army Air Force today. He has to report to Montgomery, Alabama in two weeks. I was asking him how will he get there when you walked in," Mom revealed to Dad as they sat down at the table.

"Well Sport, how will you get there?" Dad asked.

"They included a letter of authorization for me to go to the Chattanooga train depot and get my tickets to ride the train from Chattanooga to Montgomery. I will go through Atlanta on my way to Maxwell Field," Sport nervously answered.

"How long will you be away from home?" Mom asked.

"Mom, I don't know for sure at this time," Frank answered.

"Sport, you will have to help me complete the harvest of the corn crop before you leave. Mom and I can keep up with the garden," Dad pointed out.

"Hey, you can count on me working long hours to get the corn crop in," Sport proudly replied.

"Frank, do you want to have Irene over or have the neighbors bring a special dish to eat just before you leave?" Mom asked.

"Sounds OK to me," Frank nodded to his Mom.

The family and friends got together after church the last Sunday afternoon before Frank left for Maxwell Field.

The next day Frank boarded the train in Chattanooga for the journey to Montgomery.

After he arrived, he was shown his barracks.

Man, I can finally stretch out and get some peaceful rest. In the morning I will have a meal to stop the hunger pains from the trip.

Initial Basic Training.

Frank went through some very serious air cadet training, complete with sixty hours of intensive physical training before entering primary flying training. The mental and intelligence testing was secondary at this point. Frank sure was glad he had been made to work hard on the farm.

This is a long way from learning about airplanes. Nobody told me that I had to learn about physical defense among us cadets and fighting a war before I could learn how to fly or navigate airplanes. I better not write to Mom about this training. She would never forgive me. Frank thought.

After completion of basic cadet training at Maxwell Field, Frank was given additional testing as a candidate to become a pilot, bombardier or navigator. Frank gave his best efforts with the preflight school for pilots. He grew to love the idea of becoming a pilot of one of the fighter attack planes. After being there, as a cadet pilot for several months Frank decided to go into his squadron commander's office and ask about when he could expect to become a pilot with the Air Corps.

"Major, I enlisted in the US Army Air Force and set my goal to become a pilot of any airplane. Now, my primary wish is to become a pilot of one of the fast fighter planes. I have learned about everything there is to know about an airplane, but my goal continues to be a pilot," Frank said, as he expressed his determination.

"Are there any exams that I must pass, or how do I get qualified to join a fighter pilot's squadron?" Frank continued.

"Cadet Montgomery, you have shown us some high marks in most all classifications of your training here. Based upon your comments today and the discussions I had with General Longfellow yesterday, I will issue orders for you to be transferred to the Army Air Corps at Randolph Field in San Antonio, Texas where you will train in the AT-4 single engine fighters." Major Clark replied.

"Sir, you will not be disappointed. I appreciate your confidence in me." Frank said as he saluted the Major and did an about face and left the office with a skip in his steps.

Frank was given his assignment for pilot flying of fighters at Randolph Field. He packed up and caught the next available plane from Maxwell Field to Randolph Field.

Upon circling the runway and getting in line to land at Randolph Field, Frank saw more military aircraft than he had ever seen in his life. There were several Air Fields near each other in San Antonio. From his seat in the plane from Maxwell Field, Lackland, Kelly, and Randolph Air Fields looked awfully close to each other and large.

Frank became a natural when flying the AT-4 fighter. All of his superiors watched him from up close in the cockpit and from various towers around the field. They were very impressed with his rapid learning skills to maneuver the trainer. He completed his training and earned his wings. It was the proudest day of his young life.

Frank received his commission as a 2nd Lieutenant. He had to share his excitement and write Mom and Dad.

Letter Home.

November 14, 1939

Dear Mom and Dad:

I told you that I would make you very proud of me. I earned my commission as a 2nd Lieutenant and my pilot wings.

I enjoy flying my single engine fighter. Being up there in the sky where I can see for miles is a most satisfying feeling. I did not realize there were so many types and sizes of airplanes in the world.

Army Air Corps pilots, navigators and support people are all over this town. I got to move into the officer's quarters after I received my commission.

I get to fly several times each day in all types of weather. When one of those cold blue north storm fronts comes blowing through here, it can be real tricky to fly my plane in and around these Central Texas thunderstorms. The other day a bolt of lighting struck the end of my left wing and it scared me to death. Even though I had gone through classroom training, I did not know what the lightning would do to my plane. Fortunately, the engine did not miss a stroke and no fire was started in the engine. No parachute bailout for me this time.

During some of my earlier training I had to learn how to make a parachute jump from a tower. I was prepared to make one, but everything went OK and I learned something about flying in or near a thunderstorm with bolts of lighting.

My Commanding Officer, Colonel Stevens, told me about a new faster fighter that will be delivered to Randolph Field in the next few months or so. He wants me to become very familiar and learn everything about it. It is manufactured by Lockheed and called a P-38 Lightning.

This will give me another chance to earn another promotion, more pay and fly more different planes.

I hope the money order enclosed will help you have a Happy Thanksgiving.

Bye for now, I love you.

2nd Lieutenant Frank Montgomery
U. S. Army Air Corps

Frank continued to work hard and learn everything possible about his fighter trainer. The Air Corps flew in some P-40-E's for use and upgrade of the pilot training programs. Frank was chosen to go to classes to learn the features of this more advanced fighter. Curtiss developed the P-40-E. It features six 50-caliber machine guns and the maximum speed of 365 MPH with a performance range of 850 miles. Frank asked some important questions concerning the starboard elevator, single rudder, and tail section to clarify some of his concerns for maneuvering the fighter in a dogfight.

On May 2nd, 1940, Frank received his first opportunity to fly the P-40-E. His heart was beating almost as fast as the Allison V-1710 engine with 1150 horsepower. He was excited as he jumped up on to the wing and into the cockpit and pulled the canopy over his head. He fired up the powerful engine. After taxiing over to runway 17W, he pushed down the throttle and he felt the thrust as it shoved him back in his seat. When he reached eighty miles per hour, he pulled back on the stick and the plane lifted up at a steep upward angle. It was a clear blue Texas sky. It was all practice and progress after that initial flight.

Speed and maneuverability are tops on the list for fighter pilots. Frank was in heaven as he went into some steep turns and dives. Many of the new fighter cadets would come out of their Quonset hut barracks and watch whenever Frank was flying over the field while practicing some of his flying skills. Frank became known as the 'Ace' of the P-40-E's squadron.

A few days before July 4th, Colonel Stevens summoned Frank to his office.

"Colonel, you called for me to report?" Frank asked as he clicked his heels together and saluted.

"Yes sir. At ease! Frank, General Crocket and I have reviewed your excellent record and here are your papers and Captain bars."

"From 2nd Lieutenant to Captain, you are more than generous."

"Frank, the General and I have rated you as one of our more advanced fighter pilots. The people at Curtiss have told us how much they have learned from you during the testing of the P-40-E. In fact, they have made the modifications that you recommended to improve the safety and performance of the aircraft. After the holidays, General Crocket is having one of the high altitude fighters, the P-38 Lightning delivered to us. He wants you to study it from both props to the tail navigation lights. The shape of this fighter is so much different than the P-40-E. You know what pilots think about drastic design changes. However, some of us believe that we need to improve our firepower."

Lockheed's pilot flew this new designed long-range interceptor fighter to Randolph Field Saturday afternoon on July 25th, 1941. Most of the men were off the base for a weekend pass. Sunday evening the commissioned officers drove into the parking lat outside their quarters. The usual greetings and questions about how many fish you caught down at Corpus Christi or where you spent the week end was heard along the sidewalks and entrances to their buildings.

At 06:00 Monday morning Frank arrived at the officer's mess hall and loaded his plate with sausage, biscuits, scrambled eggs, butter and grits. He had developed a good taste for grits and always asked for an extra helping. Taking his tray by the coffee and juice bar he filled up with a cup of black coffee and a large glass of grapefruit juice. He spotted the large round table near the center of the mess hall and walked over and sat down to feast. A few moments later Colonel Stevens sat sown next to his left.

"Good morning Frank!"

"Good morning Sir."

"Frank, have you been out to the hanger yet to take a good look at the P-38 Lightning?" Colonel Stevens asked.

"No Sir, I didn't know it had arrived. When did it land?"

"Saturday afternoon. Most of the pilots were off the base for the weekend. When we get through our morning closed-door meeting, you and I need to go to hanger 14 and take a close look. Don't be too surprised. The Lockheed engineers and its' test pilot will be here at 09:00 to begin the schooling and flight training for this very revolutionary designed fighter. You need to keep me posted of any of your concerns about the P-38." Colonel Stevens elaborated.

"Sir, I will give you my one hundred percent attention while evaluating it." Frank replied.

"May I get you a refill on your coffee Colonel?" Frank asked as he stood up to go get his coffee mug refilled.

"Sure, yes!"

"How do you take it?"

"My blood sugar is probably low this morning after the week end long hours. Put two spoons of sugar in it, Thanks!'

The chow hall smell of frying bacon, sausage and steaks was a temptation to sit there and drink several more cups of coffee. But, duty called.

Colonel Stevens, Captain Montgomery and Cadet Novak met outside conference hall number 4 to walk over to hanger 14 to take a look at the new kid on the block. Eventually, arriving at hanger 24 the Colonel asked the enlisted watchman to unlock the door and turn on the lights. The three men walked into the lighted hanger.

"Holy Angel, different, it is more than I imagined," Frank said as he walked over to the P-38 Lighting.

"It is such a drastic change from your P-40-E design, Frank. It is faster and look at the 20 mm cannon in the nose to go with those four 50 caliber machine guns. The twin Allison V-1710-27/29 1150 horsepower engines together with those twin tail sections make for something very new." Colonel Stevens said as he pointed to the front of the plane.

"Yes Sir, I have only one of the same size engine on my P-40-E. The information that I received a few months ago described how fast the P-38 could climb with a full load. Something like 2,400 or 2,500 hundred feet per minute up to around 39,000 feet. That is higher and faster than I have ever flown." Frank responded.

Letter From Home.

August 12th, 1941

Dear Frank:

It was good to hear from you and learn about your progress in San Antonio. Irene sends her love to you. Every time we go to church she waits on us outside afterwards. We mostly talk about you. All of us are concerned about the happenings in Europe. Sounds like another war against the Germans. We pray for you several times every day. Yes, we are proud of you and what you have seen and learned. Dad and I are considering getting into the milk cow business. See the enclosed article that your cousin, William, sent to us from Pickens, South Carolina. Let us know your advice. It would be something that you could build here at home.

We are working long hours taking in the corn crop and plowing for the winter garden. The new seed corn that Dad bought last spring has produced some of the best ears of corn these parts have ever seen. We estimate that we will pick about sixty bushels an acre. That is more than twice what we harvested last year. The mailman told Dad about a used feed grinder that is run by a long belt off the tractor transmission. With all this extra corn we went into Cleveland and bought some feed sacks. The price of feed has gone up about twenty-five cents a sack this year. I think we will pay the bank off for the loan for the grinder next month.

Dad and I are thinking of going over to North Carolina to the Biltmore Dairy Farms and get a young registered Jersey bull and a few Jersey Heifers and build up a very productive dairy. You might remember the articles published in your agriculture class books about the famous herd of registered Jerseys at Biltmore Farms. In a few years we could do something like is mentioned in the article.

When are you going to get another furlough? Are you going to re-enlist? We need you here.

Love you from our hearts,

Mom and Dad

The Attached Article.

THE PICKENS SENTINEL, PICKENS, S. C.

CAROLINA COWS SERVE WELL

CLEMSON, July 6, 1941

Besides helping greatly as one of the nation's big food industries, milk from South Carolina's 166,000 dairy cows is rendering a valuable service on the home front, says C. G. Cushman, Clemson extension dairy specialist.

A considerable part of the state's total of 275,000,000 quarts annual production is consumed in homes, in new plants to build military equipment, and otherwise among a people geared to a future wartime tempo, helping to give greater vigor. As the Milk Industry

Foundation points our: Milk drinking – now widely popular in war equipment plants – lessons fatigue, reduces accidents, cuts losses in man-hours, improves production and earning power.

"Milk and its products comprise over 25 percent of the 1700 pounds of food estimated to be consumed annually by the average America," the Foundation says, "and consumers use 50 million quarts of fresh milk and cream a day through doorstep and store distribution alone."

"Americans enjoy the best milk in the world with sanitary safeguards and widespread distribution. This period of time has proved emphatically the economy and value of milk as a food containing vital components of the diet. During a war and postwar demands seem to be destined to be greater than nutritionists dreamed of in past years.

Milk receiving plant at Newberry was running 8 truck routes, according to C. O. Huey, manager.

It opened for business August 12, 1939, and got 1,300 pounds of milk that day. On its first anniversary it received 6,471 pounds, and on its third one this year it got 10,375 pounds of milk. For the coming year 15,000 pounds is the goal.

It has 189 patrons. County Agent Ezell says practically all of these are doing definite pasture improvement and are saving their good heifers. He is working on extensions for the present routes. A systematic campaign has put a good dairy bull in walking distance of every farm in the county.

The trucks were arriving when I was there. A constant flow of milk was going through the cooler and into the 1,300-gallon thermos tank on a truck that carries it to the mother plant at Chester.

Someone inquired how a new patron was coming along and the driver said. "Fine, His wife doesn't have to work in the mill now that the milk checks have started to come."

Practically all of this up there is just plain and practical farm dairying. The farmer had a few cows from which he was getting no regular cash income. He invests $13.20 that he does not have, in equipment that the plant advances to him. From there on he just sets the milk by the side of the road each morning, goes back later for the empty, and gets his check twice a month.

Looks as though real farm dairying is well on its way in he Chester-Newberry area. Despite the unprecedented demand for bottled milk, this business continues to make substantial growth.

Upon the completion of the intensive schooling and training sessions with the Lockheed engineers and its' test pilot Colonel Stevens called for Captain Montgomery to meet with him out at the hanger of the P-38 Lightning.

"Frank, I want you to take it up and get prepared for 'Dogfight' with Lieutenant Carlson in the P-40-E. I need to report to the General of your findings and final evaluation of this new designed fighter. Give me a written report each morning before you fly out again. Take as many hours as you need," Colonel Stevens instructed.

"Sir, I will give it every test that I know and get prepared for the 'Dogfight' with Carlson. The failures of the P-38 that I pointed out to Lockheed have been corrected so this test next week should give us a true result of its' current status. Have you determined where the 'Dogfight' will be flown? How many air fights will it be to determine the winner?" Frank asked?

"That is good. I am glad to learn that Lockheed has completed the modifications. Yes Sir, each of you will take off in the middle of the runway in different directions and fly out five miles and circle back over the runway approximately one hundred feet apart toward each other at five hundred feet elevation, which is your minimum altitude. Then, each of you will pull up to eighteen thousand feet at a maximum speed of each aircraft. Each will make your dive and pursue the other from the other's tail, staying within eye site of the base. All of your flying skills will be used during this important test of aircrafts. Remember, full flight suits and parachutes are required," Colonel Stevens replied.

"You forgot one important matter, Colonel."

"What's that?"

"What constitutes victory?"

"Yeah, somebody has to win the 'Dogfight'. The first pilot that forces the other to fly above the maximum or below the minimum altitudes or stays on the tail of the other for at least three seconds is the winner. The loser will acknowledge this fact by flying level and rocking his wings in submission. Each pilot will fly in different directions back to the middle part of the runway and start battle two just as battle one was done. The winner must win two out of three 'Dogfights'. When that is determined, each of you will land and taxi to a designated spot."

"Sounds like I need to get to work and learn all the capabilities and types of turns and dives that this P-38 Lightning will do," Frank replied as he walked toward hanger 14.

"Thursday is the day. 10:00 hours you and Lieutenant Carlson will meet me at the hanger to talk about the rules of engagement for the 'Dogfight'," Colonel Stevens said as he left the area.

"Yes Sir Colonel."

The 'Dogfight'.

"Good morning Colonel. How are you Lieutenant?" Frank greeted them at hanger 14.

"Good morning Frank. It is a beautiful day to conduct this competitive exercise between these two fighters," Colonel Stevens replied and observed.

"Just a little nervous, Frank. I have not done this before," Lieutenant Carlson answered.

"I am ready," Frank said.

"Do I need to go over the details of this 'Dogfight' again?" Colonel asked.

Both men answered, "No Sir. We understand."

"Lieutenant, you take the P-40-E and Captain the P38 Lightning," the Colonel ordered.

The men checked out their respective equipment and airplanes before jumping up into the cockpit. After final checkout, each pilot started their engines and taxied his plane to the middle of the main runway, Carlson in the north direction and Captain Montgomery to the south. The mock 'Dogfight' began.

Captain Montgomery pushed the throttle forward and took off flying out the required five miles and made a ninety degree turn to the left and circled back toward the starting point at 500 feet and zoomed past Lieutenant Carlson now headed south. Immediately after passing Carlson, Frank pushed the throttle completely forward and climbed almost vertical until the nose of the P-38 was pointed straight up for a few seconds until he kicked it over for a loop back toward his target.

Lieutenant Carlson turned up at a forty-five degree in the opposite direction for separation in his P-40-E.

The speed of the P-38 coming out of the inverted loop showed Frank a new method to keep the P-40-E off of his tail as he gained control and leveled out tempting Carlson to turn upward toward Frank.

Frank saw Carlson's move and suddenly pulled his plane up and into a ninety-degree turn to the west. Carlson pushed the throttle forward reaching top speed. The P-38 Lightning was more powerful and Frank used the two engines to his advantage and gave the fuel to it. Frank pulled away and out of the range of the P-40-E, advantage P38.

At this point, Frank elevated his plane vertical to fifteen thousand feet and kicked it over into a partial loop coming out of it at an angle putting him in a position to attack Carlson from the tail. He sped up and stayed on his tail for the required three seconds representing a kill. Carlson dove down to one thousand feet and rocked his wings to show his acceptance of defeat.

The heavier P-38 Lightning with a complete load of weapons had proven the better fighter in round one.

Carlson and Frank both climbed to ten thousand feet and made ninety-degree turns putting them flying straight at each other ten miles apart. Carlson tried a proven maneuver in the P-40-E by making a forty-five degree turn to the west without pulling back on the stick to allow Frank to make a high speed move around to his tail. Carlson began doing a half turn spin to the right and then to the left. This forced Frank in his much heavier fighter to take longer to zero in on the P-40-E. Frank backed off and waited for Carlson to fly level for a short time. Frank fell into the trap when he accelerated full throttle. As he got near the tail of Carlson, Carlson dropped his landing gear and flaps to force Frank to fly over him. Carlson immediately 'threw the coals' to his fighter and pulled up behind Frank for the required three seconds. Frank dove down to one thousand feet and rocked his wings to show his acceptance of defeat.

The P-40-E proved its strengths and won round two.

Colonel Stevens and General Crocket and many of the fighter and bomber pilots were enjoying the show.

The final, winner take all, round began with both pilots flying side by side out the five miles and turning ninety degrees in different directions. Frank slammed the throttle down and climbed to 18,000 feet and circled around to locate Carlson below him. He knew that Carlson would attempt a climb and dive. The P-40-E was known for its ability to made dives to avoid a kill.

In the meantime, Carlson knew his plane was more agile and could dive. However, Lieutenant Carlson did not have the experience of Captain Montgomery.

Frank cautiously made a steep dive down in the direction of Carlson with his round two defeat clearly on his mind.

Carlson saw the P-38 Lightning coming down toward him at a moderate diving speed. He decided to make a vertical climb to the point the nose of his P-40-E was straight up. Unfortunately, he either did not accelerate fully or his fighter engine misfired. The

Lieutenant lost forward speed and the plane started a tail slide. He had lost all control of his plane. As the plane fell it began to speed up causing great physical force and swapping ends. The big heavy engine caused the P-40-E to tumble end over end. Spinning and cart wheeling downward at a high rate of speed is a nightmare for any pilot, much less one without a great amount of hours flying the aircraft.

At this point, Frank and everyone on the ground were dismayed.

Carlson released his safety belt causing him to catapult out of the cockpit, luckily missing the uncontrolled fighter. As he pulled his ripcord, Frank and the men watching below were relieved to see Carlson's parachute stream out behind him allowing the chute to blossom out like an umbrella.

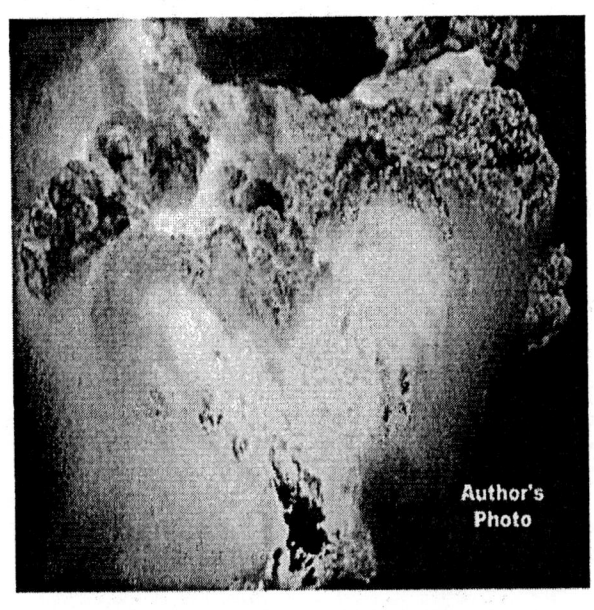

Frank keenly watched to see where Carlson landed on a nearby ranch. The Lieutenant's P-40-E crashed in a nearby ravine leaving a large hole in the rocky surface from impact and the exploding engine fuel and ammunition on board. The explosion and large ball of flames reaching several hundred feet into the air forcing the mesquite trees and brush to catch on fire.

As Frank circled low overhead, he saw Carlson stumble and fall over one of the small boulders in the area. Carlson stood up and waved to Frank signaling he was OK and walked a few steps and sat down on a flat rock.

Author's Photo

Frank turned his plane to the side as he pulled his side window open and shouted, "Stay right where you are!"

Frank continued on to the airfield and landed from the north end of the runway. He taxied his P-38 over to in front of hanger 14 and cut both engines. He stepped out of the cockpit and told his crew. "Take the supply truck and go pick up Carlson. He is just outside the air base fence just north of the smoke coming up from the crash."

Frank jumped into the jeep and drove to the review stand area looking to locate Colonel Stevens and make a report of Carlson's condition. Upon seeing the Colonel slowly walking with General Crocket about 50 yards away, Frank hollered. "Colonel, Carlson's OK."

Colonel Stevens and General Crocket stopped and turned around and walked in the direction of the Captain. Captain Montgomery walked up and saluted both men and said, "Carlson had a safe chute landing in a rough area. I told him to stay put. I sent some of my crew in the supply truck to get him."

"Excellent Captain. The three of us need to meet for supper at the officer's club and begin our talks about the events of today," Colonel replied.

"Colonel, I would like to pick up the tab for supper and join you men," General Crocket added.

"Yes Sir General!"

"Colonel, do you want me to issue emergency orders to Fire Rescue to go to that neighboring ranch and put out that spreading brush and mesquite tree fire?" Frank asked.

"No thanks! I will give that order to Major Thompson."

Home Furlough.

August 20th, 1941, Frank was called to Colonel Stevens's office where he received his first 21 days home furlough to Cleveland, Tennessee since he enlisted three years earlier. His orders authorized him to hitch a flight on a C-47 transport from Randolph to Chattanooga Air Field.

Once in Tennessee, he took a taxi to the bus station where he purchased his ticket to Cleveland. The relative short bus ride around the mountain roads and down into the valley to Cleveland took about one hour with no stops along the way. He noticed the farmers harvesting their corn crops, and it brought back memories of the long hot days that he had worked on his Mom and Dad's farm. Upon arriving in Cleveland he jumped off the bus and grabbed his luggage and went to Walker's 5 and 10-cent department store to see his Aunt Ruby.

"Look at you. The girls are going to fall at your feet. That uniform with your ribbons and Captain bars make you look bigger than life," Aunt Ruby said as she ran up and gave Frank a long hug.

"Thank you, where may I get a ride out to the farm and surprise Mom and Dad?" Frank asked.

"They don't know you are here?"

"No, I wanted to surprise them."

"As soon as Mr. Walker gets back from lunch, he or I will drive you out to the farm," Aunt Ruby responded.

"Sounds like a good plan. I noticed the town is growing fast. There are some new businesses and homes near downtown," Frank observed.

"Yes, the TVA has had a dynamic affect on our economy and growth. We are building a new larger school and going to use school buses to bus the kids from the rural area to it," Aunt Ruby said proudly smiling.

"Progress is coming to those who deserved it. Ya'll have pressured Congressman Lindsey over and over to get some of that FDR federal money to be spent down here. Being a Democrat and working to pass the agenda of President Roosevelt has worked for our communities' benefit. Nearby Senators Russell of Georgia and Byrnes of South Carolina have given Tennessee people special support for the region," Frank replied.

Shortly thereafter, Mr. Walker returned from his home and lunch. He offered to take Frank to his parent's farm. He drove his 1939 Chevy pick up around to the highway and turned off the hard-top road down the dirt road straddling the week old ruts made during the rains the previous week. As he approaches the first stream across the road, he slowed down to be sure the water running across the rocks in the stream's bottom was not too deep for his truck. He slowly drove through the stream and noticed the beautiful mountain water falls up on the left side feeding the water into the stream.

They rode past the John Paul Jones farmhouse and waved to Mrs. Jones sitting on the porch snapping some fresh green beans from their garden. As they drove into the valley looking up the mountainside, Frank could see some of his Dad's corn growing on the right side of the road and the barn and house in the distance. Around the bend and down into another wider stream crossing Mr. Walker slowly creep through the water rushing under the truck. As they rode up onto the plateau where the road leveled out, Frank looked off down into the valley where the stream they had previously crossed wound straight down the middle of the valley. Frank saw his Dad driving the small Farmall tractor with the side cutting blade mower. He was cutting the corn down on the third terrace section.

Up on the left as they were approaching Frank's Mom and Dad's home he noticed that someone had built another lean to off the main two story barn. A new six foot wooden corral fence extended out from the new barn by at least fifty feet. He noticed a new Jersey bull with a ring in his nose standing in the corral.

Mom and Dad sure didn't waste any time getting those Jerseys from Biltmore Dairy Farms. Wonder where the Jersey cows and heifers are? Maybe they are already in the dairy farming business. Frank thought.

Mr. Walker drove up into the driveway and stopped near the rear of the house. Frank's Mom looked out the kitchen window facing the barn and driveway and saw his truck. She went out the back door onto the back porch. Frank stepped out and reached around to pick up his suitcase from the back of the pick up. His Mom immediately noticed who he was.

"Frank, Frank," she yelled as she ran to greet him.

"What do you think, Mom?" Frank asked as he pulled away from the big hug and turned around modeling his proud uniform.

"You look great. You are a lot stronger and taller," Mom answered.

"Thank you Mr. Walker. Would you like to come in and have something to drink or a piece of Mom's cake or pie?" Frank asked.

"Yes, Mr. Walker come on in and let me make some coffee or ice tea and cut your choice of apple pie, chocolate cake or cherry pie," Mom added.

"Well, I need to get back to the five and dime, but I will stay for a short visit."

"Let me go ring the big bell out front to call Dad in from the field," Frank said after dropping off his suitcase on the back porch.

"Ring it five times to let him know to come immediately," Mom told Frank.

Frank went out next to the front driveway and grabbed the wheel and turned it to the right until the large ball hit the side of the two foot wide steel bell hanging under the four by four mounted on the top of the round four foot tall cedar post. When the bell rang, the loud sound could be heard half way up the mountain behind the house and all over the valley down below. After the fifth ring, his father stopped the tractor in the middle of the terrace and stood up to see Frank in his Army Air Corps uniform waving for his Dad to come. Dad waved back and turned the tractor off and pulled up the safety brake and jumped down to the ground. He walked down to the east end of the terrace and up the trail to the dirt road in front of the house. Frank had walked down and met his father in the middle of the road.

"Hi, Dad. It is so good to see you again. Give me a big hug," 'Sport' said.

"'Sport', I am sweaty and dirty from the dead corn stalks and limbs. Let's wait until I wash up and change overalls at the house."

"Dad, don't worry about that. I haven't seen you in three years. Give me a big hug. It has been too long since my last hug from you," 'Sport' replied with a tear in his eyes.

The two men hugged and walked around to the back and pumped some fresh water from the well into the small basin used for washing face and hands.

"Son, that cool water feels good. This August heat is worse this year than normal," Dad said as he took two hands full of water and splashed it over his entire head to cool off and then washed his face and hands.

"Mr. Walker is in the kitchen with Mom drinking some ice tea and eating a piece of Mom's cake or pie," 'Sport' stated as he opened the back door to the kitchen for his Dad.

"Hi, Mr. Walker, thank you for bringing 'Sport' out here," Dad said as he shook his hand.

"The main reason I came out here was to eat some of Margie's delicious apple pie. That big apple tree out back has been one of the best producing trees I have ever seen. Its reputation has spread since Margie entered her apple pie in the country fair the first year after you bought this place. And the apples get better every year," Mr. Walker replied.

They all visited around the table and ate several pieces of homemade apple pie. Mr. Walker, Frank and his Dad walked out on the back porch when 'Sport' asked, "Dad when did you build the corral for your Jersey bull?"

"Let's go out there. I want to show you and Mr. Walker how good things are going with the Jersey dairy milk operations are progressing. The Biltmore Dairy Farm people in North Carolina really wanted to work with us and get some of their Jerseys over here. Your Mom and I bought the registered Jersey bull and two registered Jersey cows and one heifer at a substantially reduced price. All we have to do is show our stock to new prospects that want to purchase dairy cows from them. They want to spread the dairy business to supply all of the new people moving in Chattanooga, Cleveland and northern Georgia region. We keep separate daily production records for the Jerseys and our mixed breed milk cows. Our daily production from the two Jersey cows equals the total from the six old mixed breeds. Also, the grade of milk from the Jerseys brings a better price.

Jack Harris Milk Products driver picks up one ten-gallon can of the Jersey milk and one ten-gallon can of milk from the mixed breed cows every morning. Based on the current demand for milk, milk prices will remain good and our livestock and milking equipment will be paid for in ten months," Dad said as they walked to the barn and corral.

"He is a beautiful bull," Mr. Walker said from his position standing on the second plank of the corral fence. "Will you use him to breed your other cows and your new Jersey cows," Mr. Walker asked.

"Oh yes, Blackie is four years old and will be available to service neighbors cows too."

"Dad sounds like you have a very profitable business."

"Let me show you my prize young Biltmore Jersey heifer. Lady has been bred by Blackie and will have her first lactation in January after the birth of her calf. I have been keeping a close watch on her near the barn. We are hoping for another heifer. Isn't she a strong looking Jersey heifer?" Dad asked as he went to the back entrance to the barn.

"She's beautiful. May I go pet Lady?" 'Sport' asked.

"Sure 'Sport', she is a little nervous around strangers. Take that bucket next to the hallway in front of her and put a little feed from the feed barrel over there in it and hold it out to her. She will smell the feed and you will be her friend for life. And while I am thinking about it, you might want to be sure to do the same when you decide to pet Blackie. Emphasis on the sure," Dad said.

"Jake, you and Frank enjoy your visit together, but I must be going now. Your usual hospitality out here has made me stay longer than I should," Mr. Walker said as he shook their hands and started to his truck. "By the way, your Jerseys and the new addition to the barn and the corral are something you must be proud of and I will let my friends and customers know where they can see it first hand."

"Thank you Mr. Walker for those comments and bringing me home," Frank replied and waved goodbye.

"Dad, where are the two Jersey cows?"

"They are in the separate harvested alfalfa pasture down the road past the house over toward the Masters place. This evening I bring all of the cows to the barn for feeding and milking. You can go with me and see how I do it."

"Will I need to get Prince and Baby saddled this evening?" 'Sport' asked.

"Yes, water them at the well trough behind the barn on the north side."

"About 18:00?"

"You mean six o'clock?"

"Yes, Dad."

'Sport' and his Dad went and sat down in the rocking chairs on the back porch and began getting caught up on three years of separation. Mom soon joined them for the happy and emotional family time. Later in the conversations, 'Sport' wanted to learn the current status of Irene. He had not heard from her for about four months. Mom told him that she had gone up to Knoxville and enrolled in the University of Tennessee studying pre-med. She had come home one time since her enrollment and came out to visit them. Mom assured Frank that Irene remained his girl and she was doing what was best for their future by obtaining her goal to become a medical doctor.

Frank shared some of his exciting pilot training moments and his continued desire to be the best pilot he could be. They discussed the support that Frank had been supplying them from his Army Air Forces Captain's pay. Frank told them that he had purchased his first automobile in San Antonio and used it occasionally to see parts of Texas and the Gulf Coast. Frank looked at the clock on the wall and noticed that it was getting close to milking and chores time.

Frank went out to the pasture behind the barn where the horses stayed. He whistled and to his amazement Prince came trotting out of the trees followed by Baby. He had to locate everything in the barn. He found the bridles, blankets and saddles hanging on assigned knobs in the hallway outside each ones stall. He grabbed a hand full of sugar and waited for the horses to reach him at the barn. Prince looked as good as ever. He held out his hand with a little sugar in it. Prince licked the sugar and raised his head and neighed. Frank gave him a big hug around the neck rubbed him behind his ears watching him lower his head for some more. After putting the bridles, saddle blankets and saddles on Prince and Baby, Frank led them through the barn and closed the gate behind him. Walking the horses over to driveway near the back porch, Frank stepped up into Prince's the left stirrup and hoped into the saddle while holding onto the bridle leather of Baby.

'Sport' hollered, "Dad, it is time to go herd the cows from the east pasture."

"OK 'Sport', I am getting some cleaning soaps together for washing the cows' utters," Dad said as he put them in the wheelbarrow.

"I see you have not forgotten how to saddle the horses."

"You taught me well a long time ago. Prince was glad to see me."

'Sport' and his Dad rode off down the dirt road around the bend to the entrance to the pasture where the milk cows were grazing. Dad whistled and the cows immediately came walking up from the valley. They knew it was time to be milked and get some feed. With the gate open, the cows walked out and made the left turn down the road past the house through the side yard to the barn. Dad and 'Sport' rode behind the cows watching for any need to move the cows over to one side of the road in case a car or truck came along. Each cow went into its' separate stall and waited for some feed to be put in the trough. 'Sport' tied the horses up on the hitching post outside the barn. Dad walked over and fetched wheelbarrow with the cleaning water and soap. Upon entering the hall of the barn, he dropped the wheelbarrow and went over to the large wooded barrel with the dairy cow feed. He lifted the lid and pulled out a gallon bucket full of feed. He went into the first stall and dumped the feed into the trough. 'Sport' seeing this, decided to take another bucket hanging on a post near the feed barrel proceeded to put feed in each stall. After plugging it in, Dad picked up the Jersey milk milking machine and milk can and put it in the stall with one of the Jersey cows. First, he cleaned the utter with the soap and then splashed some water on the utter. After taking his clean rag and thoroughly drying the tits and utter off, Dad connected the milking machine's four suction cups to the cow to complete milking the cow.

Subsequently, Dad did the same for the other Jersey cow and then put the milk can in the locked stall with the wooden floor away from the cows and varmints. Then, he competed the milking of the mixed-breed cows into a separate milk can.

"Prop and leave the barn door open at that end so the cows can either stay in or get water or graze in that pasture during the night," Dad instructed 'Sport' as they were leaving the barn.

"Yes Sir!"

"Dad, you never cease to amaze me with all the things that you have successfully undertaken in my life. I can now see why you and Mom are going to do well with this dairy farming. You have thought of just about everything," 'Sport' went on.

"Thank you 'Sport'. Sounds like you are not doing so bad yourself. Captain Montgomery sounds terrific and having men under your command is something special and you seem very pleased with reaching one of your goals in life. Your Mom and I are very proud of you. You have done things that we have no imagination for and only occasionally read about in the Life magazine. It must be something that you are considering to do for several more years. Education is one of the most important things in life. Study everything you can about any subject that is new to you," Dad proudly said and advised as they guided the horses into the north shed and corral.

After feeding the horses a little feed and turning them lose, 'Sport' and Dad walked across the yard to the back porch. It was dusk and the evening near the mountains was cooling off quickly. Mom came out and brought them some coffee and ham sandwiches and sat down and ate with them at the round wooden table on the back porch.

"'Sport', we need to get up early in the morning and milk the cows again and set the milk cans out on the walk way steps near the road for Jack Harris's driver to pick up. The cows will need to be herded back over to the alfalfa pasture for the day."

"I will be up early. That's the way we do it in the Air Force. You can count on me," 'Sport' replied.

"How long is your furlough?" Mom asked.

"I have to be back at Randolph on September 10th."

"Since Irene is 80 miles away in Knoxville and just began the new semester about one month ago, she most likely will not be able to come down here to visit. You may want to go up to see her. Anyway, you decide. We want to make your visit as nice as possible, but we have our commitments here. You and Dad could take off Sunday and drive up to Cherokee National Forest and go fishing in the Ocoee River or one of the lakes. We know you mentioned going fishing in Texas at the Gulf," Mom continued.

"We only have the one good week-end left before I have to fly back to Randolph. I would like it if you and I could go fishing together," 'Sport' eagerly said as he stood up and took a deep breath of the fresh evening mountain air.

"Here are the plans," Dad said. "Saturday night, we will milk the cows and return them to the alfalfa pasture. 'Sport', you and I will leave later and drive the pickup to the National Forest and camp out for the night. We will fish early and during the mid-morning and return here by mid-afternoon to milk the cows. Harris' driver does not come on Sunday for the milk cans. This will work just fine."

"Son, you will sleep up stairs in the big bedroom at the right of the stairs. We moved all of your things in there and are using your old bedroom for our office. If you get too cool during the night you might want to lower the windows on the east side about half way and the double windows on the south side all the way," Mom said as they said their goodnights.

The next evening, after completing the milking and putting the milk cows in the east pasture, 'Sport' was eager to leave and went to the utility house and found the fishing poles and tackle boxes. Mom had prepared a couple of lunches for them and fixed a thermos full of coffee for the trip and fishing. 'Sport' jumped into the driver's seat and started the engine. Dad loaded his other special fishing gear and some pork jerky and fresh liver for bait. After arriving at the lake, they camped out. Early the next morning, 'Sport' bought some live bait and rented a small wooden boat with a couple of oars. Upon failing to locate some good fishing holes, they passed a couple of fishermen and asked where they were biting. Just around the point in the next cove near some dead tree limbs was the recommended spot. Sure enough, Dad baited his hook and tossed it just on the edge of the limbs, the fishing trip just begun. For the next few hours, 'Sport' and his Dad were running a contest of who would catch the biggest and most fish. The fun and laughter was enormous. They were catching fish until they realized that they had to stop and return to the farm and do the milking and chores.

Author's Photo

After some rekindling of family ties, 'Sport' needed to contact the Air Field in Chattanooga and learn when the next C-47 transport would be coming through and going to Randolph. He determined that in order to meet his orders, he had to go to Chattanooga on September 8th and be back to Randolph by September 10th.

Mom said her goodbyes at the farm. Dad and 'Sport' jumped into the pickup and drove off toward the hard top road near Cleveland. He was a refreshed young man. He looked like a million dollars in his U. S. Army Air Force Captain's uniform. The C-47 transport had not arrived yet. 'Sport' and his Dad looked out across the mountains and valleys from their vantage point at the airport on top of the long flat mountain.

"Dad, you have many things to do and get here in Chattanooga and Cleveland for the farm. I appreciate that you are here, but you do not have to wait for me," Frank said.

"'Sport', give me that big hug for Mom and me."

One day in late September 1941, Frank received his orders to pack his gear for an overseas duty.

Frank set down and wrote his Mom and Dad a letter to tell them that he was leaving the US.

Letter Home

September 20, 1941

Dear Mom and Dad:

I just got my orders to pack and fly on the C-47 to San Francisco and board a ship to go to the Philippines. I will be stationed at Nichols Field in the Philippines. I read a little about the Philippines. Luzon is the large northern island. The airfield is six miles from Manila, the Philippine capital.

My Colonel told me that the US government approved the establishment of the Commonwealth of The Philippines with the provisions of the agreement allowing them to form an independent country. This agreement was passed by congress and signed by FDR. In the meantime, the United States controls these important Islands and has several military installations in the Philippines.

Tell Irene that she is my girl and pet old "Prince" on the forehead for me before you ride him. I understand that my tour of duty in the Philippines may last a year. I will be home for Christmas in 1942. Sorry I won't be home for Christmas this year.

I will write you once I arrive at Nichols Field. I bought a new camera and will take some good photos and send to you.

Hope it does not snow too much this year. Did you get the firewood cut and split in time?

All my mail will be forwarded to me. Write as often as you have a chance. It is good to hear from you and the family.

Bye for now, I love each of you.

        Captain Frank "Sport" Montgomery
        U. S. Army Air Force

On October 14, 1941, Frank arrived at the Port of Manila, Philippines.

One of his primary duties was to fly the South China Sea coastline in his P-40-E fighter. He is Squadron Commander for some twenty-eight fighters.

Frank and the guys at the Army & Navy Club would jump on the C-47 transport and get out of the tropical heat and fly up in the mountains to Camp John Hay in Baguio City, Philippines. The cool summer climate attracted many American businessmen who had been in the Philippines since President Teddy Roosevelt had purchased the Islands from Spain at the end of the Spanish American War. The businessmen conducted their business activities from Baguio and entertained Frank and his buddies. They made sure everyone ate the finest Filipino foods and made the social circles with dancing and long hours of visiting during the evenings and learning to play golf at the exquisite golf clubs in Baguio.

The steep hills and mountains with all the beautiful trees made some of the most challenging golf shots. The par three sixth hole at Baguio Country Club had them looking down about one hundred feet or so to this tiny green with sand bunkers on each side and immediately over the green. The first time Frank played this one hundred fifty five yard hole up against this tall hill of rocks some three hundred feet above them to the right, sloping all the way down to within fifty feet of the right side bunker next to the green, he sliced his high six iron up off the hillside rocks. It bounced about four times down the side of the hill and struck something hard at the foot and bounced over the sand bunker onto the green. The ball rolled up to within ten inches of the cup. He was startled.

"Men that is how you hit your shot at this hole, no straight shots into the bunkers."

One day Frank and his buddies went sight seeing in Wright Park. They saw the official residence of the first American Governor General, Governor W. Cameron Forbes, private house "Topside". The house was built of timber and stone, designed for the New England style Governor Forbes was so familiar with from his childhood in Massachusetts.

"This house is very similar to the Commandant's house back at Camp John Hay," Frank noted.

"Look at the sprawling layout of that large stone fireplace. It covers the whole wall on that side of the room. We could use some of those comfortable lounge chairs," Frank pointed out.

"I bet they did not have these beautiful cozy pine trees back in the States," his buddy, Sam observed.

"Very beautiful, the weather is cool and no humidity like we have down at the air base in Manila," Frank went on.

"Did any of you guys notice the High Commissioner's new house back at Camp John Hay?" Sam asked.

"Yea, those big white columns in front with all the bougainvillea bushes was an attempt to make you think about the wisteria we have in the US," Frank replied.

At the end of their R & R in Baguio, they went out to the airport and boarded the C-47 for the flight back to Nichols Field.

A few months had past, and the air defense in the P-40E fighters, up and down the South China Sea coast of the Philippines had become a twice daily routine when it began to rain heavy. The blowing wind and heavy monsoon rain felt good at first. Then, someone told them that they are in the direct path of a typhoon. The heavy and low clouds came in over the mountains from the Pacific Ocean and Philippine Sea.

After review one morning in the large hanger Frank sought out his weather advisor.

"What is a typhoon?" he asked.

"Captain, did any of those Gulf of Mexico hurricanes ever make it up to Tennessee?" the Sergeant asked, laughing.

"All we got were some heavy rains, and we had to go out into the fields and harvest as much corn as we could before it got ruined," Frank explained.

"Sport, I understand your nickname is Sport. From what I have been able to learn about this part of the world, we may get some very forceful winds and more rain than we can cope with. Captain, in fact you should give the orders to tie down the airplanes," Sergeant Couples added.

After the clean up and repairs of the facilities from the damage of the Typhoon, some of the men were getting excited about completing their tour of duty in the Philippines and going home for Christmas within the next month.

December 7, 1941

Most every adult American alive at the time, remembers where and what they were doing when they heard Pearl Harbor had been bombed. It wasn't any different for Frank. He was to spend Sunday with his buddies at the Army/Navy Club. Soon the peaceful atmosphere of the day turned. His sergeant sped up in his jeep and told Frank what was to be the most important alert notice he could ever have received.

"Captain, the Japanese just bombed Pearl Harbor and we must prepare for the worst," Master Sergeant Stan Roberts shouted.

"Your military career has changed," Sarge continued.

"No more simple life in the military," Captain Montgomery cautiously acknowledged.

"You bet your life on that understatement," Roberts feverously replied as he swerved back and forth down through the streets of Manila to Nichols Field.

Nobody could have told them what was in store for these young brave men. None of them really knew about the brutal war just around the corner, a few days in fact

On December 8, 1941, at high noon, mealtime, the Commander out at Iba Air Base, southeast of Nichols sent the telegram message. "Jap Zeros and Bombers attacking – scramble your P-40's now. There is death and devastation everywhere."

Captain Montgomery immediately ran to the officer's barracks and shouted out the telegram message from the Commander at Iba Air Base. He ordered all pilots to man their P-40-E's and take off as soon as possible behind him with or without ammo. Frank and a few in his squadron took off toward the northwest before the Jap Zeros and bombers arrived.

Thirty minutes later Frank and his squadron flew over Nichols Field only to find the base in a state of peace and tranquility. He led them back to runway 17 W and landed. Once in the hanger, Frank attempted to reach the aircraft warning system controller up at Clark Field without success. Frank told his men to be prepared for an attack and seek out any Japanese living around Nichols Field and bring them to him for questioning.

On December 9th, 1941 the Jap Zeros came in force as one after another squadron attacked Nichols Field. Most of the P-40-E's did not get off the ground and were destroyed in the surprise attack.

Frank was able to take off and fight back. He flew out toward the northeast and during one of his dogfights against two Jap Zeros he ended up high above Clark Field and noticed the total devastation of the American bombers destroyed on the ground.

Frank, with his exceptional training and P-40-E fighter ability shot down three Zeros within the first few hours and was able to force some of the Jap Zeros away from Nichols Field back to the north. Most of Frank's men did not have a chance against the Jap Zeros. Most of them did not return.

Frank circled out to the south of Manila toward Sangley Point and the U. S. base. He noticed that this base had not been attacked yet. He buzzed the field rocking his wings to indicate his desire to land without risking radio contact with the tower. He circled very low to keep his whereabouts from the Jap Zeros not too far to the north and landed. He taxied up to the main hanger where some U. S. Army and Navy men were waiting. He pulled back the cockpit canopy and unbuckled his safety harness. He jumped up and screamed the message that the Japs were attacking and bombing Iba and Nichols Fields. The Commander of Sangley came running out to learn what was going on. After some heated discussions for about an hour Frank jumped back into his P-40-E fighter and taxied out to the south end of the runway and took off toward Manila to the north.

Frank learned the use of 'ORANGE PLAN' was worthless because Sangley was just like he was at Nichols. The Commander at Sangley told him that the necessities of war are scattered all over Manila and so old that most of them are no good to him at all. The artillery shells that Sangley had previously found in one of the warehouses in Manila would not fire. Ammo, rations, medicines and the like were from the U. S. Military leadership in the Philippines from way back in 1898 during the Spanish/American War and Filipino/American War before World War I.

Why on God's green earth did I get sent here to fly combat fighters without proper military support? Maybe the brass in Washington thought we would never have to go to war and believed some of the politicos. Here I am flying back to Nichols without knowing what alternative plans is at my disposal. Frank thought as he took off from Sangley.

American losses were mounting out at Iba Air Base. During the night, most of the survivors from Iba were trucked to Nichols Field.

Early on the morning of December 10th, Frank had his men fuel up the six remaining P-40-E's with limited ammo and fly off toward Clark Air Base to the northeast. As they got near Clark, the Jap Zeros came over the mountains from the north by the hundreds. Frank told his men to follow him and circle out to the northwest and attack the left wing group from the rear. Flying low over the rice fields with very little cover, Frank pulled his fighter straight up and climbed to ten thousand feet and made his dive down in the back of the squadron of Jap Zeros forcing them to split up. This allowed his men to come around from the rear of the Zeros. After several successful runs, Frank and his men had shot down four Zeros. However, the main part of the Squadron of Zeros and bombers continued on to Nichols Field where the Japs handed out heavy bombardment and causing heavy loss of lives, destruction and the wounding of many military and civilians.

Frank and two of his pilots made it back to Nichols in one piece. He saw three of his men's parachutes open before hitting the ground.

The next morning Frank got the three fighters ready to go into combat. Surprising to him, the Japs did not make a bombardment run over the city of Manila and Nichols Field.

TREASURES OF WAR – CONCEALED BY THE EVIL ONES / 258

Maybe it was due to the heavy fog and rainy conditions all around Manila Bay. Frank thought.

That night the men from Iba and Nichols got together to come up with some survival plans under these horrendous conditions. Frank knew his way around some parts of Manila and some of the American and European Business people and families. All of them were fearful of the worst. All of the passenger ships in the harbor had felt the best thing to do was to stay tied up at the dock and hope the Japanese would not attack these defenseless vessels. Some of the men from Iba Air Base had been in the Philippines for several years and knew the Filipino people better than Frank. He talked with them and got their ideas of what may be next.

December 11th was not so lucky. After the first flight of Jap Zeros had made their way over Manila and toward Nichols, Frank and his two other P-40-E fighters with limited capabilities scrambled off to the west and over the mountains to the Philippine Sea. Frank told his men of his plans to make a few kills. Frank and his men battled the Jap Zero pilots for several hours until they returned to the north. All three P-40-E's were shot up pretty good. The damage to the landing wheels and starboard elevators caused two of them to make crash landings. The other one came in with a damaged smoking engine. Now, Frank and his men were left to fight from the ground.

Hanging in and around Nichols Field, Frank hung on until Christmas Day. At this time trucks and boats transported them over to the Bataan Peninsula. Some of their friends in Manila packed some bags with pork and turkey to eat for their Christmas dinner.

Frank and his men had to retreat to Bataan. In December 1941, Bataan was nothing but a tropical jungle. Frank and his buddies fought as general troops on Bataan as best they could with what they had left until the surrender of Bataan on the 9th day of April 1942.

From that date forward, including the Bataan Death March is when their hell on earth really began.

Frank and the Americans soldiers together with the Filipino soldiers, fighting till their Commanding General surrendered on Bataan, were taken prisoners of war.

The Bataan Death March began from Mariveles, Bataan, Philippines up through Cabcaben, Hermosa and on to San Fernando. Frank had to march approximately 60 miles.

The Japanese army drove the POW's very hard at all times, day and night. No water and no food, beatings and shooting of the slow walking prisoners was the normal.

Frank could not have imagined the torture, starvation, disease and murder at the hands of the Japanese during the Bataan Death March and the prisoner of war camp at Camp O'Donnell. Tens of thousands would die during the future months.

During the Bataan Death March Frank met the Fitzgibbons brothers from Texas, Elmer and older brother Reid.

"Don't give in to these criminals," Frank whispered to them with his head bowed. "Stand tall and let them believe you are strong. You will have a better chance to live by becoming one of their servants," he continued.

Japanese army guards shot everyone that made an attempt to seek water from the rice fields or escape.

The Japanese army released a few of the Filipino prisoners when we arrived in San Fernando.

Being one of the survivors of the Bataan Death March from Mariveles to San Fernando, Frank was packed into an old hot, suffocating and crowded rail car.

Some of the men died on the trains. Frank was in the second company to arrive at Camp O'Donnell near Cabanatuan City, Ecija, Philippines.

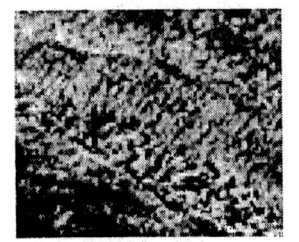

Cabanatuan "ONE" prison camp at Camp O'Donnell was where Frank had to perform burial duty. The large burial pits were used every day.

Elmer got sick, and Frank nursed him in the barracks and gave encouragement to fight the Jap's cruelty. One of Frank's dear friends, Sonny Nesloney from Arkansas, had gotten diarrhea today so bad that Frank told him to eat the burnt rice from the bottom of the cooking pans.

One of the larger typhoons in recent history was bearing down on the Central Luzon area of the Philippines. The Japanese officers knew all about typhoons. The rains came in sheets blowing the POW's over with the strong twirling winds. The palm tree limbs outside the prison camp were flapping loudly and some of them would fly off in the distance. If one of them had hit you, it would have cut you into halves. The Japanese officers and most of the guards bunkered down during the typhoon.

Sergeant Lewis "Curly" Wright had been trying to get some of the men to escape from the camp almost from the day we arrived. Now, he felt like it was an excellent time to escape while the Japs were taking cover from the storm. He talked three of his men into making the escape with him.

"Men, you know that if we get caught; it will mean torture and eventually death. There are some Filipinos out there that will feed us and hide us until we can get to the American troops that will eventually come and free us from this horror. I would rather take my chances than live like this until they starve or work us to death." He told the men he was recruiting for the escape.

"The typhoon has knocked out all of the lights. Something heavy has been blown into the north fence near the guard tower and made a large enough hole for us to walk through. Things are blowing all over the place. Any guard that might come looking tonight won't know whether a tree limb is moving or one of us. I am leaving at 20:00 tonight." He firmly stated as he pointed to the northwest corner of the prison camp.

"Bo, Dawson and I will meet you here at 20:00," Cpl. MacDonald confirmed.

"OK Mac, just bring yourself and any money you can find or borrow," Curly replied.

The next morning the Typhoon had just about blown itself out to the northwest toward Japan. The Jap officers called us out of the barracks at 09:00. 'Old Harvard', as we called the US educated Jap officer, bellowed out orders of the day over the bullhorn.

"All of you men split up into groups of six and clean up the camp. All of the broken things should be carried over to the middle of that fence line," he ordered as he turned and pointed to the area near the main gate.

"Do I have any carpenters in this group," he asked.

"Yes Sir," Frank answered as he raised his hand.

"What is your name prisoner?" he hollowed over the bullhorn.

"My name is Frank," Frank shouted.

The Jap guard nearest to Frank came over to him and punched him in the stomach with the butt of his rifle. "Yes, Sir", he shouted at me.

"Sir, my name is Frank," Frank answered again as he straightened up from the hit by the guard.

"Prisoner, you get about ten men to help you repair the roofs of our officer's buildings. See my maintenance officer to get some tools to do the work," he ordered. Then, he turned to one of his officers on the platform and told him something in Japanese. The officer stepped forward and bowed to his command. This same officer came down the steps and grabbed Frank by the arm and led him away to the tool and supply truck.

After seeing the tools Frank attempted to tell the Jap officer that he needed to go get the ten men to help him. Finally, he understood and went with Frank to round up the men.

Frank knew that one of the first things that they were going to need was a ladder. Again, he attempted to tell the Jap officer that they needed a couple of long poles or small tree trunks to make the ladder. After some gesturing and the like without success, He decided to draw a picture of the ladder on the ground. He pointed to the two long pieces needed and the Jap guard just laughed and bowed to Frank's request.

They did not see any long pieces of wood anywhere on the prison's grounds. Therefore, Frank asked one of the men to get the saw out of the tool truck. The guard went with them out the gate and down the road to an area with some tall tropical bamboo woody stalks big enough to make several good and safe ladder poles. After cutting three of the large bamboo shoots down and a bunch of the smaller bamboo shoots for ladder steps they marched back to the camp. By the time they got this part of the project done, pieces of lumber and pieces of roofing were being thrown into a pile near the gate entrance.

All day long I kept wondering what had happened to Curly, Mac, Bo and Dawson. Did the Jap officers and guards overlook roll call or were they too interested in getting their offices repaired. The longer the Japs take before they send out a search party the better chance for them to escape. I do not want to go through another hot water torture effort by them. Maybe Curly was very smart after all. Frank thought.

"Go over to the tool truck and see if you can find some twine to tie the steps onto the ladder," 'Sport' asked Sonny.

"We are in luck. Here is a bundle of twine. What do I do with this?" Sonny asked 'Sport'.

"See the two long bamboo poles. Take these short cut pieces and attach them with the twine to each side of the long poles about every two feet or so to make the ladder about ten feet tall," 'Sport' instructed as he laid out the two long bamboo poles.

"This thing should hold anyone of us. I know I don't weigh more than one hundred twenty pounds now," Sonny responded as he rubbed his skinny body.

"Yea, maybe if we fix the General's roof real good he will give us an extra cup of rice," 'Sport' said as he also showed his disgust with his skinny body.

All of the Americans went to work repairing all of the roofs damaged by the typhoon. On occasion it rained on them causing the Jap officer to run out of their office to point out where it was still leaking. Later in the afternoon, 'Old Harvard' came out and called them all down from the roofs and asked them to gather in front of him.

"Prisoners, go to your barracks for a meal break," he shouted.

Finally! He told himself. How long will these good deeds last? He wondered. This is a good triumph of our human spirit.

The next morning 'Old Harvard' sent his assistant to fetch Frank from his bunk.

Did they find Curly? What in the world is he trying to do? Frank thought as he looked around the yard as he crossed over to his office.

"Frank, you have won the respect of the General. He asked me to order you to choose forty of your strongest men for a new assignment away from the camp," 'Old Harvard' demanded without giving 'Sport' an opportunity to ask any questions. "Do it now and meet me in front of your barracks in thirty minutes," he added.

The Jap guard grabbed Frank and led him out of 'Old Harvard's office over to his barracks.

Why does he need the strongest men? Who should I choose? Frank wondered.

Frank choose ten men from his barracks building and told them to get all of their things together and meet him in front of his barracks in no more than thirty minutes. Then, Frank preceded to three other barracks buildings and did the same thing. Thirty minutes later Frank had the forty men standing around in front of his barracks. Everyone was asking all kinds of questions that Frank did not have the answers too.

The General came out of his office across the yard and shouted commands at them in Japanese. 'Old Harvard' picked up the bullhorn and shouted, "Prisoners get in line, two abreast, and march out the front gate with these guards guiding you to your next destination."

We all stood there wondering what was in our future.

"Move out," 'Old Harvard' commanded.

About three miles down the road the Americans could see some Japanese trucks along the side of the road. When they got to the trucks the Jap guards shouted for them to halt. One of the guards grabbed one of our men and pushed him up on the truck. All the POW's were tired of walking and picked out one of the trucks and jumped onto it.

Five hours later they arrived at the Port of Manila. There was a Japanese freighter docked at the pier. The trucks pulled up to the ramp and stopped.

Thank God! We are going to get out of these horrible POW camp conditions and go somewhere better. Frank thought pleasantly for the first time in almost a year.

The Americans were ordered off the trucks and up the loading ramp and down into the bottom of the ship. When Frank reached the bottom of the ship about another seven or eight hundred POW's from all around the Philippines were packed into this ship. Eventually, they arrived at the Port of Fukuoka on the Island of Kyushu, Japan. The voyage was one of the most miserable times in Frank's life. Besides surviving a terrorizing partial torpedo explosion on one side of the freighter from one of the US submarines, distasteful sanitary and eating conditions on board (no dining hall or galley for the men to eat in), and seasickness Frank was glad to see any port city. Frank was one POW in about every four POW's to survive the trip.

The Jap guards lined the POW's up on the dock. They staggered down the gangplank because of being so weak and sick from everything imaginable. In one hour, more or less, this short Japanese officer with the largest sword Frank had ever seen came jumping up onto the platform and begin to speak in excellent British English.

"You POW's have been brought out of the war zone by us to protect you from the fighting between our superior Imperial Armies. We will transport you to some POW camps here in Japan. His Imperial Majesty, Emperor Zapp, has asked me to tell you to obey your orders from us and you will be much better off. Emperor Zapp will not take action against you after his Imperial Orders are completed and your homeland is defeated and subject to his Holy rule. However, every man must work hard to support this mighty effort to win this war against the wicked forces against Emperor Zapp. Do you understand? I did not hear your response. Let me hear some enthusiastic show of support. I ask you again. Do you understand His Imperial Majesty's orders to you?" He shouted through the microphone.

The POW's were tired of standing and eager to get off the dock and get a meal and maybe a bath. Most of them gave a sound of sorts to satisfy the Japanese General. He ended up at our Fukuoka 'Omuta' POW Camp Number 17 and we later nicknamed him General Sword.

The POW's were loaded onto trucks and buses and taken the 57 miles to the bay city of Omuta, Japan. The POW Camp was a group of buildings used by Mitsui Coal Mining Company used by the Imperial Japanese Army. The POW Camp was completely enclosed by a tall wooden fence with several wires on the fence and above it. Emperor Zapp's officers used some buildings in the center of the POW Camp as their headquarters and torture chambers.

Many of the POW's arrived needing urgent medical treatment. The barracks were constructed of wood and were not airtight. Frank and soldiers from the Philippines were accustomed to temperatures between 85 and 100 degrees. The cold and damp conditions made the weak very vulnerable to further illness.

Frank was glad to see a mess hall with POW trained cooks preparing the meals. The main food was from the big electric ovens in the form of bread lofts. The bread and a ration of rice were much better than the Philippines and ships. Occasionally, the steamed rice was served with various types of vegetable soups.

A separate building was equipped with large tanks with steam-heated hot water, sometimes too hot. Immediately after taking their baths, the POW's put whatever clothes they had on and went to bed.

The septic sewer system was not maintained and caused raw sewerage to remain near the latrine building. Flies, with all sorts of diseases, were obnoxious during the summer months.

Mitsui Coal Mining Company, using Emperor Zapp's Imperial Army, forced the POW's to work in the its mines until the end of the war. They had to dig tunnels using dynamite, very dangerous work to produce the coal for commercial benefit of the company and Emperor Zapp. The inhumane treatment of the POW's began by forcing them to work 12 hours a day. Not being trained miners with proper equipment, tools and safety supplies, many of the POW's received serious lifetime injuries from breathing the coal dust to falling rocks.

This was not a POW Camp. **It was a slave labor camp.** Located on Mitsui Coal Mining Company property and only six tenths of mile from the coal mine. On the days the POW's did not return to the POW Camp to eat lunch; they were given 3 buns of bread every 2nd day to take with them to eat in the mine. A thirty-minute lunch break and back to the slave labor. Occasionally, once every ten or twelve days the POW had a day off.

When POW Camp Commander or one of Emperor Zapp's Imperial Army Guards decided to have some entertainment, POW's were beaten with sword cases, fists, clubs and boots. For no apparent reason, the prisoners would be tied on a post in the center of Camp for many hours at a time. The POW's needed every hour of rest that they could peacefully achieve. However, the Emperor Zapp's trained warriors, who believed that he was God of the universe, would come roaring into the barracks at all hours of the night and wake the POW's from their deep restful sleep.

POW's used some large wood tubs with drain boards to wash their own cloths. The scrubbing to remove the mine coal dust was never an easy chore. The coal dust penetrated the pores of their skin and became a major health hazard for the POW's.

Japanese POW Camp Officers had been trained at Emperor Zapp's Military Academy to use the POW's for his benefit and keep the morale of POW's as low as possible to defeat them and win them over to his goals to conquer the world. You could cut the depression with a knife around this POW Camp. The long hard inhumane working hours in the mines, undernourishment, beatings, torture, and short rest periods were conditions to defeat most people.

Captain Montgomery, the P-40-E trained fighter pilot, weakened to less than miserable weight of approximately 110 pounds, began to notice the B-29 bombers were flying more and more missions over the POW Camp area.

We are winning the war. It won't be long now before I don't have to go back into that coalmine. I will survive this horror! Mom and Dad will be very glad to see me, and I will be very thankful to them for their teachings to keep the faith. Frank thought.

All of a sudden on August 15th, 1945, the POW Camp Commandant and all his vicious guards disappeared. A short time later, the American bombers began dropping supplies of food and clothes over the camp. Together with this was the notice that Japan had surrendered.

The Japanese Guards bailed out of the POW Camp like a swarm of wasp had landed all over them. I decided to lead my bunkhouse out the gate. I grab some of the food packages drop by our planes and started marching down the road out of the mountains toward the nearest seaport city.

Captain Frank 'Sport' Montgomery, you made it through this horrendous war and are going to live to tell everyone about the atrocities of these Japanese, I thought. *I better stop and kneel down and pray to thank God for his mercies and grace.*

Finally, some U. S. Navy landing craft pulled up near the shoreline and we started wading through the knee-deep water while the landing gate was being lowered and could not wait to "GO HOME"!

Then, we flew to the Army hospital in Tokyo for routine check-ups.

Then, I flew on to Washington, D. C. -- Andrews Air Force Base. My plane was a four-engine prop plane. I think it was a DC-6.

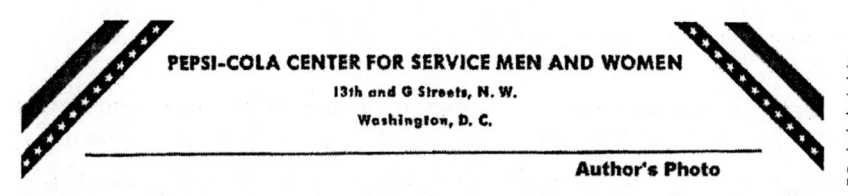

PEPSI-COLA CENTER FOR SERVICE MEN AND WOMEN
13th and G Streets, N. W.
Washington, D. C.

Author's Photo

After arriving in Washington, D. C., I was bused to the Pepsi-Cola Center for Service Men and Women. They took us to a telephone exchange and told us to tell the operators to call our family back home and we would be allowed to talk as long as we wanted.

I laughed at them, we were so far out in the country before I went into the U. S. Army Air Force -- we did not have a telephone.

They asked me if I could remember the name of a store or family that had a telephone near my home. Give this information to the operator and they will do their best to get in touch with that party and tell them to go get someone from your family to talk to you.

I contacted my mother, and she asked me when was I going to be home? I told her I did not know. They have not given us any idea. But I was in Washington D. C.

Then, we were taken into the uniform tailors and they told them to make two tailor made uniforms for all of us.

Then, I was told to go to the treasury post and get my back pay for the years I was a POW.

When I arrived at the window the man asked me what's your rating. I replied, "I don't know what my rating is, I was a Captain when I left for war."

He told me that you should be ranked at least a Colonel. I said that was okay.

I got paid and was put on 90 days leave.

I went to the train station and stood in line with all the other guys. When I got to the window I said, "I want a ticket to Chattanooga, Tennessee."

The ticket clerk looked at me kinda astonished. "You want a ticket to Chattanooga, Tennessee. You'll have to wait a couple of days."

"I want one now."

He says. "But Airman there's been a war on."

Those were the wrong words to tell me. I told him. "For a guy who had just spent almost 4 years as a POW, I know there was a war on, but I still want a ticket to Chattanooga, Tennessee!" I pounded on the window and kinda lit into him with everything I could think of.

The crowd was edging me on. "Give it to him Airman," they shouted.

So he closed the window on me.

One man stepped forward. "If you go to the airport, I think you might be able to get a ride and a ticket out of Washington, D. C," the kind and concerned man told me as he directed me to the airport.

I arrived at airport at midnight. It was almost empty. I stood there and it was the loneliest moment of my life. *Here I am standing here, I'm home, but where are all my friends.* I just felt crushed and I did not know what to do.

So, I spotted a soldier on a bench in the waiting room. I went up to him and I sat down, gave him a cigarette and we got to talking. And I asked him. "What he was doing here?

"I live in Alexandria, Virginia and I don't have any money to get home and there's no buses running or anything."

"You're in luck because I just got my pay for almost 4 years of military service."

So I got us a cab. *I was delaying going home. I was doing everything I should not do to go home.*

I took him all the way home to Alexandria and then had the cab bring me back to the airport.

I said, "Here's your fare cab driver." "Never mind Airman, you earned it"

I spent the remainder of the night on the hard bench at the airport. The next morning I was lucky and jumped a flight to Chattanooga. I hailed me a cab at the airport and told him to take me out to the farm so that I could surprise Mom and Dad. It was lunchtime and Mom and Dad had taken a lunch break and were sitting in the kitchen.

So as I looked at the house I could see a lady sitting in a chair facing the window and she had blonde hair. My mother was not blonde. So I wondered if they had moved or what had happened. The lady turned around and talked to somebody in the house. And, immediately, the door flew open, my mother came charging out of the back door, down the porch steps, slipped on a step losing her balance. She stumbled and I reached her just in time to catch her. And believe me, that was some kind of homecoming.

TREASURES OF WAR – CONCEALED BY THE EVIL ONES

Chapter Eleven

The Story of Japanese Colonel Kiyoshi Stingy

Hiding Gold Bars For Himself

And

Japanese General Tomoyuki Yamashita

In The Philippines

Author's Photo

The rapidly retreating Japanese Imperial Forces are winding their way through the trails, over the mountains, lowlands and river bottoms during the time that Colonel Kiyoshi Stingy had repeatedly struggled to keep the control of the twenty 75 kilo gold bars and three Chinese Golden Buddhas some 3 feet tall for his own personal wealth once he arrived back in Japan. Realizing that his troops were falling behind and the American Forces were coming up fast from the south, he began looking for a place to hide his separate treasure for a rainy day after the war was over.

After slowly crossing a branch of the Cagayan River during the dry season by wading in two or three feet of water and struggling to push the vehicles over the rocky bottom and finding an old farm road across the flat rice farming communities, he was on the look out for someplace to bury his treasures.

I am making good time going to the northeast. Maybe I will make it back to one of our Japanese ships at the Port of Aparri, Philippines. If I'm lucky enough to get my men to put the gold on the ship, the only thing I will have to worry about is one of the Admirals learning about it. Oh, I will just give him a few gold bars for his booty and be home free, I thought.

The retreat to the north came to a serious decision making time. When the Japanese troops reached the banks of the large Cagayan River Bridge crossing on the outskirts of Tuguegarao, I noticed that the American Army Air Force had bombed parts of the bridge.

What do I do? If that truck carrying my gold bars and Buddhas does not make it across the damaged bridge, my riches will fall into the bottom of the river and I will never be able to find it. That water is flowing very swiftly and the currents will wash them to unknown locations all along this river and possibly to the bottom of the sea, I thought to myself.

Remembering the rice farmer's hut and the water pond I saw from the road, I decided to take advantage of the delay and ask the two truck drivers to turn around and follow my orders. We drove back to the Filipino's Hut and he came out to greet me. I ordered my men to be sure nobody else was in the Hut. They found his wife and a young son and daughter. I ordered my men to march them out into the side yard under the trees and shoot all of them.

TREASURES OF WAR – CONCEALED BY THE EVIL ONES / 271

I commanded the drivers to drive to the low end of the nearby water pond.

This is a place that I can remember out here all by itself and will not be used for anything other than a water pond for a farmer's water buffalo, I thought.

I ordered one of my drivers to pick up one 75 kilo gold bar and wade out into the pond until he was chest deep in the water. As he did this he began to sink in the muddy bottom until his head went under. He immediately dropped the heavy 168-pound gold bar to the bottom and fought to free his submerged legs from the mud. He made it out. He told me that there was quick sand at the bottom and it almost pulled him under. I ordered the two drivers to walk out to about waist deep and toss the gold bars as far as they could toward the deep end. They completed burying all twenty gold bars in the bottom of the muddy pond. Then, I told the two drivers to grab one of the Golden Buddhas and take it out as far as they could and drop it to the bottom. They completed the disposal of the first two Buddhas and as they were carrying the third one out into the middle of the pond, I picked up my tommygun and began to fire on the surface of the water near them forcing them to move further into the deeper water and watched until the muddy bottom pulled them under. I waited until I knew that they had drowned and I jumped into one of the trucks and drove it back on the road and down a ways and into the ditch. Then, I ran back to the other truck and drove it back to the river crossing and joined the Japanese Troops making the crossing into Tuguegarao. As soon as I got time in Tuguegarao I sat down and drew my self a map of the location of the place where I hid the Gold Bars and Buddhas.

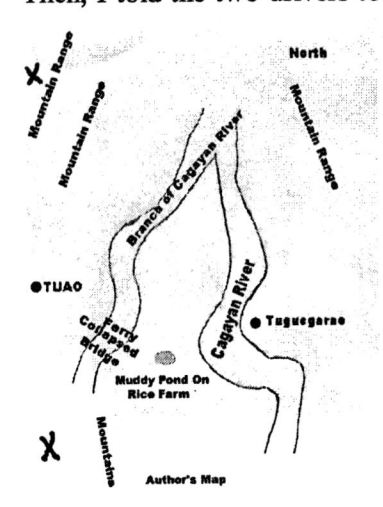

This is better for me. I will not have to share my wealth with anyone. No matter who wins the war I will be able to come back to the Philippines and retrieve my hidden treasure, I thought as I breathed a sigh of relief.

"Colonel Stingy, where are your drivers and other truck?" General Whatashi asked.

"They ran off the bridge and fell into the swift river water and drowned. After that scary event, I decided it best for me to carefully drive my other truck across."

"We have one day to reach the Port of Aparri before Emperor Evil God's Navy leaves."

General Tomoyuki Yamashita, commander of the Japanese Fourteenth Area Army, brought the treasure, and all of his field commanders, and buried the treasure with the idea of future recovery.

"YAMASHITA's Gold" as it has all come to be known. As the war reached a climax, hiding this huge treasure became a matter of urgency to senior Japanese navy officers in Manila who were responsible for its security and its shipment homeward.

It is believed that General Yamashita was chosen to bury the "Treasure" on the Island of Luzon in the Philippines. The secret treasure maps were kept in the headquarters of the Japanese high command in Manila until General Yamashita pulled out of the city in late 1943 to new headquarters at Baguio. All of the un-buried loot was taken in truck convoys to the mountains near the Benguet mines in Baguio.

There were grisly stories about **Allied prisoners --- mostly Americans, Australians, Britons, and Filipinos** --- being forced to dig these pits and tunnels during 1943 and 1944, only to be buried alive.

Japanese engineers rigged elaborate booby traps at each site, including fully armed 1,000 and 2,000-pound bombs, so that safe access to the treasure could be gained only if an excavator followed precise technical instructions described on secret maps.

The loot was hidden in tunnels or caves and sealed with concrete or buried in deep pits in over a 100 locations of the Philippines.

During the first part of April 1945 Yamashita abandoned Baguio and led his army to the Kiangan Pocket, Ifugao Province for the showdown.

General Yamashita remained in the Kiangan Pocket for months, fighting an impressive and ultimately futile rear guard action. No force was sent to relieve him. Kiangan itself was captured in July 1945, after some of the harshest mountain fighting ever. During the last month, the Americans advanced only three miles. Yamashita was neither captured nor defeated. On September 2, 1945, the same day that Japan surrendered, Yamashita surrendered.

Some treasures have been recovered during the regime of several presidents since the end of the war. Newspapers from around the world claim that **only one third** of the buried treasure in the Philippines has been found. Such findings estimated to be worth billions of U. S. Dollars.

TREASURES OF WAR – CONCEALED BY THE EVIL ONES

Chapter Twelve

The Story of Filipino Family Guarding Hidden Japanese Gold Bars

"I am claiming this land because my grandfather and parents came out here in the wilderness, cleared the land for farming a garden and rice crop and raising a few goats and pigs. They harvested the trees and bamboo used to build their home and fences. They have been paying realty taxes for more than thirty years. During the war the Japanese Navy Forces used the Polillo Strait to hide some of their naval vessels from the Allied Forces in the Pacific.

According to my grandfather, in 1944, the Japanese used the deep Agos River to unload cargo from some of their ships. The smaller Pinlac River that feeds into the Agos River goes right through the middle of our land. The Japanese Navy Forces came up to our farmhouse and took all of our stock and food.

My grandfather, grandmother, their young son, my father, fled up into the hills to a safe place that they had used for just such purposes. My grandfather, who is now dead, watched the activities of the Japanese Navy Forces for more than a month. He saw first hand the Japanese using American, Australian and other POW's to dig deep tunnels used to later bury Gold Bars and treasures. He made maps of the locations of the buried treasures.

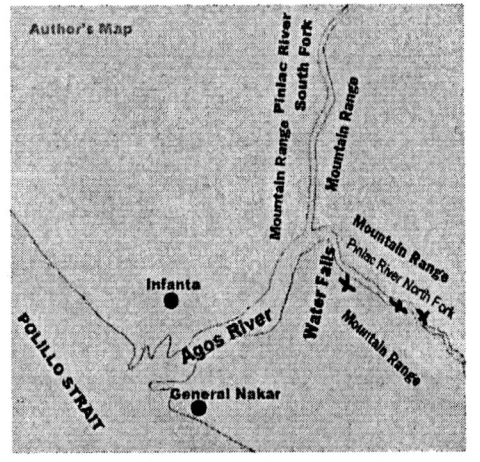

After the Japanese Navy Forces had the POW's carry the Gold Bars and precious stones into the tunnels, they brought some heavy equipment up the Agos river on a landing barge and unloaded it on the other side of the bend in the river near the site of the tunnels. The Japanese rounded up all the POW's and marched them into the tunnels. Shortly after this with the Japs standing guard, they used the heavy equipment to move some huge rock boulders onto the entrance of the tunnels. The tunnels were closed and the Japanese Navy had completed its mission to bury the treasure and kill the POW witnesses by burying them alive in the tunnels.

Then, the Japs began placing some boulders along the riverbank in a formation on both sides of the river. They located a huge flat boulder, like the top of a table, and placed it in the middle of the Pinlac River. My grandfather used these symbols to designate the location of the tunnels and buried entrances to the tunnels in the side of the hills along the river. He knew in time that the tropical growth would cover them.

He estimated the distance from the location of the water falls feeding into the Pinlac River to the huge flat boulder as 28 meters north. Then, he indicated one of the three tunnels approximately 70 meters north of the large flat boulder on the west side of the Pinlac River. The other two tunnels were dug out of the side of the bank of the River around the bend another 194 meters across from each other.

The Japanese loaded their heavy equipment and military armaments onto the barges and cruised down the Agos River to the sea. He told my grandmother and father, if anything ever happens to him, never allow any Japanese to stay on their land and not to sell the land to anyone," Oliver Tonseca elaborated.

Over the many years since the end of World War II I have wanted to uncover the Gold Bars and other Treasure hidden in the tunnels, but the many stories about how the crooked Filipino government leaders and their military servants murdering innocent landowners and peasants like my family caused me to keep this family secret of hidden wealth.

Now, the dictator has been run out of the country and the famous EDSA revolution has created a more favorable time to move the Gold Bars from the tunnels. But, how in the world am I going to get the heavy equipment up the river to remove those very heavy boulders covering the entrances? I do not have the money to undertake such a project. I am going to need some of my local people that I can trust to perform security duty from the mountainside. The local politicians will surely have their hand out and want to know what is going on out here. This is the system here in the Philippines. Who can I trust? Should I risk everything? Who would buy the Gold Bars?

Everybody is going to ask how I acquired such a significant amount of Gold Bars. I need money to pay my workers out here. What will happen if I apply for a treasure hunter license or a charter for a mining company? How much or what percent of the value of the

Gold Bars am I willing to give up? I will need some trustworthy attorney. I do not know one. I don't have the money to file for a charter?

What will I do with the bones and dog tags of the dead American POW's and other remains in the tunnels? That information will surely bring an international investigation out here. I will need money for food for all the men working on the project. Will I be able to find a trustworthy Gold broker to contact a financially able buyer? I had many thoughts and questions running through my brain.

One Year Later

The mountains were thick with tall trees and the Philippines were encouraging exports to help the balance of payments of the country.

I could get a timber and lumber license and bring the heavy equipment in under the scheme of using it for cutting some of the timber and working as a logger.

Take each 40 or 50 foot log; split them down the center from end to end. Carve out on each half several cavities one half the size of a 75-kilo Gold Bar. Place the Gold Bars in the cavities and put the matching halves back together and wrap a steel band with a banding tape machine around it in three or four locations. I could float the logs down the river and across the Polillo Strait to my new lumber mill on the Polillo Island north of the City of Polillo. Maybe the Filipino government or a U. S. Lumber Company would finance the development of such a Filipino export operation.

Once I got the logs with the Gold Bars out to the lumber mill I could have my special crew cut the steel bands and remove the Gold Bars. I could buy a big safe making people think I needed it to protect my business export documents and banking records.

I will need three or four boats to guide the logs down the river and across the Polillo Strait to a cove next to the sawmill. From the Polillo Island I can control the Gold Bars better away from suspicious visitors that will come from metropolitan Manila and any Japanese.

One of these days some of those Japanese Navy Officer's families are going to return to the Philippines as a tourist and come out here to look for their hidden Gold Bars. They will bring their father's maps and want to go out to the hidden tunnels.

Here is my opportunity. The Japanese came out here with some Filipino guide that they have hired, I took them up the Agos River and showed them the large rocks and let them look around to determine that their so-called secret locations were undisturbed and they became very eager to want to bring the Gold Bars out for their personal benefit.

I told them that I needed mobilization money for the very expensive project to dig out any treasure and large boulders from the entrance of the tunnels and bring the Gold Bars out of the mountains. I worked out an agreement with them to split the money for the eventual sale of the Gold Bars. I got their money up front for mobilization and the heavy equipment that I need for my lumber mill. I will give the Japanese a quarterly financial progress report for the project. The Filipino guide or advisor jumped through loops to get them to sign the agreement because he will not get paid much until he convinced them that the deal is excellent money to be made by them. He smells money. Then, I will delay them until I have removed the Gold Bars to the Island.

Biding my time for all the years since my father told me the story of my grandfather's maps of the hidden Gold Bars, will now pay large dividends to my family and me. The first log with the inserted Gold Bars inside will be floated down the Agos River across the Polillo Strait to the gathering cove on the Island next to the new sawmill.

I sure hope that everyone made the correct calculations for the amount of Gold Bars in each forty-foot log, and the log won't sink to the bottom of the sea. Those 10 Gold Bars weighs 1,680 pounds in each 40-foot log. I firmly believe that is very conservative and not be too heavy. It will take more than six hundred forty foot logs to move all of the Gold Bars.

I missed the opportunity to have Gold Bars for sale five years ago when the price of Gold was at an all time record price of more than $800.00 per troy ounce. Now the price is back up to $500.00 a troy ounce and it will be to my advantage to make some sales before the cycle returns to a downward trend.

The men got together and floated the first log down the river and out into the sea without problems with the water currents and guided it into the gathering cove next to the sawmill.

After I remove all Gold Bars to my sawmill on the Island, I will tell the Japanese that I have purchased all the equipment and set up the project campsite and that they should bring the Japanese team out with their secret maps to find the hidden Gold Bars. When they arrive I will take them up the Agos River to the Pinlac River and to the large rocks in the river. They will get off the boat and walk around looking for the tunnels and point out to us where they are located. They will leave their own security people at the campsite to watch over us.

A few days later, we brought the heavy equipment up to the locations that they pointed out to us and used the backhoe to pull the earth off the large boulders and hooked the crane cable around the boulder and lifted it away. The Japanese were shocked beyond belief the first time that took their high-powered flashlights and looked all over the tunnel to find it empty.

Author's Photo

They immediately began jabbering Japanese to each other and motioned for the Filipino advisor to tell us to take them back to camp. When we all reached the camp, the Japanese quickly made many long distance telephone calls to Japan. When the telephone conversations were over, they went into a portable conference room and talked loudly for more than an hour. The Filipino advisor came out and told us that they had other sites that they wanted to uncover. I told him that we would begin early the next morning. We are not leaving without the Gold Bars!

One by one, my team completed removing the boulders from the entrances in front of all of their secret tunnel locations. After the Japanese determined that their so-called hidden wealth was not there and came into my office to ask if I knew where it might have gone. My answer was very simple. I told them that the old Filipino Dictator and his military officers must have found and took it during the many years in office when my family was not living out here. I asked them what they wanted to do with the campsite and equipment. They were so upset that they told me to do whatever I wanted to do with it. One of the Japanese Navy Officer's son stepped out of the office with one of his security man's gun in his hand and rant out to the end of the dock and put the gun to his head and pulled the trigger, blowing his brains out and falling into the river.

The Japanese team and their Filipino advisor left and will probably never return.

We began to focus on moving the campsite and heavy equipment out to my sawmill company on the Polillo Island.

I worked out a deal to sell our lumber and logs to the Big Star Lumber Company in Texas. They are one of Texas' oldest and largest suppliers of interior trim materials and heavy lumber beams backed by many years of experience for supplying the construction industry. They need to keep a large inventory of lumber because of the building boom in Texas. They have plenty of orders for all types of lumber products and deep pockets to go with them. They advised me and joined me in the establishment of my sawmill and the harvesting of the timber. Besides furnishing me with the names of the best modern equipment, including the carbide and steel saws blades, that we would need to operate the timber operation; they showed me the best method for timber stand improvements for sustainable forestry for future generations profitability. I learned so much from them about protecting forests and controlling pests, diseases and other damaging agents, which would improve the long-term health and productivity of my forest. As members of the American Forest and Paper Association, they had the inside track to the best shippers of wood products at their disposal throughout the world.

This alliance helped me obtain approval from The Philippines Board of Investments for a New Domestic and Exporter of Lumber on a Pioneer Status with Non-Pioneer Incentives. These favorable incentives include a 3-year income tax holiday and a maximum of 3 % duty on imported capital equipment. The 35% savings for Federal income tax was very significant to both parties.

Upon receiving some of the funds, I decided to secure the Gold Bars in a better location. I used the large backhoe to dig out a section of the mountain 800 yards behind the office and sawmill and constructed a heavy metal framed building with a thick concrete foundation to mount the stainless steel vault that I purchased in the U. S. A. Then, I stationed my personally trained Filipino military guards in key locations around the hillsides to work shifts 24 hours a day. These guys were ones that I could trust and I saw to it that they and their families had nice houses.

I met some financially responsible precious metals brokers during the process of doing large international financial transactions with bankers in the U. S. A. and other locations for my lumber business; I took some pictures of some of my Gold Bars in one of my new vaults with me.

"Let me see the photos," Ahmed said.

"I will sell them to your buyer at an attractive discount price off the London Daily Fixed Price, but you have to send your ship to my dock at Polillo on the Island. The current London Fix Price is $498.00 per troy ounce for 24 karat Gold Bars. My bottom line price is $300.00 per troy ounce," Oli told Ahmed.

"I will send a telex to His Royal Highness today to confirm his agreement to the price," Ahmed replied.

"You may assay the Gold Bars in my offices one by one, but it has to be done under the scenario that your buyer's men are there to check out some of my lumber and the word Gold would never be mentioned outside my offices. You must keep the location of the Gold Bars secret, and I will tell you the best time for your buyer's ship to enter the Polillo Strait when the Filipino Navy patrol boats are not patrolling. You must agree to let my special team load the buggies of Gold Bars onto your buyer's vessel simultaneously with your buyer's bank wire transfer payment for the Gold

Bars to my offshore bank account in the Netherlands Antilles" Oli stated the remaining terms and conditions to Ahmed.

"I will include those additional conditions in my telex for his approval," Ahmed added.

"A better method to handle the money part would be to have your buyer issue me an Irrevocable Letter of Credit on his international Prime Bank to my offshore bank in the Netherlands Antilles in the amount of $4,823,000,000 US Dollars with provisions to allow partial deliveries and draws against it based upon his team at my offices confirming that I have delivered Gold Bars to his vessel in Polillo and his authorization notification to my bank to make the partial payment wire transfers to my account," Oli interrupted and said with more confidence.

"Okay, my buyer has the resources to issue the L/C in this amount," Ahmed emphasized.

"The target is for me to deliver a total of 500 metric tonnes of Gold Bars in this first shipment. Anything over that weight and quantity of Gold Bars would be unsafe for your buyer's vessel," Oli warned.

"Holy Cow – that's more Gold Bars than I expected for the first shipment," Ahmed observed as his eyes lit up.

One Month Later –

His Royal Highness Prince Faisal bin Sultan's private ship's captain telephoned my office in Polillo from off the coast of the Philippines in the Pacific Ocean. My man put it through to me and when I answered the call the captain said, "I am Captain Abdullah Majid. Is Ahmed in the office?"

"Yes Sir, just a minute."

"How are you Captain? Where are you at this time?"

"Ahmed, I am approximately two hours from your docks. Is the coast clear for me to enter the Polillo Strait?"

"Yes, the Philippine Navy patrol boats passed through here two days ago and will not come back here for another ten days."

"Very good, I will arrive near the docks before five this evening. Will you arrange for a tugboat to meet us about one half mile out? Tell them that my vessel number is KSA 482 and the name is Big Boy."

"Okay Captain, we will take care of that immediately. What is your international telephone number in case we need it?"

"The international number is 966-2-647-3399. You know the country details and everything."

The KSA 482 vessel docked in the evening hours.

His Royal Highness knows how to protect his investment. Look at those 50 caliber cannons mounted on the ship. I do not believe any of those pirates off this coast or when he crosses the South China Sea will attempt to rob this vessel, I couldn't help thinking.

Captain Majid's crew was armed to the teeth. They did not come ashore. Some mean looking dudes.

Everything is on schedule and everybody is working hard night and day to have a smooth operation exactly like I planned.

The end of the fourth day after my bank confirmed all payments had been transferred to my account, His Royal Highness Prince Faisal bin Sultan's private ship set sail for his country. The first Gold Bars transaction went smooth, and I learned the importance of more patience.

Finally, my many years of waiting, raising hogs and chickens, living on mangos, bread and rice are over, I gleefully thought.

TREASURES OF WAR – CONCEALED BY THE EVIL ONES

Chapter Thirteen

The Story of Mafia in Argentina During War

A neighbor of mine, a native Argentine, laughs whenever I suggest that organized crime is creeping into Perón's Argentina. "This isn't Italy," he assures me. "Businessmen here are too straight, too far away from the old country, and too freedom loving. Any gangster who tried to muscle in on somebody's business here would get it right between the eyes."

Are most of the emigrants from Europe too tough to intimidate? Yes, maybe so, but that's not the issue. The Argentina Mafia is too sophisticated to try to come out in the open and show gang style massacres.

Instead, it's pushing in and paying the political powerful Perón organization, slowly and subtly.

What makes Argentina vulnerable to Mafia infiltration these days is the smokescreen of its mushrooming infiltration of Europeans, especially Spanish, Italian and German, and its enormous need for foreign investments. Droves of new families, workers and companies are coming through the port cities every week. Confiscated assets of the holocaust victims and treasures from the conquered countries flow through the Nazis High Command and money streams into banks, corporations, and real estate developments. No one knows the real identities of the "players", who are fronted by brokers, agents, and attorneys.

Unsavory sources make up the bulk of the foreign "investments." The opportunity of the European Mafia to establish a piece of the Argentina action could not be riper. All of the attention around the world is focused on winning the war against Hitler and Emperor Zapp.

Mafia is buying into more and more legitimate businesses in Buenos Aires, Córdoba, Bahia Blanca, Comodoro Rivadavia, Mar de Plata, San Juan, Corrientes and other interior agriculture regions. The defiant and determined Mafia knows that under the conditions of being able to hide large sums of ill-gotten wealth in a country where the leadership is bribed, suckered and intimidated. They, in fact, can dig even deeper into all phases of life and swallow up the wealth of the country. All in all, a helluva experience results for the people who are being destroyed economically and socially.

"Today, Argentina means opportunity and booming business," says President Perón. "These guys are legitimate businessmen and investing in this land of opportunity, pouring a river of cash into respectable, aboveboard enterprises."

However, the true source of this wealth is from treasures of Nazi Generals and Mussolini's military officers looted from Holocaust victims and conquered countries treasures.

At the same time that the money was being poured into legitimate businesses, the mobsters were involved in the shady businesses of gambling, bookmaking, smuggling, prostitution, loan sharking, pornography, narcotics and other tacitly sanctioned vices. The massive amounts of cash these businesses generates equates to power.

Because all of these Mafia businesses, legitimate or otherwise, are all tax free, Governmental services for education, transportation, medical, military, agriculture, and international commerce are reduced to barely coming up to a poverty level for the masses.

"Violence is bad for business," Lucky told his 'family'. "We use violence sparingly," he added. "We just ask our 'Political Partner', the President, to use his military when we need to really get their attention," he further explained.

"I belong to the Jockey Club, Golf and Tennis Club, Country Club, and make contributions to the popular charities, and I am a pillar of the community, a member of the Knights of Columbus and Rotary Club," he boasted.

"Vito, you need to call the President and our 'Family' leaders and tell them that we will meet in Mendoza on November 14th," Lucky instructed. "Here is my hand picked invitees," he added as he gave him the secret list.

"We have some major decisions to be made regarding in-fighting caused by the recent actions of the President and the failed delivery of some of the Gold Bars from our Villa Krause Gold re-refining operations. One hundred eighty 12.5 kilo Gold Bars are missing." Lucky confided to Sal.

"Money makes our 'Family' organization go 'round, and it gives us instant kinship to the 'Giardalli' family," Lucky proudly stated.

"Our goal is to control practically every type of business and industry in Argentina. Currently, we have penetrated about sixty percent of the hierarchy with some specific no-holds-barred, and we have an awesome task to complete this year. We do not need Perón attempting to keep treasures for himself, allowing him to become financially self-sufficient.

We need to convey to Perón that his support will weaken over-night without our organization's support." Lucky growled as he laid out the detailed plans to Vito.

"Vito, the Giardalli family leaders must know exactly what our message to Perón will be in the meeting on the 14th. in Mendoza," Lucky deliberately emphasized.

Mendoza is the national headquarters for the Giardalli Family. It's structured like any big business. At the top is a president (Boss); beneath are vice-presidents and division executives (Under-Bosses) and staff members (Soldiers or Buttonmen). The organization is not designed around a single personality. It is corporate, self-perpetuating, built for longevity. The whole is far more dangerous that the sum of its parts.

"Sal, go over to O'Farrell Trucking Company and ask them to have three hundred wooden crates made according to these specifications," Lucky asked as he gave him the sketch. "Tell them we need these crates delivered to our Villa Krause Gold Refining operations in Villa Krause within three weeks," Lucky added.

"Yes sir. Do I go on to meet with Fräulein Schroeder while I am in her neighborhood?"

"Why don't you call Fräulein Schroeder to see if she is in," Lucky suggested.

"Good idea," Sal nodded as he went to the telephone.

"Sal, when you know that the wooden crates have been delivered to Villa Krause by O'Farrell, you need to take the CHEVY trucks and go out to San Juan near Villa Krause and check out all items on your check list for loading the Gold Bars. Stay in our place in San Juan. You will be a very short distance from the Gold re-refining plant. Once you are sure everything is in place at Villa Krause; you will take this authorization letter from me to show them that you will supervise the packaging, crating and loading of the Gold Bars for shipment to Buenos Aires." Lucky said as he handed him the letter.

"OK, I will let you know what goes down before I leave for San Juan," Sal replied.

"Will you have the military security forces from the President lined up to guard the shipment of the Gold Bars along the route from Villa Krause all the way to our bank here in Buenos Aires?" Sal asked.

"I will arrange this with General Héctor Ortiz in about a week," Lucky answered.

"You will transport the Gold Bars to the bank here in Buenos Aires and place the crates in the gold depository vault under the name of Compania La Primavera of GÉNÉVE, Switzerland in a Gold Bullion Vault Account. Be sure you take each Gold Bar out of the crate and place it on the rack in the bank's vault in the appropriately secured section for our company. Get a Gold Bullion Certificate and Warehousing Receipt for each, I repeat, each Gold Bar from Dr. Marcos Bosch, the Central Bank of Argentina's president. Do you completely understand what is required of you at the bank?" Lucky instructed and quizzed Sal.

"No sir, this is my first time to supervise the shipment from our Villa Krause Gold re-refining operations all the way here to Buenos Aires and obtain the necessary receipts from the bank for any Gold Bars," Sal replied.

"Sal, here are the copies of receipts from a previous shipment of Gold Bars. Study them thoroughly and memorize them," Lucky said as he handed several documents to Sal.

"Let's go over each one of these important documents," Lucky said looking at the copies with Sal.

"This is an excellent way to let me know what I must do and not screw up on such an important and valuable transaction," Sal enthusiastically replied.

"First, the president of the bank must sign all documents," Lucky stated in a questionable voice.

"I think so, but let me study these documents several more times to be sure I do not have any questions and understand everything," Sal interrupted.

"Then, after the Gold Bars are deposited into the Gold depository vault; the president of the bank will give you a copy of all documents. He will take the original to the Minister of the Treasury and to President Perón's office for both of their signatures on the originals. The President will call me to come and pick up the originals of all signed documents.

Second, each Gold Bar will have a Gold Bullion Aurum Utilium (AU) Custodial Receipt Number issued for it. This Gold Bullion Custodial Receipt will have a place for the serial number of each bar with it's Hallmark and our company's assay report indicating Fineness at 999.5/1000 or better, the bar size, bank officer signature place, and warehouse receipt number, complete with bar numbers and assays. For this current shipment of Gold Bars, each bar will be 12.5 kilograms.

Third, the Central Bank of Argentina will issue a Gold Bullion Certificate in metric tonnes for the total amount of the Gold Bars deposited at this one time at the Safekeeping Gold Bullion Depository Bank. Here is a copy of one of my previous Deposit Receipts," Lucky elaborated as he handed him the receipt.

DEPOSIT RECEIPT

We are holding one package in safekeeping containing the following:

Gold Bullion Certificate of Deposit – Reference Gold Bullion Certificate No. 5366090657-B. C. R, A, 602917 – One Thousand and Five Hundred (1,500) Metric Tons of Gold Bullion (Aurum Utilium) Banco Central de la Republica Argentina (BCRA), Buenos Aires, Argentina.

Package is held in favor of owner – Virgilio Hermano Foundation.

Specifications:

COMMODITY:	Gold Bullion
CERTIFICATE NO.	BCRA F. S. -- 4766520633-B. C. R. A. 602917
QUANTITY:	One Thousand Five Hundred (1,500) Metric Tons
TROY OUNCES:	Gold Bullion calculated at 32.1507428 Troy Ounces Per Kilogram
HALLMARKS:	European Hallmarks.
FINENESS:	99.999% Purity.
BAR SIZE:	12.5 and 75.0 Kilograms Bars.
TITLE:	Free and Clear of All Liens and Encumbrances, Being Fully Negotiable per Instructions of Owner.

Guarantee Of Certificate
No. BCRA F. S. 4766520633
International Transaction Deposit
From: Deutsche Europa y Banca di Roma

Got the picture?" Lucky asked.

"Lucky, I understand everything. Thank you for this opportunity to come up in the organization and earn your trust. I will use the power of the Giardalli family's name and my training out at the gun range and take whatever action I have to in order to keep the 'Family's assets secure." Sal assured Lucky.

"Sal, you do not have any choice at this point." Lucky reminded Sal as he emphasized how the 'Family' looked upon theft.

TREASURES OF WAR – CONCEALED BY THE EVIL ONES

Chapter Fourteen

The Story of Sergeant Ronald 'Cherokee' Osborne

Author's Photo   Author's Photo

I joined the Army in Tulsa, Oklahoma on December 5th 1940. I was a twenty-one year old hunk of a man, standing six foot four inches, and strong as an ox.

In April 1941, after completing basic military training at the early age of 21 and ranked as Private First Class Ronald 'Cherokee' Osborne, my superior officer told me that my orders were to report to a steamer in San Francisco for my overseas assignment in Manila, Philippines.

I went into the dispatcher's office and asked him, "Where in the world are the Philippines?"

"Private, it is way out there in the Pacific Ocean," the dispatcher replied.

"Thanks man!"

"I hope you know how to take a long boat ride without getting sea sick, hey man good luck," the dispatcher continued.

My artillery squadron, composed of 206 trained men was off to the Port of Manila.

I boarded one of the cruisers in San Francisco for my first time ocean vessel trip. I maintained my food most of the time. We all got use to it after about a week out.

It took us twenty-six days to make the journey. After I walked down the gangplank to the waiting trucks, I noticed some demonstrators holding up signs in protest of our arrival. Apparently, some of the Filipino people wanted their independence from the United States immediately.

Upon arriving at my camp northwest of Manila, review was called for all of the new arrivals in the Philippines on the field in front of the tent housing.

The commander of the camp, Brigadier General Walter 'Rip' Ripkowski, spoke to the new troops.

"We have a job here to train the Filipino Army to operate the artillery weapons that have been shipped here to the Philippines. Washington has ordered me to have the Filipinos trained and equipped to allow them to defend the Philippines for themselves in a few years when the Commonwealth of The Philippines is declared an Independent Republic.

Keep your nose and other sensitive parts of your body clean," the General ordered.

"Let me introduce you to the Chief of the Philippine Constabulary, Major General Guillermo Francisco. Let me tell you right now, he is from the 'old military tradition'. His men know that he is very strict and disciplined, and expects the same from all of his men. Don't be fooled by his youthful looks.

He is responsible for his Filipino infantry and artillery divisions here under his command. Each of you will work together with his men. All of you will receive your supplies from the U. S. Army supply warehouse over there," as General Ripkowski firmly spoke and pointed to the large warehouse building off to his left.

Since there wasn't much else to do, I worked very hard to get my next stripe. Sure enough, after four months of successfully training the Filipino soldiers, the 1st Lieutenant called me in, complimented me and presented me with my First Sergeant stripes. I was very excited. This was the first time in my life that I had received recognition for anything.

Most of the Filipino soldiers had been schooled in English. But, I could not understand anything they said in their local Tagalog language. I oftentimes wondered what they were saying to each other about me as I was training them. One day they were talking among themselves during water break time, and they began to laugh loud.

"Felipe, what are you guys looking at me and laughing about?" 'Cherokee' shouted.

"Sarge, Generosa said you were the biggest man he every saw and wondered how you could have made love to any of the small Filipino chicks," Felipe said smiling.

"You guys better not worry about my love life. You might ought to be concerned about me beating you little guys to death tonight when I sneak into your tents. Felipe, did the American school teachers sent up to your school in Urdaneta by Teddy and Governor Taft ever teach you smart guys American history and about the famous Sioux Chief Crazy Horse?" 'Cherokee' asked with a stare into the eyes of the men.

"Yes, Sarge, we learned about the American Indians," Felipe quickly replied.

"During his hit and run raids, he led his Indian forces in the Battle of Little Bighorn where he and his savage warriors slaughtered General Custer and all of his men. The massacre became known as 'Custer's Last Stand'. As you know, I am part Indian and have some of the same ancestral powers as Chief Crazy Horse. Bet you men will think twice before you have fun with my size and laugh at me again," 'Cherokee' said as he told them the water break was over.

"Attention, my orders for today are to get you prepared to use all of this heavy artillery weapons, the 'dry powder' and shells for battles during the typhoon seasons here in the Philippines. During the next few months you are going to learn first hand just how difficult it will be to move the weapons, trucks and wagons, food supplies, ammunition and fuels when the typhoon blows through here and the monsoons that follow," Sergeant Osborne promised his men.

"Secure your weapons in their proper places. You are dismissed for now. Mess call is for 17:00 hours," Sarge commanded his Filipino soldiers.

Sometime between now and the end of September, I hope that I can get these men ready to pass the strict final inspection for Major General Francisco, I thought.

Most of the Filipino soldiers were very eager to become good soldiers for the Commonwealth of the Philippines. They could not wait to be free from the control of a foreign power, the United States; and become an independent country in about five years. They were primed to learn how to defend their country.

However, in early December 1941, Major General Guillermo Francisco and all Filipino soldiers were inducted into the United States Armed Forces in the Far East (USAFFE) by an executive order of President Franklin D. Roosevelt.

General Francisco was given his orders by General Ripkowski to serve as commander of the 2nd Regimentary Division in Limay, Bataan, on the Manila Bay side of the Peninsula. He and his men trained by Sgt. Osborne moved out to their new position.

On December 8th, 1941, Sergeant Osborne was ordered to Lingayen, a port city on the Gulf of Lingayen in the Province of Pangasinan, the South China Sea side of Luzon, with G-Battery to defend against the Japanese attack. He had three fellow Americans artillery squads, 24 of the elite Filipino Scouts and 540 raw Filipino reservists, who were illiterate and could not communicate with all of the men around them.

As 'Cherokee' and his platoons were beginning to set up their defense, the fleet of the Japanese Navy vessels began their initial landing in the Philippines north of them at Aparri. More than five thousand men of the Japanese Army under the command of General Masaharu Homma began spreading out all over Northern Luzon and fighting their way south toward Lingayen.

Emperor Zapp, the sacred and inviolable, and Head of the Empire of Japan was the supreme commander (daigensui) of the Japanese Armed Forces. His Army, Air Force and Navy forces were commanded to carry out his declared war and campaign of terror that is unsurpassed in bestiality and savagery in modern times.

His orders were to destroy the Philippines within sixty days. The non-combatant Filipinos, Filipino Tribesmen, Filipino soldiers and American soldiers were being bombarded, massacred, summarily executed, beheaded, beaten and raped, stabbed, shot, hanged, tortured, boiled alive, impaled on bayonets, burnt alive, starved, and enslaved for their labor. Fierce battles erupted all over the place.

The American military plan named, WAR PLAN ORANGE by General Douglas MacArthur, was relayed to all troops a day before Christmas 1941. It was drawn up in the hope that reinforcements would come by way of the sea to assist in the battle of the invaders. Cherokee expected to see American soldiers landing on the beaches to fortify their positions.

As part of the United States Armed Forces in the Far East (USAFFE), 'Cherokee' and his platoons were ordered to retreat to Bataan.

I went into my commander's office on Bataan and asked, "Colonel, why do all the men think that help is coming? You know differently don't you?"

"Sgt. Osborne, President Roosevelt and his military advisers have decided to put America's effort in Europe first. The message that I received a few days ago is that we are on our own. Fight as long as you can," the Colonel answered.

"Sarge, you are dismissed."

I met up with some of the men from the small airfield at IBA, Zambales Province. They were giving it their best shot, but the ammunition was almost 25 years old. Grenades were something that could be effectively used in the jungle warfare on Bataan, but only about 3 in 30 worked. Men were being killed and wounded because of old WW I supplies, guns and ammunitions.

All of them were running out of supplies in the steamy and malaria infested jungle, but they were determined to cause delays in the Japanese plans to conquer the Philippines within a few months at the most.

They valiantly fought to disrupt Emperor Zapp's orders and timetable of the conquest of the Philippine Islands in order to allow the United States and Allied Forces to gain valuable time to recover from the initial onslaught by Japan at Pearl Harbor, Singapore and Hong Kong.

On Good Friday, April 3, 1942 the Japanese made its' fiercest attack on the troops. The shells and bombs rained down on Bataan.

By Easter, April 5th, 1942, after four months of fighting, nursing the wounded, some 70,000 American and Filipino troops were gathered in several lines to defend Bataan.

The highest point on the Bataan Peninsula was Mt. Samat, 4,550 feet. At about 1 PM on Easter Sunday, the Japanese planted the banner of the rising sun at the summit of Mt. Samat.

Word got out that their commander, General Douglas MacArthur and the Philippine Commonwealth President; Manuel Quezon had fled to Australia.

After four months of fierce fighting, nursing the wounded, weak, diseased, starving and with ammunition running out and with "No Momma, no Poppa, no Uncle Sam" and no sign of reinforcements coming, the "Battling Bastards of Bataan", on April 9, 1942 were ordered to surrender to the invading Japanese Armed Forces by Major General Edward P. King, commanding officer of the forces on Bataan.

Approximately 10,200 American and 65,000 Filipino fighting soldiers and 1,500 American and 2,500 Filipino wounded and sick in the Bataan's two field hospitals became Prisoners of War of the Imperial Japanese Armed Forces on that fateful April 9, 1942 on Bataan.

Early on the morning of April 11th, I was marched by Japanese Guards with bayonet rifles out to a large field outside the small town of Mariveles with about two thousand American and Filipino prisoners. We had to stand there all day long and slept in total darkness surrounded by Jap Guards.

The next day, I was one of about two hundred American and Filipino confused soldiers forcefully shoved out onto the hard concrete road leading north out of the Bataan Peninsula. I did not know any of the men near me on the march to prison camp. The scorching hot sun, with no water or rest along the way caused some of the men to drop out of column. The Jap Guards poked the men with their bayonets and shouted all types of commands in Japanese in an attempt to make the men get back in line.

After about ten kilometers down the road, I heard the shots as they rang out and hit some of the POW's.

"What in the world are they doing? I whispered to the stranger next to him.

"Better keep quiet, you will be next," the fellow prisoner replied.

The Filipino and American soldiers who had survived the fierce fighting in Bataan were forced to walk between five to eight days under the heat of the summer sun, without water, for about 98 kilometers to the town of San Fernando.

I survived by eating some of the moist leaves and grasses during the night to get my necessary fluids. I had learned this from some of my up bringing as a young Indian boy.

The Jap Guards forced about 100 prisoners to get into some very old railroad boxcars for the 4-hour train ride to Capas, Tarlac. The POW's were packed like sardines, no place to sit down and with the additional heat from fellow prisoners; it became sweltering hot.

The POW's that had survived the boxcar ride were ordered off the train by the Jap Guards and forced into two marching lines for the 9-kilometer march to Camp O'Donnell.

The now famous Bataan Death March will live forever.

General Francisco led his Filipino men on the Bataan Death March. Of the original 65,000 Filipinos it has been estimated that between 22,000 to 26,000 Filipino soldiers inducted in the United States Armed Forces in the Far East (USAFFE) were either shot or struck by lethal blows from the Japanese captors or fell dead on the wayside from exhaustion, illness or wounds from the war on Bataan.

One night inside the American concentration area, the Death Camp at O'Donnell, I had a dream in which I saw myself going home to Oklahoma and marrying a country girl and raising a family of five boys.

Tormenting Jap Guards forced many soldiers to began to believe that the dead were the lucky ones. The daily human degradation and cruelty to prisoners by the Jap Guards, together with only one water spigot for the entire prison camp which caused them to stand in the waterline all day and half the night just to get their drink of water.

Baths were forbidden because it was a waste of water for the Japanese Army to use.

During the first forty days at Camp O'Donnell between 1,500 and 1,800 Americans died. Another 23,000 to 25,000 Filipinos died. The burial detail never ended, day or night.

In July 1942, the Japanese Army Officers decided to move by train only the American POWS at the Camp O'Donnell Prison to the Prison Camp at Cabanatuan, a larger POW camp. The Filipino POWS remained at Camp O'Donnell for several more months before most of them were released. The Japanese Army Officers were attempting to win over the Filipino people.

Again, I was stuffed into a rail car and taken to Camp Cabanatuan Prison Number 2 in Nueva Ecija Province.

"I bet I don't weigh much more than one hundred pounds," I told my bunk buddies the first night in the new prison camp.

"Yea, with your size, you must have lost more than you weigh now. My name is Johnny Saunders. I am from Alabama," he replied.

"Nice to know somebody from Alabama. I am from Oklahoma. One of those rare part Indian guys," I softly spoke.

"Been through hell and back on the march from Bataan and at the prison camp at Camp O'Donnell. It was sad to see the men that made it to Camp O'Donnell die by the hundreds everyday. Where were you captured?" I asked.

"My squadron was on Corregidor. We surrendered the middle of May and were transported to Manila. Those Japs made us march right down through the main streets of Manila. They used us to show the Filipinos how brave they were," Johnny answered with tears in his eyes.

"How long have you been here?" I asked.

"Been here about two weeks before you got here today. We better get some rest before those Jap Guards come in here and play their torture games and search us again. Tomorrow you will meet Captain Tanaka, the prison commander. He has been ordered to shoot any Filipinos that came near this American POW camp," he replied.

During the horrible times at Cabanatuan # 2 Prison Camp, 'Cherokee' had malaria, very little to eat or drink, burial duty five days a week to bury his fellow soldiers; but the image from his dream kept him wanting to live.

After about six months at Camp Cabanatuan, he was trucked to the port of Manila and put into the pits of one of the "Hell" ships for the hazardous sea voyage to Japan.

'Cherokee' and three or four hundred of his fellow prisoners were packed into the POW ships. The men had to share bunk beds built from the floor to the ceiling. It became unbearable to eat, take a shit or piss, hear anything but screaming men during the battles against the attacks by the Allied submarines and the shoving and jumping up to the top bunk became a ritual during these times of horror.

They reached the Japanese port. All of the live POW's were unloaded and ordered to stay on the dock so that the Japs could wash them down with a fire hose. It seemed very strange to Cherokee for the Japs to finally clean them up for the first time in a month. Then, the Japs set up sick bays near the dock to care for the seriously ill that had survived.

"Guess they need us to work hard over here for them," I muttered to my buddy next to me.

"They did not want us to bring our diseases into their country," the buddy replied.

"Bet you are right. Never thought about that angle," I confirmed.

'Cherokee' became a slave laborer in the coalmines of Japan until the end of the war.

TREASURES OF WAR – CONCEALED BY THE EVIL ONES

Chapter Fifteen

Filipino Warrior Stories – Before -- During -- After -- World War II

Author's Photo

Most of the Filipinos were men from the hinterlands, *probinsyanos,* who were patriotic enough and eager to be a part of the military, which read and memorized the military oath without understanding a single word of it.

In 1941, as a 22-year-old student at the University of the Philippines law school, I, Bautista Cruz, was called to join the United States Armed Forces in the Far East (USAFFE). It was a thrill to be a part of the military and being trained to be part of my country's reserve forces. And maybe it was the patriot in me that made me and the other Filipinos yearn to fight and resist the invading Japanese. I had a very good Christian up bringing.

The Filipino and American soldier's belief in God would be greatly tested together with belief in themselves and the American Spirit.

Japan's Imperial General Masaharu Homma and his two divisions of veteran fighters were given orders from Emperor Zapp to conquer Luzon in only 50 days from the day they landed in Aparri on December 8, 1941.

The capitulation of Bataan came after repeated demands from the Japanese to surrender starting on January 10, 1942.

General Homma could not budge the United States Armed Forces in the Far East defensive lines on Bataan.

Emperor Zapp became "acutely worried" and sent a high-powered contingent of Imperial Army staff officers to Manila.

General Homma was "effectively relieved" from his command, and Emperor Zapp took direct leadership of the Philippine Military operations from his palace in Tokyo.

Easter is always a joyful occasion. While many Filipinos worshipped at dawn services, the Filipino and American soldiers hid from shells and bombs that rained down on Bataan, literally caught between the rock and the deep blue sea; they could not fight much longer.

After surrendering, they were made to march on the morning of April 11 and over the next few days from the airstrip in Mariveles to Balanga some 33 kilometers away. The Japanese Guards refused water and food along the march. A trail of decomposing bodies were left along the long journey from Mariveles all the way to San Fernando, some 100 kilometers down the dusty hot roads.

TREASURES OF WAR – CONCEALED BY THE EVIL ONES / 303

The Jap soldiers seemed to enjoy tormenting the prisoners. The POWs were not shown any mercy. But then, this is war and the victors made the rules.

Death came every morning to hundreds Filipino and American POW's who failed to withstand starvation and disease at Camp O'Donnell, the first prisoner of war camp. The dead were taken out in tattered blankets slung over bamboo poles and dumped in common graves.

The Japanese Guards refused to permit the POWs to wash their face in the small river that ran through the camp.

They were told the river was used for the Japs' drinking water only.

How many died today? This is truly hell on earth. I wake up every morning at O'Donnell POW camp asking myself that question, Lt. Cruz emotionally thought.

The Japanese were starving us and disease was not something we were combating well, together with malaria and dysentery.

Most of the Jap Guards got a great deal of enjoyment out of kicking a guy in the open sore or wound, then laughing very loud about it. Some of the Filipino soldiers had huge holes in their legs, no flesh right down to the bones.

The Japanese officers would not give the POWs any medication, as the brave soldiers got sicker and sicker. Some of the older Filipino tribesmen, part of the Filipino Scouts Unit, knew how to put the maggots in the wound and wrap it with rags. The maggots would eat away the entire puss and everything diseased.

Filipino POWs were lying there dying and flesh rotting off their bodies.

After six months at Camp O'Donnell prisoner of war camp, the Japanese attempted to change their thinking over night and release most of the Filipino POWs. We were allowed to clean up and go home. The Japs realized that they might need the Filipino troops to fight future battles to defend the Philippines against the Allied Forces. Also, they needed the Filipinos to support them in the Japanese propaganda that the Philippines belonged free and the Japanese would free us later.

I jumped on a Japanese truck that was going to Manila for more supplies. I was surprised to find life almost normal along the way and in Manila. The 'foreigners' had been rounded up and put in an area where the Japs could watch the 'aristocrats' and keep them from underground activities against them.

"I was captured on Bataan and made it through the Death March of Bataan to Fort O'Connell Prison. I spent five months in that Death Camp. Each morning that I woke up I thanked God that I was still alive. Many mornings I woke up to find the man beside me was already dead. I could barely move due to dysentery and other diseases when the Japanese discharged me last week," Lt. Bautista Cruz confessed to his mother and neighbors.

"If I was lucky, I got a ration of rice balls with salt once a day. I can remember more than 300 POW's died one day. They were taken out in blankets then slung over a bamboo pole and dumped into common graves. The horrors of waking up to dead men all around me each morning will last in my mind forever," Cruz explained further.

"You never gave up," his mother said with tears running down her cheeks.

"But, Mom I am going to get well and go back out there and fight with the Filipino Guerrillas. These invaders must be destroyed, forced off of our lands and pay for what they have done to us and the Americans," Lt. Cruz emotionally replied.

The atrocities committed by the Japs during the Bataan Death March would not be found out about until April 1943.

Another Filipino Story of Heroism.

Since the mid-1930's, Rico C. Holliman, statesman and renown international lawyer, industrialist and businessman, had developed extremely important trading relationships with the Japanese leaders was led down the path to open large credit lines with the Japanese. During one of his trips to Tokyo in late 1940 I attempted to negotiate some payment schedule terms for the amounts owed to me. This would enable me to have been paid by the Japanese for shipments made to them over the previous year time period.

The negotiations were very tough. I was at a point of "get my money" or cease doing business with them. The tough stance was not well received at that time by the triumphant conquerors of Asia. I did not receive any YES answers from anyone on any portion of the monies owed to me.

TREASURES OF WAR – CONCEALED BY THE EVIL ONES / 305

I hired a Japanese lawyer colleague of mine from past years working together in Japan to file several lawsuits against several Japanese companies and in two causes of actions against the Japanese government.

I symbolized Filipino valor against all odds, while my unusual actions made me a marked man.

Later, I returned to Manila. I summoned all of my staff together for a meeting in my large elaborate conference room.

"Let me tell each of you what I have decided to do. None of my companies will supply the Japanese any more materials or perform any services for anyone connected with a Japanese business. There are no exceptions. As long as the Japanese employees of my companies, residing here in the Philippines, perform their jobs and are loyal to me, you have a job," Holliman addressed the staff meeting.

"Maybe I should not ask. What happened?" Margaret asks.

"Without the details, all of the Japs refused to pay me for most of the shipments that we have made over the past year. I had to file several lawsuits against them," Holliman replied.

A year later.

In November 1941, a month before the Japanese Imperial Forces attacked and invaded the Philippines; I flew to Singapore and then on to the U. S. I was very concerned about the Japanese aggression throughout the region. I knew he was a marked man.

During my war years in the U. S., I worked with some top military and civilian officials in Washington, D. C. Before I left D. C., one of the State Department officials gave me a letter of introduction from the Secretary of War and Secretary of State, the Honorable James F. Byrnes, for my future benefit.

A few months after the end of the war I returned to Manila. Most of the buildings around my offices were completely bombed out. Fortunately, my building was only partially destroyed from the outside.

How lucky can I be? What new claims do I have against the Japanese? I wondered?

I need to go meet the top people at the U. S. Embassy. I thought.

Maybe my D. C. letters will help me get assistance to correctly file my previous claims before the war against Japan and my postwar compensation claims for the damages here.

In my first meeting at the American Embassy I met Agents David Morin and Anthony Smith from the Office of Strategic Services (OSS) and Colonel Landsdale from the U. S. Air Forces.

"Gentlemen, let me take this opportunity to introduce myself with this letter of introduction from the Honorable James F. Byrnes, the Secretary of State, and the Honorable George L. Harrison, the Special Consultant to the Secretary of War," I stated as I handed them the two letters with the proper United States government departmental seals.

"Thank you for your efforts in Washington, D. C. during the war." Landsdale responded as he looked up from reading the two letters with a smile.

"The purpose of this meeting is to learn from you and receive your assistance regarding my claims against the Japanese before the war and afterwards. Here are copies of my lawsuits I filed against the Japanese government and these Japanese companies in November 1940. I can't make contact with my lawyer colleague I knew before the war. Where and how do I go about getting some of my money?" I asked as I presented them with the causes of action against the Japanese.

"Great God in glory, I do not have a clue of what should be done to recover assets on pre-war debt transactions. At this time all financial interaction with Japan is in suspense," Agent Morin replied.

"Whether you can lawfully lay claim to Japanese assets in the Philippines, Japan or anywhere else around the world, is a question that we need to get answers," Agent Smith added.

"Let me take you to my old office, what remains of it," I suggested.

"You will understand more of who I was before the war."

"As you can imagine, we are extremely busy, but we will take some time tomorrow to go there. Your address is not far from here," Landsdale responded.

"In the meantime, I will make some contacts with some military officer buddies of mine in the Supreme Commander for the Allied Powers headquarters in Tokyo as soon as possible to seek some answers and direction for you on your pre-war claims against Japan," Landsdale added.

"Thank you very much, and I will meet you in front of my office building at 11:00 hours tomorrow," I replied with a smile from ear to ear.

OSS Agents David Morin and Tony Smith together with Colonel Landsdale of the U. S. Army Air Force met Mr. Holliman in front of his office building the next morning. As they walked around the outside looking at the damage it became apparent only the north and south sides and the rear of the building was demolished. The front entrance with double glass doors leading up the stairs to Mr. Holliman's elaborate office and conference room was in tact.

As they entered his large private office everything was as though a war had not occurred. The beautiful teak wood built-in file cabinets with some glass sliding fronts were unscratched. However, as they looked over in the far corner where Mr. Holliman's L shaped desk was, the destruction jumped out at them. The Japanese Military Officers had taken some heavy ax or hammer and chopped both sides of the L's into two pieces. The large high back executive chair had been sliced right down the middle into two pieces. The private three foot tall fireproof vault had the combination and locks blown off and all business papers and valuables removed.

"Look's like the Japanese Military were sent here to send me a message and find the documents to support my lawsuits against them for non-payment of the merchandise I had shipped to them before the war," I said describing the gruesome state of my office.

"I do not believe they mistook whose office this was," Colonel Landsdale replied.

"It appears if you had been here, you would also be in two separate pieces," Agent Morin observed.

The men continued to go about the offices noticing how the Japanese had moved things from the fourth floor down into the basement and apparently at one point used a small section in the basement as sleeping quarters with mattresses lying on the floor. The Japanese Troops had stolen souvenirs that Mr. Holliman had bought during his trips to the U. S. A. before the war. The investigation lasted three hours.

"Mr. Holliman, you obviously have claims against the Government of Japan. We will continue to learn what you must do to file those claims and let your know," Colonel Landsdale cautiously said.

"I appreciate your valuable time and will wait for your advice during these very unusual times," I replied.

A Post World War II Filipino Story.

My name is Teofilo Escobar. In 1964, I decided to go overseas to study aeronautical engineering in Japan. Throughout the year before I was to leave the Philippines, I solicited as much advice about the country I was going to spend several years of my life. Some of my relatives and businessmen I consulted with told me of many frightening stories about Japanese Military Forces atrocities in World War II committed here in the Philippines.

Uncle Alfredo came to me and told how the Japanese were forced by the American and its' allied military forces to hide lots of treasures in many locations around the Philippines.

"Teo, your grandfather saw the movement of the Japanese Armies marching American and Filipino POW's over the mountain roads in the Rizal region together with trucks loaded down and had difficulty going up the steep hills. Once, he told me that he saw some shining bars fall off the trucks. The Jap soldiers would run and point to the shining bars and command the POW to pick it up and put it back in the wooden crate on the truck." Uncle Alfredo said with a greedy grin on his face.

"You got to be kidding me," I replied with a bigger grin on my face.

"I am serious as sin. Pops Domingo told your father and I that story. In fact, he added that on several occasions when the trucks could not make it up the steep roads the Japs would make the POW's unload some of the heavy crates and carry them up to the top of the hill before reloading them back onto the truck. You have seen some of the news articles about Filipinos finding some of the hidden Gold Bars that the Japs left here during their retreat," he further elaborated.

"I wish that you would not call them Japs. I will be doing my studies over there for three to five years and I do not want to get into the habit or be tempted to say the word, Japs."

"OK, I am older and know what we had to live through during the War. I will do my best not to use that word again," Uncle Alfredo added.

"What is your best guess? Do you think that I am going to the best place to get my aeronautical engineering degree?" I asked in my doubting voice.

"I am not an expert in the field of aviation. But, those Japanese fighter and bomber pilots knew what they were doing. Somebody had to be able to build a very fast airplane. It would also be good to have you this close to home in case your father or mother needs you for any reasons. The other alternative is the USA. They are now the best, but too far away in my opinion," Uncle Alfredo said as he pointed off in the direction of the USA.

"Thank you for your candor and advice. I am excited about going to Tokyo University in Tokyo. I will be leaving in a few weeks, but I promise to write you occasionally," I said as I reached my arms around my uncle and hugged him.

Later In The Year.

After brushing up on my new found language, Japanese, I began to open up a little bit and mix with some of my classmates during my free time. I wanted to learn the language better and knew that the best place to do this was with my classmates.

By chance, my classmates were sons and daughters of high-ranking Japanese officers of the Imperial Navy and Army. They had survived the war and intermarried with local women in parts of Asia in which they sought refuge. Such nations included: the Philippines, Indonesia, Malaysia, Thailand, Vietnam, and China. The Japanese government awarded academic scholarships and monetary pensions to the children of these surviving military officers. Miss Meiko Kato, one of my classmates, was the daughter of a ranking navy officer. Her father was in hiding in Menado, Indonesia. On his deathbed, he revealed his lifelong secret about a treasure hidden on an island in the Philippines. He gave her the map that showed the location of the treasure. The secret map had been written on a cloth, which was deteriorating and becoming illegible. Miss Meiko kept the map as a keepsake of her father, not really believing the story her father had told her.

The pair sat next to each other in class and quickly became friends. The friendship between Miss Meiko and me developed into a relationship and we were inseparable. Gaining Meiko's trust, she confided in me her father's secret. They both transferred the map to paper and the cloth was burned. Each now had a copy of the secret map. The map was written with Japanese characters, which was foreign to both Miss Meiko and me. Frustrated, we sought help from a professor at our university. Humorously, the professor claimed that it was a map of some sort. His translations made no sense and were alien as far as we were both concerned. Miss Meiko and I ended our pursuit and justified its end with the skepticism we had when we first had heard the great tale.

I kept my copy and soon thereafter our relationship ended and I returned to the Philippines. I did not pursue looking for the treasure because of the political environment that pervaded the Philippines. The atmosphere during current Philippine President regime contraindicated any "poking around" and/or questioning about a treasure. The strong hand of the Filipino government would clearly interfere and seize any information dealing with a treasure with this much potential ---- billions of dollars. I soon forgot about the map, and went about an ordinary life.

One day, I went on a trip to visit some old friends from college. During the bus ride, the driver would announce the stops so that travelers would wake up if they had fallen asleep during the ride. Nearing my destination, the bus driver yelled the name of a volcano because it was one of the scheduled stops. I recognized the name but could not place it. After an hour of thought and two headaches later, I remembered that the name was one of the names on the map, which I had put out of my mind years ago.

The fire of excitement was quickly extinguished when I looked at the vast landscape and realized that I had only found a very general location. It was like trying to find a street in an unfamiliar city without a map, but at least I had found the city. Even if I had found the treasure's location, retrieval would be difficult. It would take teams of men and equipment, not to mention lots of money and engineering skill to excavate and to find the precise locations. Once again the thought came to an end.

TREASURES OF WAR – CONCEALED BY THE EVIL ONES / 311

Years later, I went to the United States. I lived a normal life but would spend my free time researching Philippine maps and history. This periodic hobby lasted for 30 years and soon became a source of entertainment rather than a quest. Through my research I learned of the many warship battles in the Philippines.

Markings on my map indicated that the treasure on his map were in the vicinity of the mountain range near the city of 'Priority Location'. I concluded that my map indicated the location of the 'unknown cargo' and is the map of the field commander's headquarters. I had also uncovered more identifying landmarks from the original map. Presently, the fall of the Filipino President's regime has eliminated a number of obstacles that were present in the past.

With the current technology in location finding devices available, a team of searchers was established to retrieve the buried treasure. The actual site has been pinpointed. Enhancements during this technology era have allowed me to facilitate and expedite the removal of a treasure.

However, the Greater Metro-Manila Pinoy Pulis authorities have ordered the deployment of secret marshals into the region. The secret marshals work as plainclothes undercover agents and bring fresh money into the community under the guise of establishing a new retail shop selling the latest radios and other electronic devices for the Filipino huts with recent installed electricity around the hillside communities. Their true motive is to keep everyone under surveillance and learn where any Treasures are hidden in the region.

Finding American POW Bones.

Bangaan, Ifugao Province --- A dusty gravel road that dead ends into a rice field in this famous "Eighth Wonder of The World" Rice Terraces has served for years as a gathering place for the local Filipinos and tourist from the Philippines and all over the world.

But in 1950, this same road served a more ominous purpose --- a place to uncover bodies. The best clue officials could have hope for to identify the victims were the distinctive wooden POW number tags issued by the Japanese to the American and Filipino POW's. These wooden I. D.'s could not be found anywhere.

The Japanese soldiers tore the American's 'Dog Tags' off of them shortly after being captured or murdered. This was a Jap soldier's souvenir indicating his warrior triumphs. He collected them to show his heroic courage.

"They are the bodies of men who were fatally shot once in the chest, but their dog tags had been removed. Some had no heads, arms, or legs. Most of the bodies had only the trunk," said Constable Rex Aso. "Everything else is gone. It looks like as though the missing body parts might have been surgically removed, without any chipping of the bone, by a swordsman with something that was very sharp, like his sword. We don't know why, but maybe it was done to try to prevent identification." He added.

"Was this done to prevent war crime charges against the Japanese officers that had POW's under their guard? The size of most of the bones indicates them to be either American or Australian POW's. Why were these POW's this far from Camp O'Donnell or Cabanatuan Prison? What had they witnessed to cause the Japs to murder them and eliminate all parts of the bodies that would identify them?" Colonel Olano of the Philippine Military Academy asked.

Circumstances surrounding the murders remain a mystery.

"We do not have enough of the bodies necessary to make an identification, no fingerprints, or dental work. This discovery is like putting together a puzzle with many pieces missing," Constable Aso sadly commented.

"The buttons, belts, belt buckles and other distinctive items sometimes found on buried POW's are missing. The location of the burial underneath the wet soil of the rice fields for more than five years destroyed all clothing. However, apparently one of the POW victims may have swallowed a small round Gold love sake heart trinket shaped with the inscription on it, 'I love you Red'," Deputy Constable Villegas went on to described.

"Constable, I have been sent here to transfer these body parts to Clark Air Force Base for further attempts to identify and to properly bury them at the U. S. Military Cemetery in Manila," Captain Townsend informed Constable Aso.

"Does the U. S. Military Forces have a way to identify soldiers by their nicknames? If so, are they able to know whom in the U. S. Forces remains missing that fought in this region?" Constable Aso asked.

"Oh, you mean whether we had anyone in our Forces with the nickname, 'Red'?"

"Yes, sir, that is the only clue that we have uncovered. Good luck in you work at Clark. Someone back in the U. S. continues to anxiously await for some answers as to where their love one was killed."

"Thank you, this is like finding a needle in a haystack. You have to take out one straw at a time and keep a positive attitude," Captain Townsend said.

"We believe the retreating Japanese Forces did these murders during the final days of the war. They did this to prevent identification that would have tied their group into the POW's that they had under their control," Constable Aso added. "We will continue to search for the old Cordillera mountain people that may have been a hidden eye witness to this horrible and senseless war crime. Somebody out there knows what happened and can help us. The Ifugaos natives have good reasons to distrust foreign military forces. The tribal women have not gotten over the crimes of rape of their young women by the Japanese soldiers, village shootings of innocent leaders to force submission and control, taking of food and livestock, scattering them to the jungles and hills and the later births after the war ended of sons and daughters from the Japs sexual assaults," Aso elaborated.

"Today, I can't imagine the fear they have for you and anyone in authority. They have many bad memories of the war years that they do not want to share with anybody," a concerned Captain Townsend replied.

"We need to keep in contact."

"Yes, Captain."

TREASURES OF WAR – CONCEALED BY THE EVIL ONES

Chapter Sixteen

Japanese Surrender to the Allied Military Forces

September 1945

315 / DON STEWART NIMMONS

INSTRUMENT OF SURRENDER

of the Japanese and Japanese-Controlled Armed Forces in the Philippine Islands to the Commanding General United States Army Forces, Western Pacific at
Camp John Hay
Baguio, Mountain Province,
Luzon, Philippine, Islands
3rd of September 1945

Pursuant to and in accordance with the proclamation of the Emperor of Japan accepting the terms set forth in the declaration issued by the heads of the Governments of the United States, Great Britain, and China on 26 July 1945; at Potsdam and subsequently adhered to by the Union of Soviet Socialist Republics; and to the formal instrument of surrender of the Japanese Imperial Government and the Japanese Imperial General Headquarters signed at Tokyo Bay at 09:08 on 2 September 1945:

    1. Acting by command of and in behalf of the Emperor of Japan, the Japanese Imperial Government and the Japanese Imperial General Headquarters, We hereby surrender unconditionally to the Commanding General, United States Army Forces, Western Pacific, all Japanese and Japanese-controlled armed forces, air, sea, ground and auxiliary, in the Philippine Islands.

    2. We hereby command all Japanese forces wherever situated in the Philippine Islands to cease hostilities forthwith, to preserve and save from damage all ships, aircraft, and military and civil property, and to comply with all requirements which may be imposed by the Commanding General, United States Army Forces, Western Pacific, or his authorized representatives.

    3. We hereby direct the commanders of all Japanese forces in the Philippine Islands to issue at once to all forces under their command to surrender unconditionally themselves and

all forces under their control, as prisoners of war, to the nearest United States Force Commander.

    4. We hereby direct the commanders of all Japanese forces in the Philippine Islands to surrender intact and in good order to the nearest United States Army Force Commander, at times and at places directed by him, all equipment and supplies of whatever nature under their control.

    5. We hereby direct the commanders of all Japanese forces in the Philippine Islands at once to liberate all Allied prisoners of war and civilian internees under their control, and to provide for their protection, care, maintenance and immediate transportation to places as directed by the nearest United States Army Force Commander.

    6. We hereby undertake to transmit the directives given in Paragraphs 1 through 5, above, to all Japanese forces in the Philippine Islands immediately by all means within our power, and further to furnish to the Commanding General, United States Army Forces, Western Pacific, all necessary Japanese emissaries fully empowered to bring about the surrender of Japanese forces in the Philippine Islands with whom we are not in contact.

    7. We hereby undertake to furnish immediately to the Commanding General, United States Army Forces, Western Pacific, and a statement of the designation, numbers, locations, and commanders of all Japanese armed forces, ground, sea, or air, in the Philippine Islands.

    8. We hereby undertake faithfully to obey all further proclamation, orders and directives deemed by the Commanding General, United States Armed Forces, Western Pacific, to be proper to effectuate this surrender.

Signed at Camp John Hay, Baguio, Mountain Province, Luzon, Philippine Islands, at 1210 hours 3 September 1945:

317 / DON STEWART NIMMONS

TOMOYUKI YAMASHITA, General, Imperial Japanese Army Highest Commander, Imperial Japanese Army in the Philippines.

DENHICI OKOCHI, Vice Admiral, Imperial Japanese Navy Highest Commander, Imperial Japanese Navy in the Philippines.

By command and in behalf of the Japanese Imperial General Headquarters

Accepted at Camp John Hay, Baguio, Mountain Province Luzon Philippine Islands, at 1210 hours 3 September 1945: For the Commander-in-Chief, United States Army Forces, Pacific:

EDMOND H. LEAVY, Major General, USA Deputy Commander, United States Army Forces, Western Pacific.

Surrender of Japanese Forces in the Philippines

Surrender ceremonies at Baguio, Luzon, Philippine Islands, 3rd of September 1945.

The Japanese commander, General Tomoyuki Yamashita, is seated in the middle on the near side of the table. Seated on the opposite side, second from left, is Lieutenant General Jonathan M. Wainwright, U. S. Army. Toward the right end of the table, immediately to the left of General Yamashita's head, is Commodore Norman C. Gillette, USN, Deputy Commander, Philippine Sea Frontier.

TREASURES OF WAR – CONCEALED BY THE EVIL ONES

Chapter Seventeen

The Story of General Virgilio Hermano

Commander of Filipino "Bulldog Guerrillas"

Retrieves Gold Bars From Caves In Philippines After War

In 1947, Virgil Hermano, the leader of the 'Bulldogs" Guerrilla group in the beginning of the war decided to retire from the military services as a Brigadier General with many honors from his war years and return to his birthplace in Darat, Northern Luzon Province.

He began seeking information of the whereabouts of some of his men from the Guerrilla war days.

One of his dearest friends, Col. Duque, had come through the village a few months earlier asking if anyone knew where Virgil was. He left a note with Mrs. Velasco, the widow of Lt. Velasco. The note had Col. Duque's address and directions to go to his village and place.

From time to time over the next three months all of the survivors from his Guerrilla Group came by General Hermano's house. The number one topic on everyone's mind and future agenda was what they should do about excavating the Gold Bars that they had witnessed being buried in caves by the Japanese Forces during the war years. These meetings resulted in the plans to organize a Filipino Foundation that Virgil and his cronies would use to obtain initial funding from the Bureau of Investment to supply the Group with enough expense money and funds to purchase heavy equipment to excavate the Gold Bars and other treasure from the well fortified caves. The Foundation was chartered in the name of Balikatan Foundation. There was a great concern regarding the need to be safe and not allow accidents from explosives, poison gas or ventilation problems.

Subsequent to the receipt of the BOI approved funds, Hermano assigned each man duties to perform for the accumulation of the construction equipment, supplies, transportation and laboratory equipment, and other miscellaneous items for the first project. They decided to establish offices near Clark Air Base at Angeles City, Manila and Darat.

Raul and Nicholas were severely wounded in the war. Nicholas hobbled around on his crutches to support himself for the loss of his right leg below the knee. Raul had lost his right eye, but otherwise was in excellent health and physical condition. Everyone of the members of the 'BULLDOGS' Guerrilla Fighters symbolized valor against all odds, who had given up their own goals in life to prove that patriotism was active and how they lived would make a difference in the future of their country.

The new organization's main purpose was summarized in the consolidation of each man's separate report of the burying of Gold Bars episodes they had witnessed during the war and in meetings with Tribesmen since the end of the war.

The excavating plans were to be intensified to secure the best results before others and the possibility of Japanese Soldiers returning to the Philippines to work out deals with landowners and make claims. The fact that under International Laws the looted countries had valid claims for their looted treasure for 13 years was being completely ignored by General Virgil Hermano. The game plan was to remove the Gold Bars from the caves, transport the heavy loads over weak bridges to the ports, and complete the export shipment out of the country on fortified military equipped vessels to prevent pirating on the South China Sea.

New Peoples Army was increasing its Communist Party activities in the mountain regions and had to be dealt with caution. They will be conducting surveillance for any activities by outsiders within their controlled mountain domiciles. The NPA is well aware of the many suspected hidden locations of Gold Bars. NPA needed funding for their illegal operations. They had established an interesting and attractive program to lure new members from small mountain towns by promising them free land and Guerrilla Force protection against any invaders into the Tribesmen clan. NPA leaders attempted bribery and torture to learn where the Yamashita Gold was hidden.

General Virgil Hermano addressed his delegates to his new Balikatan Foundation, "Men, the real problem is whether the agents of the Office of Strategic Services (OSS) and other U. S. Government officials are willing to enforce their belief that the U.S. Armed Forces had liberated the Philippines and all Gold Bars found in the Philippines belonged to the greedy Americans."

"Additionally, if anyone of you share information from our meetings with anyone, it puts all of us at risk and extremely confidential information in the hands of the Americans and NPA. The Americans already have paid informants seeking secret information from your neighbors. When they relinquish something you said to your neighbor in a casual conversation, it could be devastating to our future success. I will give each of you a tale that will keep the informants taking the U. S. Government's money and sending them chasing their tails. Some of these old Tribesmen Chiefs are wise and do not trust anybody."

"Once our project published report is given to each of you, you will guard it with your life, and all drinking and gambling will cease. Women and sex will be repeatedly offered as the ultimate temptation to you. When some father of a beautiful young Filipino girl chases you from the region, it will affect the success of each of our separate projects and bring the Philippine National Police in the picture."

Virgil Hermano deliberately passed out the project report and cautiously said leaving the meeting as Commander of the 'Bulldogs' Guerrilla Group and now Chairman and Chief Executive Officer of the Foundation, "I have shown each project by a circled code number on this confidential report I am handing out. You need to memorize the project numbers of each location. I will give you an hour or so to read over the details of our projects."

The report had a detailed organization chart with the specific assignments and duties of every member of the team. All of the men set down in a very passionate but orderly mood.

Upon the return of General Hermano, he asked all team members, "Are all of you prepared to hold up your right hand and pledge your alligiance in your performance of your obligations in each project? If anyone of you does not wish to proceed forward as a team member and carry out your responsibilities, bring your copy of the project plans to me and leave now. Nobody will think any less of you if you leave at this stage of the operations." All of the team stayed for the remainder of the meetings. General Hermano emphasized teamwork.

"Each of you identified in the organization chart as a project manager has total discretion on all decisions for your project except when it comes to the terms and conditions of the sales contract to our foreign buyers. I will give the final approval on the terms of any sales of Gold Bars," General Hermano instructed the team.

"Project Number Z-44 is the first project to be undertaken. Celso, you will need to notify me of the date the Singapore Naval Yard has completed the outfitting and mounting the 50 caliber cannons all around the deck of the ship, and you have completed your inspection together with the Singapore Vanguard Security Services Pte. LTD. and commission the vessel for duty. Immediately hereafter, I will complete the negotiation of the contract with the Singapore Vanguard Group to operate the ship throughout the transportation from the Philippines to my re-smelting operation in Dubai, UAE. The contract for completing the trip ahead of schedule will have bonus provisions for Vanguard. We must have the Gold Bars out of the cave, down the mountain, out the river to our ocean port warehouse before Singapore Vanguard Security Services leaves Singapore. The smaller patrol boats will be used to transport the Gold Bars to the anchored offshore large vessel. Singapore Vanguard will have 16 men on the ship and you see who our 4 men are that will board the large vessel with the first shipment of Gold Bars by the patrol boat to it offshore. The logistics is very critical for this project to go smooth. Due to the large quantity of Gold Bars from these caves, the insurance cost will run into the millions. The only reason I was able to obtain insurance was because of our detailed plans and most importantly obtaining the services of Singapore Vanguard Security Services Pte. LTD. This package of papers I am passing out to each of you is the detailed logistic activities and description of the duties for each project segment. Please review this data and point out any corrections that you feel needs to be made," General Hermano told his team who were so silent you could here the breeze blowing outside.

Project Number Z-44

The overall scope of Project Z-44 on the Philippine Islands shall be to facilitate the excavation, cataloguing, crating, and transportation of approximately 480 metric tons of 'test rock' material to an international shipping vessel stationed in international waters just off the Philippines coastline. The project start to completion time is anticipated to be 7-10 days while working 7 AM to 7 PM daily. Sufficient labor will be hired, necessary equipment will be purchased or leased, and necessary contracts will be executed to ensure a timely and successful project completion.

Staff

The staff for Project Z-44 will include a Project Manager, three station Managers, and approximately 20 locally hired laborers. The Project Manager shall oversee all operations pertaining to Project Z-44 and communicate as necessary with local officials and property owners. The three Station Managers will be positioned along the transportation route from the excavation area to the port of export. The Station Managers will manage specific operations at various points along the transportation route. All activity will be monitored and communicated on a regular basis from each Station Manager to the Project Manager.

Camp A Duties:

Camp A will be stationed as close as possible to the excavation area. Personnel at Camp A will include the Station Manager, one assistant manager, and eight laborers, which include a forklift operator. The personnel at Camp A will be responsible for the following:

1. Transportation of 'test rock' to packing/crating area.
2. Quick assay test and inspection of 'test rock'.

3. Catalogue and verify contents prior to crating.
4. Pack 'test rock' into shipping crates.
5. Label shipping crates according to Master Catalogue.
6. Seal crates with tamper proof screws.
7. Load crates for transport onto shipping truck to maximum weight limits.
8. Load crates for transport onto small wooden boats to prescribed weight limits.

Camp B Duties:

Camp B will be stationed approximately half way between the excavation area and the port of export. Camp B is designed to be a 'driver' exchange point and vehicle check station. Drivers from Camp A will be relieved with drivers from Camp C upon arrival at Camp B. The drivers will only be allowed to converse with the Station Managers and will not be allowed to converse at any time with other Camp personnel. Drivers will not be allowed to view the loading or unloading of the trucks. This will allow us the highest degree of security for our 'test rock' if all drivers and port laborers have no knowledge of the crate contents.

Two Camp C drivers will wait at Camp B with empty trucks until the Camp A drivers arrive. The Camp A drivers will return to Camp A with an empty truck and repeat the process. The Camp C drivers will wait for the truck to be unloaded and return to Camp B with the empty truck.

Personnel at Camp B will include the Station Manager, one assistant manager who is qualified as a truck mechanic and the four shipping truck drivers.

Camp C Duties:

Camp C will be located at the port of export and will maintain a warehouse facility. Personnel at Camp C will include the Station Manager, one assistant manager, and five laborers, which include one forklift operator. Camp C will be responsible for unloading the shipping trucks, crate storage, and the ultimate loading of the crates onto the transport ship for delivery to the offshore vessel.

As with Camp A and Camp B personnel, the Camp C assistant manager and laborers will be housed together and will dine separately from personnel in the other Camps. No communications with outside personnel will be allowed until the project is completed.

TREASURES OF WAR – CONCEALED BY THE EVIL ONES / 324

"Since Singapore Vanguard Securities has previously done some very risky operations and know and made recommendations of the equipment that we will need, they have included in their proposal the cost of much of the equipment," General Hermano said to the members of Balikatan Foundation. "Here is their proposal in specific details. You will greatly understand the real scope of this project once you read their proposal," Virgil added.

SINGAPORE VANGUARD SECURITY SERVICES Pte. LTD.
60 Ayer Rajah Arrow # 34-01
Ayer Rajah Kingdom Estate
SINGAPORE

March 1, 1947

Mr. Virgilio Hermano
Chairman
BALIKATAN FOUNDATION
Manila, Philippines

Re: Cargo from the Philippines to Dubai, United Arab Emirates

The following proposal is offered to you and your company (Code Name - BULLDOGS) for the purpose of entering into an agreement between Singapore Vanguard Security Services Pte. Ltd. for the movement and security of one certain cargo. Said cargo to be crated and delivered to the transit point by Bulldogs or its agents.

Ship charter has been arranged through Rough Seas Navigation, Inc. of Panama City, Panama. The charter party agreement will provide for the following items:

1.   **SHIP CHARTER:**

The Ship charter has been arranged. The charter party agreement will provide for the following items:

A).   Danish Flag/built 1938 --- 1700 Metric Ton Deadweight --- 2 Derricks X 22 Metric Ton Lifting Capacity.
B).   All crew and officers to be of Western European origin (A total crew of 16).
C).   Vessel to be at the disposal of Charter Company for five (5) days in Singapore for the purpose of   loading and installing equipment for the use of Charter Company.
D).   Crew change prior to sailing from Singapore.
E).   Vessel to be at one (1) safe offshore anchorage in the Philippines for five (5) days.
F).   Discharge of cargo at one (1) safe berth, Port of Jebel Ali, United Arab Emirates.

Charter Cost: USD 1,350,000 Lump Sum.

Payment Terms: Stand-by Letter of Credit for the charter cost plus other expenses. Twenty-Five percent of total freight to be bank wire transferred in U. S. Dollars to the owner's bank fifteen (15) days in advance of the vessel's arrival in Singapore. The balance of the freight to be paid at time of vessel arriving at Singapore Pilot Station --- full freight is deemed earned.

2. ADDITIONAL FREIGHT COST:

A).	Living accommodations	USD	81,000
B).	Communications equipment -- three (3) sets	USD	93,700
C).	Medical Pack Stage VII	USD	19,600
D).	Life Saving Equipment with cradles	USD	236,000
E).	Life Saving Equipment personnel	USD	14,000
F).	Installing and removal of Security Equipment	USD	42,000
G).	Meals and Catering	USD	28,800
	TOTAL ADDITIONAL FREIGHT COST	USD	515,100

TOTAL SHIP CHARTER AND ADDITIONAL FREIGHT COST   USD   1,865,100

3. SECURITY:

Security services to be provided by one of the world's leading Security Operating Companies and Security personnel are former members of special forces with excellent team leaders, properly equipped with security equipment/ship mounted, to be at one (1) safe offshore anchorage in the Philippines for five (5) days and discharging of cargo at one (1) safe berth, Jebel Ali, United Arab Emirates.

The program will provide for advance parties of two (2) man teams to be in place in the Philippines and in Singapore two (2) weeks prior to the arrival of the vessel in Singapore. Communications will be established with base operations in Dubai, United Arab Emirates.

Personnel required: 2 in Dubai, United Arab Emirates -- 2 in Singapore
                       2 in Philippines -- 16 aboard vessel

Personnel in Singapore will move to the Philippines upon the arrival of the vessel and the balance of the security team arrival.

A).	Personnel/Insurance	USD	528,000
B).	Personnel Equipment	USD	143,000
C).	Security Equipment/Ship Mounted	USD	87,000
D).	Small Arms	USD	48,000
E).	Air Freight Europe—Philippines	USD	52,600
F).	Air Travel for security Personnel	USD	34,600
G).	Hotels/Rent Cars	USD	21,950
	TOTAL SECURITY	USD	915,150

4. CARGO INSURANCE:

CARGO Insurance is by far the most costly part of the project. The present quotation for the Cargo Insurance is   USD 9,136,120.

5. PROJECT MANAGEMENT SERVICES:

The Project Management Services Company shall advise the principals of the Project during the negotiations of the Charter Party, Security and Insurance contracts. This Company will take care of all procurement (security equipment, catering, supplies, materials and etc.); human resources and logistics and provide these services to the standards required for such a project.

The fees for performing these professional services is   USD 275,000.

6. PERFORMANCE BONUSES:

Upon the timely delivery of the Cargo to Jebel Ali, United Arab Emirates the following bonuses will be paid:

A).	Security Company	USD 75,000.
B).	Project Management Services Company	USD 50,000.

7. EXCAVATION, HAUL, WAREHOUSE, DELIVERY FROM PORT:

A).	Rough All Terrain Vehicles	USD	80,000
B).	Special -- Local --- Communications Equipment	USD	4,000
C).	Patrol/ Supply Boat	USD	2,100,000
D).	Fuel and Supplies	USD	18,000
E).	Travel and Lodging	USD	42,000
F).	Crating of Commodities	USD	84,000
G).	Supervision Personnel/Insurance	USD	236,000
H).	Port and Export Fees	USD	380,000
I).	Safety Equipment	USD	6,000
J).	Excavation Equipment	USD	210,000
K).	Port of Export Command Center	USD	15,000
L).	Port of Export Warehouse	USD	12,000
M).	Loading Commodities into Supply Boat	USD	5,000
N).	Excavation Personnel	USD	36,000
O).	Food and Catering	USD	41,000
P).	Unclassified and Miscellaneous Expenses	USD	50,000

TOTAL EXCAVATION, HAUL, WAREHOUSE, AND DELIVERY FROM PORT   USD   3,319,000

327 / DON STEWART NIMMONS

8. <u>SUMMARY OF THE TRANSPORTATION COST OF THE COMMODITIES:</u>

A). SHIP CHARTER AND ADDITIONAL FREIGHT COST	USD 1,865,100
B). SECURITY	USD 915,150
C). CARGO INSURANCE	USD 9,136,120
D). PROJECT MANAGEMENT SERVICES	USD 275,000
E). BONUSES	USD 125,000
F). EXCAVATE, HAUL, WAREHOUSE & DELIVERY TO PORT	<u>USD 3,319,000</u>
TOTAL TRANSPORTATION COST OF COMMODITIES	USD 12,316,370

NOTE: The cost per troy ounce = USD .80 (USD 12,316,370 ÷ 15,432,355 Troy Ounces)

"Remember, the loads should not be heavier than the smallest weight limit for a bridge on the total trip. For example, if you need to cross 3 bridges with 20 MT signs and 4 bridges with 10 MT signs and one bridge with a 6 MT sign; the maximum weight limit load would be 6 MT. I do not want to have one of our overloaded trucks fall into the creek or river dumping the Gold Bars out in the open. We will be required to make many different trips to the port city. Eighty trips of 6 MT each will be done to remove all 480 MT of Gold Bars from the caves," General Hermano said to motivate each man.

"General, do you have a preference of materials and methods to safely open the entrance to the cave?" Jose asked.

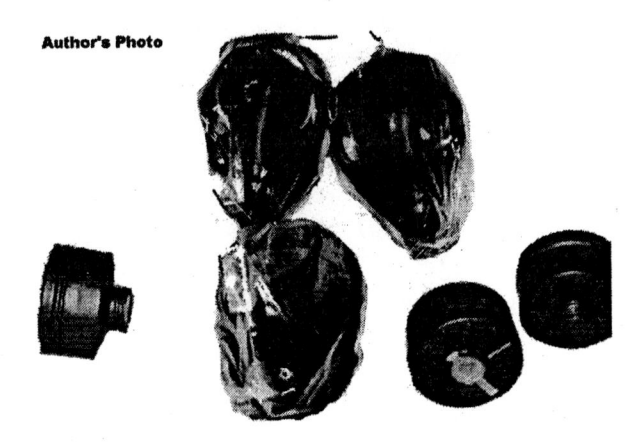

Author's Photo

"The main task is to remove the concrete in a safe manner. Some of the cave entrances may be booby-trapped. Sometimes you can use the long arm of the backhoe with the narrow bucket and reach behind the top concrete entrance wall and jerk or hammer down toward your backhoe. Should this action trigger an explosion you would be protected by the backhoe. Another recommended method would be to use the cable from the truck winch and wrap it around a section of the large concrete or boulder covering the entrance. The long cable puts you at a safer distance from any explosion," Virgil fully explained.

General Hermano directed his men as he looked out the window off into the mountain range. "Every time you enter cave you must wear one of these facemask. I also have the radiation detector that will scream loudly to let you know a dangerous level of radiation exist. The likelihood of one of these scenarios existing is remote. Some of us know that we are going to find the remains of dead Filipinos and American POW's. We are to respect these ghastly settings. All we want is to remove the Gold Bars. Later, after we have shipped the Gold Bars out of the country, I will assign someone to notify the local police that bodies were found in the cave. I envision us acquiring a significant amount of looted Gold. We must perform everything on schedule and do it exactly like I planned."

"General, how will we get paid for working on this project?" Ronell asked.

"Since Bangko Sentral ng Pilipinas is guided by our country's general banking act and the officers are not competent international bankers, they have issued regulations which require identification of all monies coming and going through the banks. Therefore, it is in our best interest to bring the smaller amount of your distribution of profits from the final sale of the Gold Bars into the Philippines. If you have a local bank account, give me the detail account information so that the Foundation might deposit pesos into your account. For those of you that do not have an account, the Foundation will notify you of a date to pick up your pesos in cash."

"Urgent, take special notice, the largest portion of your profit distribution will be set up in an offshore bank account in the name of the Foundation in Dubai, UAE. Periodically, the Foundation will make a distribution of your profit distribution to wherever you direct us. Do not forget! The looted countries have claims against their looted Gold for another 11 years. If anyone of you comes into a large amount of money all of a sudden without any explanation the Filipino government taxing authorities and others are going to come calling on you. However, the activities of the Foundation with parties outside the Philippines are normal. The directors of Balikatan Foundation will make funding decisions in the future years whereby it's funding to your specific program here in the Philippines will be made to you. The Foundation's record keeping for each of you is on going, and a current annual status report will be furnished to each of you," General Hermano warned his men.

"Virgil, one of these days in the future years I may make an application to move to the USA. How would this affect my fund balance in the Foundation?" Celso asked.

"Under normal circumstances you could have your balance of the money transferred to you in a U. S. bank account. Once you receive all of your requested funds, you would no longer have any interest in the Foundation and would execute the proper resignation papers," General Hermano replied.

"Anyone else have a question?" Okay, let's go find some Gold Bars and sell them and make some money so that the Foundation will be able to pay back this large loan in a few years and make some attractive distributions to each of you for your brave efforts during the war and now," General Hermano said as he dismissed the meeting.

LATER IN THE WEEK.

General Virgil Hermano and his men drove the trucks up and around the mountains to a spot near Project Z-44 cave entrance. No New Peoples Army agents were spotted in this region of Northern Luzon. The first action was to cut a path into the jungle off the road and set up camp. The men piled out of the trucks and began cutting a roadway back into a large flat rock area on the side of the mountain. The spot gave them a clear view over to the cave entrance as they remembered from some 3 years earlier. Tired from the long trip from the Clark Air Base area and cutting the clearing in the jungle, the men set up their sleeping tents for a good nights rest.

At 06:00 the next morning, General Hermano had 'Chief', the project manager for Z-44; call everyone to morning roll call.

"Men, from this time forward 'Chief' is the boss on this project. What he says is the law. I will be returning to headquarters," General Hermano said as he turned Camp A over to 'Chief'.

The men began cutting through the jungle around the ledge on the mountain until they reached the front of the cave entrance. They cleared out an area in front to provide space for the backhoe to maneuver.

"Benjamin, go start the backhoe and drive it over here in front of this concrete wall," 'Chief' instructed.

"Yes Sir!"

Slowly moving the backhoe on the newly cleared road to the space in front of the cave entrance, Ben asked. "What do you want me to do?"

"All of you men move back to behind that large boulder over there in the jungle. Ben, take the backhoe arm with the heavy bucket and raise it high over the concrete wall and drop it about 1 foot behind the front of the top of the wall and then use all the power that you have to pull the bucket caught in the top toward you. Let me get back before you do this," 'Chief' instructed his men and Ben.

The first dig into the top of the cave entrance made a dent about 1 foot deep. When the hydraulic pull was made by the backhoe, the backhoe's rear wheels came off the ground. Each time Ben continued this routine a larger crack in the concrete was visible. When the opening at the top reached 6 inches you could see some sort of gases flowing up the mountainside. Ben turned off the backhoe and jumped off and ran over to talk to 'Chief'.

"What do you make of these fumes and gases coming out of the cave?" Ben asked 'Chief'.

"It is probably methane gases from the bodies of the dead Filipinos and Americans POW's. It has been sealed up since they were murdered and this is the first time it could escape. If the wind changes direction and blows toward the backhoe, immediately turn it off or we will find pieces of you and the backhoe down there in the river below. Methane gas is very combustible," 'Chief' said looking straight into Ben's eyes.

Everyone in camp saw Ben's eyes light up when the danger was explained to him.

"Striking down with the backhoe arm with the heavy bucket from the top could cause a spark if you should hit the wrong kind of rock. We don't need that potential damage to occur. Since you already have a small hole in the top, put the backhoe bucket up inside it and use the hydraulics and put the backhoe in reverse gear and pull down the wall. It may take a while, but be careful and patient," 'Chief' instructed in an assuredly manner.

"I'll give it my best."

Finally, on the fourth attempt the cave entrance came crashing down and Ben immediately turned off the backhoe, jumped over the large back tire and ran over to the spot behind the large boulder to await for any explosion of any bomb set as a booby trap. After waiting 30 minutes for the dust to settle and the large cloud of methane gas to be blown up over the mountain ridge, 'Chief' took his binoculars and scoped the cave entrance to look for possible booby traps.

"Everything looks all clear around the entrance. Listen up men! The four of you that have been trained on using the gas mask should get rigged up. The remainder of you should stay back away from the cave entrance," 'Chief' ordered the men at Camp A.

Four men dressed in long sleeve jackets and long pants in new steel-toed boots came to the cave entrance.

"How do you expect to find anything in that cave without your powerful flashlights?" 'Chief' asked. "Ben, go over to supply trailer number 2 and get six of the large flashlights."

"Okay 'Chief'!"

"Take your time and go slowly down only one chamber of the cave at this time. Each of you counts how many steps you go into the cave to the first point of discovery of Gold Bars. Do not get hung up on seeing the bones, you saw many Filipino and Japanese killed during the war. Each of you picks up only one Gold Bar and return to this area over there. As you know, each of you will be washed down from head to toe," 'Chief' instructed the four men as he lead them to the entrance.

Fifteen minutes later, almost to the minute, each man returned from the cave with a heavy 75 kilos Gold Bar. They walked over to the assigned area. One of the men with the large barrel with water began pumping the water as the other man took the hose and sprayed each man down. The four men stepped over to the camp table and placed the Gold Bars on it. Then, each man took his facemask off and you could see the smiles all the way to Manila.

"How many Gold Bars did we count three years ago?" Elmer asked 'Chief'.

"The total count was 4,821 large Gold Bars," 'Chief' replied.

"We must have seen one chamber on the left some sixty three steps inside the cave with probably one thousand large Gold Bars," Nick excitedly added.

"Is the fumes from the gas all over the place?" 'Chief' asked.

"The fumes seem to be dispersing. Most fumes are hanging around the top of the cave. This cave has very high ceilings. There are some old tribal artifacts and ethnological information written on some of the ceilings and walls. 'Chief', I am ready to begin a hand-to-hand relay of Gold Bars out of the cave," Jose said in his excitement of the moment.

"Elmer, take that long rope and securely tie it around your waist. Then, I want you to leave your facemask here and return to the cave and pick up another Gold Bar. If you get woozy, turn around immediately and run out. Jose and Leo feed the rope into the cave as Elmer walks," 'Chief' ordered his Camp A men.

As Elmer began slowly walking back into the cave he yelled out. "I'm okay! I'm okay! No problem! I'm okay!" Suddenly, Elmer walked out with another large Gold Bar.

"'Chief', the gas fumes are very high and almost dissipated. It seems very safe to enter all the way to the left chamber," Elmer advised.

"Men, we need to form our brigade from the inside of the cave out to the assigned area and move the Gold Bars out of the cave. Since you four have experience inside the cave; Elmer, Nick, Jose and Leo should be the beginning of the brigade. You other men fall in line and let's see how many Gold Bars we can bring out of the cave in 30 minutes. Should anything happen to slow or stop the movement of the Gold Bars, yell out to me out here. I will yell the word Mabuhay into the cave entrance at the time that I want all of you to come outside of the cave and take a break," 'Chief' explained and ordered his men.

'Chief' ran into the mobile command center and ordered, "Celso get Junior and establish your security team in the bush around camp and be in place with your binoculars and keep a constant lookout all around the mountains and down the road for any unwanted visitors. Use you loud bird call whistle to warn me of anything spotted."

"Yes Sir, I will find Junior. He told me he was getting fully equipped to hide in the brush where nobody could see him. Let me see if I can round him up and tell him of our plans to communicate with each other."

"Mo, take one of those table clothes and

cover up the four shining Gold Bars. I do not want someone to see anything from a distance," 'Chief' ordered.

Camp 'A' team organized the hand-to-hand brigade and began moving the Gold Bars out of the cave. The large heavy 75 kilos Gold Bars were stacked in a small cutout spot in the jungle just to the right side of the cave entrance.

Thirty minutes later, 'Chief' yelled out, "Mabuhay."

The men walked over to the Camp 'A' tables and set down to have a very earned cup of coffee. 'Chief' realized the excitement among the men had taken some of the work energy from them and said. "After the break, I think it best that we begin loading some of the Gold Bars onto the trucks. Each Gold Bar weighs 75 kilos. The maximum weight for each truck should be limited to a little less than 10 metric tons. The weight limit for the bridge near Djora was 10 MT. Each truck must not have more than 130 Gold Bars on it. If we have not retrieved the necessary 130 Gold Bars from the cave, then, we will re-establish the brigade operation I want us to have at least four truckloads of Gold Bars taken to the warehouse at the port city each day. Without any further complications, it will take 30 to 45 truckloads to move all of the 4,821 Gold Bars, depending on which vehicles are available for us. At four or five truckloads per day, we should complete Camp 'A' project in 10 days."

"Nanoy, since you are the foreman of the drivers, why don't you take General Hermano's new '48 Chevy pick-up and drive it. You had better be very careful with all that unaccustomed power at your disposal. Load 20 large Gold Bars in the back of the pick-up bed. You will be able to make more trips down to the port city warehouse and back up here to make up for the number of Gold Bars the large trucks will carry. Once the men load the pick-up just to the top of the side panels at the rear, no higher, take that red tarpaulin in the supply trailer and secure it at the front of the bed of the pick-up and down each side and across the back," 'Chief' instructed.

"Sounds excellent, I wondered who was going to get the pleasure of driving the new imported Chevy pick-

TREASURES OF WAR – CONCEALED BY THE EVIL ONES / 334

up. I will let you know if 20 Gold Bars is a comfortably load in the bed of the pick-up. I will make sure it is secured and the tailgate is locked down," Nanoy replied.

"All Balikatan Foundation vehicle's license plate numbers have been given to the authorities at all check-points to prevent any search and hold-ups. If you or any of the other drivers encounter any check-point problem along the way to the port, report this to General Hermano and myself," 'Chief' explained as he turned to go back to the task of removing the Gold Bars from the cave.

Upon walking back to the Camp 'A' tables 'Chief' saw Jose finishing up his desired coffee break with one Gold Bar on the table in front of him. "Jose, it looks like you can't believe your eyes and are giving it a truly once over inspection. Believe it! You need to put your long sleeve shirt back on and be prepared to lead another hand-to-hand brigade until all of the Gold Bars are removed from the left side chamber of the cave."

"You are correct. I do not believe this wealth has come to us after all of these years waiting to Filipino and American retrieve them. The dead POW's bones are scattered all over the floor of the cave. Lot's of families are finally going to learn what happened to their love ones. I will be ready to go again in another fifteen minutes. I just had to take time to meditate."

Camp 'A' men began to work smoothly as the afternoon progressed. Enough Gold Bars were removed from the left side of the cave to complete loading the '48 Chevy pick-up, a Jeepney bus, the two Daihatsu vans and three large World War II military supply trucks with Gold Bars. A total of 250 Gold Bars each weighing 75 kilos was jotted down on the daily total shipment records being kept by both 'Chief' and by Guillermo as a double check. When all trucks were checked and secured, 'Chief' called Nanoy and the drivers into his Camp 'A' quarters.

"Take your time on this first run. I do not want to see pictures in the newspapers tomorrow of one of our vehicles crashed beyond recognition in one of the canyons below a cliff because someone was driving too fast and could not make the turn on the mountain road. Your loads are heavy. You are going down the mountain and you should remember to leave space between each of you and go slow on some of those blind turns. All of you drivers know where the rest stops are located. Take the one rest stop and all of you get together away from everyone else and talk about any problems you may have had. Then, you must drive all the way to Balikatan Foundation's warehouse in Port Casambalangan and park together in the assigned area. Alejandro lives in the small house at the rear of the warehouse building. Send Jorge to get him out of bed and instruct him to get the security detail with their appropriate weapons and come to the assigned area in front of the dock at the warehouse building. It will be in the middle of the night and dark. Tell them not to wake everybody in town. All of you drivers should sleep in your vehicle. In the morning, Alejandro and his warehousemen will unload the Gold Bars and stack them on the warehouse dock. Nanoy and all of you drivers are ready to get in high gear and get back up here for the next shipment. Are there any questions at this stage of the project?" 'Chief' asked as he looked around the room.

"Okay, you heard the man. We have a serious job to do. Let's show 'Chief' and General Hermano how good we are driving under these conditions," Nanoy replied and gave his orders to the drivers.

The five hours trip went without major incidence and everyone found the way to the warehouse. Alejandro and Jorge came around from the back of the building in one of the darkest nights of the year. He quietly greeted the drivers and had Bravo, Alfredo and Nestor go to their assigned night watch post.

At daybreak, Alejandro ordered Romeo, Olimpio and Arturo to unload the Gold Bars from each vehicle and stack them on the dock next to the south double doors. Nanoy and the drivers went to the lunchroom inside the warehouse and Alejandro's wife, Yvonne, and two of her sisters had prepared a Filipino breakfast complete with some rice and pieces of roasted pig. They gave each vehicle crew some jars of water and a snack for the return trip to Camp 'A' in the mountains.

When one of the Daihatsu trucks backed up near the dock, Arturo noticed the warning sign similar to the one next to each warehouse door entrance. "Alejandro, have these Gold Bars in the Daihatsu truck been contaminated with some type of poison by the Japanese when they left them in the cave? Do I need to protect myself from the poison?"

"No Arturo, the sign on the Daihatsu is the same one we have on the building entrances to keep people away from them."

"Okay, I did not want to get sick from something those evil Japanese soldiers who killed all of those Filipino and American POW's. We will get them unloaded as quickly as possible. But first, we are going to move some of the Gold Bars inside the warehouse."

"**No**, No, remember the plans call for us to unload all vehicles first to allow all the drivers to get on the road back. Then, we will bring the Gold Bars inside the warehouse after they leave."

"Right!"

At 09:30, all the vehicles had been unloaded and the drivers were fed and eager to get on the road again. On this day, the trip back up the mountain road was tricky and slow due to the large logging trucks coming down the mountain road and having to swing wide around many of the sharp turns. The normal five-hour trip took an additional one and half hour to complete.

As the drivers drove into Camp 'A' everyone was anxious to learn of the results of the first trip to the port city with the Gold Bars. "Nanoy, tell us the good news?" 'Chief' asked.

Nanoy called each driver into the pow wow with 'Chief' and the men in his office. "Everything went smoothly and none of us had any difficulties whatsoever. First time was a charm. We were delayed on our return by the logging trucks making the turns around the curves along the steep section of the road. They took both lanes. I only hope each trip goes as well as this one. In fact, we are ready to return with another load of Gold Bars as soon as it is loaded."

"Excellent Nanoy, General Hermano has delivered two more Jeepney buses and the old U. S. heavy duty army truck that he recently bought from the Commander at Clark Field. This should provide enough space to transport an additional 140 Gold Bars later today for the trip back to the Port Casambalangan warehouse. How did Alejandro and his men hold up their end?" 'Chief' added and asked.

"Yvonne cooks a mean breakfast," Arturo interrupted.

"Alex had to get his men organized a few times, but the results were gratifying. He had them moving the remaining Gold Bars into the warehouse as we were pulling out. By the way, here is your original receipt from him for the delivery of the 250 Gold Bars. He had not heard anything from General Hermano or Celso regarding the status of when the offshore vessel was to arrive from Singapore. He told me the fast patrol boats for transferring the Gold Bars from the docks at the port would be arriving in two days," Nanoy confidently replied.

"This tells me the offshore vessel is on the South China Seas headed this direction. We must step up the pace and make two trips per day from here to the warehouse. We cannot afford to have the offshore ship waiting on us. I am glad this cave is close enough to the port to be able to omit the establishment of a Camp 'B' driver exchange and slow things down. I will order the Camp 'A' men to begin loading all vehicles immediately," 'Chief' said as he walked out in the yard to call them together.

Gold Bars were carried out one by one by all the available men from the temporary jungle storage area outside the cave and with each driver controlling the number of Gold Bars for his vehicle loaded onto his vehicle. "Chief' and Guillermo was checking the quantities just prior to the tarps being tied down over the top of them.

"Everyone is ready to move out. What is your count?" 'Chief' asked Guillermo.

"I got a total of 390 large Gold Bars," Guillermo replied.

"That's correct. Nanoy, lead the drivers in a very safe manner. Don't forget your previous instructions concerning all of you are going down the mountain slowly instead of coming up the mountain," 'Chief' replied and warned Nanoy.

Halfway down the mountain, the Philippine's rains began to fall and the speed was greatly reduced. It was Friday night and many of the Filipinos who worked in the larger cities were returning home from a long ride by bus late at night for the weekend celebrations with family. At just about every small town, many of the local Town Folks would walk right out in front of the moving traffic on the narrow road right through the middle of town, ignoring the oncoming headlights. Traffic was a problem. There surely was some drinking of San Miguel Beers by the locals. It was early the next morning before Nanoy and all of his drivers made it to the Port Casambalangan warehouse facilities.

Alejandro and his team at Camp 'C' for Project Number Z-44 completed the unloading of the 75 kilos Gold Bars totaling 390 during the early Saturday morning hours. Yvonne and her sisters and some additional kitchen helpers fed Nanoy and his drivers and prepared them for the return trip to the mountains. No family celebrations were in progress anywhere near the Camp 'C" warehouse. Everyone was very serious and worked extremely hard. During breakfast Alejandro came over to Nanoy's table and asked. "As soon as you are finished and before you led the drivers back, let's take the '48 Chevy pick-up and go down to the dock at the port. You will very please with the surprise."

On the way to the port Nanoy thought. *The three patrol boats have arrived.*

"Turn to the left and go to our pier number 1. What do you think about General Hermano's new patrol boat, Guerrilla 1?" Alejandro asked. "Do not go any closer at this time," he added.

"I am not a sailor, but I do not think I would want to take that patrol boat straight on in a fight to pirate it. We are getting closer to the day that we get these Gold Bars out of the Philippines."

"Yes, my specific men in Camp 'C' responsible for loading the patrol boats have already practiced carry some of them onboard and into the special compartments and racks General Hermano had them fabricate in Singapore. With the boat securely tied to the pier, the men do not have problems carrying a Gold Bar and walking along side and through the door. The next practice will divide the men from the boys. When this patrol boat gets out to the large offshore ship and the waves are tossing both ships around on a stormy day, I need to have the men put the Gold Bar in a back pack or something to allow them to have their hands free to hold onto both ships. Otherwise, I will have to explain to everyone why we dumped 75 kilos Gold Bars into the ocean. That's my problem. You need to get back to the warehouse and lead the drivers back to the mountains," Alejandro replied.

On this Saturday, Nanoy and his drivers made the slow return trip back to the mountains with only a flat front tire on one of the Jeepney buses. For several weeks, the Project Z-44 team continued moving the Gold Bars from the cave and through the roadblocks along the way until all 4,821 Gold bars, each weighing 75 kilos, were safely stored in the Balikatan Foundation warehouse in Port Casambalangan.

FIRST SHIPMENT OF GOLD BARS OUT OF PHILIPPINES VIA SOUTH CHINA SEA.

Singapore Vanguard Security Services anchored the large military equipped ship in the deep-water northwest of Palaui Island in the Babuyan Channel. General Hermano had instructed them to paint the Filipino name 'ILAGA' on the bow and the stern of the ship. After the movement of the Gold Bars from the warehouse in Port Casambalangan by the patrol boats to the large ship, Celso and Cesar and some of his men were on board for additional security, supervision and communications to General Hermano. They gave the Captain the word to raise the anchor and head for Dubai, UAE. Celso gave the Captain a recent article warning of the usage of the new Filipino Patrol Boats in the South China Sea and the legalized shipping documents for the shipment of Filipino 'Marble'.

The news article effectively stated. "The recent mushrooming of illicit drug sales by Orient Velacruz Organization heightened the search and seizure policy of the Filipino Navy. Such imports average more than $10,000 a day, compared with $1,000 the previous year, when very few interceptions were recorded prior to the increased capabilities of the Filipino Navy as a result of U. S. Military Aid through the Foreign Military Sales (FMS) programs. The speed of the new Lone Star Patrol Boats allowing it to cover more sea-lane traffic is a major factor in tightening enforcement of the importation of illegal drugs into the Manila Bay area. While Indonesian --- Chinese vessels increasingly have been involved, there is no immediate indication of a direct connection to the Filipino government," Admiral Joaquin Atienza said in an interview en route to Hong Kong, where he will attend a weekend conference on ASIAN security issues. "Overall there has been an increase on the part of Orient Velacruz Organization to intensify its smuggling operations into the Philippines, and we're going to have to simply intensify our own intervention to prevent this problem," Admiral Atienza said.

He said he thinks Macau's Drug Syndicate, "will do whatever they can to try to circumvent our Anti-Drug Smuggling operations. If they can get away with it, and if there's a laxity on the enforcement part; then they will seek to exploit it."

As 'ILAGA' moved south in the South China Sea off the Philippine coastline, the Filipino Navy intercepted it in international waters looking for drug smuggling into the Philippines.

Since 'ILAGA' had the firepower advantage over the Philippine Navy Lone Star patrol boat and had shipment documents legalized by the Republic of the Philippines' Regional Trial Court at the National Capital Judicial Region in Manila, signed by Judge Hernandez for the export shipment of Filipino Marble Slabs, Captain Magsaysay contacted the Patrol Boat via radio and invited one of his crewmen to board 'ILAGA' to verify his 'legal' shipment.

The two vessels pulled along side of each other, and the Filipino Navy Captain crossed over to 'ILAGA' by the transfer line.

"Sir, here are my documents to verify my cargo. We are loaded down with heavy Filipino marble slabs. Judge Hernandez has issued his orders to whom it may concern to allow us to proceed without any delays or diversions from any government's naval vessels. Here are my shipping documents for Southern Cloud, Imperial Rose, Capistrano, Dark Rosa, Kara Classic, and Aqua Beige slabs of Filipino marble. This shipment is destined for Hong Kong. The construction of many new hotels in Hong Kong is good for the marble industry of the Philippines. I will be making this trip many times in the future. If you see my ship, your will know what we are transporting. You realize that we are in international waters and you do not have authority to intercept us," Captain Magsaysay sternly stated to the Filipino Patrol Boat Captain.

"I am obeying my Admiral's orders. I will let him know that you are not smuggling anything, just helping the cause of exports from the Philippines; and you are in international waters," Filipino Patrol Boat Captain told Captain Magsaysay.

"Thank you, the crew will secure you in the transfer seat and pull the lines to get you back on your patrol boat," Captain Magsaysay concluded.

One Hour Later…..

"Cesar, send the coded message to General Hermano and let him known that we were successful in preventing the Filipino Navy Lone Star Patrol Boat Captain from doing a search of our shipment?" Magsaysay asked Hermano's manager on board.

TREASURES OF WAR – CONCEALED BY THE EVIL ONES

Chapter Eighteen

The Story of Born of Privilege (BOP) Party

And

Initial Establishment of Supreme Commander Allied Powers

In

Tokyo, Japan

United States Senate
Office of the Born of Privilege Leader (BOP-Leader)
Washington, D. C.

While all of the celebrations and pompous victory parades were going on from New York City to Sydney, Australia, some of the trusted brains and war heroes were planning for future victories of power and wealth.

During the last half of September 1945, the Supreme Commander Allied Powers and his staff began arriving in Tokyo to establish headquarters for the many distinct divisions of the military forces. The occupation of Japan by the Allied Powers had begun.

In Washington, D. C., a special greedy political group conducted a closed-door meeting on November 14, 1945 for the primary purpose of keeping the Supreme Commander in Tokyo under surveillance and their control. They all agreed that the most important goal was to establish a system to determine just where the wealth of His Imperial Majesty Emperor Zapp was located while at the same time keep the public attitude focused on the American victory.

Due to the pressure put on the President and Secretary of War by this strong right wing political and business leaders group known as Born of Privilege, 'BOP', decided to make Mr. Bert Dover, now from the private sector, an experienced and successful Gold mining engineer in the Far East and national politician as their main man to work with the Supreme Commander and General Milton R. Salmon. The powerful 'BOP' forced the President and Secretary of War to issue a priority order to place ★★★★ General Milton R. Salmon as Deputy Commander and in charge of the task of chief intelligence officer.

Mr. Bert Dover was just the man to persuade the leaders in Tokyo to become tolerant of corruption, splitting the spoils of war. He knew from his previous successful international experiences that in the world of public corruption; it is viewed a cost of politics, the grease that makes government work. Also, he knew that just like many battles in war, a diversion plan had to be publicized to cover up the actual plan of attack.

His diversion plan was to portray His Imperial Majesty Emperor Zapp and his family as being in total despair and broke, without wealth of any kind. He figured he could accomplish this by pushing the idea that Emperor Zapp was not the force behind the military officers atrocities during the war.

If successful, Dover knew that a few selected military officers who had gone through the war were ready, willing and eager to become extremely wealthy. He was insensitive and distant to how hard he must work to exploit these men. He was sure that the selected men he would bring into his inner circle were aware of the well-publicized fortunes he had made through questionable business deals. It was inevitable that they would succumb to his decision-making abilities.

Last but not the least, Dover had the political power backing in Washington, should he need special laws passed and military memorandums issued through the Central Liaison Office in Tokyo to the Imperial Japanese Government or any other Allied Forces governments.

"We must stop the spread of Communism" was their publicized theme.

General Salmon immediately packed up and was flown to Tokyo. Upon his arrival at the air base near Tokyo, Colonel Ray Harrison met him.

"General, welcome to Japan. My orders are to lodge you in the most secured housing area that our military forces control."

"Colonel, that's excellent. I am very tired from the long trip from D. C. I hope you have a very firm long bed, long enough for my six foot five exhausted body."

"Yes sir, I had it made especially for you. Can't find many long beds here in Japan."

"Thanks."

"General, here is one of your drivers. This is Sergeant Bobby Carlson."

"Welcome, General," the Sergeant replied as he saluted the general and opened the door to the car.

"Where are you from Sergeant?" The General asked.

"Sir, I am from Louisiana."

"Reckon you can get us some good Cajun food over here?" the General asked. "I am not much for raw fish."

"Sir, let me find a good cook in the mess hall from Louisiana."

"General, I will ride with you to your secured area and get you through the checkpoints and entrance gates," Col. Harrison stated as he entered the car.

"Sergeant, take us to Base 47," the Colonel ordered.

"Right, sir."

"Colonel, you and I need to meet in a few days to discuss all of the security measures in place at base 47."

"Sir, just let me know when you are ready to meet members of your staff that have arrived so far, since we began the occupation of Japan.

Upon arrival at the gate of Base 47 Col. Harrison got out of the car and presented General Salmon's papers to the guards and told them Gen. Salmon was inside the car.

"You men should introduce yourselves to the general and know who he is," Col. Harrison said as he opened the door on the General's side of the car.

"Welcome General," the guards said in unison as they saluted the General and reached inside to shake his hand.

"Carry on, Sergeant Carlson drive me to my quarters," the General ordered.

"Yes Sir."

A few days later General Salmon sent for Col. Harrison to join some of his other officers. Upon his arrival at the General's office at 15:00 Col. Harrison walked in and stood at attention.

"At ease Colonel, have a seat," the General softly spoke.

"Yes sir, what do you want me to do for you General?" Harrison asked.

"Colonel, as you know I have been sent here to head up military and civilian intelligence for the group backing me in Washington. My mission is to determine the potentially dangerous organized crime syndicate members and military intelligence informers within Japan. My backers and I may give out some benefits to some of these men down the road. Do you get the drift of where I am going?" Salmon said as he stared out the window overlooking the quadrangle in front of his offices.

"Sir, I believe that you can count on me," the Colonel replied.

As the General whirled around to face Colonel Harrison, "Colonel, it is not a matter of believe. You have passed the highest secrecy clearance testing and investigation. I must have your undivided commitment on this project. Do I have it?" General Salmon firmly asked.

"Yes sir, I am one hundred percent committed to your orders and will defend and protect the objectives of this mission," Harrison said with a look of solid attainment.

"As most of your know my duties here in Tokyo as Deputy Commander to Supreme Commander Allied Powers include the extremely top secret job of chief intelligence officer. Therefore, my non-military colleague, Mr. Bert Dover, and I have been assigned an extraordinary secret operation to retrieve the billions of dollars of looted treasures hidden by Emperor Zapp and his family. I have personally reviewed each of your excellent records and counter-intelligence activities over the past ten years. Each of you has your various talents to get the enemy to furnish us with the information that we must have to be successful. Some of you will be required to travel around Japan and other countries in the performance of your secret duties. Only the men in this meeting will participate in recovery of Gold Bars and treasures. I will furnish each of you with 'Top Secret Clearance Passes', which will give you special authority over officers in higher rank. When I call your name please stand up. ★★★ Lieutenant General Harold Brocklesby, Major General ★ ★ Larry Broyles, Brigadier General ★ Loong Lee, Colonel Jean-Claude Araki, Colonel David Nakazawa, Colonel Ray Harrison, Colonel Billy Bob Zachry, Sergeant Bobby Carlson and Sergeant Muddy Chichibu. What we discuss and all documents presented in these meetings will not be privileged to anyone. I do not believe I have to repeat that statement to you men. I almost left someone very important out. For those of you that don't know Mr. Bert Dover and his chief liaison men, Mr. Prescott Bushel and Mr. David Clark, please stand up Bert, Prescott and David. In my absence, Mr. Dover is in charge. In the absence of Mr. Dover and myself, General Brocklesby is in charge of the operations. I trust each of you do not have any problems with carrying out our missions in the accustomed professional manner of excellent intelligence operations," General Salmon said in an assured tone.

"General, I would like to add. As the General has stated, our number one objective is to retrieve the enormous wealth Emperor Zapp and his family have hidden either here in Japan or elsewhere around the world for themselves. You will each be given the task to locate members of the inner circle of the family together with some underworld business leaders working with them. We must move silently and quickly. The War Crimes Tribunal will have the attention of the whole world. We should use this weapon to obtain the whereabouts of the Loot. Keep in mind for political purposes any treasures located will not be for publication. It is my game plan to convince Washington and the world leaders to believe that Emperor Zapp and his family are poor and cannot afford to compensate any of its War Crime Victims anything of monetary value. As you will see in the future weeks, the focus will place the blame on Military Officers of the Japanese Armed Forces without the knowledge of Emperor Zapp and his family," Mr. Dover further advised the members in the meeting.

"Thank you Bert, let's take a break for our morning tea. No, I can't get use to tea. Have you made some strong coffee like I drink?" General Salmon asked Sergeant Chichibu.

"Give me ten minutes and I will have your coffee too. There is Japanese tea for everyone now."

After the morning break, General Salmon called the meeting to order. "Gentlemen, let me begin by telling you that I am one of the best intelligence officers that ever wore this uniform. I have in my hand the initial listing of Emperor Zapp's family that we know was involved in the looting operations and movement of the loot during the war. I am handing out your specific assignment page for the family member you will be interrogating. I want each of you to carry out your findings of facts with the member assign to you. Mr. Dover and I will be doing our job on Emperor Zapp. Do not confer with each other until I have had a chance to read your initial findings. Then, I will call a meeting for the purpose to determine strategies against each member based upon what the others are attempting to collaborate.

"Resuming our meeting, the treasures were moved by ship and placed in underground tunnels. POWS did the loading and unloading of the Gold and Gems. Emperor Zapp assigned his Japanese officers to make the final decision of the sites to bury the treasures. They were commanded by Emperor Zapp to prepare and maintain detailed maps of the various locations of the Gold Bars burial operations complete with permanent markings and camouflage of the burial sites with large rocks and dirt. The Japanese military officers drew up very detailed plans for the burial of the treasures. Japanese generals conducted meetings to plan the work details for all of the POWS. In some of the tunnels concrete walls up to eighteen (18") inches thick were poured to seal the entrances. They took detailed pictures in and out of the caves," General Salmon said.

"Yeah, in many instances after the Gold Bars were buried and as the concrete was poured the POWS were shot and killed or left in the tunnels to die. The commanding general for each region retains the original maps for Emperor Zapp or his own personal greedy purposes, expecting to return after the war to recover the treasures for themselves," Lieutenant General Brocklesby agonizingly added.

"Most of the world is calling Emperor Zapp, 'The Evil God', but let me tell each of you we have to take immediate action to keep him from destroying the records and evidence that will link him and his family to the commanding of the day to day military operations since 1935 until the end of the war," "Bert' Dover described the immediate problem in a 'do not' blink your eyes manner.

"Yes, his secretary, Opium, will do her utmost to protect his neck and the necks of his family. Do not let her have any contact with Emperor Zapp's uncle, General Donkey, and allow him to burn all of his Central China Army command records. We need to keep Opium under 24 hours surveillance. Emperor Zapp will attempt to send her personally to his palace and deliver his messages and ask him to immediately bring all of the treasure locations of the looted Gold Bars, paintings, Buddhas, diamonds and currency stolen under his leadership to Emperor Zapp. If she ask any questions, tell her that I am planning everything to keep her from destroying evidence to charge Emperor Zapp with War Crimes by the Allied Forces," General Salmon ordered Colonel Harrison.

"Colonel Araki, you and your men should keep a constant surveillance on Emperor Zapp's chauffeur, Yellow Sun. I want to know the time and destination of every trip he takes from the Palace, day or night. When you see that he has been stopped and searched at one of the roadblocks during the daytime or for violating nighttime curfew, identify yourself to the roadblock military police guard and confiscate anything they found in the limo," General Salmon ordered. "At your first opportunity, send the confiscated materials to me."

"Excellent, let Emperor Zapp continue to use his influence of his position to keep his people loyal to him to force a better life for him, his family and them. The BOP Party will succeed here and raise money for us to control future politics in America for the next century," 'Bert' Dover said smiling.

"This meeting is adjourned," General Salmon ordered.

TREASURES OF WAR – CONCEALED BY THE EVIL ONES

Chapter Nineteen

Global Banking Group Created

Author's Photo

GLOBAL BANKING GROUP

The initial meeting of the Board of Directors of the Global Banking Corporation is hereby held this 31st. day of January 1934.

"Gentlemen, we are in a position to take over the gigantic private credit business in the United Sates of America. Some people fear us and are name calling us money tyrants. We are going to take command because the Federal Government, through our powerful lobbying with the BOP party members, has passed the law, which it now must operate under. Now the majority of the people think that the Global Reserve Banks are U. S. Government institutions. We shall do everything in our power to promote this impression. Our comrades are in place on the inside. They know exactly what they will earn from each of our group's money lending activities. Some of you will establish the domestic lending network with the large fund of dollars we have obtained. This will convince the people of the United States; we operate upon the highest degree of re-gaining the prosperity and stability of business, therefore, in the minds of the people, each one of them will benefit. I am passing out the listing of targeted industries that we will initially support. When the events of the international marketplace come to fruition at the desired time, our private credit monopolies will be in the right place at the right time. I have appointed the committee to bring in the foreign customers. Each of you will travel to the various foreign banks and meet with the bankers assigned to you. We will continue to lobby to maintain the issuance of money at the controlled level that will benefit our foreign customers," Robert 'Buddy' Whiteside, the Chairman, stated as he addressed the meeting.

The Secretary of Global Banking Corporation called the roll of the Board of Directors to determine all members being present: Mr. Prescott Bushel, General Jack Adams, Dr. Francisco de Luca Moro, Mr. Robert 'Buddy' Whiteside, Mr. Santana Drisco, Mr. Herbert

Dover, Mr. Jack Townsend, Mr. Carlos Burton, and Sir. Henry Willows.

"As Chairman I have passed out the ballots for the election of on-going Directors and officers for the term of two years. Mr. Dover will serve as our President. All in favor of the election of all officers raise your right hand and say aye! It carries unanimously. Thank you for your confidence and continued work under difficult times."

Mr. Herbert Dover was presented to the meeting for his acceptance speech. "Chairman Whiteside has pretty much described the purpose of Global Banking Corporation. Our focus at this time should be the establishment of private credit companies wholly owned by individuals or jointly among members only here today in this initial meeting. I will see to it that the appropriate funds are funneled out to our new private credit companies. We must continue to lobby the BOP Party and Democrats to pass additional excellent legislation for our benefit."

"Being no further business on the agenda for the meeting, I hereby adjourn this meeting," Chairman Whiteside announced.

TREASURES OF WAR – CONCEALED BY THE EVIL ONES

Chapter Twenty

The Story of Deputy Commander of Allied Powers

General Milton R. Salmon

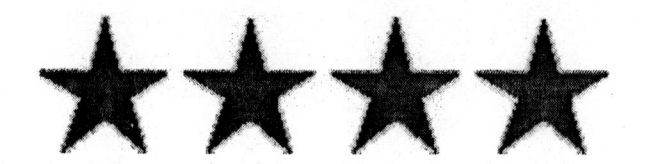

★★★★

And

BOP Party Chairman in Tokyo

Mr. 'Bert' Dover

Retrieve All Treasures From Emperor Zapp and His Family

FOR *WHO*

The Deputy Commander of Allied Powers, General Milton R. Salmon, and Born of Privilege, 'BOP', Tokyo Chairman, Mr. Bert Dover, arranged for Emperor Zapp to meet them at a specified location away from the headquarters. The initial message delivered by Sergeant Muddy Chichibu asked that Emperor Zapp come by his official vehicle with his usual motorcycle escorts.

This was done because Salmon and Dover knew that the newspaper reporters camped out near the Imperial Palace would be taking photos and the Japanese people would come swarming along the streets as he slowly passed. They needed to show the world that the Japanese people continued to worship him even after defeat.

It worked just as Dover had planned. The streets were lined with Japanese women waving the flag of the rising sun as Emperor Zapp rode by in his limo. Emperor Zapp took the long route through Tokyo and then sped off to the secret destination. As he drove up to the building chosen by Dover and Salmon his driver stopped and jumped out and opened the right rear door near the curbside. He waved to his men to give them the assurance that all was well.

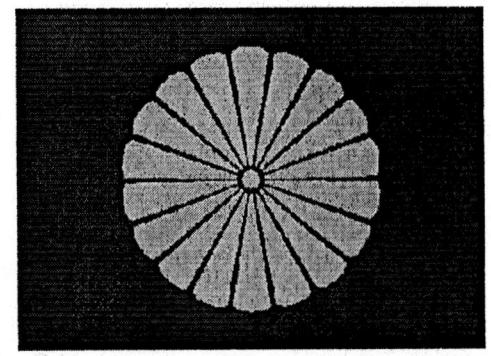

The initial meeting began with the normal introductions of all in attendance. "Emperor Zapp, you are a very important person here in Japan. You use the Chrysanthemum as your symbol of being a divine God and authority to your people. General Salmon and I have been agonizing over whether you may retain your power. I am sure that you have read some of the American politicians, such as the State-War-Navy Coordinating Committee announcement. They want us to remove you from office and take you to jail to stand trial as a war criminal. Our Allied partners, Australia, New Zealand, Philippines, China and others in the war against you are calling for your head on a silver platter. Even Senator Richard Russell presented the U. S. Congress a proposal for the U. S. to declare that all of our Allies and us should arrest you and try you as a war criminal," Bert Dover angrily announced to Zapp.

"I understand your statements, however, I do not believe that you understand our society and culture. Your occupation here in Japan is something entirely new and different to my people. We are the most advanced nation in the Far East and the United States needs us to keep peace in the region. Because of this and the close business ties with my country's progressive businesses with the American businesses, our production revolution will keep both of us stronger for many years to come. You need my influence to achieve your goals," Emperor Zapp replied in his arrogant manner.

"Do you think we are stupid? The world would hang us instead of you if we deserted all of the men and women in our Military Forces who died conquering your Evil God objectives. The massacres of millions of people in Asia and the sudden attack at Pearl Harbor and the survivors of your Death Marches and POW Camps and Slave Labor operations are very real and no one has forgotten," General Salmon replied as he constrained himself in his chair.

"The key witness in this investigation has denounced you as trafficking opium in China and hoarding large sums of money in the process. He has told us that you secretly paid him commissions through some of your large companies. He has brought more than twenty files to his interrogation meetings with me. These files included secret letters, bank statements complete with supporting checks and most importantly the deposits," Bert Dover told Emperor Zapp while sitting right next to him.

"You are bluffing! You don't have anyone in my family that has brought you anything."

Calmly, Bert Dover replied. "Some of these bank accounts are labeled as Gold Bullion Depository accounts. You and your family set up quite a sophisticated banking network in an attempt to fund your military operations. The foreign bank accounts in countries where you purchased critical materials during the war were established to have your suppliers paid locally without the international banking community being able to trace or block the flow of funds. Pretty good scheme, but the cleverest action was the transportation of cash by your couriers to make the deposits in these accounts. I bet you would have sent out your personal assassination squad to the ends of the earth and below to make a hit on any courier that did not make it to the bank with the huge amounts of cash."

"Let me see just one of those so-called bank statement."

"Using the name of American Victory Investments was real clever. You bought American equipment and supplies and had them shipped to Hong Kong and forwarded from Hong Kong to Japan."

"Huh!"

"Yea, since 1938, we have been spying on your family's banks, trustees, accountants, lawyers and fiduciary agents. My intelligence reports identify you and your brother, Major Snatch, as the asset managers of the accounts in the Hong Kong First International commerce Bank. We think that this is just a small fish out there in the big ocean. The international War Crimes Tribunal Claims already filed against you and more importantly to you personally is the forthcoming estimated millions of Civil Claims that will be filed in the future years and leave you a broken man and family in ruins. Once the lawsuits are put on the docket, the plaintiff's lawyers are going to file interrogatories seeking detailed information about where your assets have been stashed. This will go on for years. I can see one of the first motions filed against you that will be granted immediately by the Courts," Bert Dover warned as only someone with his background could do and make you believe him.

"What are you talking about?"

"The Judge will issue orders to prevent transfer and will freeze all of you and your bothers, cousins and uncles bank accounts all over the world."

"When do you want to meet again?"

"Emperor Zapp, time is of he essence! How about tomorrow morning?" Dover asked.

"I will be here at 02:00 tomorrow," Emperor Zapp replied as he hurriedly bowed and did an about face and crisply walk out to his awaiting limo.

"Fine, see you tomorrow afternoon."

General Milton R. Salmon called his military officers together after chow to discuss the events of the week. "Was your gathering of evidence from Emperor Zapp's family successful? Pass your written reports forward?" General Salmon asked.

"I am very apprehensive at this stage of the investigation," Bert Dover replied.

"Why?" General Salmon asked.

"These militant communists are on the verge of starting to disrupt everything. Emperor Zapp and the pending new government are their current targets," Dover replied.

"That just makes our gun powder a little dryer." Lieutenant General Brocklesby replied with a grin planted all over his wide face.

"What do you mean?" Colonel Nakazawa asked.

"Besides our objective and pressures, Emperor Zapp and his family members surely do not want the communists and its link with China and Russia to have any say in the future of Japan," General Brocklesby answered.

"Harold, you are exactly correct. We should use this negative communist thing during our next interrogations of the family members. Let's take a fifteen minutes break to give me time to review your reports," General Salmon instructed the team.

Subsequent to the break, General Salmon, Bert Dover and David Clark set down at the head table facing the men. "Emperor Zapp and two of his brothers seem to be the weak parties in our investigation. Emperor Zapp, Major Snatch and Prince Mikey have softened up. The others are showing their loyalty to Emperor Zapp. I recommend that you keep your urgent but confident approach in your next meeting. Bert and I have another important meeting set up on Monday with Emperor Zapp. Once he comes around, the others will follow. Does anyone have any questions or would like to make a comment? This is open for discussion of all subject matters," General Salmon spoke addressing the Team.

"General, Admiral Lavish has guilt written all over his face during our interrogations and is very ill. He brought his personal advisor with him. As you know I speak excellent Japanese, but he apparently knows that and turns to his advisor and talks to him in German. I could use someone that speaks German to go with me the next time and takes notes. Admiral Lavish participated in a region where our troops stopped the movement of all Japanese ships back toward Japan for several years before the end of the war. He must have first hand knowledge of some hidden Gold Bars and treasure from that region. He may not be around much longer. I do not want to see him take everything to his grave," Colonel David Nakazawa said in his even-tempered voice.

"David Clark don't you speak German fluently?" General Salmon asked.

"Yes Sir! I will be glad to work with anyone with the first name David," Clark replied as the members laughed.

"Colonel Nakazawa, you and David work on Admiral Lavish from this point forward," General Salmon ordered.

As Colonel Billy Bob Zachry raised his hand, "Yes, Colonel, you have the floor."

"General Salmon, this guy Prince Eye Spy is slick as a greased pig. After he finished his duties in China and returned to Emperor Zapp's headquarters here in Tokyo he gets a little squirmy and gets the jitters. Whatever he did in China must have been cold blooded and has dealt with those crimes in his mind and is a cool cat never flinching. He must have done something to double cross his brother, Emperor Zapp, here in Japan," Colonel Zachry said seeking some additional advice from members.

"Billy Bob, I can give you some suggestions for handling this slippery dude. He obviously is fearful of his brother. In your next meeting, go in with some documents prepared by yourself with a forged signature of Emperor Zapp on it and show it to him. Here are some blank letterheads and an official stamp of Emperor Zapp for your task. Tell him his brother has already acknowledged that Prince Eye Spy hid some Gold Bars for his own stash here in Japan. Put the issue of where is your private stash versus being tried as a War Criminal to him. With your phony document in front of him, he will realize that his brother will not protect him anymore," Bert Dover advised in his prosecutor/negotiator tone of voice.

"Use all of our tools to break the greedy criminals down and achieve our mission to retrieve the billions of dollars of looted treasures hidden by them," General Salmon emphasized. "I noticed in your report Major General Broyles, you might do something similar with your interrogation of General Donkey. He was a major participant in big time massacres and rapes in China, and the old fart is not that loyal to Emperor Zapp because he did not become the ruler and has a few screws loose," General Salmon disclosed.

"General, it is getting late and some of the men have early morning meetings. You and I should have our agreement with Emperor Zapp worked out this next week, which will make everyone's job easier. I make a motion that we adjourn for this week and work hard and meet again this same day next week," Bert Dover said.

"This meeting is adjourned!" General Salmon ordered.

INITIAL INTERROGATIONS OF EMPEROR ZAPP'S BROTHER, PRINCE EYE SPY.

"The Tribunal has voted to hang you for the brutal killings of tens of thousands of the Chinese women and children and old defenseless men by your Imperial Japanese Troops under your command in Nanking," Colonel Zachry told Emperor Zapp's brother, Prince Eye Spy during his first closed door interrogation.

"But I was only following the orders of my spiritual leader, my brother, Emperor Zapp."

"All of you dudes have been brainwashed to give the same identical answers to save your necks. I know you have pledged your alligiance and devotion to Emperor Zapp and are afraid of his condemnation of your spirit to eternal hell. Look man, he had already signed off he is not a divine person and your God. Your faith in him as your God has been eliminated," Colonel Zachry bitterly stated to Prince Eye Spy as he motioned for his Lieutenant to enter.

"What are you telling me? Emperor Zapp wouldn't desert all of us. My friends and members of my family died for him carrying out his orders during the war."

"How do you think he is going to save his butt? People like your brother always point to others to avoid war crime charges against themselves. I know you were assigned by your brother to operate the secret removal and transportation of Gold during your time in the Chinese Expedition."

"Who told you that I was ever in China?"

"Your brothers, Emperor Zapp and Major Snatch have blamed you for your overzealous sex drive and raping thirty young Chinese girls before you cut their heads off."

"I don't believe you. They did not tell you that garbage. I have never been to China."

"On February 13th 1945, you were shacked up in the Shanghai Expedition Hotel on the top floor executive suite with two Chinese virgins."

"Wait a minute! Somebody is lying."

"You didn't know you had some Japanese Troops with cameras wanting to take pictures of their superiors to win special recognition at a later date by Emperor Zapp's family.

It is all documented for the prosecutors during the International Military War Tribunal causes of actions."

"My brother, Emperor Zapp, is the only Holy and Supreme Power under our constitution. He is totally responsible for his orders to his Imperial Forces and the results of the brutal campaign."

"You just admitted you carried out brutal military actions for Emperor Zapp. See this article in the local newspaper? The majority of your former zaibatsu underworld business buddies are saying, you are guilty and should be executed. Does not look like you have any support to save your life."

"Those sorry corrupt bastards are in this up to their heads with all of us."

"What do you mean, all of us and in what?" Colonel asked and added. "Don't give me a bunch of your lies."

"Holy Golden Buddha! I am not saying anything more today."

"My investigation report goes to Chief Prosecutor, Mr. Adam Lincoln, first thing in the morning. You have not revealed anything to me to change my mind about your guilt."

"Do you think I am a fool? I tell you what you want to know and I'm history."

"I think you are a fool if you fail to cooperate with my investigation. Do you really think the world is not going to be looking over your shoulder for the remainder of your life? When all of a sudden you have lots of money to spend for lavish things for you and your wife and children and the International Military War Crimes Tribunal for Far East (IMWCTFE) or Office of Strategic Services (OSS) learns about your lifestyle, you and your immediate family will be brought before the courts and all of you will be sentenced to long-term harsh punishment. You are a marked man forever. Just do the right thing now and save yourself and family tons of grief."

Prince Eye Spy hastily left the meeting without saying a word.

SECOND MEETING WITH EMPEROR ZAPP.

The next afternoon, Emperor Zapp had his driver drive him to the same secret location as the first meeting. However, General Salmon had been called into an update briefing with the Supreme Commander of Allied Powers (SCAP). Mr. Bert Dover asked Mr. Prescott Bushel and Mr. David Clark to join him for the scheduled meeting with Emperor Zapp.

The meeting began with Emperor Zapp asking, "Where is General Salmon? It is very important to me for your military leaders to be included in all of our sessions."

"General Salmon has been called to meet with his boss, the Supreme Commander of SCAP. He authorized us to proceed without delay and let you know of the pressures from all over the world to have you tried as a war criminal. The Supreme Commander wants us to work out some reasonable compromise," Dover replied.

"What to you mean by a compromise?" Emperor Zapp asked.

"Emperor Zapp, you do not want to be put in prison with American and Australian military police as your guards while awaiting your war criminal trial. Some of those men lost loved ones, brothers, and best friends in the Pacific Campaign. It wouldn't take much effort to put poison in your food. When they find your body, the American Military pathologists will perform an autopsy without doing any blood work, or test of the liquids from your body or make tissue reports. Results, the world will believe their autopsy report that you died of natural causes and no one will ever care about you again. We know you took time after yesterday's meeting to confer with some of your family members, and you learned all of your brothers, cousins, and uncles have been interrogated by my team and are being included in our War Crimes charges. They know we know all about your directives to declare war, kill, loot, deal drugs, and raise money to build your military machinery in your quest to become ruler of the world. Some of them have already pointed the finger at you. Some of them have stated how they shipped Gold Bars and other valuable treasure to you here in Japan and other countries," Prescott Bushel lectured.

"Dover, you mentioned compromise. What do you mean by a compromise? How may I save my name and my family's name? There must be a better resolution than hanging me. Is it the Gold Bars and treasure you are wanting to use in your compromise?"

"You and I are going to divide some of your Gold Bullion Depository Bank Accounts. I am not greedy. We will split them fifty/fifty," Bert Dover said as he coerced Emperor Zapp.

"I don't have any problem with the fifty/fifty for the Bank Accounts."

"Not so fast! We still have the issue of the looted Gold Bars that made it back to Japan. My education as a mining engineer with my registered Professional Engineer license could benefit you greatly if we could come up with a scheme to move most of your Gold Bars located here in Japan to a safe haven and divide it between General Salmon, you and I."

"How do you suggest that we move it safely at this time?"

"That's the easiest part. I will arrange a freighter to carry the heavy 'military weapons' from the port. General Salmon will give orders to send the trucks to wherever we set up the warehouse operation to be sure the Gold Bars are properly crated and marked as weapons. Some of your men will load the trucks and the trucks will be driven to the port. The loaded trucks would be hoisted onto the freighter and delivered to the final secret destination."

"When do you want to visit the three sites for the Gold Bars here in Japan?"

"You tell me when is the best time."

"The first visit should be with you and General Salmon for your critical evaluation of the task to move it. I could be prepared to show you the local site tomorrow and the other two sites outside of Tokyo on Saturday."

"Okay, General Salmon and I will come to your palace and drive through the tall gates and around to the south side entrance. We will pick you up at 10:30, and you will direct us to the site."

"I agree," Emperor Zapp said as he bowed and left the meeting.

During the evening Dover and Salmon went to the officer's club out at Misawa Air Base to dine and thoroughly discuss the unbelievable, unexpected and very, very secret information Emperor Zapp earlier furnished Dover regarding the Gold Bars located in Japan. After reviewing all new possibilities, Bert Dover and General Salmon agreed it was in their best personal interest to take one military vehicle with the markings of a general on it without a driver to make the visit the next day. They concurred on Dover's game plan to ship the Gold Bars out of Japan.

"What are we going to do to avoid prosecution for violating the 1933 Executive Order issued by President Roosevelt on April 5, 1933," Dover asked.

"What Executive Order are you talking about?" General Salmon replied.

"The Executive Order forbids the hoarding of Gold Bullion, Gold Bars and Gold Certificates by anyone within the continental United States. Only the Federal Reserve Bank or any member of the Federal Reserve System may own Gold now," Dover replied.

"What are they going to do to you if you violate this Executive Order?"

"If found guilty, each of us could be imprisoned for up to ten (10) years, and fined $10,000 or both. Here is another important rule; a like fine, imprisonment, or both may punish any officer, director, or agent of any corporation who knowingly participates in any such violation. A U. S. citizen can not own Gold," Dover warned.

"Everybody in Washington is concerned about saving Europe from Stalin and will never know what we are doing over here. I am not going to lose a nights sleep over a thirteen year old Executive Order from a dead President," General Salmon replied.

"Don't forget I must deposit some of these funds for the politicians in Washington and the Born of Privilege (BOP) party to finance secret subversive anti-communist regimes and fund candidates running for office from the BOP party. You and I must decide on how much of our cut we are going to send to BOP," Dover said in his gluttonous voice.

"How about twenty-five percent of our portion?"

"General, I was thinking more like eight to ten at the maximum."

"Do you think ten percent will satisfy those scoundrels?"

"Since our operations have been established without any controls on us, our reports to them in Washington are of our own making. Besides, what took place over here will not be revealed to the world for a century. The ten percent amount I anticipate sending to them will be like the Easter Bunny, Santa Claus and winning the World Series all in one for them. Furthermore, we could get Emperor Zapp to take ten percent less; telling him that Washington needs ten percent more," Dover eagerly replied.

"You amaze me Dover. Where did you learn all these methods to do large transactions like this?"

"Just my human nature, this type opportunity will come by only once in your life."

SECOND MEETING WITH PRINCE EYE SPY.

Four days later Prince Eye Spy contacted Colonel Billy Bob Zachry to set up their second meeting at his secret location on the outskirts of Tokyo. Colonel Zachry asked Mr. Prescott Bushel to come along. General Salmon's driver Sergeant Bobby Carlson drove them to the meeting place. The thatch roof house could be seen behind the bamboo fence. As they walked through the bamboo gate into the garden, the Prince's gateman led Prescott, Billy Bob and Bobby down the natural stone path by the beautiful Cherry blossom trees in full bloom until they reached a point where the path divided into two directions. The path to the left led them through the garden to the fusuma or beautiful cedar moveable partition entrance door and on to the okuzashiki or inner sitting room. Prince Eye Spy greeted them and pointed to the tatami mats for the place to sit during this first meeting at one of his houses.

"This is quite different from our first meeting place at our offices. This must be away from your clay tile roof palace. I take it that you did not want anyone in your family to know that you were meeting with us," Colonel Zachry said.

"You are a brilliant officer. I use this house away from downtown to conduct all types of meetings. I have a lot of private space with my beautiful gardens out here. Maybe you will do me the honor to have tea out in my teahouse after our meeting today or some other time. I am eager to know whether you have dragged out the War Crimes claims against me and delayed your investigation report to Prosecutor Lincoln until I have had the chance to discuss all matters that you brought up in our first meeting. I trust you have not filed War Crime violations against me," Prince Eye Spy said waiting for a sudden reply.

What's this goon up too? This is a long way from his total denial and leaving without saying a word at the first meeting in our office. Colonel Zachry thought before replying.

"My name is Prescott Bushel and General Milton Salmon's driver Bobby Carlson has joined us for this meeting to warn you of the War Crimes charges. You denied everything in the first meeting, but I have brought some documents to support the fact that your brother, Emperor Zapp and Major Snatch have sworn under oath that you committed those gruesome crimes in China. Here are several of the documents under the seal and stamp of Emperor

Zapp that will be included in the filings before the International War Tribunal, and if convicted, you will be sentenced to death by a firing squad. We do not have anymore time to drag this matter out."

"What was your name again?"

"Prescott Bushel."

"Okay, I have something to offer you men to stop your investigation of me."

"It better be something beneficial to everybody," Colonel Zachry replied.

"Mr. Bushel, I have some zaibatsu partners and we have hidden some of the Gold Bars from China in a few safe places."

"How much are you talking about?" Prescott asked.

"Oh, there is almost ten metric tons of the small 6.2 kilos Gold Bars."

"Prince, you had better get back to your confession brainwaves. Let me show you another document executed by Emperor Zapp complete with his seal stamp. Do you see he has known all along you were stealing some of his Gold Bars? What is the amount of Gold Bars that your brother states that you and your zaibatsu partners have claimed for your very own," Prescott asked as he pointed on the detailed report to the total on the document that he and had prepared using Emperor Zapp's letterhead, signature stamp and official seal."

"But my zaibatsu partners have large companies for manufacturing military aircraft, tanks, troop personnel carriers and navy war ships. They will go busted without any money to re-tool its operations for peacetime engineering, design, and manufacturing of commuter train systems and vehicles for our people and possibly export them around the world. We are planning to occasionally use the proceeds from the sales of the Gold Bars to finance our new peacetime companies. I am willing to consider relinquishing forty percent of what my brother Emperor Zapp has declared that I have in my control. My zaibatsu partners will go along with me on this viable offer. Otherwise, they will tell you to stick it."

"You can tell your zaibatsu partners they will be included in the War Crimes trials as defendants together with you. Results, you and they will be busted forever," Colonel Zachry replied in a demonstration of rage. "Come on Prescott and Bobby, let's get out of this so-called peaceful setting and get the locations of the Gold Bars from Emperor Zapp and file the papers with the Prosecutor. They will rot in hell as far as I am concerned.

"Maybe, just maybe I could convince my partners to accept less. What is your deal?" Prince Eye Spy asked.

"You know exactly where all these Gold Bars are stashed and you really do not have a choice but to except our offer. You get thirty percent of the total number of Gold Bars and we move seventy percent of them to our secret locations. We have enormous expenses to handle our portion. Your decision must be made immediately," Prescott stressed.

"Man, you guys deal tough. I have one condition to add to your offer. You do not let the results of this meeting be known to anyone, especially my zaibatsu partners."

"Hey, Colonel do you have any problem with that request? My lips could be silent under the correct policy," Prescott replied.

"Prince, what you do with your thirty percent is your business. Not a soul will discuss this matter again as soon as we have our seventy percent of the number of Gold Bars in our possession. As you now understand, silence will only happen as soon as the transfers are completed. We will put a hold on the war crime charges against you and not say anything now or in the future when you deliver the complete detailed site locations of the Gold Bars here in Japan and in the Philippines to me. When we are satisfied, you can do whatever you want to with your share and we will destroy all of the war crimes documents," Colonel Zachry cautioned Prince Eye Spy.

"It is time for you to take those papers out of your briefcase and let us see the site location list," Prescott added.

"It is our custom to bow to the other party when an agreement is reached. Here is the list of all site locations of the Gold Bars, all four hundred metric tons of it," Prince Eye Spy said as he removed the list from his briefcase, handed it to Prescott and bowed toward Prescott, Colonel Zachry and Bobby.

Colonel Zachry, Prescott Bushel and Bobby Carlson all returned the bow as they looked at the detailed site location list of the Gold Bars from Prince Eye Spy.

Prince Eye Spy summoned the head of his Geisha Girls and told her to be sure everything was ready for them to go to the Tea House and have the tea ceremony.

FIRST MEETING WITH PRINCE MAJOR SNATCH.

Prince Major Snatch was summoned to Lieutenant General Harold Brocklesby's office to discuss his secret wartime operations for the control of the looted Gold Bars in China, Hong Kong, Malaya, Viet Nam, Laos, Sumatra, Java, Borneo, Singapore, Burma, Cambodia, French Indo-China, and the Philippines, especially operation 'Golden Turbo', the secret code name given to him by Emperor Zapp.

Upon his arrival, he and several of his advisors attended the International War Crimes Tribunal investigation. "Good morning, General Brocklesby, how may I assist you in your investigation? Since I did not participate in any military campaigns during the war due my illness, I do not have much information for your investigation."

"Illness, what illness are you talking about?" General Brocklesby asked.

"I have been treated for tuberculosis by my doctors for five years. Here are some of my medical records to support my whereabouts during the war while being treated in the special tuberculosis hospitals," Prince Major Snatch replied as he handed a large envelope with stacks of medical records to Brocklesby.

Laughing, General Brocklesby said. "The German Nazi SS officers are not this good. I spent a few months investigating some of the top criminals in Germany before coming here. This takes the grand prize."

"I am serious. You do not see me laughing. Here is my medicine that I have to continually take for several more years. In fact, I am not able to meet with you for long periods of time during your investigations because I become very weak. The tuberculosis has left me without much strength. I must rest four or five hours during the day," Prince Snatch said in his sheepish voice.

"Let's cut out the act and all this bologna and these lies. Your brother, Emperor Zapp, has testified about the success you had in China and Hong Kong. Did the man with the name Goose Sun have tuberculosis in Hong Kong? Also, was Alejandro Chin too sick to carry on his operations in the Philippines? The most intriguing alias you used was your banking arrangement in England. Victor Royal sounds so British not even your zaibatsu partners would have found the deposits made by you at Barclays Bank London. Maybe the damp weather in London caused your illness to get worse," General Brocklesby revealed with sarcasm.

"Your satirical suggestions offend me. There is no way that I can be considered as a suspect of hiding anything from anybody. Those medical records are dated and signed by the doctors, nurses and hospital administrators. My brother, Emperor Zapp, did not testify against me. He sent a letter to the doctor specializing in the cure therapy of tuberculosis at the hospital. Look in those letters and you will find his letter requesting immediate medical treatment for me."

"How many 'young comfort women' did you enjoy in China and the Philippines? Your sexual desires were satisfied several times every day. It is a shame you murdered them when you moved on to the next town. Your wife does not understand your daily sex drive these days. It must be frustrating to you. Reckon you could get some of those young virgins from China and the Philippines to come here and live with you? Weak! You must be getting stronger now because no tongue wagging sexual demands. Your tuberculosis is recovering fast. No harem makes a young Prince very strong," General Brocklesby said as he quizzed the Prince.

"My wife, the Princess, is a lovely woman and excellent mother to my children. Her father would kill me if you spread all of these rumors about me."

"Rumors! The formal charges against you are in these War Crimes Trial Documents."

"Let me see those papers?" Prince Snatch asked as he grabbed them from General Brocklesby's hand.

The International Military War Crimes Tribunal for the Far East (IMWCTFE) draft of the criminal complaint against Prince Major Snatch read as follows:

Count 1 – 'Leaders, organizers, instigators, or accomplices in the formulation or execution of a common plan or conspiracy .. to wage wars of aggression, and war or wars in violations of international law.'
Count 26 – Waging aggressive war against the China.
Count 27 – Waging aggressive war against Manchuria.
Count 28 – Waging aggressive war against Philippines

Count 29 – Waging aggressive war against the Untied States of America.
Count 31 – Waging aggressive war against the British Commonwealth.
Count 32 – Waging aggressive war against the Netherlands.
Count 33 – Waging aggressive war against France (Indochina).
Count 54 – Ordered, authorized, and permitted inhumane treatment of Prisoners of War and others.
Count 55 – Deliberately and recklessly disregarded their duty to take adequate steps to prevent atrocities.

Movement of the money from the sales of Opium and Drugs in your personal efforts to make the Chinese addicted to them was just the beginning of your crimes in China. Your adhesion to the rapes of young Chinese and Filipino girls and eventual brutal murders of thousands of innocent people goes down in history as the atrocities of the century.

Directly and routinely conducted massive looting of the people, banks, and government coffers of China, Hong Kong, Malaya, Viet Nam, Laos, Sumatra, Java, Borneo, Singapore, Burma, Cambodia, French Indo-China, and the Philippines and concluded the transportation of Gold Bars and treasures to your secret locations and the profiteering from the sales of them and financing the warmongering goals against the world by you and your zaibatsu partners. If you are found guilty, the sentence will be hanging by the neck until you are dead.

"Prince, you have an option to consider a way to prevent the proceedings against you from moving forward. My four star boss, General Salmon, controls the International Military War Crimes Tribunal for the Far East. Besides your cruel deeds of the past, you simply cheated a great number of people out of their wealth. I want to know where all of it is. You are covering up vital information about where all of your bank accounts and Gold Bars are hidden. It hasn't vanished. Where is it?" General Brocklesby asked.

"If I agree to an advanced compromise of the charges against me before I am scheduled to go to trial and furnish you with the financial information you need to locate everything, will my name and family be protected from further prosecution by you?"

"It depends on whether you have decided to be totally honest with us. Any advanced compromise agreement will include the understanding of the terms and conditions whereby it becomes null and void at the instant your facts are proven false and you have perjured yourself. Your cousin, Prince Count Saigon, Deputy Commander of your secret team will be interrogated by me beginning in two hours. So, the facts man, just the facts?" General Brocklesby asked.

Collaboration between Emperor Zapp, his family members and General Milton Salmon, Mr. Bert Dover, and Lieutenant General Brocklesby to locate and retrieve the confiscated loot is the primary goal at this point of the investigations.

"We must not let the world know where the Gold Bars and Bank Accounts are located. If Office of Strategic Services (OSS) agents such as Mr. Bobby Staples come to you as a representative of the United States Government or as an investigator for the International Military War Crimes Tribunal for the Far East, do not tell him anything or show him any maps in the Philippines. He does not have any authority to investigate this matter, and he is not part of Mr. Dover and General Salmon's team," General Brocklesby told the Prince in a very firm finger pointing manner.

"Tell me about the shipments of Gold Bars to the Philippines from the various looted countries. Give me the locations of the Gold Bars?"

"General, the Gold shipments under my direction were made to three different regions of the Philippines. The first ship docked at Cagayan De Oro City on the island of Mindanao. The second ship docked at Cavite near Manila. The third ship docked at Lingayen on the South China Sea coast of the island of Luzon."

"General Manila Rape was your army commander in Nanking and in Manila. How many of the Gold Bars did he keep for himself in the Philippines?"

"I can tell you lots of stories about that dude. He is scum of the earth. I had my suspicions about him hiding all that Gold for me. I can tell you where it is in the Philippines according to the maps he turned into me at my Manila office. The total number of Gold Bars is shown on each map with a code number. The total on each map equals the total Gold Bars for each separate shipment. If any Gold Bars are not retrieved from these locations or some of them come up missing from the count, General Rape is guilty as sin," Prince Snatch replied.

"Where were the Gold Bars taken from the docks?"

"Here is the map for the Cagayan De Oro Region. The cave up the Mulita River is marked by the dot on the photo taken from across the river. The photo shows a dark spot up the mountain from the dot. That is the entrance to the cave. This site has code number ZZ3724. A large number of Gold Bars was hidden is this cave. Here is the photo taken in the cave before the engineering brigade under the command of General Toyo Redball closed it."

"Looks like those Gold Bars are stacked very deep in that large cave site. How many American and Filipino POW's did you use to handle all of those Gold Bars?"

"I do not have a report or an answer for your question. I recommend we use our time wisely and proceed. According to General Redball, he reported to me that they cruised up the Pulangi River around Mt. Kaatoan and went ashore near the town of Valencia. Here is the photo taken in front of the Filipino house looking toward a mountain in the background. Directly behind this house, if you pointed to the highest point of the mountain, you would see a valley at the bottom of the mountain. The cave entrance is located some 15 meters up the mountainside. Here is the photo of the Gold Bars inside the cave prior to what ever took place before General Redball moved on to the next location."

"Prince, it looks like there are two entrances into the cave from overhead. The light is coming from the small opening above the Gold Bars. I hope they figured out a way to close that small opening. Otherwise, some Filipino Tribesman will find the Gold Bars during one of his hunts," General Brocklesby replied.

"The soldiers moved two boulders and leaned them against each other covering the small opening. The boulders on the hillside are key landmarks for locating the cave."

"What's in the cave across the Pulangi River?" General Brocklesby asked.

"This is a deep cave. A winding entrance leads down to a large cavity in the subsurface to the cave. This photo was taken by General Redball's photographer near the bottom of the cave in front of the stack of Gold Bars," Prince Snatch replied.

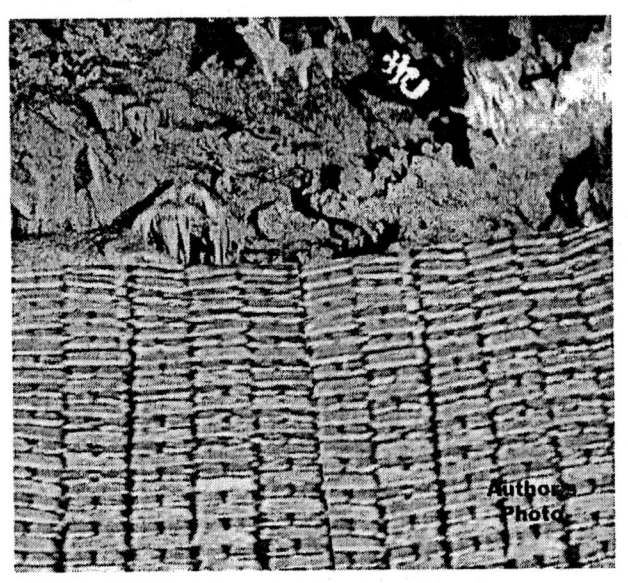

"Man, this is the largest number of Gold Bars I have seen to date. How many are hidden in this cave?' General Brocklesby asked.

"Let's see! Cave number EZ3489 was inventoried and has over 6,000 Gold Bars weighing 75 kilos each."

"They must have made many boat trips from Cagayan De Oro to transport all of those Gold Bars to this cave way up there," General Brocklesby said in amazement. "You did not want anybody to find that many Gold Bars up in the interior on the other side of Mt. Kaatoan in a deep cave," he added.

"My brother, Emperor Zapp, could have lived in luxury for the rest of his life from the proceeds of the sales of those Gold Bars. He didn't think he would lose the war and have to be accountable to anyone in the world for his looting of many countries' wealth."

TREASURES OF WAR – CONCEALED BY THE EVIL ONES / 372

"How many local Tribesmen did you have killed to keep those locations secret?" General Brocklesby asked.

"I didn't kill anyone. What General Redball did carrying out his orders from Emperor Zapp is another matter," Prince Snatch replied.

"General Redball was under your command. The second ship docked at the Port of Cavite. Who was your commander assigned to hide the Gold Bars near Manila?" General Brocklesby asked.

"General Taya Squirrelly was the commander."

"Wait just a second. You are confused. You have already confirmed General Manila Rape was your commander for Manila."

"Oh yea, General Squirrelly was in charge of Lingayen. General Rape was responsible to me for hiding the second shipload. I was in Manila most of the time this operation was undertaken. His reports to me included this photo for the San Pedro site near the small river. See the mark near the tree on the hill? The cave entrance is located south some fifty steps from the mark.

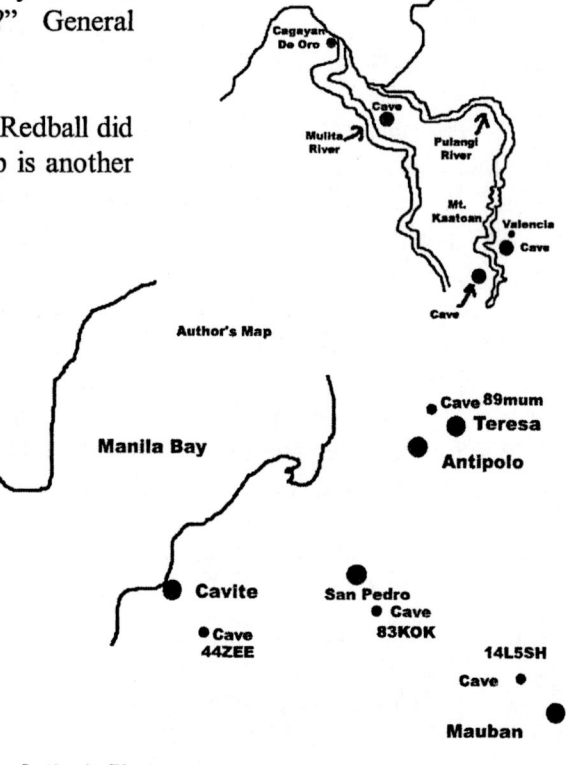

In the Manila region, we decided to provide two different routes to retrieve the Gold Bars. Mauban is located opposite the South China Sea. We could use either Cavite to the South China Sea or Mauban to the Pacific Ocean.

The largest cave had to have some blasting done out of the side of the mountain near Teresa to easily reach it with our military trucks. I personally went out there to inspect the final disposition of the Gold Bars. Eleven of our troop transport trucks were loaded with stacks of Gold Bars one meter high all over the bed of the trucks," Prince Snatch explained.

"The other site on the Manila Map is the cave near Cavite. Near the port, you must have kept a large heavy load of Gold Bars for safekeeping at a convenient nearby place," General Brocklesby said putting the pressure on Prince Snatch.

"I am shocked. I do not find a report from General Rape for the cave at Cavite."

"Prince Snatch, you find the report and have it in my hands no later than 16:00 tomorrow," General Brocklesby ordered.

"I will find it. The Yakuza, organized crime syndicate, are going to be expecting to continue making their huge profits somehow. You warned me about the Office of Strategic Services (OSS) agents. It is my duty to return the favor. Here is a listing of some of the individuals and their corrupt companies who profited from military supplier contracts during the war. Obviously, these same leeches have some knowledge of the Gold Bars and have teams scattered throughout Japan, Philippines, Burma, Java, Sumatra, Singapore and other locations working night and day and paying incentive bonuses to anyone that locates any treasures for them."

"I noticed that you left out The United States of America and Great Britain. Why?" Asked General Brocklesby. "We have information the U. S. Mafia is working hand and hand with your Japanese Yakuza. If they can get their grimy hands on ten billion dollars worth of these Gold Bars, it could finance their criminal activities around the world and expand them throughout the U. S. and buy political clout for fifty years or more."

"Emperor Zapp has worked very close with his friends in Japan and elsewhere," Prince Snatch replied.

"Back to the specific identification of your Gold Bullion Bank Depository accounts. Some of the Gold Bars you collected were delivered to Hong Kong for deposit. Earlier, I mentioned your account in Hong Kong in the name of Goose Sun and the Filipino Bank in the name of Alejandro Chin and Barclays Bank London in the name of Victor Royal. Did you make the normal Gold Bullion Trade transaction for an 'Off-the-Market' private Spot Deal as a Bank-to-Bank Transfer from your bank in Hong Kong to London, New York, Paris and Geneva?" General Brocklesby firmly asked.

"Yes Sir! I needed some money I could get to quickly. All current bank transactions in Japan are being put under the magnifying glass."

"Do you have copies of the Sale and Purchase Contracts for the AU? Did you lodge these contracts with the respective banks?"

"Since I was the seller and the buyer in some of the transfers, my seller bank officer for the Gold Bullion sent the key tested telex with the bank taking full responsibility to my buyer bank officer, it was easy to set the closing and window time for the transfer of accounts. Just used different names for myself," Prince Snatch replied. "Further, I sold some tranches of Gold Bullion whereby I affirmed and warranted the physical possession and control of Aurium Utalium bars. As many times as possible, I got the buyer to use my Hong Kong bank's correspondent bank overseas. This made for a smoother transaction."

"Prince, your buyers' bank officers issued written Certification of Funds in the amount to support the purchase of the Gold Bars. The Gold Bars physically remained at your Hong Kong bank under the name of the buyer after you received the payment in U. S. Dollars or British Pounds. I need a copy of the Declaration of Seller's Bank signed by your bank officers with the bank's seal and stamp for each and every transaction."

"General, your investigation is very thorough. I do not have those records with me today. I will bring them tomorrow."

"Additionally, I need a copy of the following attachments for each Gold Bullion bank transaction:
Certification of Ownership.
    Internationally accepted assay certificate.
    Assayer and Smelter Certified Weight List Describing Each Bar.

375 / DON STEWART NIMMONS

      Certificate of Origin.
      Gold Bullion Certificates.
      Bank Safekeeping Receipts.
I cannot wait to see what you had the bankers perjury themselves and forge for Certificate of Origin," Brocklesby said with a grin.

     "General, you mean business!"

     "Yes Prince, I can not allow you to cause any cracks to let the re-smelted Gold pour out to 'interested and unknown parties'."

     "Now, traveling up the coast from Manila to the Gulf of Lingayen, I bet the third ship load of Gold Bars was attempting to make it to your brother, Emperor Zapp's hideout here in Japan. Somebody had to have sent him a message to notify them of the U. S. Naval blockade and they diverted the shipment to Lingayen. Did you send the message from Manila?" General Brocklesby asked.

     "General Taya Squirrelly took his orders directly from my brother, Emperor Zapp."

     "Since General Squirrelly furnished you his map, he must have reported all of his gruesome killings he carried out in the Gulf of Lingayen and Tarlac regions. Those poor Filipino fishermen were robbed of their daily catches to enable Rear Admiral Hot Water and General Squirrelly and your soldiers and sailors to eat fresh fish. You broke the rules again," General Brocklesby said deliberately in a way at first was difficult to decipher.

     "I don't know what you are talking about!" Prince Snatch replied in a startled and denying voice.

     "Never mind for now, let's talk about Cave NL6291 in the mountains. Let me see the photos?"

TREASURES OF WAR – CONCEALED BY THE EVIL ONES / 376

"Here is the photo of this huge cave showing the stalactites and stalagmite sand pillars. The cave is another sight to behold, very, very nice. A note in this file warns the danger of the very venomous Filipino snakes in this cave.

This other photo shows the mountainside and the hidden cave entrance marked with an X."

"You had some American POW's working as slave laborers on road and tunnel construction in this area. Am I going to find some American POW skeletons in the bottom of this cave?" Brocklesby angrily asked.

"General Squirrelly probably carried out the religious commands of his Evil God, Emperor Zapp. He truly was not concerned about killing the evil enemy of his Emperor Zapp to satisfy his master. His report indicates his orders called for the cave entrance to be sealed with a very thick reinforced concrete wall with American POW's left inside. Maybe he left some American POW's to try to find another exit and deal with the deadly snakes."

"Those actions could be a cause of action in the War Crimes Tribunal resulting in the sentence of hanging until you are dead," General Brocklesby reminded Prince Snatch.

"I hope they found another exit from the cave and lived. If not, they did not suffer an agonizing death," Prince Snatch replied in a soft voice.

"Your tenderness is much too late to have helped those brave American warriors who survived the Death March of Bataan only to have been buried alive. What does your files indicate for the river site cave number NL1144 near Tarlac?" Brocklesby asked.

"This photo is marked with the green dot near the edge of the river on the east side of the city of Tarlac toward the South China Sea. I do not have any photos in the tunnels dug to bury the Gold Bars before it was closed by dynamite explosions."

"North of this river site is another river site near Urdaneta with the number NL441789. Do you have any markings to lead us to where these Gold Bars are located?" General Brocklesby asked.

"Unique, this is the best description of this location. See the large boulders in the river next to the bank? Colonel Torture furnished the details of where the Gold Bars were hidden. Standing on top of the boulders, facing the riverbank, point in the direction of two o'clock and measure off ninety-two meters and the entrance to a cave will be found. Once a person climbs seven meters down into the cave, they must walk along a narrow rock ledge leading into a waist deep stream of water with a hard rock bottom until they gradually walk more than one hundred meters and out into a large cave. A special red line note is on this paper.

During the heavy rainy season and monsoon rains, the cave tunnel and the cave are under water."

"General Squirrelly and Colonel Torture made a big mistake. They assumed no one would find the Gold Bars so far back in a watery cave. I bet some Filipino Tribesman that knows the river, hillsides and surroundings around Tarlac has already found the Gold Bars. Our only hope is he does not have a clue of its worth," General Brocklesby observed.

"We will determine the answer to that comment when you retrieve the Gold Bars," Prince Snatch replied.

"How in the holy world did General Squirrelly get Gold Bars up the steep mountainside near Santa Ignacia? My intelligence topography maps indicates some abrupt rock cliffs," Brocklesby asked.

"The file indicates a local Tribesman led them on a climb up from the road through the thick jungle around the front of the cliffs and to a cave entrance. Here is the photo of the mountain taken from a higher ledge. Notice this photo inside the cave. This cave was not very large," Snatch replied.

"Who killed the unlucky Filipino Aeta Tribesman? You couldn't afford to leave any living witnesses.

"The Aeta Tribesmen became friends of the Japanese troops during the war. I imagine the chief of the Aeta tribe, Salvador Morales, and his men are living today," Prince Snatch replied.

"Weird! They fought the Spanish, Filipinos and Americans over forty-five years ago to protect their people from outsiders. Now, you are trying to tell me you Japanese troops had a loveable personality with the Aeta tribe. Some of our recent War Crimes investigative reports for this region reflect during the final days of the war Aeta women and children were killed, butchered and eaten by your starving Japanese Troops. I will not ask any of you Japanese to return with us to retrieve the Gold Bars in the Mt. Pinatubo region. The Aetas tribal leaders might lynch you and me as punishment for your War Crimes. They do not mess around while punishing when it comes to crimes against their women and children. Their arrows come fast and silent. Let's finish up the maps for the Philippines. The cave number NL553 near the town of Mangatarem is the last."

"The first photo shows the winding river from the bottomland, and the second photo shows the winding river through the mountains to the cave. There are two different cave sites. Here is the photo of the POW stacking Gold Bars on top of the stack of bars."

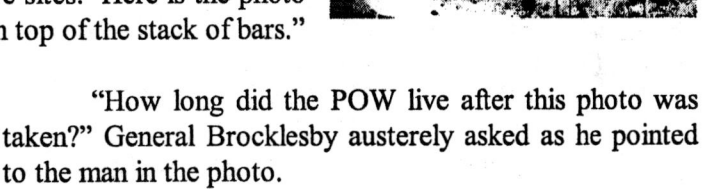

"How long did the POW live after this photo was taken?" General Brocklesby austerely asked as he pointed to the man in the photo.

Shortly thereafter, the initial meeting between General Brocklesby and Prince Major Snatch and his advisors were adjourned.

"You need to pack up your things and be ready to leave Japan with me on my military aircraft for the Philippines, Hong Kong and other unknown locations," Brocklesby demanded.

INITIAL INTERROGATION OF PRINCE MIKEY, THE YOUNGER BROTHER OF EMPEROR ZAPP.

The newspapers were publishing articles of the atrocities committed by Emperor Zapp's younger brother, Prince Mikey, in China. Brutal acts were the focus of the publications. The timing could not have been better for Major General Larry Broyles and his team of interrogators for the War Tribunal. General Broyles sent his messenger driver to the home of Prince Mikey with a message for him to attend his initial interrogation meeting at the military base the next day. The message instructed Prince Mikey to bring all records of his activities as head of Emperor Zapp's Secret Intelligence Team in the Chinese Expeditionary Forces in China. He needed to bring the codes used in his messages to Emperor Zapp in the reports of the movement of the Gold Bars and treasure looted in China.

The next afternoon Prince Mikey had his driver bring him to the military base. He used the Military Gate Pass furnished by Major General Broyles to enter the base. A special sergeant jumped on the running board and pointed the way to the meeting place building. He jumped off and motioned the driver to a reserved parking place of War Criminals near the entrance to General Broyles conference room. They entered the building and were escorted to the conference room. Major General Broyles and Mr. Bert Dover entered a short time later. Both sides expressed the normal greetings.

"First, I would like to see the copies of your reports to your brother, Emperor Zapp, for your snooping around on your family members and Military Officers during your time in China. We know you made some very incriminating reports concerning your brother, Major Snatch, to Emperor Zapp," General Broyles requested.

"General Broyles, you did not include a request for my special reports on other family members and military officers in your notice yesterday."

"Yes, but the developments here during our investigations with other family members has raised the level of what I want to discuss today."

"My name is Bert Dover and I am here to begin our interrogations for the International Military War Crimes Tribunal for the Far East to determine all of the various War Crimes you committed during the war. Indictment against you includes:
        Count 1 – 'Leaders, organizers, instigators, or accomplices in the formulation or execution of a common plan or conspiracy to wage wars of aggression, and war or wars in violations of international law.'

Count 26 – Waging aggressive war against the China.
Count 27 – Waging aggressive war against Manchuria.
Count 28 – Waging aggressive war against Philippines.
Count 29 – Waging aggressive war against the Untied States of America.
Count 32 – Waging aggressive war against the Netherlands.
Count 33 – Waging aggressive war against France (Indochina).
Count 54 – Ordered, authorized, and permitted inhumane treatment of Prisoners of War and others.
Count 55 – Deliberately and recklessly disregarded their duty to take adequate steps to prevent atrocities.

Your direct leadership in Shanghai and Nanking, China for the massive brutal killings and rapes and looting of the people, banks, and government coffers has been authenticated. In your direction of the movement of the money from the sales of Opium and Drugs and transportation of the Gold Bars and treasures our documents indicate additional atrocities occurred in the Philippines, Burma, and Cambodia and elsewhere. If you are found guilty, the sentence will be hanging by the neck until you are dead."

ADMIRAL LAVISH, COUSIN OF EMPEROR ZAPP, INTERROGATION.

From the directions furnished by General Salmon, Colonel David Nakazawa instructed his U. S. Military Auto Pool driver to take the route out to the Ichikawa section out from Tokyo for his first meeting with Admiral Lavish, the cousin of Emperor Zapp. Along the way, it became a tricky job of driving around the almost total destruction of the bombed out buildings in the roads. They recognized the Imperial Sign on the front gate to the Japanese House behind the bamboo-fenced yard. The unarmed Japanese soldier was standing at attention as they drove up in front. The elite house with the clay roof tiles was unharmed during the Allied Forces bombing of Tokyo. Apparently, the guard had been instructed to accompany the Americans inside the gate across the winding stone path across the yard to the entrance to the large house. As they got to the entrance Colonel Nakazawa ordered his driver to return to the vehicle and wait there. As Colonel Nakazawa and Mr. David Clark entered the large sitting room, Admiral Lavish welcomed them to his home.

"I am Colonel David Nakazawa and this is Mr. David Clark. We are here to begin our interrogations for the International Military War Crimes Tribunal for the Far East (IMWCTFE) to determine all of the various War Crimes you committed during the war. The pending indictment against you includes:

TREASURES OF WAR – CONCEALED BY THE EVIL ONES

Count 1 – 'Leaders, organizers, instigators, or accomplices in the formulation or execution of a common plan or conspiracy .. to wage wars of aggression, and war or wars in violations of international law.' Count 32 – Waging aggressive war against the Netherlands. Count 33 – Waging aggressive war against France (Indochina). Count 54 – Ordered, authorized, and permitted inhumane treatment of Prisoners of War and others. Count 55 – Deliberately and recklessly disregarded their duty to take adequate steps to prevent atrocities. And Count 29 – Waging aggressive war against the Untied States of America. Our authentic and reliable information supports the Tribunal's claim against you for directly and routinely conducting massive killing of POW's and looting the countries of French Indo-China, Dutch East Indies, Borneo, Burma and Java. If you are found guilty, the sentence will be hanging by the neck until you are dead. How in the world can you live with yourself? You ordered your men and even some civilians to shoot survivors of torpedoed American ships swimming ashore. Then, later you changed your mind because you realized you could use the surviving POW's as slave labor too."

"My cousin, Emperor Zapp, has told me to keep my mouth shut. He also ordered me to not admit to you where I was during the war and what I was doing for him."

"I do not believe that you were crying over the men killed that you sent into battle for your frenzied delight in carry out your obedience to Emperor Zapp and his Evil commands. Did you hear me when I said that you are guilty and will be hanged until dead? Do you think the world is going to accept and forgive you for the macabre crimes that you committed? What happened to the heroin? What happened to the Gold? I want some answers, now!" Colonel David Nakazawa said in his loud and fervent voice into the face of Admiral Lavish.

"Admiral, I have been interrogating some of your men. Your Army Commander in French Indo-China, General Yellow Belly, has been in hiding since his second meeting with me. His wife has begged us to not indict him for War Crimes. Some of your officers have seen the light and realized just whom they were fighting and who would receive all the materials things after your victory. All of your lies have now caught up with you and your family. I am personally going to parade you in the back seat of my jeep all around Tokyo with several signs on it letting the Japanese people know just how brutal you were to your men and to the POW's and the innocent men and women that you raped and killed for your personal satisfaction. Do you think that if I tied you up on a steel cross beam in the back of my jeep and had one of my men pull out a large razor blade showing that he was going to cut your family jewels out like you did to many of the American and Australian POW's when you attempted to make them talk during the battles?" Clark asked in his best threatening voice.

I did not know Clark had it in him. He is getting with the program. I'll let him keep up the aggressive questions until he convinces Admiral Lavish he has a very serious problem. General Salmon told me that this older Jap was going to be steadfast and not wither away. Colonel Nakazawa thought.

"My journeys during the war kept me busy guiding my ship through rough Pacific and South China Sea waters. That is all that I am guilty of doing. You have mistaken me for some of my brutal comrades. I am not guilty on any of the counts and especially Count 54. I did not have any POW's under my command during the entire war," Admiral Lavish replied.

"Obnoxious, you are the most obnoxious individual I have ever met in my life. The Evils have been identified precisely by a few that survived at the end of the war. You personally committed these War Crimes in French Indo-China and Burma; so say the witnesses. When the chief prosecutor calls these American and Australian POW witnesses to point their emotional and shaking finger at you during the War Crimes trial, whom do you think will be believed? Think about that question and future fact of your life," David Clark viciously asked.

"I object to your tone of voice," Admiral Lavish replied.

"Admiral Lavish, in order to achieve our goal we are going to use our most effective weapon, the public opinion of more than ninety-five percent of the people of the free world and try you and your cousin, Emperor Zapp, as War Criminals because he used his divine and supreme power under Japan's Constitution to carry out the atrocities committed by you and him. Now, if you want to cut a secret deal in order for us to accomplish our goals of learning where all the looted treasures have been hidden; you had better get prepared to do so before I report back to General Salmon. Colonel Nakazawa and I can not close the deal, but our boss will listen to our recommendations," Clark replied in his most effective warning manner.

"During your occupation here in Japan, your number one goal is to find the treasures from our defeated enemies. Why didn't you begin with that tone of negotiations? I am a very educated man and understand your main goal. I do not have such treasure information with me today. But, I must be assured you will drop all War Crime charges against me. I can furnish you with data of where some of the treasures outside of Japan are hidden for fear it would be captured by your military forces if I tried to bring it back to Japan on my ship," Admiral Lavish said with a relieved smile on his face.

"Until Mr. Clark and I see what you have to offer us, no deals will be finalized. What you bring to me had better be something worth your life," Colonel Nakazawa replied. "My boss, General Salmon has the final say so and controls the War Crimes Court's decisions."

"When do you want to meet again?" Admiral Lavish asked.

"Time is not on your side. Our final report must be presented to General Salmon and Mr. Bert Dover quickly," David Clark answered.

"Tomorrow at 13:00 at this same location will be excellent for me," Admiral suggested.

"So be it," Colonel Nakazawa ordered.

MEETING THE FOLLOWING DAY AT 13:00

Admiral Lavish brought two of his aides with him together with a small wrap-a-round folder with documents inside. Formalities were completed and the meeting began.

Author's Photo

"Before I leave here today, I must have your promise to drop all War Crime charges against me," Admiral Lavish said.

"Admiral, as I told you yesterday, my boss is the only one with authority to finalize any deals. However, I will promise you that I will ask him to approve dropping all War Crime charges against you if I see enough evidence to do so," Colonel Nakazawa replied.

"How much do you value your life?"

385 / DON STEWART NIMMONS

"This is a photo taken by my men at a cave site in Hai Phong, French Indo-China. These seventy-five kilos Gold Bars were buried near the port. We had taken them from Burma during one of my voyages. The hallmarks indicate Burma. Here is the map of the exact location of the cave site. The report indicates a total of 680 Gold Bars were buried in this cave. That is almost one million six hundred forty thousand troy ounces of Gold Bars. You figure out the value."

"Perhaps you have some other documents or photos in your folder. The potential value of the Gold Bars in your first photo will delay your execution for maybe six months," Colonel Nakazawa observed.

"How could you be so tough on someone that is Japanese? Aren't you Japanese also?" Asked Admiral Lavish.

"I am a proud American with the last name of my Japanese immigrant father. Don't try to play that card with me. That line will not be well received by me at all. I rejoice every day because I was born in America. The repugnant actions committed by the Evil Spirit of Emperor Zapp and you will taint the good Japanese people all over the world for generations to come," Colonel Nakazawa replied as he gave a haunting stare directly into Admiral Lavish eyes.

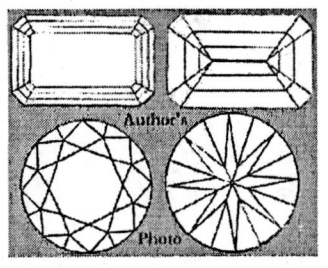

"Here is the photo of the cave entrance located four kilometers northwest of Hanoi on the road to Cao. Large stashes of large diamonds were hidden deep in this cave behind the stacks of Gold Bars. Some of the diamonds are very large. Here are the jeweler description papers of the four large diamonds types wrapped in cloth and hidden in steel boxes. Some are rectangular shaped diamonds and some are round shaped diamonds. One of the steel boxes has the large unique cut very slight imperfection diamonds and the largest being sixty-eight carats in size. The steel boxes were buried near the end of the cave chamber off to the left of the entrance. Anyone finding the Gold Bars would be so excited that they would never discover the buried boxes of diamonds," Admiral Lavish said as he described the location.

"Gold Bars! Do you have photos and quantities of these items?" Clark asked.

"Inside the cave you will find seventy-five kilos Gold Bars from Burma, Cambodia and China. The cave is very deep and a total of 1856 Gold Bars are hidden in the chambers of this cave. You may have to obtain some approvals from the French government to scavenge these Treasures for your benefit. I am sure the local people will gladly assist someone other than a Japanese military man to accompany you on your mission. You know those Frenchmen; that may be another episode. I might suggest from past personal experiences; just place a few heavy Gold Bars or nine or ten of the exquisite diamonds in the hands of the local French Governor and your trucks and ships will have the complete protection from him and all the way to General De Gaulle himself. Those local French leaders in French Indo-China live a very servitude lifestyle. They cannot wait for the opportunity to leave the jungles and return to their eloquent European culture with some extra wealth obtained during their Foreign Service duty."

"Thank you for your oration on the French. Where are the photos of the contents inside the cave?" David Clark asked again.

"Yes, I only have this one photo of the stacks of Mixed Gold Bars in the cave near Cao."

"You may have reduced your guilty verdict to a term of twenty years instead of hanging until you are dead," Colonel Nakazawa replied as he looked at the photo of Gold Bars.

"Admiral Lavish, you have danced all around the city of Hanoi. We know that you gave the orders to execute all American, Australian and French POW's in your slave labor camps the week before your cousin, Emperor Zapp, surrendered. Unfortunately for you, many of your officers decided to kill a few POW's and run for their lives. What did you and your men have to hide in Hanoi during the rapid retreat?" David Clark asked.

"The largest stash of Treasures in French Indo-China was hidden down in a sealed room off the main storm sewer line just below my headquarters in Hanoi. General Yellow Belly used some of the American POW's during the dry season from the train construction project to dig out a large room and build a short sealed door to the room where the Treasures were stored. I did not order him to kill the POW's once they completed their job. He told me later that he did not want any prisoners left alive to be able to identify the location of the valuables. I learned later that he gave orders to shoot all the POW's that worked on this project after they took the Gold Bars and other valuable Treasures down into the room. One of his Colonels came to me and told me that the bodies of the POW's and their blood were washed down the storm sewer during the first big rains out into the river. When you climb down the manhole into the storm sewer, the third Japanese marking is the mark for the room."

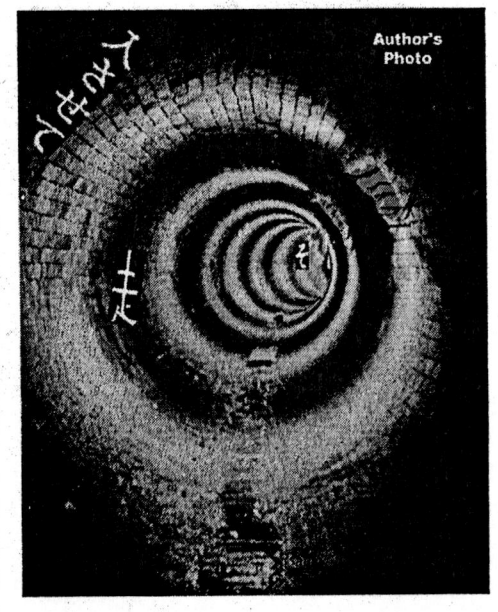

"You were arousing my support for reducing or dropping all War Crime charges against you before you told me about the execution of the American POW's down in that storm sewer. When you give an order to use POW slave labor and your commanders eventually mercilessly have them killed, you are just as much to blame as the soldier that pulled the trigger," Colonel Nakazawa sternly said.

"I hope for your sake that the hidden room below your headquarters in Hanoi contains enough treasures to make the Colonel and I forget your mutilating admission," David Clark angrily announced.

"I did not admit to any murders. I am telling you the truth of how the Evil Spirit had taken over the allegiance of our fighting men who worshipped my cousin, Emperor Zapp."

"Let me interrupt you. You were under this identical allegiance and more importantly you gave the orders," Nakazawa hastily added.

"I humble beg you to believe me and have compassion for me. Please recommend to General Salmon to drop all War Crime charges against me and let me go on with my life. I have cooperated with you and given you all that I know regarding the Treasures," Admiral Lavish pleaded.

"You must convey to all of your cousins, uncles, brothers and in-laws that there is only one way to save their necks. It is left up to my boss, General Salmon, to decide whether you are indicted or not. Thank you for your candor and copies of the documents and photos. I know that any agreements with you will be contingent upon the accuracy of the data that you have supplied to us today. So, if you have anything else or corrections to the things you have given to us; speak now or be prepared to either serve the remainder of your life in prison or hang by the neck until you are dead. This meeting is adjourned," Colonel Nakazawa announced.

Admiral Lavish and his two aids stood and bowed. Colonel Nakazawa and David Clark returned the bow and hastily left the residence of Admiral Lavish out to the awaiting U. S. Military Auto Pool driver.

IMPORTANT MEETINGS WITH EMPEROR ZAPP AROUND TOKYO.

General Salmon, Bert Dover and Prescott Bushel arrived at Emperor Zapp's palace at 10:15 to link up and travel to the three sites in Japan of the stolen loot from China.

The first site was found near the palace. Emperor Zapp led them down a wide ramp to an underground cavern. He had his fully armed palace guards standing around the large room in front of this huge vault door. The palace guards all bowed and came to attention with their rifles raised. Emperor Zapp walked over to the vault door and punched a timer

Author's Photo

button and stepped back and stood in silence for some ten minutes. He returned to the door, turned the large combination dials, reached down and pulled the lever up and ordered three of his guards to pull the vault door open. Through the vault door was a very large thick door on hinges made out of 24 karat Gold.

"What's behind the Gold Door?" Bert Dover asked.

"Yeah! I would like to see what you have stashed behind it," General Salmon added.

Emperor Zapp reached down and pushed a knob on the Gold Door and the door began to slowly swing open. He reached inside and turned on the bright lights. The left side of the room behind the Gold Door had racks of Gold Bars at least ten feet high and six feet deep and thirty feet long. The racks were constructed in a manner to allow a person to load or unload Gold Bars from both the front and the rear of the racks. Similar racks were located at the rear and on the right side of this large room. Upon completing the walk threw the large room with the racks of Gold Bars, Emperor Zapp, General Salmon, Bert Dover and Prescott Bushel just stood there looking at each other wondering what to say. Eventually, General Salmon said, "your naval forces made several profitable voyages before our naval blockade stopped the trafficking from China to here."

"Yes sir! Winning my war in China was profitable and made me a very wealthy God. It is a shame for me to have lost the Gold Bars and the war."

"General Salmon, Prescott and I took the time to study our overall cost to ship Gold Bars from here to a safe neutral offshore location or locations. We believe the fifty/fifty split we discussed between us concerning the overseas Gold Bullion Depository Bank Accounts cannot be used to determine a proper split for the Gold Bars here in Japan. We need the minimum of seventy percent. You and your Yakuza partners may split the other thirty percent between yourselves and keep it here in Japan or we will ship it to a secure offshore location," Bert Dover advised Emperor Zapp.

"You really don't have a choice in this matter," General Salmon added. "I control the

International Military War Crimes Tribunal for the Far East decisions."

"We need to drive onto the second site," Emperor Zapp said.

He is going to show us many more Gold Bars today in his attempt to entice us to raise his percentage. Bert Dover thought.

"You lead the way," Prescott replied.

Emperor Zapp's driver drove through the town of Tachikwa and turned north for two kilometers on the road to Hanno. Suddenly, he stopped quickly almost causing a pileup of the following vehicles. The driver stepped out of Zapp's car and ran back to General Salmon's driver and explained they must turn around and go back to the previous intersection in the road and turn to the right. From there, they all traveled to a section along the road with a beautiful Japanese garden. The archway over the entrance stood out from the surroundings. Each vehicle made a slow turn down this winding driveway until they reached a man made tunnel out of the side of the stone hillside. Emperor Zapp's driver jumped out and motioned for each of them to follow him into the tunnel. Slowly, each vehicle followed Zapp's driver into the tunnel turning their respective headlights on after entering. Several hundred yards down the tunnel they entered a large parking area in front of a caged area with armed palace guards on duty. Everyone parked and met at the gate leading into the caged area. Emperor Zapp asked his guards to open the gate for him and his guest to enter. He led them through a chiseled out rock tunnel to some underground offices and onto a large corner office equipped with everything Zapp needed to conduct daily business. He sat down behind his beautiful teak wood executive desk and asked his male secretary to serve tea to his quest in the very soft and cushiony and low to the floor sofas in front of him.

This dude is a smooth manipulator. No conscience at all. Short memory for all the brutal and evil deeds he has done and commanded to be done during the wars. General Salmon thought.

After taking the tea break and enjoying the artifacts from all over the world scattered around the beautiful office, Emperor Zapp led everyone through his private restroom around his fusuma behind his very deep sunken tub to a cypress floor level secret door, which he opened by pushing on three different panels on the wall next to it. The lights were turned on and to everyone's astonishment large racks containing Gold Bars lined the twelve by twelve meters room. Into the next room a fairly good size vault grabbed your attention. Emperor Zapp worked the combination and had his male secretary open it. The two large Gold Buddhas from China stared you in the face.

"Emperor Zapp, I thought you wanted to smelt down the Gold Buddhas from China into Gold Bars and destroy the God's of your enemies. Many of your fighting warriors died to steal these Chinese Gold Buddhas and transport them back to you knowing you needed money to finance and fight your evil wars with their understanding and orders that you would smelt them into Gold Bullion," Bert Dover said in an even-tempered voice. "You triumphed over the human spirit of your military forces while at the same time you had hundreds of thousands and millions of innocent people killed to have your trophies in your secret hideouts here in Japan and betrayed the ones carrying out your orders."

Ole Bert is not going to give Zapp a chance to have a one up-man-ship on us because of all of these Gold Bars all around Japan. General Salmon thought.

"Let us return to our autos and go to the third site near Mt. Fuji," Emperor Zapp instructed.

"Yeah, let's do it!" General replied.

The convoy of vehicles rolled out of the tunnel and drove on the roads around Lake Kawaguchi and through the beautiful large evergreen trees to the hillside near Mt. Fuji. This time of the year the snow and ice remained on many of the trees, the mountain and hillsides. But, Emperor Zapp knew exactly where he was going to stop. Everyone turned down this ice-covered dirt road through the trees until they came upon the clay roof Japanese house in the middle of nowhere with the icicles hanging from the roof's edges. The house had been built on a flat area dug out of the side of the hill. The back of the house was rammed up against the hillside. Emperor's Zapp's driver ran around his car and opened the door for him. Zapp motioned for the remaining parties to come with him into the house. He knocked on the door and to everyone's surprise two fully armed palace guards opened the door. Once they recognized Emperor Zapp, they bowed and opened the door. Everyone walked into this warm visiting room and was glad to get out of the cold.

As they walked back to the rear of the house to a large high door with some type of locks on them, Emperor Zapp handed the keys to one of the palace guards to unlock each separate lock.

"Where did you steal all of these USA Gold Coins? Bert Dover asked in an alarming voice. "All U. S. Gold Bullion and Gold Coins were mandated to be sold to the United States Treasury on March 16, 1933 by President Roosevelt."

Subsequent to closer inspection of some of the USA Gold Coins in various denominations, special markings were noted.

"Look's like you had your people stamp your own mark next to the date of 1907 on all of these Gold coins. What possessed you to have this done?" General Salmon asked.

Emperor Zapp thought for a moment. "My deliberate spirit led me to show the world of my conquest over the Americans by putting my personal stamp on their Gold Coins."

"When we take all of these U. S. Gold Coins out of here, the value will become greater over the years because everyone will know that they are special with your defeated stamp on them," Prescott Bushel replied.

Zapp must have looted the government banks for every country in the world to have such an inventory of U. S. Gold Coins of this enormous quantity. I wonder how many years he made this one of his evil goals? There must be more than several million U. S. dollars worth of our Gold Coins stacked in here. Bert Dover thought.

"What's in these built-in shallow wooden drawers in the files all around the two walls of the room?" General Salmon asked.

"You may just pull them open and see for yourself," Emperor Zapp replied.

Bert Dover walked over to the first row of six inch high drawers and took the handle of one about two feet from the top and pulled it open. "One hundred thousand U. S. Dollar Gold Certificates issued by Secretary of Treasury Henry Morganthau, Jr. in 1934," he said as he tossed a small stack of them on the nearby table.

"Whose head did you decapitate with your samurai sword to achieve all of these?" General Salmon asked as he opened several more drawers around the room.

"Just some good business deals with some of

your American businesses paid off well for me before the war started with you guys at Pearl Harbor," Emperor Zapp replied.

"Payola at its best!" General Salmon replied in disgust.

Deputy Commander of Allied Powers General Milton R. Salmon and BOP Party Chairman in Tokyo, Mr. Herbert 'Bert' Dover, had accomplished all of their greedy goals using the threat of indictment and conviction of War Crimes against Emperor Zapp and his family members. The two men went back to 'Bert's office to review the mass of data and status of all agreements.

"Dover, those State Department officials in Washington do not know what to do. The Administration and the Department of War and State cannot agree on a peacetime intelligence organization that is accountable to the President or have an independent agency to have its own funds and a solely consultative function. J. Edgar thinks he can catch all of the Al Capones of the world by using his Elliott Nesses in a wide world operation. The military bosses want an independent and centralized intelligence system for all foreign activities to coincide with the FBI. That proved fruitless. A real active Dog and Cat fight has begun. Each office does not know fully just exactly what powers and authority each has to use to do its important job. The National Security Council has got some truly political appointees. President Truman and Congress are establishing a bureaucratic CYA routine for all failures of foreign intelligence. Our enemies will learn to maneuver around our lack of coordinated efforts. The covert missions of the OSS will forever be secret operations without any scrutiny. Keep our intelligence connections, but make sure you do not leave any written trails to implicate you. Keep your hands clean," General Salmon warned Bert Dover.

"May I suggest that you and I keep the flashy cars and jewelry out of sight for several years," Dover replied.

"I will wear this cheap military wristwatch as long as it keeps good time," General Salmon said in his strong voice.

"The confusion in Washington will make our job much easier to distribute the Gold Bars to our secret locations and establish the offshore banks accounts for ourselves and the joint bank accounts with Emperor Zapp," Dover said smiling as he left the room.

TREASURES OF WAR – CONCEALED BY THE EVIL ONES

Chapter Twenty One

The General Headquarters of Supreme Commander For The Allied Powers (SCAP)

Issues The December 15, 1945

SHINTO DIRECTIVE

Abolition of State Sponsored Shintoism

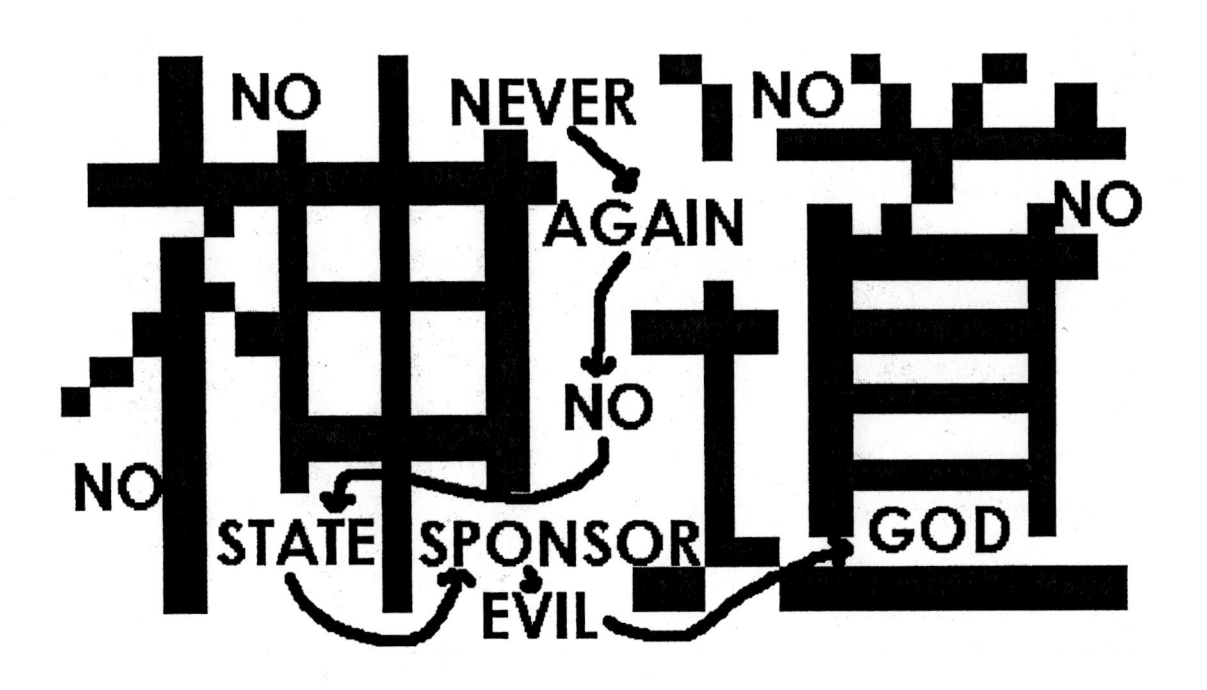

THE SHINTO DIRECTIVE

GENERAL HEADQUARTERS SUPREME COMMANDER FOR THE ALLIED POWERS (SCAP)

15 December 1945

Memorandum for: Imperial Japanese Government
Through: Central Liaison Office, Tokyo

Subject: Abolition of Governmental Sponsorship, Support, Perpetuation, Control, and Dissemination of State Shinto (Kokka Shinto, Jinja Shinto).

1. In order to free the Japanese people from direct or indirect compulsion to believe or profess to believe in a religion or cult officially designated by the state, and

In order to lift from the Japanese people the burden of compulsory financial support of an ideology which has contributed to their war guilt, defeat, suffering, privation, and present deplorable condition, and

In order to prevent a recurrence of the perversion of Shinto theory and beliefs into militaristic and ultra-nationalistic propaganda designed to delude the Japanese people and lead them into wars of aggression, and

In order to assist the Japanese people in a rededication of their national life to building a new Japan based upon ideals of perpetual peace and democracy,

It is hereby directed that:

a. The sponsorship, support, perpetuation, control and dissemination of Shinto by the Japanese national, prefectural, and local governments, or by public officials, subordinates, and employees acting in their official capacity are prohibited and will cease immediately.

b. All financial support from public funds and all official affiliation with Shinto and Shinto shrines are prohibited and will cease immediately.

   1. While no financial support from public funds will be extended to shrines located on public reservations or parks, this prohibition will not be construed to preclude the Japanese Government from continuing to support the areas on which such shrines are located.

   2. Private financial support of all Shinto shrines which have been previously supported in whole or in part by public funds will be permitted, provided such private support is entirely voluntary and is in no way derived from forced or involuntary contributions.

c. All propagation and dissemination of militaristic and ultra nationalistic ideology in Shinto doctrines, practices, rites, ceremonies, or observances, as well as in the doctrines, practices, rites, ceremonies, and observances of any other religion, faith, sect, creed, or philosophy, are prohibited and will cease immediately.

d. The Religious Functions Order relating to the Grand Shrine of Ise and the Religious Functions Order relating to State and other Shrines will be annulled.

e.	The Shrine Board (Iingi-in) of the Ministry of Home Affairs will be abolished, and its present functions, duties, and administrative obligations will not be assumed by any other governmental or tax-supported agency.

f.	All public educational institutions whose primary function is either the investigation and dissemination of Shinto or the training of a Shinto priesthood will be abolished and their physical properties diverted to other uses. Their present functions, duties, and administrative obligations will not be assumed by any other governmental or tax-supported agency.

g.	Private educational institutions for the investigation and dissemination of Shinto and for the training of priesthood for Shinto will be permitted and will operate with the same privileges and be subject to the same controls and restrictions as any other private educational institution having no affiliation with the government; in no case, however, will they receive support from public funds; and in no case will they propagate and disseminate militaristic and ultra-nationalistic ideology.

h.	The dissemination of Shinto doctrines in any forms and by any means in any educational institution supported wholly or in part by public funds is prohibited and will cease immediately.

   1.	All teachers' manuals and textbooks now in use in any educational institution supported wholly or in part by public funds will be censored, and all Shinto doctrine will be deleted. No teachers' manual or textbook, which is published in the future for use in such institutions will contain any Shinto doctrine.

2. No visits to Shinto shrines and no rites, practices, or ceremonies associated with Shinto will be conducted or sponsored by any educational institution supported wholly or in part by public funds.

i. Circulation by the government of "The Fundamental Principles of the National Structure" (Kokutai no Hongi), "The Way of the Subject" (Shimmin no Michi), and all similar official volumes, commentaries, interpretations, or instructions on Shinto is prohibited.

j. The use in official writings of the terms "Greater East Asia War" (Dai Toa Senso), "The Whole World under One Roof" (Hakko Ichi-u), and all other terms whose connotation in Japanese is in extricably connected with State Shinto, militarism, and ultra nationalism is prohibited and will cease immediately.

k. God-shelves (kamidana) and all other physical symbols of State Shinto in any office, school, institution, organization, or structure supported wholly or in part by public funds are prohibited and will be removed immediately.

l. No official, subordinate, employee, student, citizen, or resident of Japan will be discriminated against because of his failure to profess and believe in or participate in any practice, rite, ceremony, or observance of State Shinto or of any other religion.

m. No official of the national, prefectural, or local government, acting in his public capacity, will visit any shrine to report his assumption of office, to report on conditions of government or to participate as a representative of government in any ceremony or observance.

2. a. The purpose of this directive is to separate religion from the state, to prevent misuse of religion for political ends, and to put all religions, faiths, and creeds upon exactly the same legal basis, entitled to precisely the same opportunities and protection. It forbids affiliation with the government, and the propagation and dissemination of militaristic and ultra-nationalistic ideology not only to Shinto but to followers of all religions, faiths, sects, creeds, or philosophies.

   b. The provisions of this directive will apply with equal force to all rites. practices, ceremonies, observances, beliefs, teachings, mythology, legends, philosophy, shrines, and physical symbols associated with Shinto.

   c. The term State Shinto within the meaning of this directive will refer to that branch of Shinto (Kokka Shinto or Jinja Shinto) which by official acts of the Japanese Government has been differentiated from the religion of Sect Shinto (Shuha Shinto or Kyoha Shinto) and has been classified a non-religious national cult commonly known as State Shinto, National Shinto, or Shrine Shinto.

   d. The term Sect Shinto (Shuha Shinto or Kyoha Shinto) will refer to that branch of Shinto (composed of 13 recognized sects), which by popular belief, legal commentary, and the official acts of the Japanese Government has been recognized to be a religion.

   e. Pursuant to the terms of Article I of the Basic Directive on "Removal of Restrictions on Political, Civil, and Religious Liberties" issued on 4 October 1945 by the Supreme Commander for the Allied Powers in which the Japanese people were assured complete religious freedom,

1. Sect Shinto will enjoy the same protection as any other religion.

2. Shrine Shinto, after having been divorced from the state and divested of its militaristic and ultra-nationalistic elements, will be recognized as a religion if its adherents so desire and will be granted the same protection as any other religion in so far as it may in fact be the philosophy or religion of Japanese individuals.

f. Militaristic and ultra-nationalistic ideology, as used in this directive, embraces those teachings, beliefs and theories, which advocate or justify a mission on the part of Japan to extend rule over other nations and peoples by reason of:

1. The doctrine that the Emperor of Japan is superior to the heads of other states because of ancestry, descent or special origin.

2. The doctrine that the people of Japan are superior to the people of other lands because of ancestry, descent or special origin.

3. The doctrine that the islands of Japan are superior to other lands because of divine or special origin.

4. Any other doctrine, which tends to delude the Japanese people into embarking upon wars of aggression or to glorify the use of force as an instrument for the settlement of disputes with other peoples.

3. The Imperial Japanese Government will submit a comprehensive report to this Headquarters not later than 15 March 1946 describing in detail all action taken to comply with all provisions of this directive.

4. All officials, subordinates, and employees of the Japanese national, prefectural, and local governments, all teachers, and education officials, and all citizens and residents of Japan will be held personally accountable for compliance with the spirit as well as the letter of all provisions of this directive.

FOR THE SUPREME COMMANDER:
H. W. ALLEN
Colonel, A.G.D.
Asst. Adjutant General

(From: Political Reorientation of Japan)

TREASURES OF WAR – CONCEALED BY THE EVIL ONES

Chapter Twenty Two

The Compromise Agreements with Emperor Zapp and His Family

Memorandum In Support of Offer In Compromise
Based on Liability (War Crimes)
Emperor S. Zapp et al
Offer in Compromise

Joint Release and Settlement Agreement

This joint Release and Settlement Agreement (hereinafter "the Agreement") is entered into by Bert Dover, Trustee of the Estate of Born of Privilege 'BOP' and Salmon/Dover Group Interest, **AND** Emperor S. Zapp, Prince Major Snatch, Prince Mikey, Admiral Lavish, Prince Eye Spy, General Donkey, Prince County Saigon, Prince Coni-Dip, Prince Major General Shield, General Loot and General Monty.

WHEREAS, Bert Dover, General Milton R. Salmon and his subordinate military officers, Prescott Bushel, Allison D. Rumsfield and David Clark investigated and prepared War Crimes litigation in the International Military War Crimes Tribunal for the Far East (hereinafter "IMWCTFE") in Tokyo, Japan for filing; and

WHEREAS, on May 14, 1946, entered into a Protocol of Intentions for relief with the understanding as stated therein, and

WHEREAS, Bert Dover and General Milton R. Salmon (the "Co-Trustees"), on or about February 25, 1946 accepted their appointment as "IMWCTFE" Co-Trustees in the War Crimes pending case; and

WHEREAS, pursuant to the Co-Trustee's Plan and Motion to Compromise controversies (the "Motion to Compromise"), confirmed and approved by Court Order dated May 25, 1946 issued by the Supreme Commander of Allied Powers (SCAP), and incorporated herein for all purposes, the Co-Trustees (on behalf of Emperor S. Zapp et al [all alias; Foundations, Overseas Bank and Investment Accounts] and the Japanese Yakuza Partners of

Emperor S. Zapp), IMWCTFE et al have reached a settlement with regard to all as more fully set forth in the Plan and Motion to Compromise;

NOW, THEREFORE, for and in consideration of the premises, covenants, and agreements contained herein and in the Plan and Motion to Compromise, and for other good and valuable consideration, the receipt and sufficiency of which is hereby acknowledged, it is hereby agreed by the Co-Trustees (on behalf of Emperor S. Zapp et al [all alias; Foundations, Overseas Bank and Investment Accounts] and the Japanese Yakuza Partners of Emperor S. Zapp), IMWCTFE as follows:

1. Co-Trustees on behalf of themselves and their respective officers, directors, affiliates, joint venturers, insurers, employees, attorneys, agents, and assigns hereby releases and forever discharges Emperor S. Zapp et al and his relatives, agents, associates, judgments, liens, causes of action, claims, rights, and controversies, known or unknown, which they had, now have, or may hereafter acquire which relate to, are based on, arise out of, or are in any way connected with or form the basis of the subject matter of the Plane and Motion to Compromise; and from all claims and causes of action, asserted in said pending litigation in the International Military War Crimes Tribunal of the Far East or which could have been asserted therein, and all claims known or unknown, of whatever nature, whether or not accrued at the time of this release. This is a general release of all existing and possible claims and causes of action of every kind and character and is to be interpreted liberally to effective maximum protection for Emperor S. Zapp et al.

2. Emperor S. Zapp et al on behalf of themselves and their respective agents and assigns hereby release and forever discharged the Co-

Trustees and their respective employees, agents representatives, affiliates, relatives, successors, and assigns from all causes of action, claims, rights and controversies, known or unknown, which they had, now have, or may hereafter acquire which relate to, are based on, arise out of, or are in any way connected with or form the basis of the subject matter of the IMWCTFE claims and the Plan and Motion to Compromise, except for any claims to be paid pursuant to the Plan and Compromise and except for any claims which might be made by Emperor S. Zapp et al and/or his attorneys, as to which claims Emperor S. Zapp et al may raise any opposition, defenses and counterclaims. This is a general release of all existing and possible claims and causes of action of every kind and character and is to be interpreted liberally to effectuate maximum protection for the Co-Trustees and IMWCTFE, subject to the exceptions listed.

3. The undersigned parties understand and acknowledge that this is a mutual release of all claims, known or unknown, as against each other, except as set forth herein. The parties to this Agreement recognize that claims and causes of action other that those heretofore asserted in the Litigation, including, but not limited to, counterclaims and cross-claims, might be asserted by some of the parties against other parties. The parties agree that there is considerable doubt, disagreement and controversy with reference to the liability of any party to any other party regarding claims heretofore asserted or those which might be asserted, as well as for any other claims or causes of action to be settled and disposed of by this Agreement. The parties further agree

that there is considerable doubt, disagreement and controversy with reference to the amount of damages claimed by any party in the Litigation, or which in connection with any party in connection with any other claims might claim or causes of action settled and disposed of by this Agreement. In entering into this Agreement, no party is admitting liability to any other party for these claims, or for any other claims or causes of action settled and disposed of by this Agreement. Rather, each party entering into this Agreement is action in the interest of settling controversies and in the interest of peace.

4. The parties agree and understand that this Agreement is not limited to settlement of the Litigation, except as limited hereinafter, but also extends to any and all other claims and causes of action arising out of or related directly or indirectly to the facts made or which might be made the basis of the Litigation, whether or not they have accrued; and to any and all other claims and causes of action which have accrued prior to the Effective Date, except as set forth herein. The parties have entered into this Agreement for and in the consideration of the mutual benefits to accrue to each of them as expressed herein.

5. The parties agree that, simultaneously with the execution of this Agreement, Stipulations of Dismissal along with any and all documents necessary to obtain approval thereof shall be provided by Co-Trustees to be filed in IMWCTFE Litigation.

This **Release** shall be binding upon and inure to the benefit of each party hereto, and upon the respective heirs, executors, administrators, successors and/or assigns of each.

Because of the international nature of this **Release**, the parties agree that this Agreement shall be governed and interpreted as to all matters including validity, construction, and performance by the laws of Parliament of Singapore, and the British Empire.

Should any provision of this **Release** be declared or determined by any court to be illegal, invalid or unenforceable, the validity of the remaining party, terms or provisions shall not be affected thereby, and said illegal, invalid of unenforceable part, terms or provisions shall not be deemed to be a part of this **Release**.

This **Joint Release** and Compromise Settlement Agreement is executed this 25th day of May, 1946.

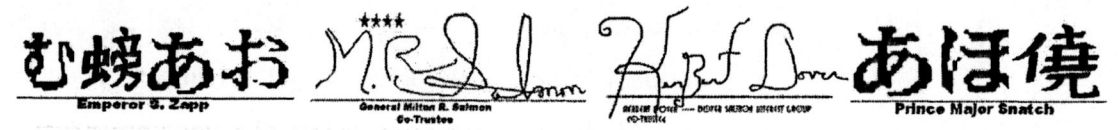

_____ _____ _____ _____
Emperor S. Zapp General Milton R. Salmon Herbert Dover Prince Major Snatch
 Co-Trustee Co-Trustee, Dover Salmon Interest Group

Certificate of Acknowledgment of Execution of an Instrument

<u>OCCUPIED JAPAN</u> §
   (Country)

<u>UNITED STATES OF AMERICA</u> §
   (Name of Foreign Service Office)

<u>INTERNATIONAL MILITARY WAR CRIMES
TRIBUNAL for the FAR EAST ("IMWCTFE")</u> §
   (Country and/or Other Political Division)

347 / DON STEWART NIMMONS

I, Chief Prosecutor Adam Lincoln, *of the INTERNATIONAL MILITARY WAR CRIMES TRIBUNAL for the FAR EAST ("IMWCTFE") at Tokyo, Japan duly commissioned and qualified, do hereby certify that on this* twenty fifth day of May, 1946, *before me personally appeared* Emperor S. Zapp, Herbert Dover, General

TREASURES OF WAR – CONCEALED BY THE EVIL ONES / 409

Milton R. Salmon, and Prince Major Snatch *to me personally known, and know to me to be the individuals – described in, whose names are subscribed to, and who executed the annexed instrument, and being informed by me of the contents of said instrument they duly acknowledged to me that they executed the same freely and voluntarily for the uses and purposes therein mentioned.*

In witness whereof I have hereunto set my hand

and
[S E A L]   *official seal the day and year last above*
written.

Adam Lincoln
Chief Prosecutor
IMWCTFE

Subsequently, Lieutenant General Harold Brocklesby and Prince Major Snatch met within a few weeks before the International Military War Crimes Tribunal for the Far East trial was to begin. General Brocklesby requested his staff to prepare the necessary agreements for Prince Major Snatch to execute and finalize the retrieving of all Gold Bullion Bank Depository Accounts and the understanding of method accepted by Prince Major Snatch regarding the disposition of the Gold Bars in the Caves in the Philippines. Due to the short time frame left to use the fear of the War Crimes Trial scare tactics, Brocklesby was instructed by General Salmon to be sure to have Mr. Bert Dover, Mr. Prescott Bushel, Mr. David Clark and Allison D. Rumsfield in attendance to pressure him to complete the successful sting.

"Prince Snatch, let me introduce some of my colleagues joining you and your advisors this morning. This is Bert Dover, the number one aid to General Salmon. Next to his right are Prescott Bushel and David Clark, Dover's top advisors. You know Mr. Allison D. Rumsfield of Overseas. Did you bring the records for all of your Gold Bullion bank transactions that I ordered you to bring to this meeting?" General Brocklesby asked.

Prince Snatch bowed to the men introduced and to General Brocklesby. "Here are all of the Certification of Ownerships, Internationally accepted Assay Certificates, Assayer and Smelter Certified Weight List Describing Each Gold Bar, Certificate of Origins, Gold Bullion Certificates, and Bank Safekeeping Receipts."

Bert Dover spoke up. "We have increased the number of War Crimes you have committed during the past eight years from 10 to 14 in the revised complaint against you being presented to General Salmon a week before the trials begin."

"You men promised me to present me with a compromise document for my consideration as long as I continued to cooperate with you and split the Gold Bullion Bank Accounts and the hidden Gold Bars in the Philippines," Prince Major Snatch urgently replied. "I just gave you all of my records of transactions for the Gold Bullion Bank Accounts. Just for your information, you were correct to warn me about that OSS agent by the name of Bobby Staples. He was snooping around and wanted to meet with me the other day."

He is scared to death and does not want to go to trial, knowing he most likely will receive a verdict of hanging until he is dead because of all the brutal crimes he has committed. David Clark thought.

"There are some new surprises in these records you handed me. Several more Gold Bullion Accounts than you led us to know about in several other countries," General Brocklesby interrupted.

"I told you I would fully cooperate with your desires to retrieve all of the war loot I had any control over. But, you promised me an advanced compromise."

"Yeah, the compromise will be discussed later. No more surprises from you. For now, here is the first of many agreements that you must execute before we get to the compromise."

OVERSEAS INVESTMENT BANK, LIMITED -- PROTOCOL OF INTENTIONS

PROTOCOL OF INTENTIONS

On this the fourteenth (14th.) day of May, 1946, the Joint-Stock Industrial-and-Commercial Bank "Overseas" (hereinafter "Bank"), represented by its President, Mr. Allison D. Rumsfield and operating on the basis of the Charter registered at the Central Bank of Hong Kong, and Individual, Prince Major Snatch, aka Mr. Goose Sun and Foundation, Whitewater

Foundation, (hereinafter "Whitewater"), represented by its Board President Prince Major Snatch and operating on the basis of constituent documents registered according to the laws of the State of United Kingdom (hereinafter "UK"), express the following intention:

1. "Whitewater" expresses the intention to transfer fifty (50%) percent of all of its holdings (hereinafter "Gold Bullion Certificates") to an international Gold Bullion Depository Bank with capabilities and experience chartered in the US and/or European countries (i.e., chartered outside of Hong Kong and Japan).

2. "Bank" will agree to make the necessary transfers all of the remaining fifty (50%) percent to the account(s) of Mr. Herbert Dover and/or his authorized assigns (hereinafter referred to as "Salmon/Dover Interest") per the written instructions of Mr. Herbert Dover and with the automatic approval without delay of Prince Major Snatch and "Whitewater".

3. Further, "Bank" will agree to provide specialized instruction and details of each transfer regarding bank servicing of these accounts in the future in Hong Kong and/or abroad.

4. "Bank" in return for the transfer services of all of the "Salmon/Dover Interest" agrees to charge the service fees for the transfers to the account of Prince Major Snatch and "Whitewater".

5. Additionally, "Bank" agrees to prepare and complete the transfer of process "Gold Bullion Certificates" concerning the legal authorization and recognition for the "Bank" with qualified foreign Gold Bullion Depository(s) according the laws, statutes, and regulations of the government of the Hong Kong. (In other words, "Bank" will legalize and record all of the transfers to "Salmon/Dover Interest" with the appropriate governmental authorities.) This is an exclusive right granted irrevocably to "Whitewater" by "Bank" for the period of ninety (90) days from the date of signing of this Protocol and/or until all subject Gold Bullion Certificates have been transferred.

6. "Bank" will not have the right to revoke or terminate this Protocol until all subject Gold Bullion Certificates have been transferred to "Salmon/Dover Interest" from Prince Major Snatch and "Whitewater".

7. All parties agree that this Protocol is directed in operation by the laws, statutes, and regulations of Hong Kong and the British Empire.

APPROVAL AND SIGNATURES OF PARTIES ON THE DATE ABOVE STATED HEREIN:

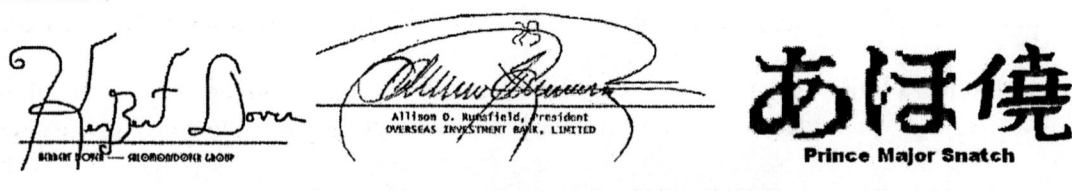

Herbert Dover — Salomondoke Loop

Allison O. Rumsfield, President
OVERSEAS INVESTMENT BANK, LIMITED

あほ僥
Prince Major Snatch

"Your attention to this extremely important matter will weigh heavily on General Salmon's final decision to try you or not for War Crimes," Bert Dover acknowledged after the signing ceremony.

"Al Rumsfield was invited to this meeting to determine if you really meant business. Here is the first Gold Bullion Certificate of Deposit in the amount of $100,000,000.00 U. S. Dollars in Overseas Investment Bank, Limited in Hong Kong, which must be assigned to Mr. Dover," General Brocklesby ordered.

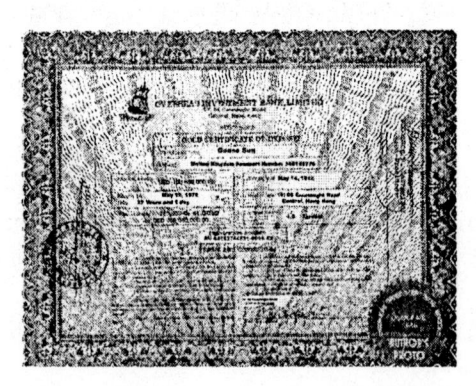

TREASURES OF WAR – CONCEALED BY THE EVIL ONES / 413

"Okay, one down and many more to go. Thirty-Six Hundred Metric Tons of Gold Bars in a London bank in the middle of 1942 took a lot of known connections in England to pull off. You spent a great amount of time there before the war in Europe broke out. I told you before. Victor Royal and your phony British passport was genius. Somebody had to assist you in London. See the back of this Special Certificate of Deposit for the assignment and transfer form to be completed by you and executed. In the For Value Received section you need to put both the names Prince Major Snatch and Victor Royal in the space provided. You do hereby irrevocably constitute and agree to sell, and transfer unto Mr. Herbert Dover and General Milton R. Salmon, U. S. citizens with these U. S. Passport numbers. Additionally, You must indicate me as the party to transfer the said Gold Bars on the Books of the within named Bank with full power of substitution in the premises and date it today." Bert Dover instructed Prince Snatch.

"Prince Snatch, you must assign and transfer the 5,800 metric tons Gold Bullion Deposit dated September 6, 1942 from Hongkong and Shanghi International Bank Limited to Dover and myself," General Brocklesby said as he pulled out the original document.

"I thought that we had already handled this one earlier," Prince Major Snatch replied.

"NO! NO! The back of this one issued by Hongkong and Shanghi International Bank Limited has not been executed. The one for Overseas Investment Bank Limited has been endorsed and assigned and completed.

"Okay, you can't blame me

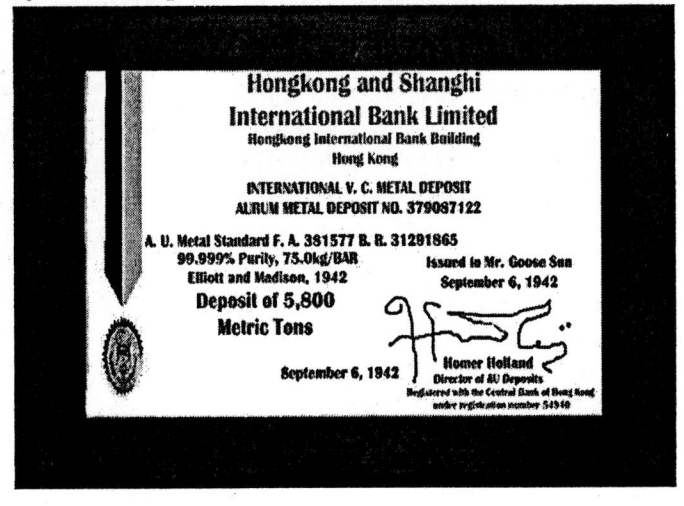

for trying. Where do I sign the other one," Prince Major Snatch said laughingly.

"Your agreed upon portion of the Gold Bullion Bank certificates back to you and the others will be issued upon the final execution of the War Crimes Court's Top Secret Compromise," Bert Dover replied.

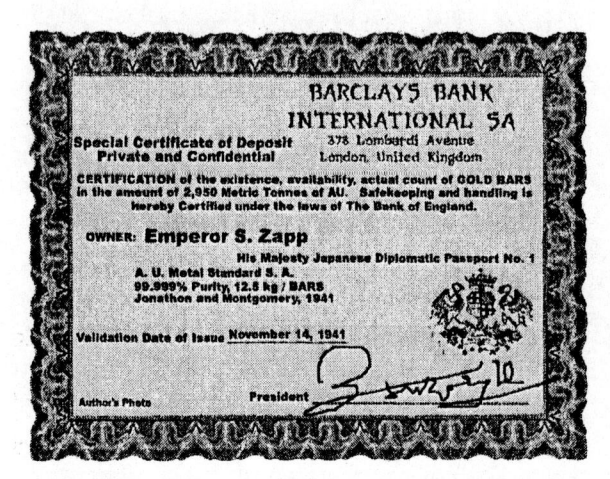

"Now Emperor Zapp, it is your time to begin signing over some of your Gold Bullion Certificates of Deposit to General Salmon and Bert Dover," General Brocklesby eagerly said as he handed Emperor Zapp the original CD's. "Sign the back of this Special Certificate of Deposit for the assignment and transfer form. Also, in the space For Value Received section, you need to put the name Emperor S. Zapp. You do hereby irrevocably constitute and agree to sell, and transfer unto Mr. Herbert Dover and General Milton R. Salmon, U. S. citizens with these U. S. Passport numbers. Additionally, You must indicate Mr. Dover as the party to transfer the said Gold Bars on the Books of the within named Bank with full power of substitution in the premises and date it today."

"The Power of Attorney that you executed the other day to the New York bank has been implemented in New York and they have followed your instructions and issued the new Certificate of Deposit for the 6,200 metric tons to be held jointly in your name and General Salmon's name. This wraps up all of these negotiations. Now, my team has the task to locate all those Gold Bars in the Philippines and ship our share of your Gold Bars here in Japan to our top Secret locations around the world," Bert Dover said as the meetings were adjourned.

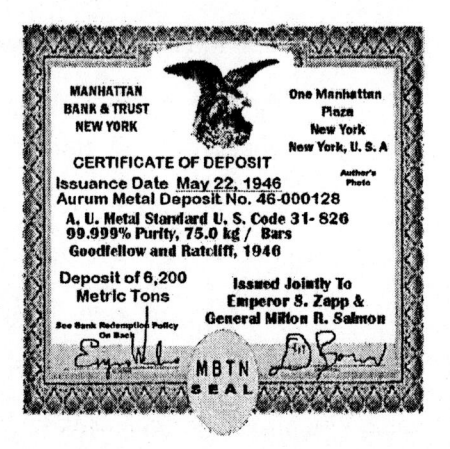

TREASURES OF WAR – CONCEALED BY THE EVIL ONES / 415

IN THE INTERNATIONAL MILITARY WAR CRIMES TRIBUNAL for the FAR EAST
TOKYO, JAPAN

IN RE: §
§
EMPEROR S. ZAPP AND FAMILY ET AL, §
§ CASE NO. 46-000001-TJ-5
DEFENDANTS, §
§
§
§

MEMORANDUM AND ORDER

This order is an unusual case in which an Evil Individual elevated himself to the position of majestic and sovereign **Evil God** of his people's faith, who deliberately waged unmerciful and aggressive wars against mankind in violations of international law under a mighty military allegiance and pledge to be willing to die for the **Evil God** for victory with unquestionable mystical spiritual obedience and loyalty with falsely perceived promises motivating the rejoicing in the strength that **Evil God** had given them, with ominous consequences. This order is a compromise of controversy. It is more unusual in that the Allied Powers oppose the compromise, having been proposed by the Co-Trustees of I M W C T F E.

The compromise addresses settlement in War Crimes lawsuits, which had progressed to the point of commencing the proceedings filed or threatened.

The testimony in the hearing on compromise has been lengthy; the Defendants have sought to introduce extensive information as to the merits of their innocence in the lawsuits. Following extensive discovery disputes, violations relating to specific war crimes and failure to provide the Court with the information requested by the Court at hearing as to the nature of the case and the requested war crimes claims.

The compromise proposes to dispose of the Court's litigations. It proposes to distribute some of the Defendant's property to Co-Trustees of I M W C T F E and to leave unchallenged the small amount of property claimed by Defendants. In the view of the War Crimes Court, the compromise is in fact generous to the Defendants, in arriving at results, which are not likely to be more favorable to Defendants than is the Compromise no matter what the ill feelings between the Defendants and the Governments of the Allied Powers.

To the extent any of the findings of fact contained herein are considered conclusions of law, they are hereby adopted as such. To the extent any of the conclusions of law contained herein are considered findings of fact, they are hereby adopted as such.

Facts

In 1926, Emperor S. Zapp, Defendant herein, became Emperor and **Evil God**. In 1931, according to the Findings 1) Defendants were instrumental in the planning, preparation, initiation or waging of a declared or undeclared war against Manchuria. 2) Defendants were the originator for planning, preparation, initiation or waging of a declared or undeclared war against China for the expansion of his empire. 3) Defendants established the planning, preparation, initiation or waging of a declared or undeclared war against the Western colonial powers of Southeast Asia and Dutch East Indies. 4) Defendants were the leaders in the planning, preparation, initiation or waging of a declared or undeclared war against the United State of America by attacking Pearl Harbor on December 7, 1941. 5) Defendants were instrumental in carrying out crimes against Humanity (murder, extermination, enslavement, deportation and other inhumane acts). 6) Defendants wrongfully looted the treasures of the invaded governments and individuals and other banking and private entities and hid the loot after Defendants gained control of the Looted Treasures. 7) Defendants conduct toward the Looted Treasures has been permeated with malice.

In spite of these findings, however, Emperor S. Zapp feels grievances of his own against his military commanders and supporting officers. However, Emperor S. Zapp was by training a military genius. He kept tight control of his military. Testimony of Emperor S. Zapp himself demonstrated that Emperor S. Zapp insisted that every military expenditure decision over one million dollars be first approved in writing by himself.

Defendant, Emperor S. Zapp, also believed that members of his family, who remained in important and secret positions in his Empire, have authority and signatory rights on family assets banks accounts for the Looted Treasures.

Emperor S. Zapp, a Defendant, finally contends that the financial declarations presented to these hearings did present a fair picture of Defendants finances.

Testimony of Co-Trustee, General Milton R. Salmon, was credible and of assistance of the Court in evaluating the possible time and cost of continuing litigation. A significant factor in I M W C T F E willingness to settle claims against Defendants is based in part on both the expense of further litigation and the difficulty to all parties of undergoing the continuing strain of litigation.

The Compromise

The major terms of the proposed compromise are as follows:

1. All litigation between the parties will be dismissed.
2. Defendants will release all claims up to sixty percent (60%) of the value of all Gold Bullion Depository Bank Accounts throughout the world and will agree to subordinate their claims against it to Co-Trustees, Mr. Bert Dover and General Milton R. Salmon.
3. Defendants will furnish Co-Trustees, Mr. Bert Dover and General Milton R. Salmon, the detail location maps, photographs and explicit

4. identifications for all looted Gold Bars located in the Philippines, Japan and elsewhere.

5. Defendants will release all claims up to a maximum of seventy percent (70%) of the total quantity of all looted Gold Bars, Diamonds and other items of a treasure nature to Co-Trustees, Mr. Bert Dover and General Milton R. Salmon, located in Japan, the Philippines and elsewhere in the world.

6. All properties identified in Article 2, 3, and 4 above will be taken by Co-Trustees, Mr. Bert Dover and General Milton R. Salmon, tax and debt free and not subject to any liens on them.

7. Defendants will receive their release of War Crime Claims, and retain their interest in forty percent (40%) of the value of all Gold Bullion Depository Bank Accounts throughout the world and in thirty percent (30%) of the total quantity of all looted Gold Bars, Diamonds and other items of a treasure nature located in the Philippines, Japan and elsewhere; their palaces and personal property.

The proposed benefits of the Compromise are the litigation risks will be eliminated, the Defendants release of War Crime Claims will be preserved, and unnecessary delay will be avoided.

Discussion

"Compromises are a 'normal part of the process of International Military War Crimes Tribunal for the Far East.'" While compromises and settlements are typical in normal court proceedings, it is less common to find a War Crimes Trial which succeeds or fails contingent on approval of the Compromise. Nevertheless, "the fact the Courts do not ordinarily scrutinize the merits of Compromises involved in International War Crimes litigants cannot affect the duty of the Court to determine that a proposed Compromise is fair and equitable."

Additional factors include the "difficulty to be encountered in the matter of the distribution of the Looted Treasures from the various countries during the declared or undeclared wars against them and in the paramount interest of the Claimants and a proper deference to their reasonable views in the assets."

An evaluation of the Compromise between Defendants and everybody leads this Court to conclude that the Compromise is in the best interest of all parties, including the Defendants personally.

After evaluation of the testimony and other evidence presented regarding the complexity and likely duration of the litigation for another three to five years, accompanied by mounting legal fees and expenses to all parties, and other relevant factors, this Court is of the opinion that the Compromise will reduce litigation time and costs to all parties. There should be an end to litigation which wastes away the resources of all parties, to the extent that no party emerges victor. Accordingly, this Court approves the Compromise of Controversy.

It is so ORDERED.

SIGNED at Tokyo, Japan on this 26th day of May, 1946.

Judge Jesse Clarkson

_____
General Milton R. Salmon
Co-Trustee

_____
Emperor S. Zapp

_____
Prince Major Snatch

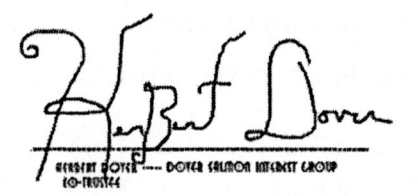

_____
Herbert Dover — Dover Salmon Interest Group
Co-Trustee

Certificate of Acknowledgment of Execution of an Instrument

<u>OCCUPIED JAPAN</u>　　　　　　　　§
　　　(Country)

<u>UNITED STATES OF AMERICA</u>　　　§
　　　(Name of Foreign Service Office)

<u>INTERNATIONAL MILITARY WAR CRIMES
TRIBUNAL for the FAR EAST ("IMWCTFE")</u>　§
　　　(Country and/or Other Political Division)

I, Chief Prosecutor Adam Lincoln, *of the INTERNATIONAL MILITARY WAR CRIMES TRIBUNAL for the FAR EAST ("IMWCTFE") at Tokyo, Japan duly commissioned and qualified, do hereby certify that on this* twenty fifth day of May, 1946, *before me personally appeared* Emperor S. Zapp, Herbert Dover, General Milton R. Salmon, and Prince Major Snatch *to me personally known, and know to me to be the individuals – described in, whose names are subscribed to, and who executed the annexed instrument, and being informed by me of the contents of said instrument they duly acknowledged to me that they executed the same freely and voluntarily for the uses and purposes therein mentioned.*

In witness whereof I have hereunto set my hand and official seal the day and year last above written.

[S E A L]

Adam Lincoln
Chief Prosecutor
IMWCTFE

TREASURES OF WAR – CONCEALED BY THE EVIL ONES

Chapter Twenty Three

The Story of The Shipments of Gold Bars and Other Treasures

From Japan and Philippines

By The Evil Ones

Author's Photo

All of the money financiers who loaned substantial amounts of money to Emperor Zapp before and during the war were pressuring BOP (Born Of Privilege) Tokyo Chairman, Mr. Herbert Dover, to keep Emperor Zapp in power. The plan was working very well. The 'Top Secret' deals with Emperor Zapp and his family had been secretly negotiated and executed. They understood that BOP would see to it that Tokyo would be used as their Asian base and would continue to pour additional money into the continued development of the Japanese industries. The splitting of the large looted treasures had been completed and Emperor Zapp was left with a substantial quantity of loot in reward for his agreement to the 'Top Secret Deals'.

"Thank you for meeting with me in my Florida headquarters at such short notice and for making arrangements with your local BOP chairman. I contacted Prescott Bushel early Monday morning on my arrival in the US, and he kindly agreed to drive up to my hotel near L. A. Airport to meet before I headed south to Florida. We had approximately three hours of discussions together and ended with a re-introductory meeting with 'Buddy' Whiteside, Clayton Riley and General Jack Adams. Prescott explained the situation and outlined that a project involving the transportation of the BOP's portion of the Gold Bars to new facilities to be designated in this meeting today was the most immediate task in hand," Bert Dover advised and instructed the loyal members.

"Bert, this is some new mansion you have built with elaborate security. It reminds me of an ancient castle with water completely surrounding it and only the lowered bridge was the enemy's way of fighting their way into the castle and taking everything inside," 'Buddy' said as he stood looking out across the bridges to the mansion.

"Thank you! Watch out for the alligators when you attempt to swim across and sneak in during the night," Dover laughingly replied.

"David Clark undertook to liaise with the various 'Top Secret' entities within Hong Kong, Tokyo, Manila, London, New York and South America, including the proper groups and to prepare a preliminary proposal and statement of capability to complete the movement of the Gold Bars in time for his presentations to the government on the 25th of next month. The presentation is more of a private meeting with key figures in the various capable Gold Bullion banks and to outline our proposals, identify the overseas groups with which we feel comfortable and intend to work out in detail all matters," Bert continued the agenda in a non-lenient voice.

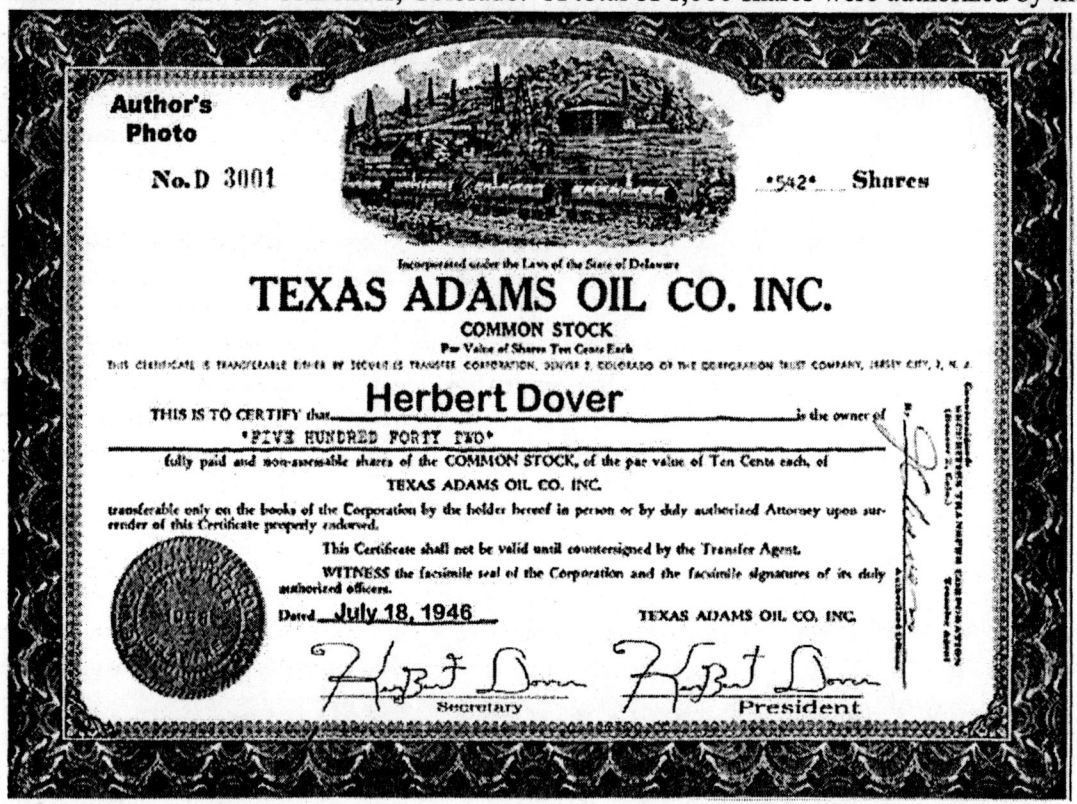

"I gave 'Buddy' Whiteside some papers from Prescott indicating that the proposed commercial structure involves the formation of a new State of Delaware company, which will be invited to act as management consultants and turnkey contractor for our project. As of today the state government approved the entity and issued its' charter. It will be called Texas Adams Oil Co. Inc. out of Denver, Colorado. A total of 1,000 shares were authorized by the State of Delaware. Here is the initial stock certificate issued in the corporation. It is issued to me in the amount of 542 Common Shares of Company Stock. I will be President and Secretary, Prescott Bushel and David Clark will serve as Vice Presidents in my absence only. General Salmon, Lieutenant General Brocklesby, will join Prescott, David and I as Directors. I reserve the first right of refusal for any other Director positions. Since the Generals remain in the US Army, it will not be reasonable for them to be shown as officers of this company at this time. Here are each of your Stock Certificates in the Company representing the agreed upon percentage of ownership and for the distribution of profits from the sales of the Treasures," Bert Dover said as he called the first meeting of the company to order.

"Looks like you have got total control of everything," Prescott said as he looked at the reverse side of the stock certificate.

"Yes, each of you must execute the back side of the stock certificate where it states 'Do hereby irrevocable constitute and appoint Herbert Dover and/or his assigns Attorney to transfer the said stock on the Books of the within named Corporation with full power of substitution in the premises'. I do not want to be fighting any of your wives lawsuits against the corporation. Discovery could raise a lot of red flags," Dover explained and put everyone as ease.

"Here is the flyer for one of the 'Front' companies. Oil Investments into the Salmon Dover Interest, Inc. in Colorado at this point of our history is not going to attract much outside attention from anybody in Washington. Each of you should be cognizant of this entity. Some of the 'Treasures Profits' will be funneled through this company as an investment," Dover said as he passed out the flyers to all in attendance.

"Various selections have been oriented toward the most professional and capable teaming arrangements. Let's proceed with the project. I pledge my one thousand percent support for your plans," 'Buddy' Whiteside replied.

"Our aspirations are centrally focused, and I am agreeable to pursue the project in cooperation with all of my associates attending the meeting today," David Clark enthusiastically said.

Author's Photo

OIL INVESTMENTS
WORKING INTERESTS
PRODUCTION
ROYALTY
LEASES

A MEMORANDUM OF INFORMATION

Prepared and Presented
By
The Oil Department of
SALMON DOVER INTEREST, INC.
Farmers Union Building
Denver 3, Colorado
Phone: AMhurst 6-0543

"In order to best orientate the initial submissions our attention is to complete the next shipment of Gold Bars to my nearby warehouses here in Florida and to the mountain resort near Highlands, North Carolina. The risk created by the Democrat's Gold ownership law, led General Salmon and I to conclude that it not be in our best interest to put any Gold Bars in US Banks. I have several Gazebos constructed with fortification on the island next to me. I suggest that we adjourn the meeting here inside my home and go over to inspect the Gazebos," Bert told the inner circle.

"Before we go to see the Gazebos let me describe our Highlands operations. The resort house is a few miles out from downtown Highlands in the mountains. However, the large mansion in downtown was built like a fortress in 1898. It has a huge basement with two secret doors leading to it. The storage or barn building out back has a direct entrance from the street with a hidden floor trap door and tunnel leading to one of the entrance doors to the basement of the mansion. The other secret basement entrance is from within the mansion. After a truck with Gold Bars crates makes the difficult trip up the mountains to Highlands from Savannah, all the driver has to do is meet our mansion manager and be told to back the truck into the barn building and walk downtown to take a break to the café in town while our men unload the Gold Bars," Prescott said describing the mansion in Highlands.

Subsequent to the inspection of the Gazebos on the reinforced island across from Bert Dover's mansion in Florida, all of the members met in the center Gazebo and were served coffee and sandwiches.

"I hope this keeps all of you adequately informed and the reminder of the extremely important and constant need to the secrecy of all phases of our operations for many years to come," Dover told the team.

"Impressed is not a strong enough word. To just be able to dock a boat at the pier or go inside the boathouse on the backside of the island is something that occurs thousands of times everyday here in Florida. No one would ever dream of what the boat was carrying onto the island. People can drive around the area at a distance and point at the beautiful private Gazebos on the island and wonder who the rich dude is that lives out there," Major General Larry Broyles said stating his opinion of the location.

"Are you going to look into the availability of additional locations in Europe and Scandinavia?" Sir. Henry Willows asked.

"It might be useful to establish documentation for other entities offering future evidence of credible locations around the world as I determine at a later stage," Bert replied.

Looks like Dover has cut some private deals he is not sharing with all of us. 'Buddy' thought to himself.

"I have been serving overseas for more than five years. Tell me what you meant by the risk of the Democrat Gold Ownership Executive Order. Does the US President and our government have the powers to seal all safe-deposit boxes and bank vaults containing Gold of any form or fashion owned by private entities or individuals?" Lieutenant General Brocklesby asked Bert Dover.

"The only thing exempted from Roosevelt's Executive Order in 1933 were rare coins and jewelry. All other forms of Gold are considered illegal to be owned by a US citizen. The criminal penalties are very serious. Ten years in Leavenworth Federal Prison is not something any of us should take lightly. Did any of you take your military training at Fort

TREASURES OF WAR – CONCEALED BY THE EVIL ONES / 428

Leavenworth? If you did, you know just how gruesome a place on the hillside Leavenworth Federal Prison appears to everyone passing by. Do not forget the meaning of 'Top Secret' operations. A picture of that famous penitentiary in your minds will make you one of the most cautious persons in the world, I hope!" Dover replied.

"I do not remember my name much less where I have been today or what I have heard and seen," Prescott said as he pointed all around the room at everyone.

"Let's walk down this ramp to the underground storage warehouse. You will see the trunks of 'Bombs', which contain some of our Gold Bars and Gold Buddhas. General Salmon used some of the US aircraft carriers to transport them to the US. I have one trunk brought from the port warehouse by my boat to this location, which is more secure. I do not believe anyone will attempt to mess with armaments," 'Bert' Dover said as they walked into the dark room and pulled the lever to turn on the lights.

"May we see what's inside one or two of them?" 'Buddy' Whiteside asked.

"Sure, 'Buddy' take this large key and open the locks at each end and lift the lid. That one has Gold Bars and that one has Gold Bars with Gold Buddhas stacked on top," 'Bert' replied as he pointed to two separate trunks.

"You have seen some of it. Everyone get on the boat that you came over to the island on and pick up any of your belongings at my home. I will see you in one month at the BOP national meeting in Washington," Dover said in his convincing voice.

"Brocklesby, please meet with me in my private office in two hours. I have some very important confidential data I want to share with you," Dover said as he put his arm around Harold.

Later in the after noon, "Here I am!"

"General Salmon and I are fully convinced that you are the most qualified and capable man on our team with excellent leadership skills in case something happened to either one of us. Every since you came on board, you have devoted your un-flinching efforts and without straying off course with dignity and precision. Therefore, he and I wish to appoint you as a Vice-Chairman and Co-Trustee of several of our Trust. Here are the executed appointment letters appointing you as Trustee to both the Herbert Dover Trust and the Dover/Salmon Interest Group Trust. Obviously, if you need to perform your duties as Co-Trustee of these Trust, you need to have selected information concerning the assets of the Trust Funds and know some of the bankers that you may be doing business with in the future. Here are copies of two Safekeeping Receipts where we shipped some of the Gold Bars from Japan and the Philippines. Keep these in your safest place possible. You understand what that means," 'Bert' Dover said in his assuring and firm tone.

"I know that I have been trained well and carried out my assignments without delays and interference from those selfish people all around us in this operation. Thank you for your confidence in me. I will carry out my duties as Vice Chairman and Co-Trustee of these two Trust Funds without failing my fiduciary responsibilities under your and General Salmon's direction," Lieutenant General Brocklesby (Ret.) replied.

SAFEKEEPING RECEIPT

We are holding one package in safekeeping containing the following:

Gold Bullion Certificate of Deposit – Reference Gold Bullion Certificate No. 379087122 B. R. 31291865 – Five Thousand Eight Hundred (5,800) Metric Tonnes of Gold Bullion (Aurum Utilium) Hongkong and Shanghi International Bank Limited (HSIBL), Central Victoria, Hong Kong, British Crown Colony.

Package is held in favor of owner – Herbert Dover Trust.

Specifications:

COMMODITY: Gold Bullion

TREASURES OF WAR – CONCEALED BY THE EVIL ONES / 430

CERTIFICATE NO.	HSIBL F. A. – 381577 -B. R. 31291865
QUANTITY:	Five Thousand Eight Hundred (5,800) Metric Tonnes
TROY OUNCES:	Gold Bullion calculated at 32.1507428 Troy Ounces Per Kilogram
HALLMARKS:	Elliott and Madison, 1942
FINENESS:	99.999% Purity
BAR SIZE:	75.0 Kilograms Bars.
TITLE:	Free and Clear of All Liens and Encumbrances, Being Fully Negotiable per Instructions of Owner.

Signed By:
SAFEKEEPING BANK

SAFEKEEPING RECEIPT

We are holding one package in safekeeping containing the following:

Gold Bullion Certificate of Deposit – Reference Gold Bullion Certificate No. 42681-B. L. 548077 – Three Thousand Five Hundred (3,500) Metric Tonnes of Gold Bullion (Aurum Utilium) Universal Bank International of Switzerland (UBIS), Gènève, Suisse.

Package is held in favor of owner -- Dover/Salmon Interest Group Trust.

Specifications:

COMMODITY:	Gold Bullion
CERTIFICATE NO.	UBIS F. S. -- 42681-B. L. 548077
QUANTITY:	Three Thousand Five Hundred (3,500) Metric Tonnes
TROY OUNCES:	Gold Bullion calculated at 32.1507428 Troy Ounces Per Kilogram
HALLMARKS:	Not Identified by Internationally Recognized Hallmarks.
FINENESS:	999.5/1000 or Lesser.
BAR SIZE:	12.5 and 75.0 Kilograms Bars.
TITLE:	Free and Clear of All Liens and Encumbrances, Being Fully Negotiable per Instructions of Owner.

Signed By:
SAFEKEEPING BANK

"I know you will. One of the main things you and I should keep abreast too is the fluctuation of the price of Gold around the world. The President has increased the price about 21 percent. You and I both are cognizant of the fact that the international money markets are going to create a tremendous change in the price of Gold because central banks around the world are going to attempt to slow inflation by taking its' weak currencies and buy Gold. We will do our best to make this happen." 'Bert' Dover said with a laugh.

"Yes, we have to work everyday to accomplish our goals. I know better than most that General Salmon's days are spent with politicians and his military officers. He does not have time to personally keep up with the daily price of Gold. I will study the international Gold markets around the world and become an expert Gold trader in the next thirty days," Brocklesby replied as he was gaining momentum in his new duties.

"Well done! I will see you out and later in Washington, D. C. Keep me posted on a daily basis," 'Bert' Dover said as he led Harold out of his Florida mansion.

TREASURES OF WAR – CONCEALED BY THE EVIL ONES

Chapter Twenty Four

CIA Attempts to Confiscate General Virgilio Hermano's Maps

And

Gold Bars

Photos Provided By National Archives and Records Administration
And
National Security Agency/Central Security Services

"The reason that I called all of you together here at our mountain camp is to discuss recent developments by the government leaders and police who are following the US Military and Central Intelligence Agency commands. The Philippine National Police together with the Americans raided the homes of several suspected treasure hunters in Quezon City last week. They arrested several men who had bought a few Gold Bars from one of the tribesmen from Mt. Arayat. Apparently, they were trying to sell the Gold Bars to a Filipino businessman to fund one of their treasure hunts. You must be aware that I have worked out a plan with the top government leaders whereby I will split the money from the sale of the Gold Bars overseas in exchange for protection and special privileges at the ports and airports," Virgil explained.

"Since these treasure hunters in Quezon City are not part of my group, the government informed the US officials about their activities in order to keep them happy and not looking so close at us. Therefore, each of you should not be too alarmed about what you have heard or read in the newspapers. However, promise me you will not let your guard down and get caught by the US Military or Intelligence Agency," Virgil requested.

"We promise we will keep our activities top secret to all outsiders," 'Chief' reassured Virgil.

"Thanks men. I take it that you noticed that Chief Superintendent Velasco quoted the US Military and Central Intelligence Agency as saying that they kept the suspected ringleader of the treasure hunter company under surveillance for more than six months. They are looking for the Yamashita Gold and Precious Stones that were buried all over the Philippines during 1942, 1943, 1944 and 1945. If the US officials find it, the Filipinos and our government will never receive anything for it. The Americans will ship it out of here and no telling what will happen to it, right men?" Virgil shouted.

All of the men shouted a loud YES in response to Virgil's question.

"The confidential information disclosed to me by the top government officials indicates two seventy five kilo Gold Bars with Chinese markings were recovered. The assay test revealed eighteen karat purity," Virgil told the men.

"Jose, don't you have additional information on this deal?" Virgil asked.

"Yes Sir! May I have your permission to address the men?" Jose requested.

"Yes, Jose tell them exactly what you and I planned discussing today," Virgil replied.

Men, the CIA agents have begun torturing these men from Quezon City to learn where the Gold Bars came from and whether they could produce treasure maps locating the big find. They seized everything in their homes and storage sheds. The men had guns on themselves at the time of the raid. Each of you can see that we must be very careful and keep our lips shut about our activities," Jose cautioned the men.

"Thank you Jose, one final comment, should you get arrested or notice that you are under surveillance, you need to have one or two individuals designated to contact me at my place in Manila or by phone there. Each of you should have my numbers. If you do not, see me after the meeting. My top officials will protect you by making the appropriate contact with the appropriate government officials that are our silent partners. You will not need to do anything else or tell anyone anything, everybody understand?" Virgil asked.

"I heard that the CIA needs money to conduct some of its secret operations in South America, Japan, Europe and the Soviet Union," Celso shouted out from the floor of the meeting place.

"Celso, I am sure that you are correct and they also want to protect their individual hides and get some of these riches to unknown political persons in the USA," Virgil replied with his squeamish grin.

"Who is this guy named Prescott Bushel that we keep seeing in some very peculiar activities in this part of the world?" Ronell asked from the audience.

"Your guess is as good as mine," Virgil replied. "Just avoid him if he comes to town."

Four Months Later...

"Cesar, the CIA team led by Agent Dwayne Hunter, code name, 'Deadeye', is watching you and every move you make. They have established a wiretap on your telephone and bugged your home, office and car. That is why I asked you to come down here in the basement of the central operations. They have not succeeded in breaking our security yet. Now, here is the plan for transferring the 'Maps' at the airport. Since some of the customs inspectors at the airport have been paid off by the CIA and are not loyal to the government anymore, and have been furnished a short list of individuals to be searched; you can not take the maps in your luggage at all," Virgil Hermano explained.

"Yes Sir," Cesar responded.

"One of our key men, 'Chief' has his team disguised as part of the cleaning crew at the airport. He has obtained airport clearance for all of his men. After you go through security and have been searched; go to gate 4 area and sit down to receive your signal from 'Chief'. He will be wearing a Ram cleaning company overalls. He is going to drop the envelope containing the 'Maps' folded up in a newspaper in the white trash can just in front of the concrete pillar to the left of gate 4. Do you understand everything so far Cesar?" Virgil asked.

"Yes Sir."

"Before 'Chief' signals you by dropping the newspaper with the 'Maps' inside into the white trash can, 'Chief' will receive a signal from one of his men that he has hung a garbage bag inside the handicap stall in the men's restroom south of gate 4 area. Then, shortly after 'Chief' drops the newspaper in the white trashcan, one of his men will be making clean up rounds and dump the contents into the waste cart. He will move down the corridor to the men's restroom. He will pull the newspaper from the trash and place it in the garbage bag in the handicap stall for you to pick up. From where you are sitting, as soon as you see the cleaning man with his cart get near the door to the men's restroom, make some conversation with some of the people around you as you stand-up. You will have six or more CIA agents watching you from around the area. Make them hear that you must make a pit stop to the restroom. Be sure that you take your briefcase with you to the restroom. You will be followed. As soon as you go inside the handicap stall, stand and make them know that you are taking care of business. While doing so, remove the envelope containing the 'Maps' from the folded newspaper and secure it in your briefcase," Virgil instructed, turning to Cesar.

"Agent Hunter and his team of CIA agents want to find out who all of our contacts are. I will come to the airport at 11:00 AM for my flight. After clearing security inspection I will go to gate 6 for the PAL flight number 334 to Hong Kong. I know that one of Agent Hunter's men will go out to purchase several tickets for flight 334 for his men to follow me to Hong Kong. At about 12:30 PM, I will go over to any man from India in the crowd near me and introduce myself and shake hands with him, sit down next to him and talk with him for about ten minutes. As we talk I will pick out a Chinese man in the crowd and point at him as we talk. Then, after talking with the man from India; I will go over to the Chinese man and say a few words to him and walk away," Virgil said, demonstrating his plan to Cesar.

"Cesar, this is your clue to go back into the men's restroom and into the handicap stall leaving the door unlocked. I will walk to the handicap stall and open the door and enter. You will hand me the envelope with the 'Maps'. I will place the envelope in my newspaper and excuse myself and go to another stall. Do you clearly understand?" Virgil quizzed.

"Yes, I understand everything and the timing necessary to make all connections go off without a hitch. I will not need to write anything down on paper that may be found later by the enemy," Cesar assured Virgil.

"You should leave the airport taking a few of the CIA agents with you. I will return to gate 6 and board the plane to Hong Kong with my first class ticket near the front of the plane. At about this same time 'Chief' will get a hostess at Gate 4 to page a Mr. Mangue. Just before the aircraft door is closed I will get off the plane, explaining that I received an emergency page as I was boarding the plane. After explaining to the agent at gate 6 that I have an emergency at home and will not be making the flight, I will go to gate 11 and board the next flight to Davao City leaving the CIA agents on the plane to Hong Kong," Virgil reveled.

"Virgil, you will fool all of them and leave them behind. This is a well thought out plan to get the 'Maps' to the proper people in the organization and prevent them from raiding your place to search for them," Cesar observed.

"On a more serious matter that I want you to take care of while I am out of the country concerns our man, 'Tiger'. 'Tiger' is being pressured by the CIA to testify against us. We need to make sure that 'Tiger' does not tell what he knows. He knows some of the locations of the Gold Bars and too much about our operations. The only way to be sure that he keeps his mouth shut is be sure he does not live too long. Cesar, take Skooter and several men to the hotel where he is staying, remember he now has two bodyguards, and shoot him in the head. Also, it would be better to kill his bodyguards at the same time. No witnesses," Virgil threateningly stated.

"We will enter the hotel from the delivery entrance and use our silencers in their room which always has loud music playing. At the time of night we take care of this critical job, it will be the next afternoon when the cleaning lady comes around before anyone even suspects no movement from the room and the killings are discovered," Cesar assured General Hermano.

TREASURES OF WAR – CONCEALED BY THE EVIL ONES

Chapter Twenty Five

Global Banking Corporation After World War II

Control -- Control

Author's Photo

Eleven Years Later After Global Banking Corporation Was Created and Many Benefits for It Were Passed By Congress:

PRESIDENT ROOSEVELT'S MESSAGE TO CONGRESS ON BRETTON WOODS MONEY AND BANKING PROPOSALS

February 12, 1945--New York Times.

TO THE CONGRESS OF THE UNITED STATES:

In my budget message of Jan. 9 I called attention to the need for immediate action on the Bretton Woods proposals for an international monetary fund and an international bank for reconstruction and development. It is my purpose in this message to indicate the importance of these international organizations in our plans for a peaceful and prosperous world.

As we dedicate our total efforts to the task of winning this war we must never lose sight of the fact that victory is not only an end in itself but, in a large sense, victory offers us the means of achieving the goal of lasting peace and a better way of life.

Victory does not insure the achievement of these larger goals-it merely offers us the opportunity-the chance-to seek their attainment. Whether we shall have the courage and vision to avail ourselves of this tremendous opportunity-purchased at so great a cost-is yet to be determined. On our shoulders rests the heavy responsibility for making this momentous decision. I said before, and I repeat again: "This generation has a rendezvous with destiny."

If we are to measure up to the task of peace with the same stature as we have measured up to the task of war, we must see that the institutions of peace rest firmly on the solid foundations of international political and economic cooperation. The cornerstone for international political cooperation is the Dumbarton Oaks proposal for a permanent United Nations.

International political relations will be friendly and constructive, however, only if solutions are found to the difficult economic problems we face today. The cornerstone for international economic cooperation is the Bretton Woods proposals for an international monetary fund and an international bank for reconstruction and development.

These proposals for an international fund and international bank are concrete evidence that the economic objectives of the United States agree with those of the United Nations. They illustrate our unity of purpose and interest in the economic field. What we need and what they need correspond-expanded production, employment, exchange and consumption-in other words, more goods produced, more jobs, more trade and a higher standard of living for us all.

To the people of the United States this means real peacetime employment for those who will be returning from the war and for those at home whose wartime work has ended. It also means orders and profits to our industries and fair prices to our farmers. We shall need prosperous markets in the world to insure our own prosperity, and we shall need the goods the world can sell us. For all these purposes, as well as for a peace that will endure, we need the partnership of the United Nations.

The first problem in time, which we must cope with, is that of saving life and getting resources and people back into production. In many of the liberated countries economic life has all hut stopped. Transportation systems are in ruins and therefore coal and raw materials cannot be brought to factories.

Many factories themselves are shattered, power plants smashed, transmission systems broken, bridges blown up or bombed, ports clogged with sunken wrecks, and great rich areas of farm land inundated by the sea. People are tired and sick and hungry. But they are eager to go to work again, and to create again with their own hands and under their own leaders the necessary physical basis of their lives.

Emergency relief is under way behind the armies under the authority of local Governments, backed up first by the Allied Military Command and after that by the United Nations Relief and Rehabilitation Administration. Congress has approved our participation in the UNRRA. But neither UNRRA nor the armies are designed for the construction or reconstruction of large-scale public works or factories or power plants or transportation systems. That job must be done otherwise, and it must be started soon.

The main job of restoration is not one of relief. It is one of reconstruction, which must largely be done by local people and their Governments. They will provide the labor, the local money and most of the materials. The same is true for all the many plans for the improvement of transportation; agriculture, industry and housing that are essential to the development of the economically backward areas of the world.

But some of the things required for all these projects, both of reconstruction and development, will have to come from overseas. It is at this point that our highly developed economy can play a role important to the rest of the world and very profitable to the United States. Inquiries for numerous materials and for all kinds of equipment and machinery in connection with such projects are already being directed to our industries and many more will come. This business will be welcome just as soon as the more urgent production for the war itself ends.

The main problem will be for these countries to obtain the means of payment. In the long run we can be paid for what we sell abroad chiefly in goods and services. But at the moment many of the countries that want to be our customers are prostrate. Other countries have devoted their economies so completely to the war that they do not have the resources for reconstruction and development.

Unless a means of financing is found, such countries will be unable to restore their economies and, in desperation, will be forced to carry forward and intensify existing systems of discriminatory trade practices, restrictive exchange controls, competitive depreciation of currencies and other forms of economic warfare. That would destroy all our good hopes. We must move promptly to prevent it's happening, and we must move on several fronts, including finance and trade.

The United States should act promptly upon the plan for the international bank, which will make or guarantee sound loans for the foreign currency requirements of important reconstruction and development projects in member countries. One of its most important functions will be to facilitate and make secure wide private participation in such loans. The articles of agreement constituting the charter of the bank have been worked out with great care by an international conference of experts and give adequate protection to all interests. I recommend to the Congress that we accept the plan, subscribe the capital allotted to us, and participate whole-heartedly in the bank's work.

This measure, with others I shall later suggest, should go far to take care of our part of the lending requirements of the post-war years. They should help the countries concerned to get production started, to get over the first crisis of disorganization and fear, to begin the work of reconstruction and development; and they should help our farmers and our industries to get over the crisis of reconversion by making a large volume of export business possible in the post-war years.

As confidence returns private investors will participate more and more in foreign lending and investment without any Government assistance. But to get over the first crisis, in the situation that confronts us, loans and guarantees by agencies of Government will be essential.

We all know, however, that a prosperous world economy must be built on more than foreign investment. Exchange rates must be stabilized and the channels of trade opened up throughout the world. A large foreign trade after victory will generate production, and therefore wealth. It will also make possible the servicing of foreign investments.

Almost no one in the modern world produces what he eats and wears and lives in. It is only by the division of labor among people and among geographic areas, with all their varied resources, and by the increased all-around production which specialization makes possible, that any modern country can sustain its present population. It is through exchange and trade that efficient production in large units becomes possible. To expand the trading circle, to make it richer, more competitive, more varied, is a fundamental contribution to everybody's wealth and welfare.

It is time for the United States to take the lead in establishing the principle of economic cooperation as the foundation for expanded world trade. We propose to do this, not by setting up a super-government, but by international negotiation and agreement, directed to the improvement of the monetary institutions of the world and of the laws that govern trade.

We have done a good deal in those directions in the last ten years under the Trade Agreements Act of 1934 and through the stabilization fund operated by our Treasury. But our present enemies were powerful in those years too, and they devoted all their efforts not to international collaboration, but to autarchy and economic warfare. When victory is won we must be ready to go forward rapidly on a wide front. We all know very well that this will be a long and complicated business.

A good start has been made. The United Nations monetary conference at Bretton Woods has taken a long step forward on a matter of great practical importance to us all. The conference submitted a plan to create an international monetary fund, which will put an end to monetary chaos. The fund is a financial institution to preserve stability and order in the exchange rates between different moneys. It does not create a single money for the world; neither we nor anyone else is ready to do that. There will still be different money in each country, but with the fund in operation the value of each currency in international trade will remain comparatively stable. Changes in the value of foreign currencies will be made only after careful consideration by the fund of the factors involved.

Furthermore, and equally important, the fund agreement establishes a code of agreed principles for the conduct of exchange and currency affairs. In a nutshell, the fund agreement spells the difference between a world caught again in the maelstrom of panic and economic warfare culminating in war-as in the Nineteen Thirties-or a world in which the members strive for a better life through mutual trust, cooperation and assistance. The choice is ours.

Therefore, recommend prompt action by the Congress to provide the subscription of the United States to the international monetary fund and the legislation necessary for our membership in the fund.

The international fund and bank together represent one of the most sound and useful proposals for international collaboration now before us. On the other hand, I do not want to leave with you the impression that these proposals for the fund and bank are perfect in every detail.

It may well be that the experience of future years will show us how they can be improved. I do wish to make it clear, however, that these articles of agreement are the product of the best minds that forty-four nations could muster. These men, who represented nations from all parts of the globe, nations in all stages of economic development, nations with different political and economic philosophies, have reached an accord, which is presented to you for your consideration and approval. It would be a tragedy if differences of opinion on minor details should lead us to sacrifice the basic agreement achieved on the major problems.

Nor do I want to leave with you the impression that the fund and the bank are all that we will need to solve the economic problems, which will face the United Nations when the war is over. There are other problems, which we shall be called upon to solve. It is my expectation that other proposals will shortly be ready to submit to you for your consideration.

These will include the establishment of the food and agriculture organization of the United Nations, broadening and strengthening of the Trade Agreements Act of 1934, international agreement for the reduction of trade barriers, the control of cartels and the orderly marketing of world surpluses of certain commodities, a revision of the Export-Import Bank, and an international oil agreement, as well as proposals in the field of civil aviation, shipping and radio wire communications. It will also be necessary, of course, to repeal the Johnson Act.

In this message I have recommended for your consideration the immediate adoption of the Bretton Woods agreements and suggested other measures, which will have to be dealt with in the near future. They are all parts of a consistent whole.

That whole is our hope for a secure and fruitful world, a world in which plain people in all countries can work at tasks which they do well, exchange in peace the products of their labor and work out their several destinies in security and peace; a world in which Governments, as their major contribution to the common welfare, are highly and effectively resolved to work together in practical affairs and to guide all their actions by the knowledge that any policy or act that has effects abroad must be considered in the light of those effects.

This point in history at which we stand is full of promise and of danger. The world will either move toward unity and widely shared prosperity or it will move apart into necessarily competing economic blocs.

We have a chance, we citizens of the United States, to use our influence in favor of a more united and cooperating world. Whether we do so will determine, as far as it is in our power, the kind of lives our grandchildren can live.

FRANKLIN D. ROOSEVELT

THE WHITE HOUSE,
February 12, 1945.

The Annual Shareholders and Board of Directors Meetings of Global Banking Corporation December 8, 1946.

The letters to Shareholders, notice of Annual Meeting of Shareholders, Proxy Materials and Financial Reports had been hand delivered or mailed out to all shareholders thirty days in advance of the meetings according to the provisions of the corporate by-laws. Appropriate identical letters and notices were included to each member of the Board of Directors. No proxy vote replies had been received by the Secretary of the Corporation prior to the meetings.

Anticipation for everyone eligible to attend these critical meetings was expected. The post war policies of the Corporation were the main focus to be resolved by the shareholders.

The Notice of Annual Meeting of Shareholders of Global Banking Corporation listed the Matters to be voted on:

1. Election of directors.
2. Ratification of the Global Banking Corporation 1946 International Banking Plan.

3. Approval of the Global Banking Corporation 1947 Investment and Incentive Plan.
4. Any other matters properly brought before the shareholders at the meeting.

The Secretary of Global Banking Corporation called the roll of the issued and outstanding registered shareholders entitled to vote according to the Stock Certificates Ledger of the corporation, noting the number of shares of voting power of each member being present: Mr. Santana Drisco, General Jack Adams, Mr. Jack Townsend, Mr. Robert 'Buddy' Whiteside, Sir. Henry Willows, Mr. Clayton Riley, Dr. Francisco de Luca Moro, Mr. David Clark, Mr. Wilhelm 'Willie' von Hindenburg, Mr. Sinan Sabancitz, Mr. Carlos Burton, Mr. Claude Rappaport, Mr. Abraham 'Abe' Osman, Mr. Jean-Yves Benoit, Mr. Prescott Bushel and Mr. Herbert Dover.

"This joint meeting of shareholders and directors is hereby called to order. First, before we get into the election of directors I would like to see the hands of anyone that did not receive your respective additional or new purchased shares of stocks certificates that were authorized by the Secretary of State. Excellent, I was concerned some of you not receiving them. We did not receive all of the mail receipts back from you. Second, you have the ballots for the election of the Directors for the next two-year term. Please vote and sign them and pass them forward for tallying the votes," 'Buddy' Whiteside stated in his normal smooth manner before an audience.

All shareholders voted one vote for each share of stock owned. A total of nine board members were being elected to serve out the new term. Due to the number of shares owned by 'Bert' Dover, David Clark, 'Buddy' Whiteside, General Jack Adams, and Prescott Bushel they were assured to be elected as five of the directors. Thereby, controlling the actions of the Board of Directors for the next two years.

"Mr. Chairman, I request to open the discussions before we ratify our 1946 International Banking Plan," Clark asked.

"The major focus of our policy is to have the new postwar governments establish laws controlling the discovery of buried or hidden looted treasures from the war. We do not want any fortunes coming under the control of anyone except our handpicked leaders around the world. You know that the Communist Bloc countries are taking control of any treasure found in their countries," Chairman Whiteside told the meeting.

"Could you give us a concentrated view of what our objective is?" New board member Clayton Riley asked.

"Excellent question, Prescott Bushel and I have been under many years of focused activities and the time has come to make some changes in objectives," Board member Dr. Francisco de Luca Moro replied.

"Yes Riley, the Global Banking Group plans must be appealing to these world leaders. The new laws that they must get put on their books will provide strict ways to control treasure hunter activities including the requirement to obtain permits and contracts prior to the hunt; governmental intervention and security at the time of discovery, including its military and police forces; recording of maps; maximum entitlement limits in the amount of fifteen percent to the treasure hunter for treasure found on public property; maximum entitlement limits in the amount of twenty-five percent to the treasure hunter when the treasure is found on private property; both federal and local approvals for each separate identified treasure expedition; severe punishment for violating the treasure hunting laws and smuggling activities, making a public example out of each violator," Whiteside summarized.

"What we want to accomplish with the local authorities is convince them that we are the only route to trade the treasures found by one of their local citizens. We offer the best place for these authorities to put these acquired riches in a very safe bank away from their country. We have the use of these funds in our banks. They have access to wealth without anyone local asking all kinds of questions and causing them problems," 'Bert' Dover explained.

"A hypothetical example would be when several or a group of treasure-hunters, using expensive, sophisticated, modern equipment and techniques undertakes to go on a treasure-hunting expedition without obtaining a costly local government permit that would divulge everything. A discovery is made. After spying on the hunters, the local corrupt government leaders and in most cases the police or military forces is sent in by these leaders to secure the location. Once secured, the local and federal corrupt officials remove all the treasures. Then, it is taken and hidden in their private treasure chest. Later, the story is leaked out to the media about treasure hunters dying in deep caves or tunnels attempting to find the treasures," General Adams further explained part of Global Banking Corporation's new policy.

"Okay 'Buddy', how is this going to effect the promotion of world peace by the leadership in Washington, D. C. that is being presented to the public by the press and radio?" Board member Drisco asked.

"Santana, I am glad you asked that question. It only emphasizes the need to let everyone of the leaders know that this is extremely confidential and must not be shared with the media. These leaders will need our financial assistance for many years to come and they will pressure us to let them in on this program," Whiteside answered.

Concerned about the impact of the plan Prescott reminded them, "Lobby, Lobby, Lobby and Lobby is one of the most important weapons we have to control all post war governments."

"General Jack Adams, it is your assignment to travel to Germany, Holland, Belgium, Switzerland, France, Italy, and Portugal for the purpose of presenting this extremely important and confidential policy of the Global Banking Group to the new leaders of these countries," Chairman Robert "Buddy" Whiteside stated as he presented the confidential package to Adams.

"I will study the contents thoroughly and discuss all details with you before I make my travel plans," Adams replied.

"Good, I am at your disposal, just call me to set up a meeting time."

The meeting on Global Banking Group's efforts to take control of the treasures of the world immediately after the end of World War II was getting into high gear.

"Another method which focuses on the purpose of this organization in the control of the money supplies and economies of the less educated countries is as follows:

1. We shall have the stronger countries purchase the goods and services of the weaker countries and make payment to them in dated currencies.

2. Periodically, we shall advise the various strong countries to have the currency of certain weaker countries demonetized without all the less educated countries having full knowledge of these activities. We will publish the dates in advance that the currency will be demonetized.

3. Then, after the expiration of these dates the currency will be worthless to the weaker countries.

The details of this policy is included in the 1946 International Banking Plan," 'Buddy' advised.

After standing and receiving acknowledgement from Chairman Whiteside, 'Abe' Osman said. "Since we are going to be able to control the movement of all currencies around the world, I make a motion to ratify the Global Banking Corporation's 1946 International Banking Plan."

"I second the motion," Prescott responded.

The motion carried by a unanimous vote.

"Let's all stand and give 'Bert' three cheers for his superb performance for the management of most of our investments around the world. I hereby make a motion to accept the company's 1947 Investment and Incentive Plan with 'Bert' continuing to lead us," Clark told the members as they all cheered for 'Bert'.

"I second the motion based upon the fact we all have the opportunity to receive that incentive bonus from the large company profits at the end of the fiscal year by just taking care of business," General Jack Adams greedily replied.

The approval of the 1947 Investment and Incentive Plan was unanimous. Being no further business the Shareholders and Board of Directors meeting was adjourned.

TREASURES OF WAR – CONCEALED BY THE EVIL ONES

Chapter Twenty Six

The Story of Filipino Investments In Argentina

By Virgilio 'Bulldog' Hermano Foundation

Author's Photo   Argentina Government Property

BANCO CENTRAL REPUBLICA DE LA ARGENTINA

GOLD MEMORANDUM RECEIPT

GMR

This Certifies that there have been deposited in the Treasury of Banco Central Republica De La Argentina Four Thousand Metric Tons

Upon arrival in August 1973 at the Buenos Aires International Airport, Mr. Ronildo Cattaui, the senior Central Bank crony of the President of the Philippines, was met by Sr. Eduardo Gomez Morales, the personal financial advisor to President Perón and President of Banco Central Republic of Argentina. The red carpet was laid down on the tarmac at the exit ramp of the PAL Boeing 707 jet together with all of the senior dignitaries representing President Perón's VIP airport greeting party. More than three thousand people were kept behind the temporary barriers along the walkway into the terminal, all waving and shouting slogans such as "VIVA HERMANO" and "WELCOME TO BUENOS AIRES".

The new luxurious 1974 black CADILLAC stretch limo was awaiting us at the VIP arrival terminal. Once we had completed greeting each dignitary, I was told that a surprise Argentina luncheon was planned for us at a nearby ranch house restaurant, complete with a "Gaucho" setting.

After the convoy of limousines followed the motorcycle police escort for about three miles from the international airport terminal, our driver turned at the crossover and circled back a short distance and entered the driveway and drove up to this old, old ranch house under the huge oak trees. The ranch house had been converted into a restaurant. The patio setting under the shade of the old oak trees provided a perfect place for the old dome shaped baking ovens made from special mortar and rocks. Open pit cooking grills with stacks of the famous outdoor cooking and smoking firewood already burning gave off a unique aroma that everyone seemed to appreciate. Old wooden tables and chairs built to last forever and a special dancing floor made of thick wooden flooring elevated on blocks about two feet high made the complete Argentine Ranch House setting.

"Please sit here at the head table," Sr. Morales politely ask Mr. Cattaui, pulling out his chair.

"Thank you, I bet that you and a lot of the members of the Chamber of Commerce have been praying a long time for beautiful weather like this for this occasion. There is not a cloud in the sky and the temperature is fabulous. This beautiful setting will make you forget your jet lag, relax, and enjoy this great atmosphere," Cattaui said, speaking for the first time at the restaurant.

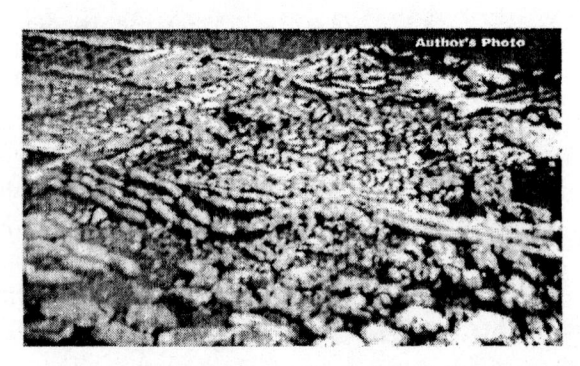

"Yes, a lot of prayers have been answered," Sr. Morales, laughed, looking and pointing up to the heavens.

The maitre d' and all the waiters dressed in typical Gaucho dress brought out the wine glasses to each guest. All of the guests were given an opportunity to taste some of the fine Argentine wines and determine whether they preferred a red or white wine as an aperitif.

The Argentine white wines are largely Chardonnay, Chenin, Rieslings, Geweurtztraminer and Torrontes; and the red wines are Bordeaux, Cabernet Sauvignon, and Malbec.

"Mr. Cattaui would you prefer a white wine as your aperitif," the maitre 'd asked, recommending the Torrontes developed in Argentina.

"Sounds good to me," he replied with a smile.

After all the guests were served their wines Sr. Morales stood up and proposed a toast for Mr. Cattaui and his Filipino delegation.

"All of you are welcome to Argentina. May your first visit be a pleasant one and very profitable and you and your families continue to have good health. The President is looking forward to receiving each of you as his personal guest tonight. Let all of our Argentine people applaud and salute you; hip, hip hooray; hip, hip hooray; hip, hip hooray," as Sr. Morales toasted each table with Filipino guest, looking first at Mr. Cattaui's table.

With the red-hot glowing coals from the special firewood being just right for cooking the meats over the parrillas (grills), the Chief Chef and his cooks brought out buckets of empanadas (meat pastries), chorizos (spicy pork sausages) and morcillas (blood sausages), an assortment of mollejas and achuras (sweetbreads) of course, these being only the appetizers.

At the same time the famous Argentine bifes (steaks) were brought out to several special parrillas (grills) with several levels of grills, where the bifes could be cooked slowly and for the different taste request (rare, medium, medium well or well done) of the guest.

The bife de chorizo (T-bone steak), bife de costilla (a large thick steak cut from the underside of the rib roast), tira de asado (a thin strip of rib roast), brochettes and enormous filet migon steaks were placed on the grills to cook. The slight breeze blowing through the trees sent the aroma of these mouthwatering steaks throughout the patio area.

While the guest were sipping their wines, the two dancing couples accompanied by the eight piece orchestra stepped onto the dance floor and began to entertain the guest with a dance of passion. The two young beautiful female dancers were dressed in high heel shoes, flowing shirts, colorful scarfs and long sleeved decorative blouses.

This tango orchestra was made up of the bando-neon, a close relative of the accordion, several guitars, violins, flutes and a trumpet.

The two young handsome male dancers were dressed in their Gaucho outfits, complete with the characteristic apparel of the Gaucho, including the flat brimmed hat; baggy trouser over his boots; a wide belt of silver ornaments, coins and a large buckle; a woolen poncho; and a very bright multi-colored scarf.

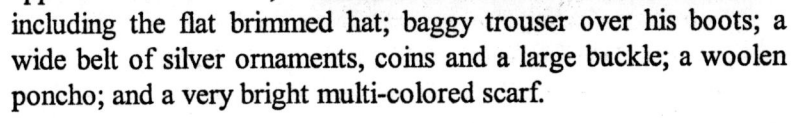

The Gaucho stands as one of the best-known cultural symbols of Argentina. A proud cousin of the North American Cowboy is maintained in Argentine culture as the perfect embodiment of *argentinidad*. He lives on as a heroic figure in the folklore, music and has been elevated to the level of myth.

The Chief Chef motioned to the maitre d' to bring his waiters over to the parrillas and pick up some serving trays with platters of a selection of the freshly cook appetizers and some of the sweetbreads baked in the famous Argentine ovens.

The maitre d' and one waiter took these appetizers, sweetbreads and local butter over to Mr. Cattaui's table and served him and Sr. Morales. After tasting the sweetbread, Mr. Cattaui expressed his delight in the taste of this bread.

"This bread reminds me of our Filipino pita bread, but this has a special taste and is excellent."

"Please enjoy, do not think about how much you are eating. We have plenty more in the ovens," the maitre d' said with a broad smile.

About fifteen minutes later the waiters began serving the steaks that each guest ordered. No steak sauce was requested by anyone. The thick steaks were so tender that you could have cut them with your fork.

"More bread" was heard from most of the tables.

"Do you have anymore of the spicy pork sausages?" came from several of the Filipinos who love their pork.

The desserts were a combination of Dulce de leche (milk jam), which is very sweet, Queso y Membrillo (combination of cheese and sweet potato preserves) and fruit salad.

The Filipinos loved the Membrillo.

All of a sudden the Gaucho dancer jumped to the center of the dance floor with two lassoes with hard balls secured near the ends of the lassoes. He lifted his hands to his waistline on each side of his body. The lassoes were held in the palms of each hand. After the introduction by the orchestra, suddenly the orchestra began to play a very fast and loud song, and the Gaucho dancer began to dance rapidly tapping his feet loud and the wooden outdoors dance floor. Then, he began to twirl the lassoes with each hand in a vertical motion to his sides like a Cowboy whirls his lariat over his head. After a moment or two, he began to whirl both lassoes and balls in about every direction that you could imagine.

I turned to one of the Argentines and ask him what was this extremely fast dance. He told me that this is the famous Boleadoras Dance of the Argentine Gaucho. He further explained that the Boleadoras consisted of three stones or metal balls attached to the ends of connected thongs. Thrown with phenomenal accuracy by the Gaucho, this flying weapon would trip the legs of the fleeing prey. The Gaucho used them to catch wild horses, cattle, wild boars, vicuñas, ostriches, deer and other animals. The Gaucho skills were used to round up, brand and maintain the herds.

As the dancer twirled the bolas, he allowed them to tap lightly on the floor, timing them with his tap dancing, stopping with the beat of the orchestra by dropping his arms causing a loud bang of the balls against the wooden floor. Then, raising his hands upward he saluted the audience.

The guests jumped up and shouted various applause slogans of the Gaucho and clapped for several minutes. It was a moment to remember.

After the guests sat down, the two attractive young dancing couples stepped onto the dance floor and passionately danced to several Argentina favorites.

When the two couples finished and bowed to the guest, we stood and cheered them.

"Mr. Cattaui, we should go to the limousines for our ride into downtown where your hotel reservations have been made. We will get you and your delegation checked in. You can rest the remainder of the day, and I will send the drivers to pick up all of you at about 8 P. M. They will bring you to the internationally famous Teatro Colón, the opera house, for a private presentation by the National Symphony Orchestra and the National Ballet," Sr. Morales told Mr. Cattaui as he handed him a program for the evening performance.

"Let's go, we surely need the rest from our long trip, and no doubt we will be able to go to sleep very fast since our stomachs are so full from this excellent meal," he replied.

The convoy of limousines, escorted by the special VIP police forces, made its way downtown and parked three abreast along the wide street in front of the hotel.

At about 7:30 P. M. the special VIP Police Force began arriving in front of the hotel. They went about the task of blocking off all traffic in both directions, occasionally directing one of the limousine drivers to park in several lines in front of the hotel.

The Filipino delegation began congregating on the steps of the hotel entrance and on the sidewalk under the wide protruding cover out past the curb of the street from the hotel. When everyone was accounted for, they entered the limousines for the ride to the opera house nearby.

Upon arriving at the Teatro Colón, they were greeted at the entrance by Sr. Morales. The Teatro Colón is the symbol of the city's high culture. Its acoustics, which are said to be near perfect, and the interior, includes some great colored glass domes and elaborate European chandeliers.

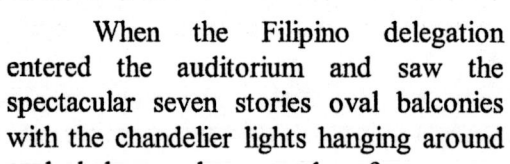

When the Filipino delegation entered the auditorium and saw the spectacular seven stories oval balconies with the chandelier lights hanging around each balcony about twelve feet apart, they were speechless and overcome by the beauty of the opera house. You could hear a pin drop.

"Mr. Cattaui, we have made complete arrangements for you and your delegation to be seated on the third story next to the center box, including an open bar with enjoy a food buffet and an assembly area right behind your box seats across the hallway. Your people may choose any boxes to the right or left of the center section of boxes where President Perón and his entourage will be sitting. The ushers will take you up to the third floor now and guide you to your boxes and seats," Sr. Morales announced as he turned to motion the conductor of the National Symphony Orchestra to play some music.

"You are a great host Sr. Morales, thank you very much for this opportunity to learn more about your culture," he replied.

455 / DON STEWART NIMMONS

At about 9:00 P. M. President Perón and his close cronies entered the center section boxes on the third level from a private entrance to the opera house. He motioned for the conductor to play. The Filipino national anthem began, and the Filipino delegation was more than pleased as they stood up and began to sing.

Afterward, the program began and everyone sat back and relaxed. During the performance by the Orchestra and the National Ballet, both the Filipinos and the Argentines occasionally met out in the third floor foyer to have a drink and talk. On one occasion Sr. Morales met with Mr. Cattaui.

"Tomorrow, at about 11:00 A. M. I will send one limousine with escorts to the hotel to pick up you and your select staff members and take you to Casa Rosada for the important business meeting with President Perón. Should you or your staff need anything at anytime such as having documents copied for the meetings; just call room 605 at the hotel and ask for Henrique Roca. He will take care of any of your needs while you are visiting us and be close by for a quick response. In the meantime, enjoy the ballet performance," Sr. Morales said deliberately, in a way to put Mr. Cattaui at ease for the evening and first meeting the next morning.

"Thank you again, and I send my thanks to President Perón for this special performance for us. I will contact Mr. Roca in the morning for any of our needs," Mr. Cattaui replied as he returned to his box.

The next morning just as planned the VIP Police Forces escorted the limousine to the entrance to the hotel. Mr. Cattaui and his staff were driven to Casa Rosada.

Upon entering the large conference hall, greetings were exchanged between President Perón, his cronies and Mr. Cattaui and his staff. Everyone sat down in his or her respective places.

"Mr. President, the first thing we want to do is get your permission to go to the Gold Depository vault at Banco de la Nación and investigate the security of the facilities. When we ship 2,000 metric tonnes of 24 carat Gold Bars to your bank for safekeeping, President Hermano, his companies and I want to be sure the assets are safe and secure. I have been instructed to personally look into this matter and the vault's security before any agreements are signed between us," Mr. Cattaui demanded without giving The President a chance to interrupt him.

"Sr. Morales, take Mr. Cattaui and his staff to the bank right now," Perón instructed.

"Ruth, I need you to come to the conference room immediately," Perón called his private secretary on his intercom.

Ruth entered the conference room with her stenography pad ready.

"Type this message on my presidential letterhead,

To: Dr. Arturo Gabriel, Secretaría de Hacienda, Banco de la Nación Argentina -- you know the address –

Dear Dr. Gabriel: This letter is to authorize the visit by Mr. Cattaui and two of his Filipino staff members to visit and evaluate the security system of the public section of the Gold Depository vault at the central bank. Also, they have access and may look from the doorway into the international Gold Depository vaults, but may not enter these vaults at this time. This authorization is limited for the time period between today and the end of this week.

Be sure the instrument is dated today. The presidential stamp and seal will be affixed to the letter after I have read it and signed it," Perón dictated to Ruth.

"Is that quick enough for you," Perón asked Mr. Cattaui smiling.

"You responded as I hoped that you would."

"Sr. Morales, you should have planned this event before Mr. Cattaui arrived. When you or I travel overseas to transact such asset business, safety and long-term security is our number one priority. To allow things to go smoothly you forgot this part of your checklist of subjects during Mr. Cattaui and his staffs meetings with us," Perón scolded him in front of everybody to make an impression.

A few moments later Ruth came into the conference room with the prepared authorization letter to Dr. Gabriel.

"Mr. President, you need to sign here and I will witness your signature," Ruth whispered to him as she handed him the letter on the President's letterhead.

Perón read the letter, signed it and stamped the presidential seal on the bottom.

"Just for you, Mr. Cattaui, now you may see just how secure our Central Bank Gold Depository Vaults are," Perón announced as he handed him the letter in his official envelope.

"For time sake would it be possible for your escort and chauffeur to take us to the bank right away?" Cattaui asked the president.

"Colonel Cordoza, escort Mr. Cattaui and his party to Banco de la Nación as soon as we finish here," Perón ordered his Chief of Protocol Escort, Colonel Cordoza.

"I am at your service Mr. Cattaui," Cordoza greeted Cattaui.

"Thank you very much. Let me say our adios to everyone here and then I will be ready to go," he replied.

Mr. Cattaui went around the conference room shaking each person's hand, thanked them for their courtesies and expressed his desire to ship some of the Gold Bullion in the Philippines to Argentina.

As he was leaving Casa Rosada, Mr. Cattaui spoke privately with President Perón.

"As soon as I have verified the security status of your bank today; we will make our plans to fly back to Manila tomorrow. I will advise you when and how the shipment will be made. I have hired an international security group to take the necessary steps to complete the shipments without everyone in the world knowing about it. You must, I repeat, must not acknowledge this secret transaction to anyone outside your inner circles," Cattaui instructed Perón.

Author's Photo

"No problem, you and your people in the Philippines can rest assured that I know how to handle secret transactions as important as this," Perón confidently replied.

Mr. Cattaui walked down the steps to the waiting limousine and was driven off to the bank. On the way to the bank he noticed some of the old buildings with large holes in the side of the marble and stone.

The VIP escort team of three motorcycles, two military trucks, and two cars began to clear the way with their sirens, flashing lights and horns honking at each intersection for the drive to the bank.

Along the way he turned to the chauffeur pointing to the buildings and asked. "Are those bullet holes on the buildings?"

"Yes, when President Perón and his military comrades staged the coup d'état and seized power in 1943 some of the holes were made then. Again, in 1955 when the Argentine military ousted him; some more of the holes were made. Looks like a brief battle to scare the people more than anything else is what happened here," the driver, replied.

"Does not sound like a very safe place," Cattaui answered. "In fact I noticed this limo has bullet proof windows."

"It's safe, we Argentines learn from our mistakes and keep revolutions from happening all the time. Yes, you are correct about the bulletproof windows. The President had this limousine specially equipped by an armament company from the United States prior to its delivery to Buenos Aires. Since President Perón returned in 1973, he has proven to everyone in the world that he is a strong and honest leader," the driver responded in his voice of conviction and loyalty.

"Also looks like they did not miss the Central Bank building with their target practice, Mr. Cattaui told his staff and the driver as they pulled up along the curb in front Banco de la Nación. Immediately, the police escorts with their sirens blaring blocked off the streets around the bank. The Colonel Cordoza jumped out of the limo and opened the doors for Mr. Cattaui and his aids.

"Here we are Sir. Follow me into the bank and I will lead you directly into Dr. Gabriel's offices. He is expecting you." Colonel Cordoza said as he took Mr. Cattaui by the arm and led him through the large doors to the bank.

"Gee, look at the sculptures and beautiful paintings up there," Mr. Cattaui enthusiastically said as he pointed to the huge dome lobby ceiling reaching some one hundred feet high or more.

"Beautiful, I have never seen something more striking and absolutely beautiful," his Filipino aid replied.

"The old world architecture is truly evident here in Buenos Aires," Mr. Cattaui further observed.

"We are very proud of our heritage Mr. Cattaui. These old buildings were constructed back in the early days of this century. The Spanish and Italian influence was very powerful in those days. Did you notice the broken sculptured statues imported in the 18th century from all over Europe placed around the ground floor lobby?" Colonel boasted and asked.

"Here is the entrance to the vault. Please feel free to step inside and look around in the first section. Not already being a Gold Depository customer of the bank, you may only glance through the doors into the Gold Depository sections."

"Colonel, you and your people know the proper diplomatic method to welcome your foreign guest. I need to have a picture taken for President Hermano of the entrance with the message for him together with the beautiful flower arrangements."

"We will take a photo from outside the bank's vault, but none will be allowed inside."

Subsequent to viewing the security of the Central Bank, the men walked up from the basement back into the lobby. "It goes without saying, but should President Hermano decide to complete the transaction of moving some of his Gold Bars here. No Diplomatic welcoming will be shown in the future. Everything will be done in complete confidentially. I hope that

TREASURES OF WAR – CONCEALED BY THE EVIL ONES / 460

you make that clear to President Perón." Mr. Cattaui firmly pointed out to the Colonel.

"I will make this a dominant subject in my report to him of our meeting here," Colonel Cordoza replied.

"It is difficult to keep from noticing these statues. Some of the very beautiful white statues have broken arms or the heads are missing and have blackened marks on them. Did you have a fire or something to cause these damages?" Mr. Cattaui confessed and asked.

"In one of the coup d'états, the strong opposition parties revolted against the image of the wealthy people. Storming the old Jockey Club was one of the first things that were done in the revolt. Many of these statues were thrown out from the upstairs windows of the Jockey Club into the streets and broken. The people ran around picking up a piece of a statue here and there. Then, they disappeared into the night with these historical artifacts of Argentina. Many years later an effort was made to find as many of them and put them back together. Some pieces were never brought forward. No telling where they might be today," The Colonel eagerly answered.

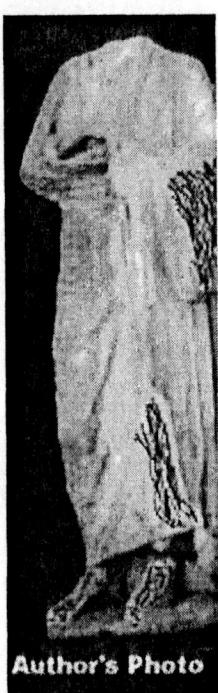

"Stunning, explain the blackened statues."

"Oh, those statues did not make it out of the Jockey Club before it burned to the ground."

"Your history has some violent periods also. I thought the Spanish American War and World War II were destructive days for the Philippines."

"I learned something today about your country here that I had no idea existed. Tomorrow morning I need you to have the limos pick us up at the hotel and take us to the airport for our return trip to Manila," Mr. Cattaui told Colonel Cordoza.

Two Years Later.

The Virgilio Hermano Foundation made several shipments of Gold Bars to Argentina to support some of his investments in Argentina.

DEPOSIT RECEIPT

We are holding one package in safekeeping containing the following:

Gold Bullion Certificate of Deposit – Reference Gold Bullion Certificate No. 5366090657-B. C. R, A, 602917 – Two Thousand and Five Hundred (2,500) Metric Tons of Gold Bullion (Aurum Utilium) Banco Central de la Republica Argentina (BCRA), Buenos Aires, Argentina.

Package is held in favor of owner – Virgilio Hermano Foundation.

Specifications:

COMMODITY:	Gold Bullion
CERTIFICATE NO.	BCRA F. S. -- 5366090657-B. C. R. A. 602917
QUANTITY:	Two Thousand Five Hundred (2,500) Metric Tons
TROY OUNCES:	Gold Bullion calculated at 32.1507428 Troy Ounces Per Kilogram
HALLMARKS:	Not Identified by Internationally Recognized Hallmarks.
FINENESS:	99.999% Purity.
BAR SIZE:	12.5 and 75.0 Kilograms Bars.
TITLE:	Free and Clear of All Liens and Encumbrances, Being Fully Negotiable per Instructions of Owner.

**Guarantee Of Certificate
No. BCRA F. S. 5366090657**

TREASURES OF WAR – CONCEALED BY THE EVIL ONES / 462

International Transaction Deposit
From HK&SIBL Bank

This **Author's Photo** **Argentina Government Property** *Certifies that there have been* BANCO CENTRAL REPUBLICA DE LA ARGENTINA *deposited in the Treasury of Banco Central Republica De La Argentina Four Thousand* **GOLD MEMORANDUM RECEIPT** *Metric Tons*

GMR

TREASURES OF WAR – CONCEALED BY THE EVIL ONES

Chapter Twenty Seven

The US – Japan Agreement of 1951

Article 14 and 15 of Chapter V – Claims and Property

WHY! WHY!
?   ?

And

Treaty of Mutual Cooperation and Security Between Japan and The United States of America

January 19, 1960

TREATY OF PEACE WITH JAPAN

Signed at San Francisco, 8 September 1951
Initial entry into force: 28 April 1952

WHEREAS the Allied Powers and Japan are resolved that henceforth their relations shall be those of nations which, as sovereign equals, cooperate in friendly association to promote their common welfare and to maintain international peace and security, and are therefore desirous of concluding a Treaty of Peace which will settle questions still outstanding as a result of the existence of a state of war between them;

WHEREAS Japan for its part declares its intention to apply for membership in the United Nations and in all circumstances to conform to the principles of the Charter of the United Nations; to strive to realize the objectives of the Universal Declaration of Human Rights; to seek to create within Japan conditions of stability and well-being as defined in Articles 55 and 56 of the Charter of the United Nations and already initiated by post-surrender Japanese legislation; and in public and private trade and commerce to conform to internationally accepted fair practices;

WHEREAS the Allied Powers welcome the intentions of Japan set out in the foregoing paragraph;

THE ALLIED POWERS AND JAPAN have therefore determined to conclude the present Treaty of Peace, and have accordingly appointed the undersigned Plenipotentiaries, who, after presentation of their full powers, found in good and due form, have agreed on the following provisions:

CHAPTER I

PEACE

Article 1

(a) The state of war between Japan and each of the Allied Powers is terminated as from the date on which the present Treaty comes into force between Japan and the Allied Power concerned as provided for in Article 23.

(b) The Allied Powers recognize the full sovereignty of the Japanese people over Japan and its territorial waters.

CHAPTER II

TERRITORY

Article 2

(a) Japan recognizing the independence of Korea, renounces all right, title and claim to Korea, including the islands of Quelpart, Port Hamilton and Dagelet.

(b) Japan renounces all right, title and claim to Formosa and the Pescadores.

(c) Japan renounces all right, title and claim to the Kurile Islands, and to that portion of Sakhalin and the islands adjacent to it over which Japan acquired sovereignty as a consequence of the Treaty of Portsmouth of 5 September 1905.

(d) Japan renounces all right, title and claim in connection with the League of Nations Mandate System, and accepts the action of the United Nations Security Council of 2 April 1947, extending the trusteeship system to the Pacific Islands formerly under mandate to Japan.

(e) Japan renounces all claim to any right or title to or interest in connection with any part of the Antarctic area, whether deriving from the activities of Japanese nationals or otherwise.

(f) Japan renounces all right, title and claim to the Spratly Islands and to the Paracel Islands.

Article 3

Japan will concur in any proposal of the United States to the United Nations to place under its trusteeship system, with the United States as the sole administering authority, Nansei Shoto south of 29deg. north latitude (including the Ryukyu Islands and the Daito Islands), Nanpo Shoto south of Sofu Gan (including the Bonin Islands, Rosario Island and the Volcano Islands) and Parece Vela and Marcus Island. Pending the making of such a proposal and affirmative action thereon, the United States will have the right to exercise all and any powers of administration, legislation and jurisdiction over the territory and inhabitants of these islands, including their territorial waters.

Article 4

(a) Subject to the provisions of paragraph (b) of this Article, the disposition of property of Japan and of its nationals in the areas referred to in Article 2, and their claims, including debts, against the authorities presently administering such areas and the residents (including juridical persons) thereof, and the disposition in Japan of property of such authorities and residents, and of claims, including debts, of such authorities and residents against Japan and its nationals, shall be the subject of special arrangements between Japan and such authorities. The property of any of the Allied Powers or its nationals in the areas referred to in Article 2 shall, insofar as this has not already been done, be returned by the administering authority in the condition in which it now exists. (The term nationals whenever used in the present Treaty includes juridical persons.)

(b) Japan recognizes the validity of dispositions of property of Japan and Japanese nationals made by or pursuant to directives of the United States Military Government in any of the areas referred to in Articles 2 and 3.

(c) Japanese owned submarine cables connection Japan with territory removed from Japanese control pursuant to the present Treaty shall be equally divided, Japan retaining the Japanese terminal and adjoining half of the cable, and the detached territory the remainder of the cable and connecting terminal facilities.

CHAPTER III

SECURITY

Article 5

(a) Japan accepts the obligations set forth in Article 2 of the Charter of the United Nations, and in particular the obligations

> (i) to settle its international disputes by peaceful means in such a manner that international peace and security, and justice, are not endangered;
>
> (ii) to refrain in its international relations from the threat or use of force against the territorial integrity or political independence of any State or in any other manner inconsistent with the Purposes of the United Nations;
>
> (iii) to give the United Nations every assistance in any action it takes in accordance with the Charter and to refrain from giving assistance to any State against which the United Nations may take preventive or enforcement action.

(b) The Allied Powers confirm that they will be guided by the principles of Article 2 of the Charter of the United Nations in their relations with Japan.

(c) The Allied Powers for their part recognize that Japan as a sovereign nation possesses the inherent right of individual or collective self-defense referred to in Article 51 of the Charter of the United Nations and that Japan may voluntarily enter into collective security arrangements.

Article 6

(a) All occupation forces of the Allied Powers shall be withdrawn from Japan as soon as possible after the coming into force of the present Treaty, and in any case not later than 90 days thereafter. Nothing in this provision shall, however, prevent the stationing or retention of foreign armed forces in

Japanese territory under or in consequence of any bilateral or multilateral agreements which have been or may be made between one or more of the Allied Powers, on the one hand, and Japan on the other.

(b) The provisions of Article 9 of the Potsdam Proclamation of 26 July 1945, dealing with the return of Japanese military forces to their homes, to the extent not already completed, will be carried out.

(c) All Japanese property for which compensation has not already been paid, which was supplied for the use of the occupation forces and which remains in the possession of those forces at the time of the coming into force of the present Treaty, shall be returned to the Japanese Government within the same 90 days unless other arrangements are made by mutual agreement.

CHAPTER IV
POLITICAL AND ECONOMIC CLAUSES
Article 7
(a) Each of the Allied Powers, within one year after the present Treaty has come into force between it and Japan, will notify Japan which of its prewar bilateral treaties or conventions with Japan it wishes to continue in force or revive, and any treaties or conventions so notified shall continue in force or by revived subject only to such amendments as may be necessary to ensure conformity with the present Treaty. The treaties and conventions so notified shall be considered as having been continued in force or revived three months after the date of notification and shall be registered with the Secretariat of the United Nations. All such treaties and conventions as to which Japan is not so notified shall be regarded as abrogated.

(b) Any notification made under paragraph (a) of this Article may except from the operation or revival of a treaty or convention any territory for the international relations of which the notifying Power is responsible, until three months after the date on which notice is given to Japan that such exception shall cease to apply.

Article 8

(a) Japan will recognize the full force of all treaties now or hereafter concluded by the Allied Powers for terminating the state of war initiated on 1 September 1939, as well as any other arrangements by the Allied Powers for or in connection with the restoration of peace. Japan also accepts the arrangements made for terminating the former League of Nations and Permanent Court of International Justice.

(b) Japan renounces all such rights and interests as it may derive from being a signatory power of the Conventions of St. Germain-en-Laye of 10 September 1919, and the Straits Agreement of Montreux of 20 July 1936, and from Article 16 of the Treaty of Peace with Turkey signed at Lausanne on 24 July 1923.

(c) Japan renounces all rights, title and interests acquired under, and is discharged from all obligations resulting from, the Agreement between Germany and the Creditor Powers of 20 January 1930 and its Annexes, including the Trust Agreement, dated 17 May 1930, the Convention of 20 January 1930, respecting the Bank for International Settlements; and the Statutes of the Bank for International Settlements. Japan will notify to the Ministry of Foreign Affairs in Paris within six months of the first coming into force of the present Treaty its renunciation of the rights, title and interests referred to in this paragraph.

Article 9

Japan will enter promptly into negotiations with the Allied Powers so desiring for the conclusion of bilateral and multilateral agreements providing for the regulation or limitation of fishing and the conservation and development of fisheries on the high seas.

Article 10

Japan renounces all special rights and interests in China, including all benefits and privileges resulting from the provisions of the final Protocol signed at Peking on 7 September 1901, and all annexes, notes and documents supplementary thereto, and agrees to the abrogation in respect to Japan of the said protocol, annexes, notes and documents.

Article 11
Japan accepts the judgments of the International Military Tribunal for the Far East and of other Allied War Crimes Courts both within and outside Japan, and will carry out the sentences imposed thereby upon Japanese nationals imprisoned in Japan. The power to grant clemency, to reduce sentences and to parole with respect to such prisoners may not be exercised except on the decision of the Government or Governments which imposed the sentence in each instance, and on recommendation of Japan. In the case of persons sentenced by the International Military Tribunal for the Far East, such power may not be exercised except on the decision of a majority of the Governments represented on the Tribunal, and on the recommendation of Japan.

Article 12
(a) Japan declares its readiness promptly to enter into negotiations for the conclusion with each of the Allied Powers of treaties or agreements to place their trading, maritime and other commercial relations on a stable and friendly basis.

(b) Pending the conclusion of the relevant treaty or agreement, Japan will, during a period of four years from the first coming into force of the present Treaty

(1) accord to each of the Allied Powers, its nationals, products and vessels

(i) most-favoured-nation treatment with respect to customs duties, charges, restrictions and other regulations on or in connection with the importation and exportation of goods;

(ii) national treatment with respect to shipping, navigation and imported goods, and with respect to natural and juridical persons and their interests - such treatment to include all matters pertaining to the levying and collection of taxes, access to the courts, the making and performance of contracts, rights to property (tangible and intangible), participating in juridical entities constituted under Japanese law, and generally the conduct of all kinds of business and professional activities;

(2) ensure that external purchases and sales of Japanese state trading enterprises shall be based solely on commercial considerations.

(c) In respect to any matter, however, Japan shall be obliged to accord to an Allied Power national treatment, or most-favored-nation treatment, only to the extent that the Allied Power concerned accords Japan national treatment or most-favored-nation treatment, as the case may be, in respect of the same matter. The reciprocity envisaged in the foregoing sentence shall be determined, in the case of products, vessels and juridical entities of, and persons domiciled in, any non-metropolitan territory of an Allied Power, and in the case of juridical entities of, and persons domiciled in, any state or province of an Allied Power having a federal government, by reference to the treatment accorded to Japan in such territory, state or province.

(d) In the application of this Article, a discriminatory measure shall not be considered to derogate from the grant of national or most-favored-nation treatment, as the case may be, if such measure is based on an exception customarily provided for in the commercial treaties of the party applying it, or on the need to safeguard that party's external financial position or balance of payments (except in respect to shipping and navigation), or on the need to maintain its essential security interests, and provided such measure is proportionate to the circumstances and not applied in an arbitrary or unreasonable manner.

(e) Japan's obligations under this Article shall not be affected by the exercise of any Allied rights under Article 14 of the present Treaty; nor shall the provisions of this Article be understood as limiting the undertakings assumed by Japan by virtue of Article 15 of the Treaty.

Article 13
(a) Japan will enter into negotiations with any of the Allied Powers, promptly upon the request of such Power or Powers, for the conclusion of bilateral or multilateral agreements relating to international civil air transport.
(b) Pending the conclusion of such agreement or agreements, Japan will, during a period of four years from the first coming into force of the present Treaty, extend to such Power treatment not less favorable with respect to air-traffic rights and privileges than those exercised by any such Powers at the date of such coming into force, and will accord complete equality of opportunity in respect to the operation and development of air services.
(c) Pending its becoming a party to the Convention on International Civil Aviation in accordance with Article 93 thereof, Japan will give effect to the provisions of that Convention applicable to the international navigation of aircraft, and will give effect to the standards, practices and procedures adopted as annexes to the Convention in accordance with the terms of the Convention.

CHAPTER V
CLAIMS AND PROPERTY
Article 14
(a) It is recognized that Japan should pay reparations to the Allied Powers for the damage and suffering caused by it during the war. Nevertheless it is also recognized that the resources of Japan are not presently sufficient, if it is to maintain a viable economy, to make complete reparation for all such damage and suffering and at the same time meet its other obligations.
Therefore,

1. Japan will promptly enter into negotiations with Allied Powers so desiring, whose present territories were occupied by Japanese forces and damaged by Japan, with a view to assisting to compensate those countries for the cost of repairing the damage done, by making available the services of the Japanese people in production, salvaging and other work for the Allied Powers in

question. Such arrangements shall avoid the imposition of additional liabilities on other Allied Powers, and, where the manufacturing of raw materials is called for, they shall be supplied by the Allied Powers in question, so as not to throw any foreign exchange burden upon Japan.

2. (I) Subject to the provisions of subparagraph (II) below, each of the Allied Powers shall have the right to seize, retain, liquidate or otherwise dispose of all property, rights and interests of

(a) Japan and Japanese nationals,

(b) persons acting for or on behalf of Japan or Japanese nationals, and

(c) entities owned or controlled by Japan or Japanese nationals,

which on the first coming into force of the present Treaty were subject to its jurisdiction. The property, rights and interests specified in this subparagraph shall include those now blocked, vested or in the possession or under the control of enemy property authorities of Allied Powers, which belong to, or were held or managed on behalf of, any of the persons or entities mentioned in (a), (b) or (c) above at the time such assets came under the controls of such authorities.

(II) The following shall be excepted from the right specified in subparagraph (I) above:

(i) property of Japanese natural persons who during the war resided with the permission of the Government concerned in the territory of one of the Allied Powers, other than territory occupied by Japan, except property subjected to restrictions during the war and not released from such restrictions as of the date of the first coming into force of the present Treaty;

(ii) all real property, furniture and fixtures owned by the Government of Japan and used for diplomatic or consular purposes, and all personal furniture and furnishings and other private property not of an investment nature which was normally necessary for the carrying out of diplomatic and consular functions, owned by Japanese diplomatic and consular personnel;

(iii) property belonging to religious bodies or private charitable institutions and used exclusively for religious or charitable purposes;

(iv) property, rights and interests which have come within its jurisdiction in consequence of the resumption of trade and financial relations subsequent to 2 September 1945, between the country concerned and Japan, except such as have resulted from transactions contrary to the laws of the Allied Power concerned;

(v) obligations of Japan or Japanese nationals, any right, title or interest in tangible property located in Japan, interests in enterprises organized under the laws of Japan, or any paper evidence thereof; provided that this exception shall only apply to obligations of Japan and its nationals expressed in Japanese currency.

(III) Property referred to in exceptions (i) through (v) above shall be returned subject to reasonable expenses for its preservation and administration. If any such property has been liquidated the proceeds shall be returned instead.

(IV) The right to seize, retain, liquidate or otherwise dispose of property as provided in subparagraph (I) above shall be exercised in accordance with the laws of the Allied Power concerned, and the owner shall have only such rights as may be given him by those laws.

(V) The Allied Powers agree to deal with Japanese trademarks and literary and artistic property rights on a basis as favorable to Japan as circumstances ruling in each country will permit.

(b) Except as otherwise provided in the present Treaty, the Allied Powers waive all reparations claims of the Allied Powers, other claims of the Allied Powers and their nationals arising out of any actions taken by Japan and its nationals in the course of the prosecution of the war, and claims of the Allied Powers for direct military costs of occupation.

Article 15

(a) Upon application made within nine months of the coming into force of the present Treaty between Japan and the Allied Power concerned, Japan will, within six months of the date of such application, return the property, tangible and intangible, and all rights or interests of any kind in Japan of each Allied Power and its nationals which was within Japan at any time between 7 December 1941 and 2 September 1945, unless the owner has freely disposed thereof without duress or fraud. Such property shall be returned free of all encumbrances and charges to which it may have become subject because of the war, and without any charges for its return. Property whose return is not applied for by or on behalf of the owner or by his Government within the prescribed period may be disposed of by the Japanese Government as it may determine. In cases where such property was within Japan on 7 December 1941, and cannot be returned or has suffered injury or damage as a result of the war, compensation will be made on terms not less favorable than the terms provided in the draft Allied Powers Property Compensation Law approved by the Japanese Cabinet on 13 July 1951.

(b) With respect to industrial property rights impaired during the war, Japan will continue to accord to the Allied Powers and their nationals benefits no less than those heretofore accorded by Cabinet Orders No. 309 effective 1 September 1949, No. 12 effective 28 January 1950, and No. 9 effective 1 February 1950, all as now amended, provided such nationals have applied for such benefits within the time limits prescribed therein.

(c) (i) Japan acknowledges that the literary and artistic property rights which existed in Japan on 6 December 1941, in respect to the published and unpublished works of the Allied Powers and their nationals have continued in force since that date, and recognizes those rights which have arisen, or but for the war would have arisen, in Japan since that date, by the operation of any conventions and agreements to which Japan was a party on that date, irrespective of whether or not such conventions or agreements were abrogated or suspended upon or since the outbreak of war by the domestic law of Japan or of the Allied Power concerned.

(ii) Without the need for application by the proprietor of the right and without the payment of any fee or compliance with any other formality, the period from 7 December 1941 until the coming into force of the present Treaty between Japan and the Allied Power concerned shall be excluded from the running of the normal term of such rights; and such period, with an additional period of six months, shall be excluded from the time within which a literary work must be translated into Japanese in order to obtain translating rights in Japan.

Article 16

As an expression of its desire to indemnify those members of the armed forces of the Allied Powers who suffered undue hardships while prisoners of war of Japan, Japan will transfer its assets and those of its nationals in countries which were neutral during the war, or which were at war with any of the Allied Powers, or, at its option, the equivalent of such assets, to the International Committee of the Red Cross which shall liquidate such assets and distribute the resultant fund to appropriate national agencies, for the benefit of former prisoners of war and their families on such basis as it may determine to be equitable. The categories of assets described in Article 14(a)2(II)(ii) through (v) of the present Treaty shall be excepted from transfer, as well as assets of Japanese natural persons not residents of Japan on the first coming into force of the Treaty. It is equally understood that the transfer provision of this Article has no application to the 19,770 shares in the Bank for International Settlements presently owned by Japanese financial institutions.

Article 17

(a) Upon the request of any of the Allied Powers, the Japanese Government shall review and revise in conformity with international law any decision or order of the Japanese Prize Courts in cases involving ownership rights of nationals of that Allied Power and shall supply copies of all documents comprising the records of these cases, including the decisions taken and orders issued. In any case in which such review or revision shows that restoration is due, the provisions of Article 15 shall apply to the property concerned.

(b) The Japanese Government shall take the necessary measures to enable nationals of any of the Allied Powers at any time within one year from the coming into force of the present Treaty between Japan and the Allied Power concerned to submit to the appropriate Japanese authorities for review any judgment given by a Japanese court between 7 December 1941 and such coming into force, in any proceedings in which any such national was unable to make adequate presentation of his case either as plaintiff or defendant. The Japanese Government shall provide that, where the national has suffered injury by reason of any such judgment, he shall be restored in the position in which he was before the judgment was given or shall be afforded such relief as may be just and equitable in the circumstances.

Article 18

(a) It is recognized that the intervention of the state of war has not affected the obligation to pay pecuniary debts arising out of obligations and contracts (including those in respect of bonds) which existed and rights which were acquired before the existence of a state of war, and which are due by the Government or nationals of Japan to the Government or nationals of one of the Allied Powers, or are due by the Government or nationals of one of the Allied Powers to the Government or nationals of Japan. The intervention of a state of war shall equally not be regarded as affecting the obligation to consider on their merits claims for loss or damage to property or for personal injury or death which arose before the existence of a state of war, and which may be presented or re-presented by the Government of one of the Allied Powers to the Government of Japan, or by the Government of Japan to any of the Governments of the Allied Powers. The provisions of this paragraph are without prejudice to the rights conferred by Article 14.

(b) Japan affirms its liability for the prewar external debt of the Japanese State and for debts of corporate bodies subsequently declared to be liabilities of the Japanese State, and expresses its intention to enter into negotiations at an early date with its creditors with respect to the resumption of payments on those debts; to encourage negotiations in respect to other prewar claims and obligations; and to facilitate the transfer of sums accordingly.

Article 19

(a) Japan waives all claims of Japan and its nationals against the Allied Powers and their nationals arising out of the war or out of actions taken because of the existence of a state of war, and waives all claims arising from the presence, operations or actions of forces or authorities of any of the Allied Powers in Japanese territory prior to the coming into force of the present Treaty.

(b) The foregoing waiver includes any claims arising out of actions taken by any of the Allied Powers with respect to Japanese ships between 1 September 1939 and the coming into force of the present Treaty, as well as any claims and debts arising in respect to Japanese prisoners of war and civilian internees in the hands of the Allied Powers, but does not include Japanese claims specifically recognized in the laws of any Allied Power enacted since 2 September 1945.

(c) Subject to reciprocal renunciation, the Japanese Government also renounces all claims (including debts) against Germany and German nationals on behalf of the Japanese Government and Japanese nationals, including intergovernmental claims and claims for loss or damage sustained during the war, but excepting (a) claims in respect of contracts entered into and rights acquired before 1 September 1939, and (b) claims arising out of trade and financial relations between Japan and Germany after 2 September 1945. Such renunciation shall not prejudice actions taken in accordance with Articles 16 and 20 of the present Treaty.

(d) Japan recognizes the validity of all acts and omissions done during the period of occupation under or in consequence of directives of the occupation authorities or authorized by Japanese law at that time, and will take no action subjecting Allied nationals to civil or criminal liability arising out of such acts or omissions.

Article 20

Japan will take all necessary measures to ensure such disposition of German assets in Japan as has been or may be determined by those powers entitled under the Protocol of the proceedings of the Berlin Conference of 1945 to dispose of those assets, and pending the final disposition of such assets will be responsible for the conservation and administration thereof.

Article 21

Notwithstanding the provisions of Article 25 of the present Treaty, China shall be entitled to the benefits of Articles 10 and 14(a)2; and Korea to the benefits of Articles 2, 4, 9 and 12 of the present Treaty.

CHAPTER VI
SETTLEMENT OF DISPUTES

Article 22

If in the opinion of any Party to the present Treaty there has arisen a dispute concerning the interpretation or execution of the Treaty, which is not settled by reference to a special claims tribunal or by other agreed means, the dispute shall, at the request of any party thereto, be referred for decision to the International Court of Justice. Japan and those Allied Powers which are not already parties to the Statute of the International Court of Justice will deposit with the Registrar of the Court, at the time of their respective ratifications of the present Treaty, and in conformity with the resolution of the United Nations Security Council, dated 15 October 1946, a general declaration accepting the jurisdiction, without special agreement, of the Court generally in respect to all disputes of the character referred to in this Article.

CHAPTER VII
FINAL CLAUSES

Article 23

(a) The present Treaty shall be ratified by the States which sign it, including Japan, and will come into force for all the States which have then ratified it, when instruments of ratification have been deposited by Japan and by a majority, including the United States of America as the principal occupying Power, of the following States, namely Australia, Canada, Ceylon, France, Indonesia, the Kingdom of the Netherlands, New Zealand, Pakistan, the Republic of the Philippines, the United Kingdom of Great Britain and Northern Ireland, and the United States of America. The present Treaty shall come into force of each State which subsequently ratifies it, on the date of the deposit of its instrument of ratification.

(b) If the Treaty has not come into force within nine months after the date of the deposit of Japan's ratification, any State which has ratified it may bring the Treaty into force between itself and Japan by a notification to that effect given to the Governments of Japan and the United States of America not later than three years after the date of deposit of Japan's ratification.

Article 24

All instruments of ratification shall be deposited with the Government of the United States of America which will notify all the signatory States of each such deposit, of the date of the coming into force of the Treaty under paragraph (a) of Article 23, and of any notifications made under paragraph (b) of Article 23.

Article 25

For the purposes of the present Treaty the Allied Powers shall be the States at war with Japan, or any State which previously formed a part of the territory of a State named in Article 23, provided that in each case the State concerned has signed and ratified the Treaty. Subject to the provisions of Article 21, the present Treaty shall not confer any rights, titles or benefits on any State which is not an Allied Power as herein defined; nor shall any right, title or interest of Japan be deemed to be diminished or prejudiced by any provision of the Treaty in favour of a State which is not an Allied Power as so defined.

Article 26
Japan will be prepared to conclude with any State which signed or adhered to the United Nations Declaration of 1 January 1942, and which is at war with Japan, or with any State which previously formed a part of the territory of a State named in Article 23, which is not a signatory of the present Treaty, a bilateral Treaty of Peace on the same or substantially the same terms as are provided for in the present Treaty, but this obligation on the part of Japan will expire three years after the first coming into force of the present Treaty. Should Japan make a peace settlement or war claims settlement with any State granting that State greater advantages than those provided by the present Treaty, those same advantages shall be extended to the parties to the present Treaty.

Article 27
The present Treaty shall be deposited in the archives of the Government of the United States of America which shall furnish each signatory State with a certified copy thereof.
IN FAITH WHEREOF the undersigned Plenipotentiaries have signed the present Treaty.
DONE at the city of San Francisco this eighth day of September 1951, in the English, French, and Spanish languages, all being equally authentic, and in the Japanese language.

For Argentina:
    Hipólito J. PAZ

For Australia:
    Percy C. SPENDER

For Belgium:
    Paul VAN ZEELAND SILVERCRUYS

For Bolivia:
    Luis GUACHALLA

For Brazil:
>Carlos MARTINS
>A. DE MELLO-FRANCO

For Cambodia:
>PHLENG

For Canada:
>Lester B. PEARSON
>R.W. MAYHEW

For Ceylon:
>J.R. JAYEWARDENE
>G.C.S. COREA
>R.G. SENANAYAKE

For Chile:
>F. NIETO DEL RÍO

For Colombia:
>Cipríano RESTREPO JARAMILLO
>Sebastián OSPINA

For Costa Rica:
>J. Rafael OREAMUNO
>V. VARGAS
>Luis DOBLES SÁNCHEZ

For Cuba:
>O. GANS
>L. MACHADO
>Joaquín MEYER

For the Dominican Republic:
>V. ORDÓÑEZ
>Luis F. THOMEN

For Ecuador:

    A. QUEVEDO
    R.G. VALENZUELA

For Egypt:

    Kamil A. RAHIM

For El Salvador:

    Héctor DAVID CASTRO
    Luis RIVAS PALACIOS

For Ethiopia:

    Men YAYEJIJRAD

For France:

    SCHUMANN
    H. BONNET
    Paul-Émile NAGGIAR

For Greece:

    A.G. POLITIS

For Guatemala:

    E. CASTILLO A.
    A.M. ORELLANA
    J. MENDOZA

For Haiti:

    Jacques N. LÉGER
    Gust. LARAQUE

For Honduras:

    J.E. VALENZUELA
    Roberto GÁLVEZ B.
    Raúl ALVARADO T.

For Indonesia:

    Ahmad SUBARDJO

For Iran:
> A.G. ARDALAN

For Iraq:
> A.I. BAKR

For Laos:
> SAVANG

For Lebanon:
> Charles MALIK

For Liberia:
> Gabriel L. DENNIS
> James ANDERSON
> Raymond HORACE
> J. Rudolf GRIMES

For the Grand Duchy of Luxembourg:
> Hugues LE GALLAIS

For Mexico:
> Rafael DE LA COLINA
> Gustavo DÍAZ ORDAZ
> A.P. GASGA

For the Netherlands:
> D.U. STIKKER
> J.H. VAN ROIJEN

For New Zealand:
> C. BERENDSEN

For Nicaragua:
> G. SEVILLA SACASA
> Gustavo MANZANARES

For Norway:
> Wilhelm Munthe MORGENSTERNE

For Pakistan:
> ZAFRULLAH KHAN

For Panama:
> Ignacio MOLINO
> José A. REMON
> Alfredo ALEMÁN
> J. CORDOVEZ

For Peru:
> Luis Oscar BOETTNER

For the Republic of the Philippines:
> Carlos P. RÓMULO
> J.M. ELIZALDE
> Vicente FRANCISCO
> Diosdado MACAPAGAL
> Emiliano T. TIRONA
> V.G. SINCO

For Saudi Arabia:
> Asad AL-FAQIH

For Syria:
> F. EL-KHOURI

For Turkey:
> Feridun C. ERKIN

For the Union of South Africa:
> G.P. JOOSTE

For the United Kingdom of
Great Britain and Northern Ireland:
> Herbert MORRISON
> Kenneth YOUNGER
> Oliver FRANKS

For the United States of America:

>Dean ACHESON
>John Foster DULLES
>Alexander WILEY
>John J. SPARKMAN

For Uruguay:

>José A. MORA

For Venezuela:

>Antonio M. ARAUJO
>R. GALLEGOS M.

For Viet-Nam:

>T.V. HUU
>T. VINH
>D. THANH
>BUU KINH

For Japan:

>Shigeru YOSHIDA
>Hayato IKEDA
>Gizo TOMABECHI
>Niro HOSHIJIMA
>Muneyoshi TOKUGAWA
>Hisato ICHIMADA

TREATY OF MUTUAL COOPERATION AND SECURITY BETWEEN JAPAN AND THE UNITED STATES OF AMERICA

Japan and the United States of America,

Desiring to strengthen the bonds of peace and friendship traditionally existing between them, and to uphold the principles of democracy, individual liberty, and the rule of law,

Desiring further to encourage closer economic cooperation between them and to promote conditions of economic stability and well being in their countries,

Reaffirming their faith in the purposes and principles of the Charter of the United Nations, and their desire to live in peace with all peoples and all governments,

Recognizing that they have the inherent right of individual or collective self-defense as affirmed in the Charter of the United Nations,

Considering that they have a common concern in the maintenance of international peace and security in the Far East,

Having resolved to conclude a treaty of mutual cooperation and security, Therefore, agree as follows:

ARTICLE I

The Parties undertake, as set forth in the Charter of the United Nations, to settle any international disputes in which they may be involved by peaceful means in such a manner that international peace and security and justice are not endangered and to refrain in their international relations from the threat or use of force against the territorial integrity or political independence of any state, or in any other manner inconsistent with the purposes of the United Nations.

The Parties will endeavor in concert with other peace-loving countries to strengthen the United Nations so that its mission of maintaining international peace and security may be discharged more effectively.

ARTICLE II

The Parties will contribute toward the further development of peaceful and friendly international relations by strengthening their free institutions, by bringing about a better understanding of the principles upon which these institutions are founded, and by promoting conditions of stability and well being. They will seek to eliminate conflict in their international economic policies and will encourage economic collaboration between them.

ARTICLE III

The Parties, individually and in cooperation with each other, by means of continuous and effective self-help and mutual aid will maintain and develop, subject to their constitutional provisions, their capacities to resist armed attack.

ARTICLE IV

The Parties will consult together from time to time regarding the implementation of this Treaty, and, at the request of either Party, whenever the security of Japan or international peace and security in the Far East is threatened.

ARTICLE V

Each Party recognizes that an armed attack against either Party in the territories under the administration of Japan would be dangerous to its own peace and safety and declares that it would act to meet the common danger in accordance with its constitutional provisions and processes.

Any such armed attack and all measures taken as a result thereof shall be immediately reported to the Security Council of the United Nations in accordance with the provisions of Article 51 of the Charter. Such measures shall be terminated when the Security Council has taken the measures necessary to restore and maintain international peace and security.

ARTICLE VI

For the purpose of contributing to the security of Japan and the maintenance of international peace and security in the Far East, the United States of America is granted the use by its land, air and naval forces of facilities and areas in Japan.

The use of these facilities and areas as well as the status of United States armed forces in Japan shall be governed by a separate agreement, replacing the Administrative Agreement under Article III of the Security Treaty between Japan and the United States of America, signed at Tokyo on February 28, 1952, as amended, and by such other arrangements as may be agreed upon.

ARTICLE VII

This Treaty does not affect and shall not be interpreted as affecting in any way the rights and obligations of the Parties under the Charter of the United Nations or the responsibility of the United Nations for the maintenance of international peace and security.

ARTICLE VIII

This Treaty shall be ratified by Japan and the United States of America in accordance with their respective constitutions,Œ processes and will enter into force on the date on which the instruments of ratification there of have been exchanged by them in Tokyo.

ARTICLE IX

The Security Treaty between Japan and the United States of America signed at the city of San Francisco on September 8, 1951 shall expire upon the entering into force of this Treaty.

ARTICLE X

This Treaty shall remain in force until in the opinion of the Governments of Japan and the United States of America there shall have come into force such United Nations arrangements as will satisfactorily provide for the maintenance of international peace and security in the Japan area. However, after the Treaty has been in force for ten years, either Party may give notice to the other Party of its intention to terminate the Treaty, in which case the Treaty shall terminate one year after such notice has been given.

IN WITNESS WHEREOF the undersigned Plenipotentiaries have signed this Treaty.

DONE in duplicate at Washington in the Japanese and English languages, both equally authentic, this 19th day of January, 1960

FOR JAPAN:
Nobusuke Kishi
Aiichiro Fujiyama
Mitsujiro Ishii
Tadashi Adachi
Koichiro Asakai

FOR THE UNITED STATES OF AMERICA:
Christian A. Herter
Douglas MacArthur 2nd
J. Graham Parsons

Houston, Texas --- Parade in 1949

TREASURES OF WAR – CONCEALED BY THE EVIL ONES

Chapter Twenty Eight

Florida BOP Infighting

and

Herbert "Bert Junior" Dover, Jr. – Permission To Sell Illegal Gold

To

Secretary of U. S. Treasury

United States Senate
Office of the Born of Privilege Leader
(BOP-Leader)
Washington, D. C.

Mr. Executive Director, the reports you have received over the past forty-eight months concerning the Born Of Privilege (BOP) have been many and varied. More than likely the contents of these reports held half-truths, etc. due to the many intra-mural actions taken by people who sought recognition be either on one side of the managerial political fence or the other.

I am going to chronologically report certain areas you are aware of and express/suggest changes that are essential to the success of this operation. I realize that I am jeopardizing what little position I have by submitting this report to you.

THIS IS A ONE MAN SHOW -- daily stated by our present manager along with such phrases as 'if you don't do this or that, heads are going to roll around here', again, stated daily and the ending statement to every staff meeting. Naturally, the personnel here have heard these quotations so often that it goes in one ear and out the other.

Personally, I am ready to return to Washington immediately as any suggestion or advice granted in behalf of BOP is taken with sarcasm and instead of a quiet discussion concerning the pros and cons of the subject a great oration covering the qualifications, brilliance and merit of the manager ensues. We have an individual here who at one time was a used car salesman and it is his belief that the tactics used on the show room floor are the same as those that should be employed to sell our contributions. There is no appreciation for anyone's intelligence whatsoever; this includes personnel in Florida, California and Washington, D. C. At this present time, it is my personal feeling that when two people are at cross-purposes with each other, as we are, no real accomplishments can be realized.

I have definite reasons for stating the foregoing and an explanation of why I feel this way requires entering into personalities and performance. Delving into this area is necessary, but certainly one that I do not particularly care for.

There are many examples of mismanagement here; they include the treatment of ESSO, General Auto and Trucks, Burton Oil and Gas and Clayton Agriculture and Food. While working on the Clayton cotton problem certain simple discoveries were made that I reported to Bushel and yourself. The minute that Prescott saw a 'close' coming about, he immediately enforces a golf date with the management of Clayton. This was all done, at a time when we were/are just arriving at certain financial conclusions and are far from the final solution. Well, 'Mr. Big Shot', like he did at General Auto and Trucks, shoots off his big mouth about the competition, which at the time we do not even have to worry about and furthermore have no reasons to consider. This is an area that I was handling cautiously due to past experience with the Clayton group. We are not dealing with 'babes in the woods' as the Clayton group here has excellent operations and like California – they need to be treated with caution and respect. All comments made by us will have to be backed up and explained factually. We will get contributions from Clayton – but as I reported earlier, the amount will be a far cry from any five hundred thousand dollars. The reason for a miscalculation here is that no one knew the insiders like I do.

The ESSO situation deserves 'Stellar Recognition'. One of my men reported that Charlie would make the final decision with regard to the approach they would take in resolving their political contribution problems. They informed us that Charlie is the man to contact. We knew that Charlie was in Connecticut and no decision or further study would be made until he returned. I told Prescott this would be a reprieve from out standpoint insofar as it would allow us time to contact other petroleum companies and thereby qualify our position in relation to resolving ESSO's problems.

I left early last Friday in order to check out an idea I had that may help us utilize our investment capabilities further (this is another story). The minute I left, according to our office personnel, Prescott came running into David's office saying – 'lets go to ESSO' – David, naturally, asked why I was not going and received a moot reply.

I found out about all of this by our driver that same night, as even he felt something was wrong. Anyhow, Prescott made a call on Dr. Morrow, whom you met, and shot the works. He offered the establishment of a complete investment package and so confused Dr. Morrow that he become lost in the ordeal and had Prescott repeat the whole deal over and over again and finally said that he would have Charlie look it over when he returned from Connecticut. All of this was done at a time when we know that ESSO has money for political contributions and the day after the U. S. government protest on tax benefits were published. Then, Prescott pushes the whole darn mess over on me – which is typical – after he completely destroyed what little we had built. As far as I am concerned all efforts directed toward ESSO will have to begin anew.

I confronted Prescott about all of this and received his version as well as David's. From what I can see – I repeat – this was handled with no regard to staff suggestions. Yes – 'THIS IS A ONE-MAN SHOW'.

As you recall when you were here I questioned our entry into ESSO until we learned more about the ancillary divisions and the nature of them. We are not qualified to talk intelligently about all of these types of operations and furthermore, we only place our ignorance on public display by even attempting such an endeavor without coordinating the joint goals of BOP and ESSO.

Sir, we have a man here who rarely arrived at the office before 4 pm last year and only on rare occasions does he arrive before 11 am now. He would deliver me at home and agree to pick me up 7:45 am the next morning. In all the time that I have been down here he has never arrived before 9:30 am at the earliest. Therefore, I confronted him about this many times – I have taken taxis after waiting an hour to two hours – in other words. I have insulted him in every way possible in order to get some type of reaction from him, but to no avail. This action is not due to his lack of transportation. Soon after you left he bought a Rolls Royce for his personal use and I was to have his driver at my disposal for client contact. This is a laugh – I realized this when Sam Mancuso and I arrived at the airport and the driver had taken our manager to the country club rather than meet us. I do not take this as a personal affront, but Burton Oil and Gas personnel are difficult to contact and we passed up a beautiful opportunity to establish some good contacts at their base in Dallas. I have happily resorted to taxis and catching rides with other members of our staff. Because of this I feel my effectiveness down here has been reduced by 65%.

THIS IS A ONE-MAN SHOW – again, repeated when the Florida Power Industries and Development deal came up; however, he did follow my advice by contacting our attorney and having him ask about the necessary Florida requirements thereby allowing a qualified person the opportunity to refute any underhanded comments or traps Florida might offer, - to have someone there who knew our position and would not confuse our efforts further. This he does to – but now, he checks with the attorney then makes statements protecting us as of his origin. This may be well and fine in many areas; however, in this regard no chances should be taken and all the facilities we have should be open for BOP use. He is in Tallahassee now with directions from the attorney on the essentials but – still – 'THIS IS A ONE-MAN SHOW'. As he says, 'Washington, D. C. will screw it up'.

In his efforts to build his self esteem he calls and reports to the attorney clan that he is going to bring in the Lindsey group and many other diversifications. Here too, I have confronted him on his approach and his reply is a childish 'Oh well – I just want to keep them shook-up'. We are a long way from shaking these people as evidenced by their control on our entrances and exits in their domain. Our biggest hope in order to survive this year will be the Coop deal – without the strong local respected BOP political influence on this we don't have a Chinaman's chance in a pickle barrel.

If the Coop deal can be closed we will have plenty of funds to increase our investment portfolio and finish out the year. Prescott has our boys contacting the small companies. The irony to all of this is that the smaller ones are being bought-up by the financially stronger and larger companies and our men are trying to win over the smaller ones. Why?

Where does this leave us? We can expect two things. One, like other industries around the country, only the large will survive and they will of necessity have to expand. This expansion will probably take place in three years from now.

Personnel problems continually plague us. The main skeleton crew here has been well spoiled in that as far as I am concerned they are overpaid for what they produce. Salaries are much too high and I've made very effort to get his over to the men. As far as I am concerned we should plan to replenish much of our staff with new people – hungrier men should replace the present ones who definitely have conflicting interests. These problems I agree, were here while my father, 'Bert' Sr., was here, yet, after this year it will be time to begin a phase out.

Our administrative staff is poor. Our advertising staff is terrible as you know – here again, this is a case where these people know one leader. They cannot be expected to operate as efficiently as our Washington, D. C. crew but it does seem that they could use a little of their own imagination.

Another area is developing new clients in other industries. We are just renewing our efforts to get the same people. This was tried once before with Father's people but with no success for new clients. This will be a progressive program on our part as we grow in critical states.

If you remember – when I was in your office discussing some of the staff problems down here, I discredited the export market companies. There are many reasons for this, namely, which have money now to buy our goods. All of these problems cannot be solved over night – it will take years. My point is that they must improve the export facilities from military to non-wartime immediately, as they cannot adequately supply our own needs for construction and household appliances that are shipped abroad. Continued industrial development will help them improve their export markets and at the same time help solve their financial problems.

Handled properly and by working closely with the large companies and the like, I believe we are on the threshold of an extremely large, lucrative and sustaining period of growth. The BOP message of growth through proper leadership can be the backbone or our future down here – few opportunities like this come along – imagine – the life of many industries is short – need I say more.

This whole operation down here could be presented by a very small group of qualified fundraisers. We should organize meetings with the large companies – and present our policies and go from there. When I discussed this with ESSO and Burton they both agreed they needed this type of program in order to plan correctly for political contributions. Only after these steps have been taken will BOP Florida ever begin making inroads toward exploiting our potential. Great enthusiasm has been expressed by some of the clients we have contacted thus far; likewise great enthusiasm will be required to keep a program like this going.

Harold, reports of this nature are certainly not my cup of tea, but after having worked with men like Milton, and you, I can only say one thing in closing – Get a new manager down here – someone we can work with. This is the main ingredient to the success of any organization and this operation has never had a good overall manager before. Prescott has some excellent qualities – but they do not include leadership. I cannot blame Bushel for everything wrong here, we both know that he inherited many problems and the working conditions at BOP Florida are less that ideal; however, aside from yelling, threatening and passing the buck, little has been done about the internal problems. Prescott is not big enough for this job and his lack of humility will probably always keep him from achieving his goal. Clients like Clayton avoid him like the plague – I've seen this many times and so have you – you cannot force yourself in on people every time you come in contact with them. Prescott is on his way now to see Clayton – Heaven knows what new Utopia this meeting will bring.

BOP Florida is in trouble. It will require a rebuilding program much like that of the initial BOP board.
Regards,

Herbert 'Bert' Dover, Jr.

"Prescott, thank you for coming up here to meet with me for our quarterly meeting. Rest assured that you are doing a very, very good job managing the Florida Branch of BOP. However, please do not jump to any conclusions and tell me to shove it after you read a letter that was mailed by 'Bert Junior' for me to receive just before you arrived for your meeting with me. Remember, let's talk before you storm out of this office and get some lethal weapons to take care of the problem. Take your time and read this letter," General Harold Brocklesby (Ret.), new Executive Director of the BOP Party, said in his usual calm voice as he stepped out of his office to ask his secretary to get him a cup of coffee and dictate a letter to a colleague over at the capital building.

Upon his return to his corner office from the secretary pool area General Brocklesby (Ret.) asked. "What do you think about this 'Coxcomb'"?

"You described him perfectly. Yeah, he wants to strut around the chicken yard as the number one rooster."

"Without question, he wants your job to run the BOP Florida operations."

"My family and I have done without and gone out of our way to provide support to him in everyway. I loaned him my driver to use exclusively for his private and business purposes. He has eaten dinner in our house on an average of four times a week. The contribution reports contradict his vicious lies, and the money transferred up to you at national headquarters supports my statement. 'Bert' would turn over in his grave if he saw this letter."

"True, 'Bert' did so much to develop a network of relations between high-ranking civil servants, judges, politicians, bank directors and most importantly our financial supporters," Harold replied.

"This is a serious problem for the future of the Florida BOP operation," Prescott said in an urgent tone of his voice.

"Yes, my main concern is whether he has poisoned any of your staff against you or not. If he has done exactly what he said he has done with some of the important contributors, those parties are intelligent enough to see through him. I recommend that you return to Florida and proceed as though nothing has happened here and that you did not even see the letter or talk to me about his report. During this time period be sure to casually talk and meet with your other staff members and learn of any disenchantment on their part toward you. I will call 'Bert Junior' next weekend and order him to return to D. C. for another assignment. After he leaves, call all of your staff together and set the record straight and terminate any other problems. I don't have to tell you what you need to do. You know how to regain any authority that you may have lost due to this problem," Harold suggested in a convincing manner.

"You sure I don't need to take some of your best former military men with me?" Prescott asked jokingly.

"Let me give you the names of some of them now. No, 'Bert Junior' has a very frustrating problem before him and does not know how to handle it. He has almost 24 million troy ounces of Gold Bars from his father's deals with Emperor Zapp and General Salmon that he inherited worth approximately one hundred million dollars today. As you know, these Gold Bars are illegal to own by an American citizen. He wants to get permission to sell them to the U. S. Treasury and be paid in U. S. Dollars. This will enable him to go on with his life and maintain his investments solely under his control. He thinks U. S. Dollars are the strongest currency in the world and if he scatters the money around and opens up some new banks around the states and with the F. D. I. C. insuring some of it; he sees this as the best route for him to go. I personally pushed for the approval of the new Secretary of Treasury's appointment. I know that I am in a position to lobby him and the President to look the other way, ignore the law and approve the purchase of the one hundred million dollars of Gold from 'Bert Junior'," Brocklesby announced to the startled Prescott.

"The risk for 'Bert Junior' is insurmountable. But with your political stroke maybe the risk is diminished. His passion for this money must have led him to try to work it out for himself by taking over BOP Florida and working his way up here to Washington. Now, I understand why he did not replace his father as a fellow director with me on the Global Banking Group's board," Prescott concluded.

"What I have to do is convince the President and the Secretary of Treasury that it is okay for them to buy and sell Gold in the way, in amounts, at rates, and on conditions the Secretary considers most advantageous to the public interest and approve the deal without any political ramifications," Brocklesby added.

"Yeah, they should have some sort of out. Maybe since the current world price of Gold is slightly more than what the Secretary has been authorized by the President to pay for Gold, the political ramifications for buying illegal Gold Bars from a U. S. citizens will be over looked," Prescott Bushel surmised.

"Back to the real world of Florida BOP party politics. Here is the latest publication of How To Hold A Precinct Convention.

1. The Born Of Privilege (BOP) Precinct Committeeman will call the Precinct convention to order promptly at 7:00 o'clock p.m. at your polling place or in the immediate vicinity thereof.

2. Any qualified voter in the precinct (holder of a poll tax or exemption in the precinct) may participate in the Precinct Convention and no pledge may be exacted from him or her as a prerequisite to participating in the Convention.

3. The first order of business is the election of a Chairman of the Convention. The Precinct Committeeman may be elected Chairman of the Convention if those present agree on him, or those present may elect some other person as Chairman.

4. The second order of business is to elect a Secretary of the Convention. (Note: Prior to the Precinct Convention our people in the precinct should have a caucus, select a floor leader and decide for whom they will vote for Chairman of the Convention and Secretary of the Convention. This information should be circulated among our friends prior to the Convention.)

5. The next order of business is the selection of delegates to the County Convention. Your precinct is entitled to a fixed number of votes in the county Convention, but you may name an unlimited number of delegates to cast these votes. (Note: At the caucus held prior to the Precinct Convention a slate of delegates should be agreed upon and at the Convention any move to add names should be registered unless the suggestion to add names comes from a friend and we are firmly in control of the Convention.)

6. If desired, the delegates to the County Convention may be given instructions on various matters, and, if we have control of the Precinct Convention, a motion that the delegation vote as a unit at the County Convention should be offered. If we are in the minority we should resist the unit rule and attempt to slip some of our friends onto the delegation.

7. A motion to adjourn is then in order. This motion is not debatable. Do not bring up controversial matters. We will have plenty of time at the County Convention to discuss controversial matters.

You have a copy of the Florida Election Laws in pamphlet form. Pass out this How To Hold A Precinct Convention and the Election Laws to all in the caucuses and in attendance at the Precinct Conventions," Brocklesby instructed Prescott as they began walking out of the national headquarters in D. C.

"I hope my patience upon my return to Florida is at its best. I know that I cannot tell my wife about 'Bert Junior's letter to you. She would probably make the newspaper headlines for something that would not help the party's political agendas in Florida. I will tell her at a chosen later date and we will have a big laugh together. I am sure 'Bert Junior' will have ants in his pants upon my arrival and be at the airport with my family and other staff members to greet me. Thank you again for your candor and confidence. We have been through too much to accept infighting as the normal way of future relationships," Prescott said as he shook Harold's hand.

"You are welcome and correct. I must continue to lobby and one of these days the law for U. S. citizens to own Gold will be taken off the law books. Then, you and I may enjoy our lives without some of the constant fears we share," Brocklesby replied.

TREASURES OF WAR – CONCEALED BY THE EVIL ONES

Chapter Twenty Nine

The Mafia Continues to Roam In Argentina

December 1954 --- Buenos Aires --- The Ministry of Foreign Affairs together with the Secretariat of Finance ordered the expulsion Monday of the West Germany diplomat linked to the German-born, Argentina immigrant, named Brazo Mauro Melmo, arrested in Mendoza on charges of smuggling "Nazi Gold" into Argentina and the 'Aryanization' programs in which he forced the German Jews to sell their properties and businesses at very cheap prices. He was a former SS officer.

The diplomat, whose name was not released, was given three days to leave the country, spokesman Roberto Guzman said.

The West Germany official was ordered out of the country for activities "criminal in nature and not compatible with his diplomatic status," Guzman said.

However, Guzman was very tight-lipped and refused to go into details concerning what had been uncovered and where any of the Gold was located. Guzman said the Minister of Foreign Affairs did not divulge any further details and had acted against the West Germany diplomat in response to evidence presented by the Argentina Federal Police under the direction of President Perón.

A news release from the West Germany State Department offered no comment on the ordered expulsion but said the allegation of West Germany smuggling Nazi Gold is a tremendous defamation of our new Republic. It said the purpose of the West Germany mission is to introduce new investments into Argentina and to promote better relations between West Germany and Argentina.

The release also said it is no co-incidence that the smuggling accusations are being leveled at a time when the corruption and central bank swindle charges and other internal battles against President Perón is reaching a critical stage. More public demonstrations have been organized and are scheduled in the coming week in the major cities and in the capital of Buenos Aires.

This is the first West Germany diplomat asked to leave Argentina. One Argentine official, who asked not to be identified, said that Guzman told him that they had been investigating SS officer Melmo, who has been known to make some pretty large imports of "equipment" from Europe, over the past six or eight years; but would not say how much Nazis Gold he had been importing.

In early 1955, more than 2,000,000 flag-waving demonstrators crammed a Buenos Aires square Saturday at noon in the largest protest yet against President Juan Perón's far right dictator activities.

Throughout the day, tens of thousands of protesters gathered for smaller rallies at different sites throughout the country.

Others shot off their rifles and handguns into the air, honked their horns, and draped slogan banners from buildings and shouted slogans critical of the government.

Later, they converged on Avenida 9 de Julio with one group breaking off and moving down Avenida de Mayo toward the Plaza de Mayo area with a large and very vocal group of them surrounding the monumental fountain of Los Dos Congresos. The leaders worked the crowd up to fever pitch in front of the Casa Rosada.

"We have to stop the corruption of President Perón from taking all of our wealth from the people of Argentina," General de Luca Moro, head of one of the opposition groups from the south told the hundreds of thousands in front of the fountain.

One of the banners hung from the Banco de la Nación read: "Perón is a Thief".

Overall, the demonstrations were peaceful.

The atmosphere varied throughout the country, from festive in the rural towns where shooting into the air was considered very revolutionary --- to downtown Buenos Aires where an earnest political rally outside government buildings took place. The main avenues around Buenos Aires were a sea of mostly hand-painted, colorful banners.

'Argentina, you have been stolen blind by corruption of Perón and his buddies;' 'Give back Democracy, Not Dictator;' 'Promises, how long do we suffer? You took away our promises'.

'It is a scandal that these crimes have been legitimized by Perón people.'

The Next Morning In Mendoza, Argentina.

"This meeting of the Giardalli 'Family' is called to order," Lucky announced as he came into the Board of Directors office.

"President Perón, thank you for attending this important meeting," Lucky addressed the President.

"Thank you for inviting me and my top brass to come to Mendoza and enjoy your hospitality. I needed a change of scenery from all the busy activities in Buenos Aires. I would not have missed it for anything, maybe a good FUTIBOL match," Perón laughed.

"Let's get to the first order of business. The 'Family' understands that you have made a request for a $500,000.00 dollars contribution to you in cash. Where and how do you want this money deposited?" Lucky asked the President.

"Yes, I need the money in two ways. First, have $400,000.00 transferred to my company, Confederation General del Descamisados of Hong Kong. The CITIBANK Central on Queen's Road in Hong Kong is the bank. My account number is shown on this paper," Perón replied as he handed it to Lucky.

"It is time to discuss this matter and vote on it. I will ask you to vote first. All in favor of making this contribution to President Perón, raise you hand?" Lucky asked as he polled the 'Family' delegates.

Slowly all but three raised their hands.

Why in the world is that blond hair German, Rudolf, not raising his hand, Lucky thought as he looked around the room?

"Raúl, what is your objection to this request for funds from The 'Family' to President Perón?" Lucky quickly asked.

"Boss, we need to know what President Perón has to say about the missing shipment of 180 -- 12.5 kilo Gold Bars from our smelting plant to the bank in Buenos Aires," Raúl responds, as he looks straight into Perón's eyes.

"Good question," as Lucky agreed and pointed to Perón.

TREASURES OF WAR – CONCEALED BY THE EVIL ONES / 505

"I do not know anything about any missing shipment of Gold Bars. Please furnish me with the details of this problem, and I will make it one of my priorities and get to the bottom of this immediately," Perón hastily replied.

"Carlos, you have the data on the missing shipment of Gold Bars. Give the details of the questions that 'The Family' has from point A to point Z to President Perón and stay on top of it with him until the Gold Bars are found and accounted for," Lucky instructed Carlos in front of all in attendance.

"Yes Sir, Boss, I will carry out your orders."

"We own these Gold Bars, find them now," Lucky forcefully expressed to Perón.

"I will locate them this next week," Perón eagerly replied.

"Ramón, what is your objection to 'The Family' making this requested contribution to Perón?" Lucky asked.

"Boss, President Perón has not had his people issue to us in a timely fashion the necessary permits on most of our important projects causing costly delays," Ramón points out to 'The Family'.

"Why do we continue to have these costly problems Perón?" Lucky asked the President.

"Well, I have recently taken steps to correct this problem by appointing General Jose Rosas to head up a new office to have all Cabildos (town councils) report to him. He has been given my personal orders to issue all of your permits for your projects without any delays whatsoever," Perón proudly stated. "General Rosas is a very capable leader to perform this function well".

"I urge and encourage you to put this problem right at the top of your priorities under the missing shipment of Gold Bars. I do not ever want to have to bring this up again in future meetings. It has cost us unspeakable amounts of money," Lucky warned the President.

"Rudolf, does your objection to the President's request for funds persist?" Lucky asked.

"Boss, both of my concerns with President Perón have been temporarily settled," Rudolf observed with a serious look.

"Now, all in favor of making this bank transfer to Hong Kong for Perón, say aye, oppose no?" Lucky asked them to voice their vote.

All of the delegates said aye.

"President Perón, what about the remaining $100,000.00 dollars contribution request? Did 'The Family' understand correctly that you needed a total of $500,000.00?" Lucky quizzed the President.

"Yes, I need the other $100,000.00 in cash taken to Banco de la Nación Argentina at Bartolomé Mitre 326 in Buenos Aires and deposited into the account for Dr. Ernesto "Che" Guevara.

"Let me have all hands in favor of this $100,000.00 cash contribution to President Perón," Lucky asked.

"We have invested a great amount of 'The Family's' money in your government. Sounds like you need to get control of the people in Buenos Aires immediately. We will make these two contributions to you. But calm the political waters and find our missing Gold Bars. Do you understand me?" Lucky asked Perón in a very frustrated tone of his voice.

TREASURES OF WAR – CONCEALED BY THE EVIL ONES

Chapter Thirty

Post World War II -- ERA

CIA In Fighting and Funds for Foreign Covert Projects

From the Sale of World War II -- Gold Bars

Photo Provided By National Archives and Records Administration
And
National Security Agency/Central Security Services

The stony silence by the CIA in the United States regarding military coups in several countries have brought grave concerns to Mr. Herbert 'Bert' Dover and General Milton R. Salmon. The two men decided to meet ten miles from Dover's Florida mansion at an apartment complex owned by them. They knew that they were under occasional surveillance by both the FBI and the CIA.

"Did you have a pleasant trip down from Washington?" 'Bert' asked Salmon.

"We had to fly around most of that hurricane, 'Bertha', pounding South Carolina that missed you here in Florida. It got pretty bumpy for about one solid hour. Other than the hurricane rains and winds the trip was okay. Speaking about storms, what do you make of the activities of the British intelligence sharing their efforts to complete the latest military coup?"

"As long as the British government and our banking partners keep control of the financial institutions over there, I personally do not think we have a problem with the ownership of the Gold Bars and Gold Bullion Certificates of Deposits in London. As long as those jocks focus on destabilizing governments and playing games of intrigue with nations, they will not even notice our wealth around the world. Remember, they think they stole most of the hidden Gold Bars in the Philippines right after the end of the war. If they only knew," Dover replied in one of his most sarcastic moods.

"I guess they know what they are doing. But, to pose as Communist Party members to win the confidence of rebellious people could back fire on them. They are supposed to be performing secret anti-communist operations. They are even funneling millions of dollars from the sale of some of its' Gold Bars to support new regimes in several places. My intelligence reports concludes that the CIA has begun an effort to flush out Swiss Bank Account holders for some of the over thrown government leaders. If they are successful in penetrating Swiss security and confidential rules and regulations, we should be concerned. Maybe we should change the name of our Gold Bullion Depository account in Switzerland," General Salmon elaborated.

"I will fly to Geneva and check things out with our bank officer," 'Bert' replied.

"Sounds credible, let's sneak out to the back boat ramp behind Martha's apartment and crank up the engines and go deep sea fishing," Salmon said with a gleam in his eyes.

"You deserve to try to catch some fish. I remember the last time you and I fished off the coast of the Philippines. Do you recall the number one fisherman on that trip?" Dover

TREASURES OF WAR – CONCEALED BY THE EVIL ONES / 509

asked with a grin from ear to ear.

"Luck, Luck, just pure Luck!"

"We shall see."

After The Florida Visit Was Over and Several Years Had Passed.

Actual Notes From A CIA Conference In Paris.

          Le Grande Hotel, Place de T'Opera
          F-75 Paris 9, Paris Telex: 22875
          March 19, 1972

SECOND CONFERENCE

REF: GB-MT-HDMRS—SHIP
    Commonwealth of the Philippines
    GOLD BULLION Certificates-Gold Bars
    Retrieve for the United States-C.

    SUBJECT: INHERENT POWER, RESPONSIBILITIES AND INSTRUCTIONS SINCE 1969.

        "INNATUS VIRES, OBLIGATUS ET INSTITUTUIO ABHING 1969"

Reference used in this conference:

    1. {Postfach}, Zurich Conference, Zurich Switzerland, May 19, 1969;

    2. Letter, Chicago, Ill, U. S. A. October 20, 1969;

    3. Letter, Chicago, Ill, U. S. A. August 2, 1970;

    4. Continuing Authority, 1969 to 1976,

510 / DON STEWART NIMMONS

      Insbruck, Germany, September 11, 1970'

5.   Carte Blancha r. l. Celso Condato,
Berne, Switzerland, November 26, 1970;

6.   Guidelines in closing Contract and
The Ratification of Patrick S. Strauss,
Berne, Switzerland, December 15, 1970;

7.   Transshipment of Gold Bullion In and Outside
the Philippines and the Redemption of the U. S.
Federal Government, Duffield, Winnipeg, Canada,
April 17, 1971;

8.   Invitation to Zurich through Davidson and Rossenberg,
Nathan Road, Kowloon, BCC,
July 21, 1971;

9.   Letter of Inquiry c/o BS 999-9 Orient,
Chicago, Ill, U. S. A., August 29, 1971;

10.   Signatories of Documents since Zurich and U. S. A.
November 5, 1971;

11.   SECOND CONFERENCE, Le Grande Hotel Place de
T'Opera, F-75 Paris 9, Paris, France
March 19, 1972

      Followed by:

      Certification of Continuing Authority, March 20, 1972
and other documents, same conference.

BRIEF POINT OF YOUR RESPONSIBILITY

1. You are the Chief Negotiator and Principal Transactor for a period of not less than five years or more, Agreement concluded by you should be authenticated by a minister

or official of any embassy to make it bankable and binding to both parties concerned. ZURICH, 1969.

2. We firmly believe that our new friend will be moving on a different phase of time and in a different environment. It would be better for IC-6-874/Celso Condato, a Filipino, not to drive the wagon backward. HAMBURG, 36, HAMBURG. 1969.

   We are leaving the discretion to you. I have the firm belief you will, time and again consult that authority from Zurich. There are Europeans and those from U.S. going to Manila inquiring about this Stuff. Beware of the waggling unauthorized agents. CHICAGO, BL.

3. Sir, Wilhelm sent me the picture of Don Celso Condato, Florida, 1970.

   Write me of your plans and activities. Utmost care should be exercised al all times. Don't push the wages against the winds. CHICAGO, 1970.

4. You are now enjoying a continuing authority from 1969 to 1976. The big holders of the items sanctioned this authority. Your name is registered in the banks concerned. You know whom to appear in submitting your contracts for ratification. You may appoint one

   {1} of your Foreign Liaison Officers. All your official acts are duly recognized deemed proper and binding. We confirmed and abide to your authority and re-affirm our full cooperation, INNSBRUCK, 1970.

5. We consider that your identity as a Co-Seller is established and you have our full backing and recognition. Protect our interest and carryout your responsibility as you have acknowledged from us. Buyers have the ability to understand our situation. An agent or Trustee of the Buyer should prove their identity with documents. Keep on looking for a better contract. You soon will find the right party. SWITZERLAND, 1970.

6. We are putting straight forward on your shoulder the responsibility in signing a "Contract" or an "Agreement". You have this instruction since Zurich Conference. Know your guidelines. Please be guided on the payment, the vault-by-vault transactions; the validation and representatives on both sides. "Contract of

Exchange", you executed is irrevocable. Take such contract to nearest embassy office. Ratification is important, SCHWEIZER 1970.

7. We've explained to you how these Treasures circulated "In and Outside the Philippines". Disclaim in writing any amount not within our given quotation in fairness to the Buyer and Associates. Register to the proper agencies as the law requires in a certain country or Country of Origin of the contracts that our claim in exchange is just and lawful. You have to do this for the protection of both parties.

8. As a result of your meetings with Davidson and Rossenberg in British Crown Colony, you were invited to Zurich. Our purpose is to introduce to other Depositor, Holders etc. Advocate is right.

9. The first inquiry was made by BCC and Singapore. During those intervening times, all were inquiring about your activities and how you are getting along. Cheer Up! CHICAGO, 1971.

10. Our Certification about the communications or documents you are receiving was placed in a clear picture. Depositors, Holders and others are residing in different places. It took S. G. W. and U to travel two years to know the whole of HDMRS. We have no other way to protect ourselves except to adopt a system not to reveal our true identities. You knew this senior. CHICAGO, 1971.

Having been engaged in business, the tremendous amount invested at times is bothersome. Most of us feel uneasy and how to recover. The only Gold Bullion that stayed astray. The disposal had been dragged and the only thing left is possession. We knew our bearings, since the endorsement. And, in this conference, through secret law firm in Washington, we are pinning down our hope and future through your efforts.

Through your reports, you displayed a rare ability and control of the situation. Furthermore, appear innocent looking to the inquiries, you're best jealous and backtracking against unjustified officers is equivalent in defending your own property. We studied the by-lines of your communications and your feeling is well defined. We meet you knowing you denied an audience to a stranger in our country a year ago. That man is an internationally dangerous manipulator. So far, we heard nothing to the contrary.

TREASURES OF WAR – CONCEALED BY THE EVIL ONES / 513

Because of your exemplary behavior, we spelled out what is beyond our feeling in dealing with you, the third foreigner and the first Filipino to enjoy our trust and confidence.

We enumerated the important facts of your documents; we pointed out in brief your bearing prior, during and after concluding a contract. Your authority is absolute, complete and carried our unanimous consent. No other party shall {in the strict sense of your power} enjoy such except you. Definitions simple as we can, are clearly manifested, irrevocable and continuing.

Our assurances were clearly written, had given our vote of confidences. Unanimously, the legalization of our decision and written statement could well be taken and to be registered at your discretion. The competence of our action and disposition rest largely on your ability to feel and understand what we have officially extended to you as our Co-Executor. Your position having been drawn left us no other alternative or any workable devices except for you to defend the sanctity of our unending confidence. With those documents you now have, coupled with the strain of your signature lies the future of those Gold Bullion Certificates of Deposits. While in the business parlance, we do not mix sentiments. This particular venture, we do.

We reply and have relied on your intelligence, capability, and understanding. Whence, in the course of time someone shall question your authority, stay calm, be firm and examine carefully why. For at times of trial and disappointment, your only weapon is your capability to discharge the proof of your claim and the law. It is therefore, at your finger tips the downfall and success of a commodity worth billions. Aware you are the bearer of courage, firmness and fairness, is equally our constant prayers for you not to alter. When you can clearly define in your mind and actuation the law of men and the law of God, then you will be vulnerable – everybody will.

Your responsibility is even greater than any combined efforts and investment we made. Your undertaking in this particular venture is so great. CANADA, 1971.

PATRICK S. STRAUSS
A52 763 GB-5000MT

General Salmon and Herbert 'Bert' Dover's replacement, Lieutenant General Harold Brocklesby (Ret.) met at 'Bert's former mansion in Florida. As the two men sat down to have a cool one Salmon said. "When 'Bert' was alive, he led a very secret life. Now, the CIA is finally getting its' act together and has begun some extremely sensitive covert activities. What do you think about the Paris conference report that you just read?"

"Where did you obtain this document?" Brocklesby asked.

"One of my military intelligence officers in the Philippines plays golf with some Filipinos that are friends of the guy that is mentioned in the report of the Paris meeting, Celso Condato."

"Interesting!"

"More than just interesting, the Filipino that brought this copy of the Paris CIA meeting report to my officer explained their concerns. Condato firmly believes that as soon as he does what the CIA wants him to do, they are going to slowly poison him until he dies."

"Condato sounds very neurotic and paranoid. Maybe his high salary and underground fees are getting the best of him. He wants the good life, not offered to most Filipinos, in which he gets to travel all around the world, meet the beautiful ladies of the night, stay in the best hotels and eat in the exclusive restaurants and clubs. And, it does not cost him one penny. Now, he must earn his keep and produce for the CIA."

"Brocklesby, I believe you are correct. Plus, the normal way of the government doing things in the Philippines in recent years after the war is to take any discovered treasures away from the locator and put a bullet in his head to keep from sharing it."

"Give them credit. The CIA is holding him in high esteem and negotiated an agreement that he cannot refuse to perform his duties. Yet, he probably has witnessed the final actions of agency in other covert activities. He also knows the importance of increasing the wealth of the CIA for its' future undertakings."

"Salmon, this Filipino is out on that famous limb, and he knows it. Once his job is complete and he puts the millions of dollars in the CIA secret bank accounts from the sales of the Gold Bars, he is expendable."

"I have a recommendation to get a message to him from his Filipino friend through my intelligence officer at our Subic Bay military base. The message would ease his concerns about the financial well being of his family in the Philippines in case he dies. At this point, I firmly believe that he is in a position to demand some U. S. dollars up front. Say, one million dollars. What do you think?" Salmon asked Brocklesby.

"The CIA needs him to sell the Gold Bars under his control. Million dollars, well it may be a good starting point to begin the negotiations. But, I bet it will work and you will have a line of communications with the Filipinos that you did not have before. We might need that contact in the future," Brocklesby replied.

"I don't know about that. The constant power structure and struggles at the CIA's headquarters in Washington causes bureaucratic entanglements on a daily basis. The number one objective of the CIA right now is to keep ahead of the nuclear threats from countries experimenting with such weapons of destruction. This could lead to severe problems for the US and keeps them in need of funds to pay foreign people off in the interest of national security," Salmon said in a very military manner.

"I cannot disagree with that statement. Why don't we get dressed casually and go out to the finest Florida seafood restaurant and pig out," Brocklesby replied.

"Let's have a ball tonight before we have to return to Washington; you to the BOP headquarters and me to my military career duties," General Salmon happily replied.

TREASURES OF WAR – CONCEALED BY THE EVIL ONES

Chapter Thirty One

Late In Life Story of Master Sergeant Arvil Steele (Ret.)

517 / DON STEWART NIMMONS

FLASHBACK

Every since my Daddy died in 1931 when I was only 11 years old and left my Mother with very little material things, my younger brother, Bob, and I worked many hours in the sharecropper's cotton fields plowing the land and turning up the furrows to make the rows to plant the cotton. Then, during the long hot summer days in Texas we picked cotton every day and got paid by the pound. My hands were so cut up and bleeding at the end of the day that I had to put them down in the cool creek at the end of the cotton field to reduce the pain and stop the bleeding before going to the bunk house to eat some of the fresh garden food and off to bed.

One of the happiest times in my life was at the age of 12, a year after my daddy's death, and my mother decided to have me and my 3 sisters and younger brother, Bob, move off the sharecroppers farm in Texas to her mother's big house up in Mena, Arkansas. Our grandmother had a large house in town.

Photo Courtesy M/Sgt Arvil Steele
1954 Greenville Miss. AFB

Spring of 2001, interview by author of U. S. Air Force M/Sgt. Arvil Steele (Ret.).

Photo Courtesy M/Sgt. Arvil Steele (Ret)

"As I look back at the situations facing us today, Iraq and etc. I can't help to think how people are trying to help the men who are over in Saudi Arabia. As for ourselves being over there in the Philippines and in Japan for almost 4 years; we did not receive one piece of mail from our loved ones, nor were we allowed to write and send letters back to our families. Those men and women over there now can send and receive mail even and up to phone calls. They also are able to eat plenty and buy the necessities they need. I believe as I did as a young man in wartime on the threats of war. You are not there to be pampered by all, but to be ready and able and that alone for fighting a war. It hurts me to know and read of all that's being done for them by families and etc. For me, the best thing I remember and know from that long time ago period of my life; was prayers were the only way to survive. I believe that it is very good for all the soldiers today to receive letters and to write back, but above all that counts, **is all of**

your prayers go out to them. I continued my service with our Armed Services after getting back from P. O. W. camp. During my 42 months as a Prisoner Of War, **my mother only knew** I was Missing In Action.

After my POW recovery and home leave, I married and was assigned to the U. S. Army Air Force Transportation. Thereafter, I served several tours of duty in Europe. Here is a copy of my 1958 orders to return from European duty in France and Germany."

1272D AACS SQUADRON (MATS)
UNITED STATES AIR FORCE
APO 253, New York, New York

SPECIAL ORDERS)   **24 MARCH 1958**
NUMBER   29)

      1.   MSG ARVIL L. STEELE, AF 6861252 (CAFSC 73170)
ASSIGNMENT; Is relieved permanent duty station 1272-1 AACS DEI (MATS), APO 84, USAF and assignment this unit; assigned 7011TH PERPRON (P/L) (USAFE) Bremerhaven, Germany for transportation to destination} relieved therefrom and assigned 1501st Air Transport Wing (MATS), Travis Air Force Base, California.
REPORTING DATA: Ann will PROBOUT 29 March 58. Report to commander, 7011th SUPPRON Bremerhaven, Germany not later than 0900 hours, 31 March 58 for scheduled departure on the USS Buckner. Report to the commander 1501st Air Transport Wing (MATS), Travis Air Force Base, California not later than 43 days after date stamped on this order by CONUS Post ACCT Unit.
EDCSA to 7011th SUPPRON: 7 April 58. EDCSA to 1501st Air Transport Wing:
16 May 58. 30 days DDALVP.
GENERAL INSTRUCTIONS: Authority: Message AAGSP 21-C-92, Subject: CONUS Assignment for MSG L. Steele.
TRANSPORTATION: PCS. TDN. 5783500 048-132   P531.9-02,03,07   S99-999 Dislocation allowance other. Transportation of Dependents) EVELYN B. STEELE, USCITPP # 119217, wife, CATHY JANE STEELE, USCITPP # 119217, DOB 8 MAY 49, daughter, ROBERT B. STEELE, USCITPP # 119217, DOB 16 Nov 53, son, WAYNE L. STEELE, SCITPP # 119217, DOB 26 Aug 56, son, is authorized concurrently with sponsor under the provisions of JTR. TPA WITH 13 days travel time is authorized. If POV is not used, travel time will be the time of the common carrier used. Travel by military aircraft authorized. Travel by commercial air, rail, and/or bus is authorized. Excess baggage will be shipped in accordance with AFR 75-33.

Airman and dependents will meet basic immunization requirements as stipulated by AFR 160-102. Customs declaration forms will be filled out on all cabin and hand baggage at home station. Custom will be held at USARPEB. Airman and dependents over 12 years of age AUTH two pieces of hand baggage. Dependents under 12 years of age AUTH one piece of hand baggage. Hand and cabin baggage will not be shipped as checkable baggage. Personnel arriving without hand baggage will be deleted from vessel and held until baggage arrives USARPEB.

Shipment of POV is authorized.

                        Originally signed by: MARVIN L. DULL

DISTRIBUTION: Captain, USAF

"A"   Commander

I was honorably discharged from the United States Air Force. I retired from the United States Air Force in 1966 after 30 years of faithful service."

During my twilight years I reach out to the young students in the elementary and middle schools in the Houston Heights and tell them about the bitter war I fought in the Philippines beginning December 8, 1941, the Bataan Death March and POW camps in the Philippines and Japan.

I am very proud of what my fellow POW's and I have accomplished in our lives. I stay in contact with several of them on a regular basis. God put us in some very difficult places during our lifetime and fortunately for some of us, we survived.

Photo Courtesy M/Sgt. Arvil Steele (Ret)

U. S. Air Force M/Sgt. Arvil Steele is a very unique warrior. He shows his colors everyday. His Texas license plate tells it all. His small rented cottage behind a house on

TREASURES OF WAR – CONCEALED BY THE EVIL ONES / 520

Cortlandt Street in the Houston Heights with the American Flag on the meekly covered porch next to the entrance sends a message from an eighty two year old World War II veteran. Notice the two extra lawn chairs. He will sit and talk with you for hours. The big screen TV connected to his cable provider gives him comfort or confusion, especially when he watches CSPAN.

The Following is the June 26, 2002 interview of U. S. Air Force M/Sgt. Arvil Steele by Don Stewart Nimmons, the Author.

Author – "If you had the opportunity to speak to Congress right now what would you tell them?"

Steele – "I'd like to spend about an hour with them, because of ... I've wrote several letters. I've wrote to Senator Reid and Senator Hutchison. I just told them I pray that they let me go up there and spend one hour. I'd have their heads hanging low by the way they are treating us starting off fighting that Bataan War. It wasn't Guadalcanal that began the war in World War II. We starting right there in Bataan and fought it four and half months and got captured. But it's never mentioned, only Guadalcanal. We started and he (President Bush) promised us this and promised us that. You don't have the funds to give us besides ... aah ... our aah disability pay ... our other regular retirement with it ... which is everybody you know knows we deserves that and I'd tell them that you ... you people get it and everybody else that's retired in two different places are for full disability ... gets it. And yet you're saying that ... aah ...President Bush signed it all right but underneath it he wrote funds not available. I'd say you got funds alright to give to all the enemy countries that we have over in the Middle East, Africa and wherever there is ... aah ... a dreadful enemy of ours you give them a hundred million ... a five hundred million to Egypt ... some to Israel, that's alright ...all of them ... so many ... Mexico ... five hundred million or a billion ... every year for NOTHING ... FOR WHAT? ... there is enemism ... they send in ... everyone that are having this done to us now ... and yet you can give them money for nothing and yet not give us our ... you know ... aah ... our regular retirement pay to go along with our disability ... they hang their head down low and answer us that ... and here we are dying off at a thousand a day ... and the most that you could pay us is about five to eight years. You'd be getting it back anyway. But you owe us the courtesy what's due us. I'd be ashamed of myself ... and hang your head down and go home tonight and pray to God ... be ashamed to yourself of what you are doing to us. That's the exact words I'd tell them and I could talk for one solid hour and have them aah ... aah ... I guess have them go home like a goat with his tail up his rear end ... being so ashamed of their selves."

Author – "Explain to me what this bill is that President Bush signed that doesn't have funds for it?"

Steele – "It's the one HR ... let me see if I can find it right fast here... aah ... If they don't pass it this time they're supposed to work on it before first of October ... see ... Then it will be another year before they bring it up again ... then, we'll all ... mostly all be dead ... It's sickening Don ... the way they are doing us........... Well see here is where it starts, see ... and its goes from there and then some amendments ... But it starts right there."

Author – "So it's the HR-303?"

Steele – "Unh haw!"

Author – "Pay restoration formerly called concurrent receipts."

Steele – "Concurrent insured."

Author – "Each .... retiree requires retired for disability to be eligible for longevity retirement."

Steele – "Unh haw!"

Author – "This bill has been reintroduced to remit retirees for over twenty years of service including those who retired for disability and have service connected disability to receive compensation from the VA concurrently with retire pay without any offset. In other words, you are not getting that now?"

Steele – "Unh-unh! No."

Author – "In other words the S-170 by Reid, he is the co-sponsor of the Retired Restoration Act S-2051 by Reid to remove a condition for preventing authority for concurrent receipt of military retired pay and veterans disability compensation from taking effect. It would provide full concurrent receipt of payments including those with disability ratings of 10 to 50 percent. Is that right?"

Steele – "Yes!"

Author – "So you are not getting that?"

Steele – "Unh-unh, no ... See I get 100 percent disability ... but see what it does."

Author – "You get 100 percent disability?"

Steele – "Uh-huh, yes."

Author – "From the military?"

Steele – "Uh-huh, yes from the VA."

Author – "From the VA."

Steele – "So then amah ... your amah ... thirty year retirement in the Air Force they took that off of you and give it to the VA. So if we get ... I do anyway ... 100 percent is $2,300."

Author – "So what are you missing out on?"

Steele – **"Missing my regular retirement which is about which is $1,700 a month."**

Author – "More than the $2,300."

Steele – **"Yeah, on top of that."**

Author – "Okay, explain that to me again."

Steele – "Well, see you would get your normal retirement ... like your thirty year retirement."

Author – "And they took that away from you!"

Steele – "They took that away from us and gave us 100 percent disability whereas we want both of them ... **because you earned both of them** ... now, here in civilian life you get both of them."

Author – "Okay!"

Steele – "See like the Congressmen, they got retire from their ... See they know ... like railroad people retire and get concurrent"

Author – "Right!"

Steele – "They been putting this off ... here about a little over a month ago they had Reid on here (pointing to TV) and about two or three other senators ... and they were talking about this right here (pointing to TV) ... Let me tell you all something this bill ... we got to pass it this time before October or else we got to hang our head in shaaammme ... what we've done to these people ... what they went through ... and we are going to be sorry and shamed as what we do here if we don't get this through it ... no fiddling around ... no arguing about it ... no adding no nothing to it ... we going to get it through. And that was about a month ago. He was up there telling his comrades ... we are going to get it through ... we're going to bind it."

Author – "Senator Harry Reid, he is from!"

Steele – "Nevada!"

Author – "Okay!"

Steele – "He was right here (pointing to TV). See, I done wrote him a letter and he was almost stating the letter I wrote him. You ought to be ashamed of your sorry selves ... and he was saying that. I keep telling others and that guy, my POW comrade, up there in New York ... asking me if I think we are going to get it ... from what I've heard and letters from Senator Kay Bailey Hutchison ... I've got done there (pointing to his cigar box under his coffee table) from her ... they're pretty sure that ... that ... they got to give it to us."

TREASURES OF WAR – CONCEALED BY THE EVIL ONES / 524

Author – **"How long has this been due to you?"**

Steele – "It's amah … amah … the time we retired. We should have got both of um."

Author – "And you retired when?"

Steele – "Aaah … retired 1966!"

Author – **"So that's amah … thirty six years ago."**

Steele – "YEAH! See it is all just passing the buck … they took OUR money and give it to the VA and the VA cut us down to full disability which is pretty good … I think my is $2,385.00 a month … but you say add $1,700.00 a month on top of that for retirement … you would be getting about thirty five … over four thousand a month."

Author – "You could live decent, then."

Steele – "SURE! But what could we do with it? … we're so old … you can't go out and have fun … you are going to kick off and they are going to get it back. I mean it would be stopped."

Author – "Yeah, so they conned you out of the retirement stuff for thirty something years."

Steele – "Yeah, see …see the main thing that I wrote … what I write I sit down here … you ought to watch me … I don't just write a note or something to read … there is about eight pages … I've had one … I never got a reply … but I know he got it … to President Bush … I had twelve pages … I had about ninety cents worth of stamps on that bugger. And amah …Hutchison … I write her real often anyway… she answers me back … says we're working on it … we're going to … we're going to get it."

Author – "How do you know that Bush got your letter?"

Steele – "Because it would have been returned to you. So, amah … however they do that. Oh yeah, he bound to have got it. I just told him how the cow eats. But I have told them all. Reid, like I said, I sitting here (watching CSPAN of TV) I just almost, man he is reading my letter cause he is telling them… we'll be ashamed of ourselves … now we been fighting … putting this off … said now look'ie here we got other things that's more important … this here war is going on ... and I kept putting in that letter ... this ain't no stinking darn war ... we are the ones that fought a war ... this is terrorism which'll be going on forever anyway ... this is not war ... Bush ain't signed no declaration of war ... I said quit calling it war ... just say terrorism ... don't call it war ... we fought your war."

Author – "What ah ... do you think about the young people today about and what they think about what World War II veterans did for them? What do they think?"

Steele – "Ah these ... most of the ones you know that you can talk to either their Daddy or Grandpaw was in World War II and they told us something about it ... everything ah ... I said ... Yeah, you'll ought to understand enough and you save papers and want to talk to us and do this and that on a ... say a Memorial Day or a Flag Day or Pearl Harbor Day or one day like that ... the following day you would not give us the time of day ... you wouldn't spit on us ... I said ... I tell all of u'm ... I tell all of u'm ... well I am going to try (quoting the young person) ... Yes, you don't know us otherwise ... Your Daddy or Grandpaw might have went through it, but you done forgot about that ... us ... you know that we were in World War II. Some of them talk nice to you and some of u'm wont ... and I tell them ... naah ... I tell them what you are ... I have asked you ... gray hair and this message on my cap ... and then one of you say ... who is he ... otherwise I'd say ... could you give me the time, I left my ... who are you ... I'd say that's how you'll are ... you don't care about us ... There're some that does, but mostly don't ... cause these young college and congress ... and wherever they don't give a CRAP ... and not, I bet it ain't ten in the house up there ... that's in World War ... none of the wars ... and try to tell us something ... like Bush and all of them ... Viet Nam was nothing compared to Bataan cause I got a bunch of buddies that were in Viet Nam ... Nothing compared to Bataan and then of course Prison ... besides that ... that was a dad blame political war ... it was not a World War ... what was Korea .. political, political it was no World War, it just political ... and Gulf War, nothing but amah ... political .. COMPLETE POLITICAL over oil ... and that's ... amah ... I said I pulled maneuvers in Louisiana, ha! Ha! ... worse than that God Darn thing ... let along Bataan. And I'll see them down there at that VA and I see them on TV. I see them sometimes on streets. I know they ain't twenty-three ... twenty-five years old at the most ... with a half a chest full of medals ... and I want to know what war give them that medal??? They ain't fought no war. Have you noticed them?"

Author – "Oh Yeah!"

Steele – "Oh, I seen u'm ... hero citations ... one over here and one over there ... and medals hanging down to here with them ... and young ... they ain't fought no stinking war ...

TREASURES OF WAR – CONCEALED BY THE EVIL ONES / 526

I called that New York Bataan buddy of mine yesterday and we got to talking about like you and I are now … he got to laughing … he said … Steele … I tell you what I think they do … they let them do as they please … they just buy them at the PX or the Army/Navy store and hang whatever they want to on there … I said I believe that."

Author – "What do you think about what the Japanese ought to do for you guys that were?"

Steele – "They not ever gonna … they ain't gonna do a stinking thing. Yea, we got lawyers and still trying to their …"

Author – "But, what do you think they should do?"

Steele – "I think the big steel like Mitsubishi … who was … had that damn … and I still I guess it's theirs … developing that electricity for all that part of Japan … should pay us … we were working for them … we wasn't working for the government of Japan."

Author – "Right!"

Steele – "Or some subcontractor … we were working for Mitsubishi … they should … it should be them … but they done got the thing set down …"

Author – "I know about the agreement in 1951."

Steele – "Well … but … that should have nothing to do with that."

Author – "That is right."

Steele – "Cause that was … soldiers … being POW's we got paid … for being like normal pay … but we … but other … like Blacks picking or me picking cotton … they should pay us for working cause … that took the place of their soldiers that was … soldiers go on into service … and us fill their place … in fact we was working for their DARN Army, Don."

The interview ended as Arvil Steele answered the telephone.

EPILOGUE / 527

A generation of Americans has grown to maturity largely unaware of the political, social, and military implications of a war that, more than any other, united us as a people with a common purpose. Highly relevant today, World War II has much to teach us, not only about the profession of arms, but also about military preparedness, global strategy, and combined operations in the coalition war against fascism and terrorism.

In the ravages of the greatest war the world had ever seen, the young tyrants learned to lead its followers by the practice of systems of unethical, collusive, corrupt, criminal, underworld, thievery, and dishonest political and cultural traits; thereby establishing 'a way of life' for many generations to come.

These 'criminal' enjoyments were bred into the young men and women coming of age after the end of the war.

Once the tyrants won the confidence of the young and naive, they had to continue their purge of the 'old' values of honesty. This was accomplished by hand picking some of the best military heroes of the war.

Many of God's innocent people are killed or lives destroyed by following an individual who portrays himself as a Spiritual Leader or a God. Freedom of Fanatical Religions whose aim is to conquer a democratic society must be disallowed.

It becomes perpetual and unstoppable until all forces against Evil join efforts and destroy them eternally.

Swearing to be true to one another, three hoodlums scurry off to slay the villain, death. They meet an old man who tells them that Death is waiting up the road for them. Hurrying, they find too their surprise a stockpile of Gold. When the promise of a rich life enters the picture, all loyalty, trust, camaraderie, and truth quickly depart.

Incensed with greed, dishonesty, deceit, and cunning now take over. Each man seeks all the Gold for himself, and consequently, these partners manage to destroy each other. Lord, to think I might have all the treasure to myself, alone! Who would have thought today would be my lucky day?

No culture or society has an eternal history which prevented Evil Ones from being conquered in time.

Hindus, Islam, Jews, Shinto, and Christians are all religions that profess peace among all nations. However, when a radical group seeks power in one or more nation, they must revert to suicide, terror, murder, looting and fear to conquer and secure its followers. Fear tactics were a main source of securing followers. People wanted to live. Living under the Japanese or the Germans was an evil and very deadly time for all of society.

Do we Americans think only foreign warriors commit war crimes?

This nation should use its' God given powers to combat and remove fanatical groups who have the goal and main purpose to use terrorist methods to conquer and destroy our freedoms and democratic society -- before these Evil individuals develop a large number of brainwashed followers. The United States actions against Evil Ones should commence immediately upon learning of the threats.

The United States of America must promptly combat all worldwide-consecrated enemy zealots whose primary purpose is to annihilate and shift our freedoms and democratic society thereby preventing a greater future threat within our nation.

"I will not return to my country for the purpose of fighting a religious war for the benefit of a few fanatical earthly Gods." Quote of a Devout Muslim from Lebanon.

Faiths are shaken by Evil Members actions.

Think what would have happened to our fighting forces, if we had lost the war!

The years just prior to and during World War II will forever be the foundation in the structuring of the Lost Generation of the future. Due to the struggles of the masses of people all over the world and the maniac methods used by the tyrants and leaders, many learned that the good things in this life would be achieved by working out a "deal" with the tyrants.

The universal knowledge of the use of bowing to the wishes of the tyrants in order to survive was learned first hand by those that became the leaders of the "Lost Generation".

The driving force and continuous passion for control and wealth were motivating factors for the "Chief" tyrants.

No compromise, no greedy deals with the criminals.

When the individuals or leaders of society do not save something of value, evil takes over.

"Through love and faithfulness sin is atoned for; through the fear of the Lord a man avoids evil." Proverbs 16:6

Are we ready for it to happen again OR are we prepared to go in and win wars against anyone fighting religious wars aimed at the society of the United States of America?

Why did all of our sons, daughters, fathers, mothers, uncles and aunts suffer and die to make some select tyrants around the world independently wealthy?

Set our individual future goals in life very high, and be willing to sacrifice to obtain them.

Don Stewart Nimmons

Printed in the United States
61367LVS00004B/139-186